Developing ASP Components

ANDRZEJ WODZIŃSKI

Developing ASP Components

Shelley Powers

O'REILLY®

Beijing · Cambridge · Farnham · Köln · Paris · Sebastopol · Taipei · Tokyo

Developing ASP Components

by Shelley Powers

Copyright © 1999 O'Reilly & Associates, Inc. All rights reserved.
Printed in the United States of America.

Published by O'Reilly & Associates, Inc., 101 Morris Street, Sebastopol, CA 95472.

Editor: Ron Petrusha

Production Editor: Ellie Fountain Maden

Printing History:

        April 1999:   First Edition.

This book is printed on acid-free paper with 85% recycled content, 15% post-consumer waste. O'Reilly & Associates is committed to using paper with the highest recycled content available consistent with high quality.

ISBN: 1-56592-446-0   [6/99]

Table of Contents

Foreword .... *xi*

Preface .... *xiii*

I. Introduction *1*

1. Writing ASP Components *3*
A Little History *5*
ASP: What It Is and How It Works *8*
ASP and ASP Components *10*
Integrating MTS with ASP Components *15*
Accessing Data with ASP Components *19*
Further Reading *22*

2. Setting Up and Maintaining the ASP Development
Environment *24*
Creating an ASP Test Application Virtual Directory *25*
The IIS Metabase *31*
The IIS Admin Objects *32*
The ADSI Container Object Properties and Methods *45*
The IIS Base Admin Object *46*
For Further Reading *46*

3. ASP Components and COM *48*
A Very Brief Overview of COM *49*
How COM Is Implemented *55*

Implementing COM in Visual C++, Visual Basic, and Visual J++ *63*
How COM Is Implemented with Visual C++ *63*
A COM Component Implemented with Visual Basic *68*
A COM Component Created with Visual J++ *70*
Further Reading *74*

4. *ASP Components and Threads* *75*
What Are Threads? *76*
Are Single-Threaded or Multithreaded Components Better? *82*
The Single-Threaded and Multiple-Threaded Apartment Schemes *85*
Further Reading *99*

5. *Components, Transactions, and the Microsoft Transaction*
Server *101*
Developing Component-Based Systems *102*
MTS, MTS Components, and Transactions *103*
Creating MTS-Aware ASP Components *105*
Creating an MTS Test Environment *111*
Installing and Monitoring an MTS Component in an ASP Environment ... *113*
MTS as a Component Management Tool *117*
Further Reading *120*

6. *Overview of the Intrinsic (Built-in) Objects* *121*
The Application Object *123*
The Session Object *127*
The Server Object *130*
The Request Object *133*
The Response Object *141*
Further Reading *147*

II. *Developing ASP Components with Visual Basic* *149*

7. *Creating a Simple Visual Basic ASP Component* *151*
Creating an In-Process or Out-Of-Process Component *152*
Component Instancing *153*
Component Execution and Threads *156*
Creating the Component Methods *159*
Generating, Registering, Installing, and Testing the Component *162*
Adding Error Handling *166*
Further Testing and Debugging Techniques *169*
Further Reading *171*

8. *The Visual Basic Built-in Object Interfaces* *173*
   Accessing the Built-in Objects in IIS 3.0 .... *174*
   The ObjectContext Interface *180*
   The Application Object Interface *190*
   The Session Object Interface *193*
   The Request Object Interface *196*
   The Response Object Interface *201*
   The Server Object Interface *206*
   Further Reading *209*

9. *Creating VB Data Access Components* *211*
   Using ActiveX Data Objects (ADO) *212*
   Accessing Data from a VB ASP Component *220*
   Creating Interactive Database Query ASP Components *225*
   Building a Library of Data Access Components *231*
   Further Reading *234*

10. *Creating N-Tier ASP Components Using Visual Basic* *235*
    What Is an N-Tier Application, and Why Is It Necessary? *236*
    Passing a Result Set to the ASP Page *238*
    Creating a Presentation Layer "Helper" ASP Component *242*
    Updating Multiple Tables Within One ASP Component *246*
    Simple Inserts Within an ASP Data Component Layer *252*
    Deleting Rows and Foreign Key Constraints *254*
    Database Updates with ASP Components and ADO *258*
    Further Reading *263*

III. *Developing ASP Components with Visual C++* *265*

11. *Creating a Simple C++ ASP Component* *267*
    ATL or MFC *268*
    Using ATL AppWizard to Generate the Basic ASP Component Project *269*
    Adding an ATL Object *274*
    Adding Methods to the Interface *279*
    Error Handling *288*
    Further Reading *293*

12. *The C++ ASP Built-in Interfaces* *294*
    Accessing Built-In Objects in IIS 3.0 .... *295*
    IIS 4.0, MTS, and ObjectContext *299*

The Application Object Interface *315*

The ISessionObject Interface *318*

The IRequestObject Interface *322*

The IResponse Interface *326*

The IServer Interface *330*

Further Reading *333*

13. *Integrating Data Access in C++ ASP Components*
**   *with OLE DB*** *334*

OLE DB, ADO, and the OLE DB Templates *334*

OLE DB Basics *336*

Using the ATL OLE DB Templates *337*

Integrating OLE DB and ASP with MTS *342*

Creating a Parameterized Stored Procedure Call *347*

Updating Data *352*

Further Reading *355*

14. *Persistence with ASP Components Using ATL and MFC* *356*

Combining MFC and ATL *357*

File Access from ASP Components *359*

Creating a Serializable Class *363*

Persistence Through Object Serialization *366*

Using Threads for Background Processes *370*

Further Reading *374*

IV. *Developing ASP Components with Visual J++* *375*

15. *Creating a Simple Java Component* *377*

What Are JavaBeans? *378*

Component Execution and Threads *379*

Creating the Java Class *380*

Registering and Installing a Java Component Using javareg *385*

Examining and Altering Component Properties with the
OLE/COM Viewer *387*

Testing the Java Component *389*

Invoking a COM Object in a Java Component *391*

Adding Error Handling *398*

Further Reading *399*

16. *The Java Interfaces* *401*
    IIS 3.0 and the IScriptingObject Interface *402*
    IIS 4.0 and the IObjectContext and IGetContextProperties Interfaces *405*
    The ASP Built-In Object and Helper Interfaces *412*
    The Java Component Framework *431*
    Further Reading *433*

17. *Integrating Java ASP Components with ADO and MTS* *434*
    DAO, RDO, OLE DB, and ADO *435*
    Connecting to a Data Source with ADO *437*
    Querying the Data *444*
    Updating the Data *449*
    Multiple SQL Statements and Batch Updates *452*
    Transaction Management Across Multiple ASP Components *460*
    Further Reading *464*

18. *Java ASP Components and J/Direct, Native Code, and*
    Marshaling *465*
    The Different Native Code Approaches *466*
    An Overview of J/Direct *467*
    Further Reading *477*

Index *479*

Foreword

Most ASP programmers build components. Some may never be able to. Why? Mostly because building a component with a half a dozen pages of Microsoft documentation is like getting an eyedropper full of water before that multimonth trek across a desert. People need a lot of examples and detailed explanations to enter the world of component building.

Some may write components sooner and learn the truism that "Pioneers are the folks with lots of arrows in their backs." However, the component-building pioneers get much better performance from their sites, along with many other benefits that script builders just can't match, including cleaner and richer syntax and the numerous additional commands and features from their underlying language.

Fortunately for component builders, Visual Basic is popular enough that simple components can be built with little documentation. But these handcrafted components often have limited capabilities, since they are built with so little information. C++ and Java programmers have even less documentation. And given this minimal documentation, making MTS-compliant components—a necessary ingredient for large web sites—is for most developers an insurmountable undertaking.

Now, in this book, Shelley provides us with a camel and a couple of months' supply for our trip to the desert. Heck, she even shows us how to walk *around* the desert and avoid all that heat and sand.

This book tells Visual Basic, C++, and Java programmers how to start from the very beginning and reach a pinnacle of knowledge that will enable them to build components in all their glory—components that get the full power of their languages, plus the ASP objects and MTX objects.

I am now confident that I can tell my scripting friends just to buy this book and begin to build components immediately. I used to tell them to wait a couple of months, in the meanwhile studying and learning more, and even then it would be tough to build them, with the scant resources on the web and bookstores...

My script tutorials at *www.activeserverpages.com* teach tens of thousands how to write scripts daily, but overshadowing those scripting lessons is the glaring absence of lengthy component-building tutorials for all three languages. It would take more research and energy than I have, yet the burning need is there, unfulfilled, in hundreds of thousands of script writers who want to graduate to component building but need plenty of help to take that leap.

I feel privileged to thank Shelley for this book before the huge line of people arrives to thank her. It is going to be a long line indeed. Now the knowledge of component building has come into everybody's hands through this book!

Charles M. Carroll

creator of *www.activeserverpages.com* and *www.asplists.com*

Teacher, Public Speaker, Programmer, and Microsoft MVP

Preface

Developing ASP components requires knowledge not just of one tool or of one technology, but of many. You have to become familiar with one or more development tools, such as Visual Basic, Visual C++, or Visual J++ (this book covers all three), and of course you also have to become familiar with the tool's underlying language. However, you can't stop there.

ASP components are nothing more than specific types of COM-based components; that is, they're COM components designed to interface with Active Server Pages and, most commonly, with Microsoft's Internet Information Server. Consequently, you need to develop a certain level of familiarity with COM, the Component Object Model that underlies much of Microsoft's technology. Becoming familiar with COM development in turn requires that you become familiar with threads, so that you can understand how a COM component interacts with a client and what performance issues are involved with clients and components that are based on similar or different threading models. This understanding of threading models will have a major impact both on your design decisions and your development efforts.

Once you've become familiar with working with a tool that supports COM component development and become aware of some of the issues involved with COM development, you still have other new technologies to learn. As you develop ASP components, you need to become familiar with web-based development in general, and with the ASP environment in particular. The way in which your components interact with the world they find themselves in—with the web server, the browser, or the web page reader—all occur through the built-in objects and the object model that Microsoft has provided for ASP development.

Originally, the built-in objects could only be instantiated based on specific event handlers, but starting with Internet Information Server (IIS) 4.0, the built-in objects can be accessed from Microsoft Transaction Server (MTS) objects, so you are going to need to become familiar with MTS, and, to some extent, transactions as well.

If you need to provide support for data access—and an increasing number of web server applications do rely on data access—then you need to become familiar with new data access technologies from Microsoft, specifically OLE DB and the data access technology built on OLE DB, ActiveX Data Objects (ADO).

Then, once you become familiar with the programming language used for the component, the tool used to build the component, what developing a COM-based component implies, what functionality is available through built-in and MTS-supplied objects, and how you can access data; then, and only then, can you take on adding the additional functionality—such as file input and output, object serialization, access to other Windows facilities, and so on—that your component needs to provide.

So, do you feel tired before you even start? Well, I want to tell you that developing ASP components really isn't all that bad. In fact, you are about to start having some fun. Not only are you about to start having some fun, you are also going to learn to work with technology that faces directly onto the road racing to the future: the road to distributed computing and component-based development.

This book introduces you to working with COM development, as well as working with threads and those pesky little "not threads, not process" apartments. It also provides an overview of the ASP operating environment, as well as some things you need to know about MTS and how to work with it. To complete this "environment overview," the book also provides a reference to the ASP built-in objects by using the objects from a scripting environment, thus introducing you both to the objects and to ASP scripting—at least enough to get you started testing your components.

Following this overview, the book then provides three complete and stand-alone sections on developing ASP components in the tool/language of your choice: Visual Basic, Visual C++, or Visual J++. If your organization is like so many others nowadays, your group is probably not using just one tool in its web development efforts. It's not that unusual for shops to program in C++ and Java, or Visual Basic and Java, or Visual Basic and Visual C++. Rather than focus this book on one language, we picked the three tools/languages most likely to be used. Each of these sections provides an introduction to building components in the specific language and using the specific tool, and also provides a detailed section on accessing the ASP built-in objects from the specific language. Each section also discusses using ADO or OLE DB from the component because data access is such an integral part of web development. Finally, each section takes on other tasks that can be accomplished from an ASP component, such as accessing the Win32 SDK from Java, or handling input and output to a file from C++, or creating complex n-tier applications with Visual Basic.

Who This Book Is For

This book is geared to the developer who has worked with one of the target languages/tools, but either has not created COM objects before, or has not worked with developing ASP components or ASP applications prior to reading this. I hope the book provides enough of an introduction to COM and threads to make you feel more comfortable with these topics if you haven't worked with them before, and to provide a good review if you have. The book does not provide an exhaustive overview of MTS and developing MTS components, but does provide, again, enough of an overview that you can feel comfortable working as a developer in an MTS environment.

The book also provides a comprehensive overview of the ASP component environment, including using tools and wizards in each language/tool to assist in creating the components, and covering every aspect of accessing the built-in ASP components essential for your development effort. In addition, the book provides good coverage of ADO from Visual Basic, ADO through the Windows Foundation Classes (WFC) from Java, and OLE DB from Visual C++. If you haven't worked with ADO before, the coverage in this book, plus a review of several resources listed at the end of the data access chapters, should provide enough information for you to get started with data access from ASP components.

Finally, each chapter also provides URLs to resources you can access to get more detailed information about the topics covered in the chapter. These, combined with this book, should be all you need to become a proficient ASP component developer.

Conventions in This Book

Throughout this book, we've used the following typographic conventions:

`Constant width`
> Constant width in body text indicates a language construct such as a language statement (like `try` or `for`), an intrinsic or user-defined constant, an enumerated type, a user-defined type, an interface name (like `IUnknown` or `IResponse`), an attribute, a class name, or an expression (like `dElapTime = Timer()-dStartTime`). Code fragments and code examples appear exclusively in constant-width text. In syntax statements and prototypes, text in constant width indicates such language elements as the function or procedure name and any invariable elements required by the syntax.

Constant width italic

> Constant width italic in body text indicates parameter and variable names. In syntax statements or prototypes, constant width italic indicates replaceable parameters.

Italic

> Italicized words in the text indicate intrinsic or user-defined functions and procedure and subroutine names. Many system elements such as paths, filenames, database names, and component names are also italicized, as are URLs. Finally, italics are used to denote a term that's used for the first time.

 This symbol indicates a tip.

 This symbol indicates a warning.

Obtaining the Sample Programs

All the sample programs presented in the book are available online and can be freely downloaded from our website at *http://www.oreilly.com/catalog/devaspcom*.

How to Contact Us

We have tested and verified all the information in this book to the best of our ability, but you may find that features have changed (or even that we have made mistakes!). Please let us know about any errors you find, as well as your suggestions for future editions, by writing to:

> O'Reilly & Associates
> 101 Morris Street
> Sebastopol, CA 95472
> 800-998-9938 (in the U.S. or Canada)
> 707-829-0515 (international/local)
> 707-829-0104 (FAX)

You can also send messages electronically. To be put on our mailing list or to request a catalog, send email to:

nuts@oreilly.com

To ask technical questions or comment on the book, send email to:

bookquestions@oreilly.com

Acknowledgments

This book lived through releases of new versions of the tools, as well as new versions of the web server and most of the technology. I want to thank both Michael Fenbert and Mark Anders from Microsoft for doing their best to answer the many questions I had during the beta period for Visual Studio 6.0. Mark, in particular, also acted as technical editor for a few of the chapters, though I am responsible for any "gotchas" that snuck through the editing process.

In particular I want to thank my long-suffering editor, Ron Petrusha, who managed to keep me going through yet another release of another one of the tools, or another version of the web server, or the pending litigation between Sun and Microsoft. Ron kept his cool, and I am grateful. He was also one of the best editors I have ever had—thanks for that also, Ron.

I also want to thank Troy Mott and Tara McGoldrick, members of the O'Reilly editorial staff, for retaining *their* cool when I got decidedly cranky towards the end of the book, and keeping their senses of humor when mine was strained.

The people who suffer the most during the writing of a book are those who have to live with the author. I also want to acknowledge my wonderful, patient husband, Robert (Rob), for providing support, encouragement, and much-needed backrubs. Oh, and thanks for keeping me from throwing the computer out the door, Rob.

Lastly, thanks to my readers—I'm here because you're here.

I

Introduction

1

Writing ASP Components

When Microsoft first released Active Server Pages (ASP) with the company's web server, Internet Information Server (IIS), the functionality included with this early release amounted to little more than an ability to handle server-side scripting. If you haven't worked with server-side scripting, it is the inclusion of script, such as VBScript or JScript, in web pages so that the script is processed on the server rather than on the client. This early ASP release soon gave way to the ASP we have now, a sophisticated server-side application-building environment that still supports server-side scripting, but also includes integration with other Microsoft server products, such as Microsoft Transaction Server, and also allows ASP pages to access COM objects.

This book is about writing COM objects to work within this specialized ASP environment. Since they are COM-based, you know that whatever functionality you can perform with COM components, you can also perform with ASP components. This means that you can create an instance of an ASP component and use that component instance to do things such as query a database, open a file, or print a file to a printer. However, ASP components are created for a specialized environment, and there are certain things you might consider doing with COM objects that you probably wouldn't consider doing with ASP components. For instance, because an ASP component resides on the server, you aren't going to use any message windows to communicate with the user; all communication is handled through IIS.

In addition, as part of the ASP environment, ASP components have access to built-in objects that contain information not normally available to a "standard" COM object—information such as form field values submitted from an HTML form, the type of browser being used to access the page, or even the language, such as English, preferred by the client.

The information available to an ASP component is also available to ASP scripting blocks, so why use components when you can use scripting? Especially since scripting is fairly simple to use and can be learned relatively quickly?

The first and foremost reason to use ASP components over in-page ASP scripting blocks is reusability. It's difficult to package an ASP script in such a way that it can be used over and over again in many different pages. Additionally, if you or your company is considering packaging some ASP functionality for resale or distribution, the use of ASP scripting becomes insupportable. You probably won't be in business long if people can not only see the source code for your packaged functionality, but can modify it for themselves.

Another reason to use ASP components is that the components themselves can reside virtually anywhere, even on different machines. You can create an ASP application that may update a customer database and that uses one component to update the person's address and another component to update the person's preferences. One or both of these components can reside on the same machine as the web server, but one or both of these components can as easily reside on other machines, with DCOM being used to access the component. While you can distribute web pages containing script on various machines, the maintenance and access issues become much more complicated and usually require hardcoding the physical addresses of the pages within the application. With COM-based functionality, only the operating system COM manager needs to know where the ASP components reside. Moving components is a matter of changing the location of a component once on the client machine; all accesses to the component now occur at its new location.

An additional reason to use ASP components is that they can incorporate the fullest range of functionality on the server, including database access, file access, archiving, messaging, and other functionality difficult or impossible to do with script. You can even transcend object systems and access CORBA-based components with the support of products such as Iona's COM-CORBA Bridge.

 Though ASP can be used with a web server such as the Personal Web Server from Microsoft, this chapter and this book focus on ASP as it is implemented within IIS. If behavior differs based on the web server used, I'll try to add a note to that effect.

Now that I've battered you with some of the reasons to use ASP components, let's take a little look at the history of web development, and see where ASP and ASP components enter the picture.

In the sections ahead, this chapter provides a little more of the history leading up to ASP and an overview of the technologies used when writing ASP components.

A Little History

It wasn't long after the first web browser was released for public use that organizations began to consider how they could use the web for applications beyond downloading single, static pages. Application development proceeded in two different directions: on the client with client-side scripting using JavaScript, and on the server with server-side applications. The earliest server-side web applications used a specification called CGI, or Common Gateway Interface, to create applications that would be executed when they were accessed, and which generated web pages to be returned to the viewer.

The earliest forms of web server development used CGI to perform some functions on the server. CGI is relatively simple in operation. A URL contains a reference to an application rather than a web page. With the application request usually comes data, such as the data from an HTML form being submitted by the web page reader. A separate instance of the CGI application is started to process the request, and the output generated by the application is returned as an HTML page to the viewer. CGI applications can perform simple tasks, such as redirecting the browser to another site or to another web page based on certain factors such as browser type. Or CGI applications can be complex, such as processing an order for an online store. Any programming language can be used for building a CGI application, with the Perl scripting language the popular favorite because of its powerful, if cryptic, capabilities.

To quickly demonstrate CGI, Example 1-1 shows a simple Perl script written for a web site using the Apache web server for Unix. In this example, the host actually has two domains pointing to the same IP address. The script checks to see which domain was used by accessing one of the standard HTTP web server environment variables, **HTTP_HOST**, and redirecting the browser to the page appropriate for the domain. This Perl script is a small, quick, and efficient little application that performs one specific task.

Example 1-1. A Simple CGI Script That Performs Redirection Based on Domain

```
#!/usr/local/bin/perl
#
# index.cgi
#
# Application will check for the existence of certain
# key terms to determine which browser the web page reader
# is using.
#
```

Example 1-1. A Simple CGI Script That Performs Redirection Based on Domain (continued)

```
# The CGI environment variable HTTP_HOST is accessed
# and certain substrings are matched against it. If
# a match occurs, the browser is redirected to the
# document that matches the browser.
#
# If no match is found, the browser is directed to a text-
# only web page.
#
# Access environment variable
$browser = $ENV{'HTTP_HOST'};
#
# check for Internet Explorer
if (index($browser,"dynamicearth") >= 0) {
    print "Location: http://www.yasd.com/dynamicearth/dynaearth.htm\n\n";
} else {
    print "Location: http://www.yasd.com/plus.htm\n\n";
}
```

Even without knowing Perl, it is relatively easy to determine what is happening with this script. After the host variable is accessed and loaded into a local variable, *$browser*, it is matched against a specific domain request, in this case a domain containing the word "dynamicearth." If found, redirection is used to point the browser location to one page; otherwise, redirection is used to point the reader to another web page.

Though still the most widely used server-side development technology, CGI is not necessarily the most efficient. Its major problem is that a new instance of the CGI application needs to be loaded for each server request. Several people making several requests at the same time impact the performance of both the CGI application request itself as well as the overall performance of the web server.

Returning to Example 1-1, each person who invokes the *index.cgi* application at the web site must wait for the CGI application to be loaded and run before receiving a response back. While the performance of this approach is acceptable, especially for simple uses such as this, starting up a new server application for every page, form access, or bit of functionality will soon disrupt overall server performance, and can actually lead to server failure or server page request timeouts.

 Security issues about CGI arose fairly early on, particularly concerning where CGI applications reside and what operations they allow. Read more on security and CGI at *http://hoohoo.ncsa.uiuc.edu/cgi/ security.html.*

The real key to improving the performance of server-side applications is to provide a technique that loads a server-side application into memory only when the application is not already loaded, and which can allow multiple accesses to the same application from different sources. Among the approaches taken to do this were those that included creating web server extensions that exist as part of the web server itself, rather than as separate applications. With this approach, add-ins to the server could be created using an exposed API, and these add-ins would become integrated with the server rather than existing outside the server. Most web server manufacturers, such as Netscape and Microsoft, soon created proprietary methods for extending their servers.

Microsoft's first web server extension was the Internet Server Applications Programming Interface (ISAPI). ISAPI is quick, in that the ISAPI application runs within the same process as the web server, and communication between the server and the application is very fast. Additionally, once the ISAPI extension application is loaded into memory, it stays in memory, and all client accesses to the extension are made to the same ISAPI process. The only time the ISAPI application is unloaded from memory is if IIS is shut down or regular memory management removes it.

Though fast and efficient, ISAPI does have its limitations. First, it is easy to begin building an extension, but difficult to finish. By this I mean that it is relatively easy to use Visual C++ to start an ISAPI component, since Microsoft has provided a built-in ISAPI wizard to create the framework for the ISAPI DLL. However, building on the framework the wizard provides is not so simple. And ISAPI is limited to C++ programming, leaving the Visual Basic and Java folks out in the cold.

Microsoft was aware of the disadvantages of using ISAPI and fairly quickly provided another approach to creating web-server-based applications: Active Server Pages (ASP). ASP provides for simple and easy server-side scripting that allows web developers to use a combination of HTML, along with JavaScript, VBScript, or any other popular scripting language, to create server applications. A key feature of ASP, though, is that in addition to scripting, it also provides for component-based development by allowing the inclusion of COM-based server components.

About the same time Microsoft rolled out ASP, it also rolled out a combination tool/API service to provide for component and transaction management, the Microsoft Transaction Server (MTS). MTS provides for transaction management for COM-based components, ASP or otherwise. In addition, MTS is an effective component management tool, providing not only component registration services, but also server and client migration. With the release of MTS 2.0 and IIS 4.0, Microsoft also provided for an optional integration of the two servers, with IIS providing the web interface and MTS providing component and transaction management.

The use of ASP and MTS is further enriched with the release of OLE DB, which provides for generic data access regardless of data structure, and which also provides for cross-process transaction management with database engines that support MTS. To assist developers wanting to use OLE DB, Microsoft provided the OLE DB Templates for Visual C++ developers and ActiveX Data Objects (ADO) for all developers.

ASP: What It Is and How It Works

Microsoft created ASP in answer to the need for a scalable and efficient web server application technology that is also relatively safe. ASP is fairly simple to use, and all of the applications can actually be created with server-side script using languages such as JavaScript/JScript or VBScript. If some functionality is needed that can't be provided by scripting, ASP components can be used.

How does ASP work? ASP pages are created with a default extension of *.asp*. When IIS gets a request for a page with an *.asp* extension, the web server accesses and compiles the script contained within the page and loads the compiled code into memory. The script then performs some processing, which usually generates HTML that is then written out to the ASP page. To perform its processing, the script has access to several built-in ASP objects that contain considerable information about the ASP environment, and which allow the script to communicate back to this same environment. The static and script-generated HTML of the ASP page is then returned to the client using a regular HTTP transaction. To the application user, the page looks no different than another static HTML page except for that *.asp* extension. This is because all processing of the script has taken place on the server.

 The ASP built-in objects are covered in detail in Chapter 6, *Overview of the Intrinsic (Built-in) Objects.*

As a quick example, the ASP page shown in Example 1-2 has a small VBScript script block that uses two of the built-in ASP objects accessible to ASP script and components: the Response and Request objects. These are discussed in more detail later in the book, but for now, the Response object provides a way to communicate from the server application to the user, and the Request object is used to communicate from the ASP environment and the user to the server application. In Example 1-2, these objects are used to create a variation on the traditional "Hello World" program.

Once the page containing this script is saved to a file named *hello.asp* and copied to an existing IIS directory, the work for this ASP application is finished. Access-

Example 1-2. VBScript Block with a Variation of the Traditional "Hello World" Program

```
<HTML>
<HEAD>
<TITLE>Server Variables</TITLE>
<STYLE type="text/css">
    BODY { margin: 0.5in }
</STYLE>
<BODY>
<H1> Hello World </H1>
<p>
<strong>
<%
   Dim strng
   strng =  "and hello to you, too, connecting from "
   strng = strng & Request.ServerVariables("REMOTE_ADDR")
   Response.write strng
%>
</strong>
</BODY>
</HTML>
```

ing the page displays "Hello World" on the browser, with some variations, as shown in Figure 1-1.

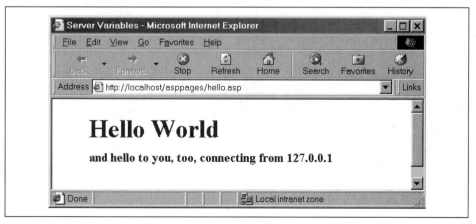

Figure 1-1. The output generated by hello.asp

If the ASP page is accessed from a client located at the IP address 127.0.0.1, the HTML that is returned to the browser is similar to that shown in Example 1-3.

Example 1-3. HTML Returned to Browser by the Script in Example 1-2

```
<HTML>
<HEAD>
<TITLE>Server Variables</TITLE>
<STYLE type="text/css">
    BODY { margin: 0.5in }
```

Example 1-3. HTML Returned to Browser by the Script in Example 1-2 (continued)

```
</STYLE>
<BODY>
<H1> Hello World </H1>
<p>
<strong>
and hello to you, too, connecting from 127.0.0.1
</strong>
</BODY>
</HTML>
```

 The IP address 127.0.0.1 is also known as *localhost* or the *loopback* address and can be used when accessing web pages from a local web server.

An ASP page usually exists as part of an ASP application. An ASP application is really all the pages and associated content of a real or virtual directory, whether the pages have *.asp* extensions or not. An ASP application can be created by creating a real or virtual web site within IIS, and setting some of the properties for the site, as discussed in more detail in Chapter 2, *Setting Up and Maintaining the ASP Development Environment*. To change one of the pages within the application is as simple as opening the page in a text editor and making the change, then copying the modified ASP page to the directory where the ASP application resides. When IIS next opens the ASP page, it can determine that the page has changed and recompile the scripts, if the page has any.

 Unfortunately, making a change to an ASP application running from the Personal Web Server is not as uncomplicated, and usually requires a reboot of the server in order to pick up the changes.

As stated earlier, sometimes the functionality for an ASP application can't be created within an ASP scripting block, and a more full-featured programming language or tool is needed. When this situation occurs, the functionality can be incorporated into the ASP page as an ASP component.

ASP and ASP Components

The beginning of this chapter introduced you to ASP components. This section continues this introduction, but in greater detail.

What Are ASP Components?

As stated earlier, ASP components are COM-based components that encapsulate a specific functionality and are invoked either directly from an ASP page or indirectly via some other ASP component. If you have worked with COM before, ASP components don't use any additional technology, but they can use additional objects available only within the context of an ASP application. However, if a component does not access the ASP-specific objects provided through the ASP object model, it can be used within a distributed application, from other components (whether or not they're part of an ASP application), or even within a flat one-tier application, with no involvement with ASP or IIS or even the Internet. From this point of view, this book could actually be about writing COM components, but with a specific focus.

Having said that an ASP component is really no different than any other COM component, I want to add that the focus of writing an ASP component can alter how that component is created. First of all, the component will usually reside on the same server as the "client" of the component, with the client for ASP being the web server. I say "usually" with some reservation, since there is no requirement that ASP components *have* to reside on the same server as the client application.

In addition, an ASP component is almost always an in-process (ActiveX DLL) component. As you will see in Chapter 3, *ASP Components and COM*, using an out-of-process component (an ActiveX executable) directly from an ASP page actually requires that the IIS installation be modified. ASP is optimized for in-process access of components.

As in-process COM objects, ASP components are usually created using apartment-, free-, or both-threaded models. ASP components are not and should not be created using the single-threaded model, since the component locks down all access to a single thread, which causes access problems in a multi-user environment such as the web and a multi-user application such as a web server. In addition, when using multithreaded models, the ASP components must be thread-safe. What's a thread-safe ASP component? One that does not contain global data, does not yield control internal to the processing of the component, and is safely reentrant. Chapter 4, *ASP Components and Threads*, goes into more depth on threads and apartments.

Now that you have a basic idea of what ASP components are, the next section discusses why you would use ASP components instead of creating the ASP application using scripting exclusively.

Why Use ASP Components?

In the beginning of the chapter, I started listing some reasons to use ASP components instead of scripting. In this section I want to discuss this in a little more detail.

From a perspective of usage, an ASP component can be used in place of scripting where scripting is just not workable or efficient. For example, your ASP application may need to make direct calls to the Windows internals through the Win32 API, or to manage file input and output. These operations cannot be done from within a scripting language such as JScript or VBScript. The IIS scripting engine can be extended to other scripting languages, such as Tcl or Perl, which do support direct file system access or calls to the Win32 API. However, the use of these scripting languages comes at a cost: the code is a little more difficult to read, a little more difficult to maintain, and a whole lot more difficult to secure against editing from external sources. If the code needs to remain unaltered, perhaps to enforce standards compliance or universal data access, the code should be contained within binary components.

Along with implementing functionality that is either unsupported or not easily supported by scripting languages, ASP components are also developed to be reusable and to wrap routines that are commonly called in ASP applications. It is true that ASP scripts can also be reusable; however, this requires copying and pasting the script and duplicating it in all the documents that need its functionality. This means that if the code needs to change, the change then needs to be propagated to all the pages that use the code. In contrast, reusable code is more easily and efficiently managed through components. All ASP applications can access a single physical component. And when that component needs to be modified or revised, the change needs to be made in just a single place. So for code that needs to be reusable, an ASP component is a better choice than ASP scripting.

ASP components can be used to modularize an application, splitting off discrete, manageable bits of functionality that can then be coded by several people in parallel or even purchased from some other party. An additional advantage to modularization of code in components is that the components can themselves be distributed on different machines, and component access can be handled remotely through DCOM or some other equivalent technology. This approach ensures that the application is more scalable and will be able to handle increasingly larger numbers of accesses. If the ASP components are also configured and coded as MTS components, transaction management for all of the components can be handled directly by the Distributed Transaction Controller (DTC) regardless of where the component resides. Though transactions can be used with scripting, and ASP pages can be located on other machines, the management of doing both with pages containing straight scripting blocks instead of components can become more complicated.

If an organization is considering building an n-tier application rather than fitting within the traditional client-server paradigm, ASP components are an excellent tool to use to implement one or more of the application layers. A classic approach is to implement the business layer of an ASP application as one or more ASP components, and to handle the presentation layer in the web page using HTML and client-side scripting, including the newer Dynamic HTML (DHTML). The data access layer would be contained within the database used in the application.

Finally, ASP components are a handy way of ensuring uniformity of an application. For example, if database queries are formatted for output into HTML tables with a certain look, the data presentation functionality can be maintained within ASP components in a layer between the web pages and the business logic, and used for all database queries.

Once sold on using ASP components, as I hope you are, the next choice is the tool or language to use.

Choosing the Language: Java, C++, or Visual Basic

In actuality, there is no "right" tool or language to use for writing ASP components. Any tool capable of creating in-process COM objects can be used to create ASP components. This includes Visual C++, Visual J++, and Visual Basic from Microsoft. This also includes Delphi from Inprise (formerly Borland), Power-Builder from Sybase, and a host of other tools. However, if a company has chosen ASP as an application development environment, it is more likely that the company is using a Microsoft tool for developing the components, which is why this book covers writing ASP components using the Microsoft tools.

 Though this book covers Microsoft tools, the technologies and the samples, though not necessarily the framework or the step-by-step instructions, can be used with any C++ tool that supports COM or, like C++Builder from Inprise, that supports the use of ATL. The same applies to Java; if a tool supports the new Java WFC classes and Java-wrapped COM access, and can run with Microsoft's Java VM, it can be used to develop ASP components that work with IIS.

As for which language to write the component in, there is no one choice that stands out clearly over the others. Writing ASP components using Visual Basic exposes less of the underlying functionality than writing the same component using Visual J++ or Visual C++. Because of this, Visual Basic is the easiest tool to use, particularly for a shop that has primarily used tools such as PowerBuilder or Visual Basic for most application development. If a shop is porting a traditional Visual Basic client-server application to an n-tier system, the continued use of Visual Basic also makes sense. Chapter 9, *Creating VB Data Access Components*, and Chapter 10, *Creating N-Tier ASP Components Using Visual Basic*, provide coverage of writing ASP components for this type of environment.

However, for a Java shop, it makes no sense to switch to Visual Basic when using Visual J++ or a comparable Java-based development tool is just as effective. Microsoft has provided a set of Java wrappers for the ASP built-in objects, and Visual J++ handles all COM interfaces automatically. The main concern of a Java developer writing ASP components is to ensure that all data types used for parameters are CORBA-compliant, which also makes them relatively safe for COM. Chapter 15, *Creating a Simple Java Component*, covers the Java/COM concerns, and Chapter 16, *The Java Interfaces*, discusses how to access the built-in ASP objects. In particular, Chapter 18, *Java ASP Components and J/Direct, Native Code, and Marshaling*, covers native API access, which could be important for some of the components you might develop.

 At the time of this writing, Microsoft is being sued for its extensions to the Java language. Wherever possible, notes are inserted into the Java chapters that detail what may or may not change based on the outcome of this lawsuit.

Visual C++ exposes more of an ASP component's underlying COM architecture and can be used to create the most efficient and speedy components. However, that same exposure to COM also makes using Visual C++ a more difficult choice. If the shop creating the components has no C++ or Visual C++ experience, this approach becomes prohibitive. However, if a shop has used Visual C++, then Microsoft has provided the ActiveX Template Library (ATL) to assist in implementing ASP components; it handles almost all of the details associated with the implementation of a COM component. Using ATL and accessing the ASP built-in objects are covered in Chapter 11, *Creating a Simple C++ ASP Component*, and Chapter 12, *The C++ ASP Built-in Interfaces*. In addition, Chapter 14, *Persistence with ASP Components Using ATL and MFC*, also provides coverage of file I/O in addition to serializing information for persistence beyond the life span of an ASP application.

As for concerns about interoperability, considering that ASP components are COM components, they are by their very nature interoperable within a COM environment. Even within an organization that uses CORBA rather than COM, there are

COM-to-CORBA bridges to handle communication between the two component management/communication approaches.

The underlying language used to create the component does not matter because ASP components are based on a binary interface, not a language-specific interface. This does, however, limit their portability to only those systems that have COM support.

> Needing COM and working with ASP does not necessarily mean that an ASP component will only reside on a Windows NT or 9X platform. Chili!Soft has implemented a product called Chili!ASP to process ASP pages from servers such as Netscape, including Netscape running on a Unix box. See the Chili!Soft web site at *http://www.chilisoft.com/* for more information. In addition, Software AG, with a web site at *http://www.softwareag.co.uk/*, has ported DCOM to Unix, and there is an interesting article on building COM components on Unix at *http://msdn.microsoft.com/developer/news/feature/vcjune98/unixcom.htm.*

Integrating MTS with ASP Components

MTS is a component/transaction management system that can be used to register components, package them for transportation and installation, expose the objects for remote client access, and work with the DTC to actually manage transactions. In addition, MTS also provides support for *stateless* components and resource pooling, concepts discussed in this section, as well as in Chapter 5, *Components, Transactions, and the Microsoft Transaction Server.*

Transaction Management

Late in 1997, Microsoft released version 4.0 of IIS and version 2.0 of MTS. The company also provided for transaction management within and between ASP components through the use of an MTS built-in object called *ObjectContext*. ObjectContext can be used to commit or roll back transactions, and the built-in ASP objects can be accessed directly through ObjectContext in order to include them within the transaction processing.

If an ASP component performs a task that begins and finishes within a single function call, transaction management is not that much of an issue. However, ASP components can call other components and perform other actions such as database activity, each of which requires some form of overall transaction support.

One of the problems with a distributed application (an ASP application can be distributed) is transaction management across several different application components, and potentially across several different machines. For instance, one component can update an address in a database, and another component can update an associated name. If the address update fails, the associated name update should also fail in order to maintain consistency of the data. If both of the updates occur within the same component, this isn't a problem, since both database transactions can be *rolled back*. Rolling back a change means that the impacted database data exists in the same state as it did before the change was attempted.

If the updates occur with two different components, transaction management becomes more complex. One possibility is to use one database connection for both components, and one of the components—the one making the name update—calls the other component that performs the address updating. The component performing the address update returns a value signifying success or failure of its operation. If the update failed, the first component would not make its update. Though workable, the approach is cumbersome, and neither component is able to work independently of the other.

Another approach is to handle transaction management within an ASP page or by a third component that creates both updating components, tests the return state of both components, and commits or rolls back all of the changes based on the results returned by either component. This is a better solution, since now both components can make their updates without having to worry about what is happening with any other component. However, in a larger application that makes multiple changes of this type, having the application itself maintain consistency between the data updates of all the components can become overwhelming at some point.

The best solution of all is to have some other process manage the transaction state of the components and test to see whether each component has succeeded in its operation or whether one of the components has failed. If any one of the components fail, then the changes made by *all* of the components are rolled back. This is where MTS and the Distributed Transaction Controller (DTC) come in.

The DTC is an NT system service, first introduced with Microsoft SQL Server 6.5, that provides for two-phase transaction management of all data updates. A two-phase commit transaction management ensures that all participants in a transaction complete successfully, or none of the participant updates are committed. You might say that this first phase of the commit operation consists of a pass made of all participants in a transaction to ask if they are ready to commit their changes. The second pass then checks to make sure all of the components have made updates without errors.

The DTC was also incorporated into MTS to extend transaction management to all components regardless of whether they perform data updates to SQL Server or some other data store. MTS can provide transaction management for components even if the components are distributed over various machines and environments.

ASP applications can participate in MTS transactions, and transaction management can occur within an ASP page, an ASP component, or both. A transaction can be created within an ASP page that is then used for all of the components created directly from the page, or created from within another component accessed in that page. Failure in any one component means all of the updates made by all of the components within the transaction are rolled back. Components themselves do not have to create transactions directly, but can be registered with MTS in such a way as to participate in an existing transaction or have MTS automatically create a new transaction for the component when the component is created.

To control transactions from within a component, all the component needs to do is complete its code. To participate in resource management, if the component uses the MTS transaction methods setComplete and setAbort, the component is basically providing information to MTS that it has finished its processing and can be unloaded from memory. The following code is an example of using setAbort from within a Java component:

```
IObjectContext iObjContext;

// get instance of ObjectContext associated with ASP component
iObjContext = (IObjectContext)MTx.GetObjectContext();
...
iObjContext.SetAbort();
```

By using the ObjectContext object's SetAbort method, MTS knows that the component has finished its processing, but that the processing was not successful. In a two-phase commit paradigm, the object passes the first phase successfully; it is finished with its processing. The second pass of the process would operate on the information that this component failed, which means the transaction failed and none of the updates made by any component in the transaction are committed.

Using the SetAbort method also lets MTS know that it can unload the component from memory even if the client of the component still maintains a pointer to the component. When the client next accesses the component, MTS loads a new version of it and passes all component references to the new component. This concept of *just-in-time activation* is a product of another aspect of MTS, which is its resource control and pooling service, discussed in the next section.

Resource Management

To understand what MTS can provide for resource management with an ASP application, you'll need an introduction to the concepts of resource pooling, resource dispensers, and resource managers. These topics are covered in Chapter 5, but an overview of the technologies would be useful now.

Resource pooling recognizes that some resources—such as database connections, threads, or other finite resources—are expensive. By preallocating a pool of resources, access to the resource happens more quickly. Since quick allocation of the resource is assured, the developer will most likely write code that allocates the resource, uses it, and releases it as soon as possible. When the developer uses this type of coding practice, the pool of available resources can be kept small. By keeping the resource pool as small as possible, the whole system performs better, and the developer receives positive feedback—a nicely performing application or component—encouraging the developer to continue using the sound coding practices that actually assist in the well-behaved application or component. This is just the kind of cycle that should be encouraged with development.

By utilizing resource pooling, expensive and time-consuming resources such as database connections can be created when the application is started and can be used for all resource access, rather than having to create a new reference every time the application wants to create a new connection. Based on resource pooling, the connection happens more quickly, and the system is more scalable, since limited resources are managed finitely and controls are maintained on the number of resources allocated.

Database connections are the most widely known resource that participates in resource pooling, but any resource can be managed in this manner by creating the appropriate resource dispenser. MTS provides for resource pooling of ASP or other components by providing an object called ObjectControl that actually allows the component to be used within a resource-pooling context. Additionally, for specific resources, developers can actually create dispensers that manage allocating the connections for any resource they think would benefit from this process.

In addition, to support resource pooling, MTS also provides for just-in-time activation, which means that when a client makes a connection to a component managed by MTS, it is really getting a connection provided by MTS and not directly by the component. If the component signals that it is finished with its process, using SetComplete or SetAbort on the component's associated ObjectContext object, MTS knows that it can mark the component for release, even while the client still maintains the connection to the component. When the client next accesses a method on the component, MTS loads a new instance of the component and the client is never aware that it is no longer using the original "component reference."

Accessing Data with ASP Components

There are few applications, Internet-based or otherwise, that do not perform data access in one form or another. ASP applications are no exception. There are actually several methodologies that an ASP application and an ASP component can use to manage or query data.

RDO and DAO: Earlier Data Access Techniques

First of all, an ASP component may access data through a set of APIs provided by the data source engine that allows direct access to the data. Though efficient, the problem with this approach is that the data access is locked into the particular database engine. An additional problem is that there is no guarantee that the API may not change over time, forcing changes to the component using it. An example of using a direct call-level interface is DB-Library for SQL Server.

If the data source has an ODBC driver, the ODBC call-level interface could be used instead. The advantage to using ODBC is that the same techniques to query and manage data for one data source can also be used for another data source, as long as both data sources provide a compliant and compatible ODBC driver. However, this technique does require a fairly in-depth understanding of ODBC.

Microsoft provided the Data Access Objects (DAO) for access to the Jet database engine that ships with Visual Basic and Access. The advantages of DAO are that it is optimized for ISAM or Jet database access, and it can support single queries against multiple data sources. The disadvantages to using DAO are that it is not an optimum approach to access data from relational data sources, and it requires more memory than other approaches such as the Remote Data Objects (RDO) discussed next. Also, before the release of ODBCDirect, DAO could not be used with ODBC data sources. ODBCDirect now provides RDO functionality from DAO objects, though the other limitations remain.

RDO are really wrapper objects for the ODBC API, but lessen the complexity of using ODBC. RDO provides for powerful functionality, including the use of local cursors and batch operations. RDO is fast and efficient, but its performance can actually degrade or it can even fail when used with ISAM data sources.

Data access techniques tend to support certain particular types of data access. Some, like DAO, are geared for ISAM data access, and others, like RDO, are geared more towards relational database access. In addition, none of the approaches are designed to access data from text files, email, or any other of the many data sources that we use on a day-to-day basis. To address the gaps in data access, Microsoft proposed the concept of Universal Data Access, discussed next.

Universal Data Access

Universal Data Access is nothing more than a single data access technology that can be used with different types of data, regardless of the format or structure of data source. This means that the same objects can be used to access an ISAM data source, a relational database, a text file, and even data from email.

To support the concept of Universal Data Access, Microsoft used COM as an implementation paradigm and created OLE DB. OLE DB is a set of interfaces based on COM that provide for data access through *data providers* that produce and control data, and *data consumers* that use the data. In this context, SQL Server is considered a data provider, and an ASP component that uses OLE DB directly is a data consumer. Chapter 13, *Integrating Data Access in C++ ASP Components with OLE DB*, covers using the new OLE DB templates to access OLE DB from a Visual C++ component. As a demonstration of how uncomplicated OLE DB can be with the use of these templates, Example 1-4 displays a component method implemented in Visual C++ that uses the OLE DB templates to create a table query and process the returned result set.

Example 1-4. Creating a Query and Processing the Results

```
STDMETHODIMP CobjFive::test()
{
    // variables
    CDataSource connection;
    CSession session;
    CTable<CAccessor<CAuthorsAccessor> > authors;

    _variant_t vbreak;
    vbreak = "<p>";


    // Define the DB Property Set
    CDBPropSet dbinit(DBPROPSET_DBINIT);

    // Set the connection properties
    dbinit.AddProperty(DBPROP_AUTH_PERSIST_SENSITIVE_AUTHINFO, false);
    dbinit.AddProperty(DBPROP_AUTH_USERID, OLESTR("sa"));
    dbinit.AddProperty(DBPROP_INIT_CATALOG, OLESTR("pubs"));
    dbinit.AddProperty(DBPROP_INIT_DATASOURCE, OLESTR("MARVIN"));
    dbinit.AddProperty(DBPROP_INIT_LCID, (long)1033);
    dbinit.AddProperty(DBPROP_INIT_PROMPT, (short)4);

    // initialize the database connection
    connection.Open(_T("SQLOLEDB.1"), &dbinit);
```

Example 1-4. Creating a Query and Processing the Results (continued)

```
    // open the session
    session.Open(connection);

    // open the rowset
    authors.Open(session, "dbo.authors");

    // move through the records and output last name
    authors.MoveFirst();

    while (authors.MoveNext() == S_OK) {
        CComVariant vt(authors.m_aulname);
        m_piResponse->Write(vt);
        m_piResponse->Write(vbreak);
    }
    return S_OK;
}
```

OLE DB is very fast and efficient, but not necessarily simple to understand or use outside of the OLE DB templates for Visual C++. To assist developers in using OLE DB, Microsoft also provided the ActiveX Data Objects (ADO), a set of objects implemented on top of OLE DB that can be used with any programming language or tool that has COM access.

ADO consists of a very small set of objects (only seven) that can be accessed either hierarchically or directly. One of the disadvantages of both DAO and RDO is that their objects form an enforced hierarchy, and any one object can only be accessed from its parent objects within the hierarchy. With ADO, an object like a result set can be accessed and used directly without having to access it from either a command or a database connection, unless this hierarchical access is what you want.

The seven ADO objects are:

Connection object

Creates data source connections and maintains connection information

Command object

Holds data source commands, including those that execute without a returning result set

Recordset object

Holds query information and maintains row data and information about the rows

Field object

Holds information about a specific column within a result set

Parameter object
>   Used to map program parameter information to the parameter passed with a
>   database command

Property object
>   Built-in information about each of the ADO objects

Error object
>   Holds information about any errors that result from some data action

The one major limitation to using ADO is that the objects can only be used for
data manipulation such as queries and updates or stored procedure calls. ADO
cannot be used for defining data structures, such as creating or dropping tables.

In Chapter 9, ADO is used to demonstrate basic data access techniques with ASP
components created using Visual Basic. In addition, using ADO with Java is demonstrated in Chapter 17, *Integrating Java ASP Components with ADO and MTS*.
However, both of these chapters assume a basic familiarity with data access techniques in general, as well as with SQL.

Further Reading

For additional reading about the topics covered in this chapter, check out the following:

*   A good resource on COM is the Microsoft COM web site, located at *http://
    www.microsoft.com/com/*.

*   Microsoft also has a separate web site covering IIS, including a set of articles
    and other references, at *http://www.microsoft.com/ntserver/web/default.asp*.

*   If you do not have Windows NT 4.0 or above, or don't have access to IIS, you
    can still work the ASP examples in this book by downloading the Personal
    Web Server for Windows (and for the Mac) at *http://www.microsoft.com/
    windows/ie/pws/default.htm*.

*   You can read more about CGI and security at *http://hoohoo.ncsa.uiuc.edu/cgi/
    security.html*.

*   If you have not worked with database access technologies before, you might
    want to read the online articles and white papers Microsoft provides at *http://
    www.microsoft.com/data/*.

*   As stated earlier, Software AG, with a web site at *http://www.softwareag.co.
    uk/*, has ported DCOM to Unix, and there is an interesting article on building
    COM components on Unix at *http://msdn.microsoft.com/developer/news/
    feature/vcjune98/unixcom.htm*.

- Again, as stated earlier, Chili!Soft has also ported ASP to web servers other than IIS, and to other environments such as Solaris, as well as NT. You can get more information about Chili!Soft's products at the company's web site at *http://www.chilisoft.com/*.

2

Setting Up and Maintaining the ASP Development Environment

Internet Information Server (IIS) version 4.0 contains several technologies to facilitate ASP application development:

- *Application isolation* allows an ASP application to be created in a separate directory and then stopped and started without having to stop and start IIS. The advantage to this, particularly in a development environment, is that a virtual web site can be created for testing ASP components. The virtual web site can then be stopped and unloaded from memory each time a component needs to be recompiled.

- The Microsoft Script Debugger, released with Internet Explorer 4.0 and IIS 4.0, can be used for client- or server-side script debugging. Though script debugging cannot help with debugging a component internally, it can be useful for debugging scripts that invoke a component, and can be used to test how a component interacts with that script. This and the debugging support provided by the development environment of the language used to create the component make an effective debugging team. This chapter covers how to install and run the Microsoft Script Debugger.

- The IIS Metabase stores persistent information instead of relying on the Windows Registry. The information stored in the Metabase is loaded into memory when the ASP application is accessed. In addition, the Metabase information can be set and accessed from within ASP scripts or from ASP components. Based on this, a set of ASP components can be developed and used locally or remotely to control the behavior of IIS.

- Control of IIS, including controlling the web, SMTP, and FTP servers, occurs through the use of IIS Admin Objects. The Admin objects can be accessed from within an ASP page script or through Visual Basic or Java components, and through the use of the IIS Base Admin Object, accessible with C++.

Before working with ASP pages, you or your webmaster will need to set up a web test environment. This chapter details setting up a test environment for IIS 4.0. If you are using any other web server that supports ASP for testing, you should follow the instructions for that web server.

Microsoft is building tight integration and interdependency between many of its products. As you will see in Chapter 5, *Components, Transactions, and the Microsoft Transaction Server*, ASP and MTS are now integrated. Another form of integration is that between IIS and the Active Directory Service Interface, or ADSI. As you will see later in this chapter, ADSI is actually a part of accessing and setting the IIS Metabase Administration objects.

This chapter includes sample ASP component code, primarily to demonstrate how to access the IIS administration objects from within components. However, the details of creating the components themselves are covered in detail in later chapters. You can return to the demonstrations in this chapter and review them after reading through the chapters on creating simple ASP components in the Visual Basic, Visual C++, and Java sections.

Creating an ASP Test Application Virtual Directory

Unlike IIS version 3.0, version 4.0 can run applications in separate process spaces, which means the application can be restarted without having to restart the IIS web server. This is particularly attractive when developing ASP components. Previously, developers had to restart the web server to install a new version of a component because the component was "locked" against change once it was accessed within an ASP page. In a development environment in which one compiles a new component, tests it, makes adjustments, and compiles it again, this change now means the server does not have to be restarted between component compilations.

Personal Web Server does not allow web applications to exist independently of each other. To unload the ASP application, you will need to shut down the server itself.

In order to facilitate component development, a test application can be created in its own virtual directory. To do this for your own environment, open the IIS Management Console and click on the default web server in the left-hand frame window. Click the right mouse button, and select New, then select Virtual Directory from the context menu. A dialog opens that asks for the name to give the Virtual Directory. You can name it whatever you want, but to continue with this example, name the component test environment "test." The next dialog that opens asks for the physical path for the virtual directory. This can be any physical location you want; however, I created my test environment as a subdirectory of the main web server directory in order keep all my ASP applications in the same general location.

 The default web server may be named to something else. Figure 2-1 shows that the default web server is named "Top," and the test application and virtual subdirectory are named, appropriately enough, "test."

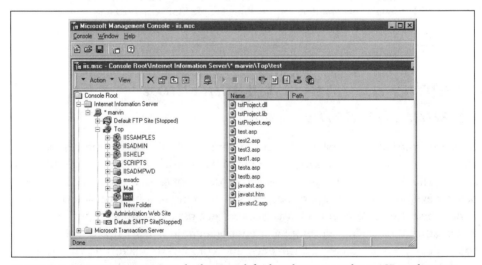

Figure 2-1. IIS Management Console showing default web server and test ASP application

The next dialog asks for the permissions to grant the new virtual directory. Since this directory will contain executable code, check all of the permissions except for Allow Directory Browsing, as shown in Figure 2-2.

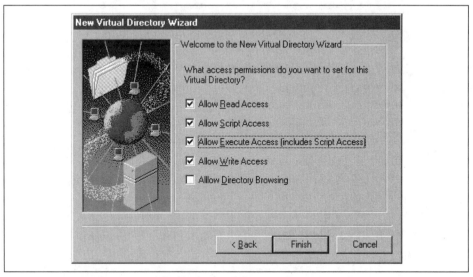

Figure 2-2. Setting permissions for new virtual directory

At this point, click the Finish button so that IIS creates the virtual directory. To complete the test environment setup, select Test Virtual Directory in the left frame and open the Properties dialog by using the context menu.

In the Virtual Directory tab, which is shown in Figure 2-3, a set of options in the top part of the dialog defines how a connection is made with the directory. The choices are that the directory is located on another, shared machine; the location of the site can be found via URL redirection; or the directory is located on the local machine. For the test environment, the directory is located on the machine local to the development environment.

The next set of options includes the physical path of the directory and the virtual directory access permissions, which were set when the directory was created. There are also options that determine whether logging is turned on for the application, whether users accessing the virtual directory can browse the directory, and whether the contents of the virtual directory are indexed by Microsoft Index Server. For the test directory, only logging is turned on at this time.

The final set of options allows you to name the application, set it to run within its own process space, and control the application access permissions.

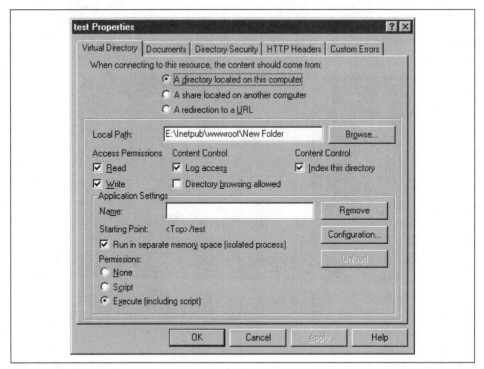

Figure 2-3. Virtual directory property page for the test environment

From Figure 2-3, below the Starting Point label, a checkbox can be selected that will run the application in a memory space separate from the web server. You definitely want to check this for your ASP component test environment, since this allows you to shut down the test environment separately from the web server. At the end of the property page is a set of options that control the application's permissions. The choices are:

- None, which means no application can be run within the virtual directory

- Script, meaning that script-engine based applications, such as ASP applications, can be run

- Execute, allowing access to *.exe* and *.dll* files

For the test environment, the access permission is set to Execute to allow all types of applications to run.

The other property pages for the ASP component test application control what pages are opened by default and control mappings to file types. Since these don't impact the test environment, you can accept the default values for all the other property pages.

Once the ASP component test environment is created, ASP test pages can be placed in the physical subdirectory mapped to the environment, and the pages can be accessed using the `localhost` loopback IP mnemonic. While testing ASP components, reinstalling the component or recompiling the component after making a change can be accomplished by selecting the Properties page of the test application and clicking the Unload button. This unloads the application, including any associated components, from memory.

> The loopback IP address is defined, by default, as 127.0.0.1. Within NT and other environments, this IP address is automatically named `localhost`, and you can use `localhost` instead of having to specify the actual IP address.

You can try out your test environment by creating a simple in-process component and an ASP page that accesses it. For demonstration purposes, I created a Visual Basic ASP component that does nothing more than return a value of 1. Example 2-1 contains the code for this extremely simple component.

Example 2-1. ASP Component with One Method That Returns a Hardcoded Value of 1

```
Option Explicit

Function ReturnOne() As Integer
    ReturnOne = 1
End Function
```

The details of creating the component are covered in Chapter 7, *Creating a Simple Visual Basic ASP Component*, but for now, create the component as an in-process (ActiveX DLL) component. After registering the component using the *regsvr32.exe* utility if the component is running on another system, create an equally simple ASP page to instantiate the object and run the code, as shown in Example 2-2.

Example 2-2. Instantiating the Object from Example 2-1 and Calling Its Only Method

```
<HTML>
<BODY>
<%
Dim obj
Set obj = Server.CreateObject("Simple.Object")
Dim I
i = obj.ReturnOne
%>
</BODY>
</HTML>
```

Use your browser to load the ASP page from the test directory. Next, modify the component to return a value of 2, and try to regenerate the DLL. You should see a message similar to the one shown in Figure 2-4, which indicates that permission to recompile the DLL is denied. The reason this message appears is that the component is still loaded in memory after it has been accessed by the ASP page.

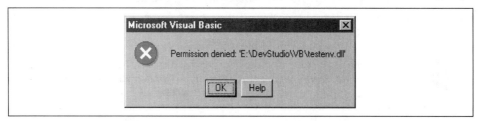

Figure 2-4. Could not recompile ASP component

To recompile the Visual Basic ASP component, open the Internet Server Manager, select the test environment, and open its property sheet. Unload the test environment application from memory by clicking the Unload button shown in Figure 2-5. After this, the VB component can be recompiled.

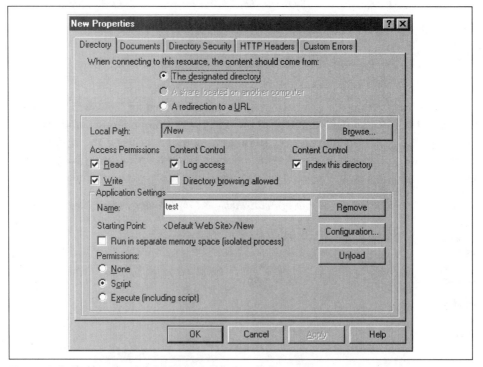

Figure 2-5. Clicking the Unload button releases a lock on an ASP component

Once your test environment is set up, you can create ASP pages and add to your ASP application just by moving the pages to the physical address defined for the test web site. You can also move your ASP components to this directory, though this is neither necessary nor desirable. ASP components can be installed anywhere on the system, and the system locates them when they are accessed within ASP pages.

For most situations, once the ASP environment has been created, no other administrative tasks are necessary, outside of regular maintenance handled by the IIS administrator. However, the IIS environment itself can be customized through the IIS Metabase objects, discussed next.

The IIS Metabase

Prior to the release of IIS 4.0, administrative information was stored in the Windows Registry, an online binary database containing name-value pairs accessible via paths. With IIS 4.0, Microsoft added the IIS Metabase, which is a memory resident data store that is quickly accessible and contains configuration and administration information for IIS.

As with the Registry, Metabase entries are found via paths, or *keys*, similar to those used with file paths. These paths, also referred to as ADsPaths, have the same structure as the paths used within ADSI, and comply with the following general structure:

```
IIS://machinename/service/service_instance
```

where *machinename* can be LocalHost for the local machine or a specific name, *service* can be something such as W3SVC (a web service), and *service_instance* can be a specific instance of that service, such as a web site. To access the Metabase object associated with the test web directory created in the last section, you would use the following ADsPath:

```
IIS://LocalHost/W3SVC/1/ROOT/test
```

This path breaks down into the virtual web site called "test," located off the root subdirectory of the first web instance on the local machine.

Metabase properties are small enough in size that they can be memory resident because they are based on inheritance by default. This means that information about all properties for all objects does not need to be maintained in memory except when the default property value is overridden. As an example, if the top level web service has a ConnectionTimeout property set to 900 seconds, all child nodes, such as virtual web sites created from this top level service, automatically inherit a timeout of 900 seconds unless a different value has been explicitly defined.

The Metabase objects, as well as their properties and methods, can be accessed from within an ASP script, a Visual Basic component, or a Java applet using the IIS Admin Objects, discussed next.

The IIS Admin Objects

 Accessing the IIS Admin Objects from within ASP components is demonstrated using Visual Basic in this chapter, primarily because VB components are least impacted by language-specific implementation details.

IIS can be administered using IIS Administration objects, which can be accessed the same way any other active ASP object is accessed. The advantage of exposing administration tasks to ASP applications is that organizations can create their own ASP administration applications, customized to the organization's needs or to a specific application's needs. Another advantage is that the ASP application and the IIS installation can actually be configured and managed remotely.

The IIS Admin objects most likely to impact an ASP application are the following:

IIsComputer
> Sets global metabase values for the IIS installation. An instance of this object is created for the local host and for each physical machine.

IIsWebDirectory
> Sets metabase values for a specific web directory.

IIsWebServer
> Controls the metabase values for a specific web virtual server, and properties for virtual directories, actual directories, and files.

IIsWebService
> Sets the metabase values for virtual web servers and directories.

IIsWebVirtualDir
> Sets properties for one or all virtual web servers.

The biggest disadvantage to using the IIS Admin objects is that they expose IIS administration tasks to remote access, so the objects should be used with care. Microsoft recommends placing the applications accessing the objects in a secure subdirectory and setting the permissions to that subdirectory to NT Challenge/ Response, which means that anonymous access is disallowed and NTFS security is used to verify access to the subdirectory.

To demonstrate the IIS Admin Objects, Microsoft provides a sample program that lists the IIS Admin Objects available on the local machine and their associated properties. The program can be accessed from the IIS documentation, found by opening the NT Option Pack documentation. From the documentation, selecting the Microsoft Internet Information Server section from the list in the left frame and choosing the Programmer's Reference provides a list of documentation for ASP programmers. From the hierarchy that opens, select the IIS Administration book, then select IIS Admin Objects. From the page that opens, the sample program can be accessed by clicking on the link labeled Sample Program. The hierarchy to follow to find this sample program is:

```
Windows NT Option Pack Documentation
  -Microsoft Internet Information Server
    -Programmer's Reference
      -IIS Administration
        -IIS Admin Objects
          Sample Program is a link within the page
```

Access this program, copy the code to an empty text file, and save the file as an ASP file (with an *.asp* extension). To run the file, it must be installed in an IIS administration subdirectory, and it can only be run by a person with administration privileges. The administration subdirectory is the same subdirectory where the HTML version of the Internet Service Manager is located. This is most likely installed within the Windows main subdirectory and has the following path for Windows NT:

C:\WINNT\system32\inetsvr\iisadmin

The exact path for the sample program with the documentation dated February 21, 1998, is *http://localhost/iishelp/iis/htm/sdk/aoii09bh.htm.*

Once the sample program is installed within the administration subdirectory, access it from within a web browser to get a printout of IIS Admin Objects on the local machine.

 The next few sections will be more meaningful if you also run the Admin Object sample program on your installation and examine its values as you read through the sections.

Each IIS Admin Object has six general ADSI properties: Name, ADSI Path, Class, GUID, Parent, and Schema. These are discussed in more detail in the next section. In addition to properties, each object also has the same methods, also discussed later in the section "The IIS Admin Object Methods." Other properties depend on which service is accessed; these are surveyed in the section "Other IIS Admin Object Properties."

The ADSI Properties

The IIS Admin objects support the ADSI interface by implementing the Name, ADSI Path, Class, GUID, Parent, and Schema properties. For the example program to begin the list of objects and their properties, a reference to the Admin objects must be made by creating an instance of the object from the local machine. The code to do this is:

```
Dim IsInheritableObj
Set IsInheritableObj = GetObject("IIS://LocalMachine")
```

The *GetObject* function (rather than the CreateObject method) is used to return a reference to an existing object.

The general ADSI properties are covered in the following sections.

Name

The Admin object name is the name used to refer to the object within a given namespace. As an example, the name "W3SVC" refers to the **IISWebService** class, which is the web service. The name is also used to represent specific instances of any particular service, except that "name" in this case represents the number of the instance rather than a user-defined name. For instance, if more than one web service is running on a machine, each individual web service can be accessed by a number representing its location within the web service listing, as well as a descriptive name mapped to the instance.

For example, on my machine I have two instances of the web service running, one for administration and one for external access. The external access web server is located before the administrative web service, so it is given the label "1." It is also mapped to its Description, "Top."

The Name property can be accessed from ASP components as well as from an ASP scripting block. Example 2-3 shows a method that accesses the IIS Admin object from an ASP component created using Visual Basic (for detailed information on creating a Visual Basic ASP Component, see Chapter 7). The method displays the value of the Admin object's Name property. The value displayed by the method call is W3SVC, which is the name given to the IIS Web Service.

Example 2-3. Accessing the Admin Object with Visual Basic

```
Sub MyIISProperties()
    Dim objContext As ObjectContext
    Set objContext = GetObjectContext()
    Set objResponse = objContext("Response")
```

Example 2-3. Accessing the Admin Object with Visual Basic (continued)

```
    Dim myObject
    Set myObject = GetObject("IIS://LocalHost/W3SVC")
    objResponse.Write (myObject.Name)
End Sub
```

Once an in-process ASP component is compiled, it can be registered using the *regsvr32.exe* utility from a command line in the same subdirectory where the component is located if it is deployed on another system:

```
    regsvr32.exe theObject.dll
```

This registers the in-process ASP component for access as a COM component. Note that changing the Visual Basic subroutine implementation does *not* require reregistration of the component.

To use this object, create an ASP page that instantiates the object and calls the object's methods, as shown in Example 2-4.

Example 2-4. ASP Page to Instantiate Component That Accesses IIS Admin Object

```
<HTML>
<BODY>
<%
Dim currentobj
Set currentobj=Server.CreateObject("theObject.myObject")
currentObj.MyIISProperties()
%>
</BODY>
</HTML>
```

The ASP page shown in Example 2-4 can be used for all the examples in the rest of the chapter by shutting down the IISADMIN web page, changing the code for the *MyIISProperties* subroutine, and recompiling the DLL.

ADSI path

Access to IIS Admin objects occurs via the ADSI path, which Microsoft refers to as the ADsPath. This path usually has the configuration of "IIS://" followed by the computer name (or **LocalHost** for the local IIS installation), followed by the specific service, such as **W3SVC** for the web service. To access the first web site on the local machine, the following path would be given:

```
    IIS://LocalHost/W3SVC/1
```

The 1 at the end of the path accesses the first web site installed on the local machine. A value of 2 accesses the second, and so on. From the specific web instance, a virtual directory can be accessed by extending the path, as the following demonstrates for the ASP component test environment:

```
    IIS://LocalHost/W3SVC/1/root/test
```

The different services, such as W3SVC, are equivalent to the different IIS Admin objects.

Class

The class is the name of the schema class, and is not unique for service instances. For example, each virtual web service, such as the test web site created earlier in this chapter, has a class name of `IIsWebVirtualDir`, and each top-level web service has a class name of `IIsWebServer`.

GUID

The Globally Unique Identifier (GUID) is the unique identifier for the specific class. Like the Class, the GUID is unique only for the specific schema class, not for each instance. For example, the GUID for the `IIsWebServer` class on my machine has the following format:

```
{ 8B645280-7BA4-11CF-B03D-00AA006E0975 }
```

Parent

The parent for an administrative object is the ADsPath of the IIS administrative object that contains it. For example, the parent for the local machine `LocalHost` is only shown as IIS:. And since the ADsPath for the top-level web service is:

```
IIS://LocalHost/W3SVC
```

the Parent for this object would then be:

```
IIS://LocalHost
```

The parent-child relationship is important because the IIS Metabase is based on inheritance. Most properties are inherited from an object at a higher level, and this object can be found by retrieving each object's Parent property.

Schema

The documentation for IIS states that the Schema property is the ADsPath of the object representing the schema class. For instance, the value for the Schema property for the top-level web service is:

```
IIS://LocalHost/schema/IIsWebService
```

The IIS Admin Object Methods

The IIS Admin Object methods are used to access and set Admin object properties. Each of the methods can be used with any Admin object, and can be used to access or set any property. The methods are discussed and demonstrated in the following sections.

Get

The Get method returns the value for a specific property. The property name is passed as a parameter to the method. For example, Example 2-5 displays the value of the AspCodepage property for the virtual web site named "test."

Example 2-5. The Admin Object's Get Method, Used to Retrieve AspCodepage Property

```
Sub MyIISProperties()
    Dim objContext As ObjectContext
    Set objContext = GetObjectContext()
    Set objResponse = objContext("Response")
    Dim myObject
    Set myObject = GetObject("IIS://LocalHost/W3SVC/1/Root/test")
    Dim codePageValue
    codePageValue = myObject.Get("AspCodepage")
    objResponse.Write (codePageValue)
End Sub
```

With VBScript and Visual Basic, the property can also be accessed using the *object.property* syntax, using something similar to the following:

```
    codePageValue = myObject.AspCodepage
```

GetEx

The GetEx method can be used to access single or multi-valued properties. An example of a multivalued property is HttpCustomHeaders, which returns a list of strings formatted in name/value pairs.

Put

The Put method sets the value for a specific property. As with Get, the property name is passed as the first parameter to the method, and the new value is passed as the second parameter. Example 2-6 demonstrates this using the AspException-CatchEnable property:

Example 2-6. The Put Method, Used to Alter an IIS Admin Object Value

```
Sub MyIISProperties()
    Dim objContext As ObjectContext
    Set objContext = GetObjectContext()
    Set objResponse = objContext("Response")
    Dim myObject
    Set myObject = GetObject("IIS://LocalHost/W3SVC/1/Root/test")
    Dim disableError
    disableError = False
    myObject.Put "AspExceptionCatchEnable", disableError
    myObject.SetInfo
End Sub
```

Again, as with Get, the property can be set directly in the object from within VBScript or Visual Basic:

```
myObject.AspExceptionCatchEnable = False
```

PutEx

As with GetEx, the PutEx method is used to set a property that has single or multiple values.

SetInfo

The SetInfo method is used to save any changes to the metabase properties. The method saves only changed properties.

Other IIS Admin Object Properties

Other IIS Admin Object properties are dependent on the type of IIS Admin object. For example, the MaxBandWidth property can be used with the IIsComputer object and the IIsWebServer object, but not with the IIsFtpService object. Each of the IIS Admin Objects and its respective properties is listed in the documentation that comes with IIS. However, the ASP-specific properties of the IIsWebServer/ IIsWebService and IIsWebVirtualDir objects can be especially useful when setting up the IIS test environment or when creating ASP components for Internet or Intranet development. These properties are discussed and demonstrated in the following sections.

AspAllowOutOfProcComponents

By default, only in-process components can be accessed from within ASP scripting blocks. In-process components are Dynamic Link Library (DLL) components that share the same address space as the application that invokes them. However, by setting this Boolean property to **True**, out-of-process components—those compiled into separate executables—can also be accessed.

To illustrate setting the AspAllowOutOfProcComponents property to **True**, use the Visual Basic ActiveX EXE project type to create a simple out-of-process ASP component. This component does nothing more than return the hardcoded value 2, as shown in Example 2-7.

Example 2-7. Method of an Out-of-Process ASP Component

```
Function theTest() As Integer
    theTest = 2
End Function
```

After creating the component, compile it.

Next, use Visual Basic to create a second ASP component, except make this component in-process (i.e., an ActiveX DLL). It accesses the AspAllowOutOfProcComponents property of the "test" virtual web server and sets this property to True, as shown in Example 2-8. After this Visual Basic DLL is coded, you should compile it and register it with *regsvr32* if it will run on the non-development machine.

Example 2-8. Setting the AspAllowOutOfProcComponents Property

```
Sub MyIISProperties()
    Dim objContext As ObjectContext
    Set objContext = GetObjectContext()
    Set objResponse = objContext("Response")
    Dim myObject
    Set myObject = GetObject("IIS://LocalHost/W3SVC/1/Root/test")
    objResponse.Write ("Before " +
                    CStr(myObject.AspAllowOutOfProcComponents))
    myObject.AspAllowOutOfProcComponents = True
    myObject.SetInfo
    objResponse.Write ("<p>After " +
                    CStr(myObject.AspAllowOutOfProcComponents))
End Sub
```

When this component is accessed within an ASP script block and the *MyIISProperties* subroutine is called, the resulting web page has the following text:

```
Before False
```

```
After True
```

The subroutine sets the AspAllowOutOfProcComponents property to True, which means that an out-of-process ASP component can be accessed directly from ASP script from within an ASP page. This can be tested by calling the out-of-process component's theTest method, which returns a value of 2. The component does not need to be registered using *regsvr32* and can be accessed using the ASP page shown in Example 2-9, which instantiates the out-of-process component using its project and class names.

Example 2-9. ASP Page to Access an Out-of-Process Component

```
<HTML>
<BODY>
<%
Dim tst
Set tst = Server.CreateObject("Project1.Class1")
Dim two
two = tst.theTest
Response.Write(two)
%>
</BODY>
</HTML>
```

The only limitation in accessing the out-of-process component *Project1.exe* is that it must be located where the ASP page can find it. For this example, the component is placed in the *Test* directory. Because the *Test* directory was set to allow execution within the subdirectory, out-of-process components can be run from the directory.

Once AspAllowOutOfProcComponents is set to True, it will remain True even if the web server is shut down and restarted. The only way to set the value back to False is to access and change the property. This property can be applied to the IIsWebService, IIsWebServer, IIsWebVirtualDir, and IIsWebDirectory IIS Admin Objects.

AspAllowSessionState

When a user accesses a web page from an ASP application for the first time within an Internet session, an ASP Session object is created. This object can be used to store and access session-level information, making this information available while the ASP session is in effect.

The AspAllowSessionState property can be used to enable or disable the session state. If the property is set to True, the default, the session state is created, and session information can be maintained. In addition, the Session_OnStart and Session_OnEnd event handlers can be programmed in *global.asa*, a file that maintains global scripting for an ASP application.

However, if no session level information needs to be tracked for the application, the AspAllowSessionState property can be set to False to stop session state maintenance.

AspBufferingOn

ASP buffering prevents any output being sent to the client until all the output is collected. This approach can be used to throw away output for an incomplete transaction or to discard or modify output based on application results. ASP buffering can be turned on or off using the Response object, discussed in more detail in Chapter 6, *Overview of the Intrinsic (Built-in) Objects*, or it can be altered by setting the AspBufferingOn metabase property.

The AspBufferingOn property is set to False by default, which means buffering is not enabled and output is sent directly to the web client as it is generated.

AspCodepage

Specifying the codepage controls what character language mapping is used within a web page. By default, the value of the codepage for an ASP application is zero (0), which is designated as CP_ACP, System ANSI.

Individual ASP applications can alter this by supplying a codepage specification within a scripting block, or by setting the CodePage property of the built-in Session object. However, overall control of the codepage for a specific web or virtual web server can be handled through the use of the AspCodepage property. Setting this property overrides any other codepage specification for an ASP application page accessed by the web service, server, or virtual web server.

 Setting a property at the web server that overrides local settings within ASP pages can be a frustrating experience for the ASP developer, especially if the developer is not aware of the global setting. Use global settings with caution, and document and publish the settings when the default values are altered.

This property can be applied to the IIsWebService, IIsWebServer, IIsWebVirtualDir, and IIsWebDirectory IIS Admin Objects.

AspEnableParentPaths

By default, relative paths can be used when specifying URL locations relative to a given location. As an example, a web page can be located using the absolute path *http://www.yasd.com/scripting/vbscript/*.

To access a web page within the scripting subdirectory, a reference can use a relative notation such as *../index.htm*. This is equivalent to providing the full path, *http://www.yasd.com/scripting/index.htm*.

However, relative paths can actually cause a security risk, since pages can be accessed outside of the directory defined for the virtual web site. To prevent the use of relative paths, the AspEnableParentPaths property can be set to `False`.

This property can be applied to the IIsWebService, IIsWebServer, IIsWebVirtualDir, and IIsWebDirectory IIS Admin Objects.

AspExceptionCatchEnable

To enable the Microsoft Script Debugger, the ASP component developer can turn on debugging from within the IIS administration tools, or the developer can set the AspExceptionCatchEnable property to `True`. This turns on the script debugger until the property is specifically set to `False`.

This property can be applied to the IIsWebService, IIsWebServer, IIsWebVirtualDir, and IIsWebDirectory IIS Admin Objects.

AspLogErrorRequests

In order to track client access errors within an ASP application, error codes can be written to a log file. This logging is enabled by default, but it can be turned off by setting the AspLogErrorRequests property to **False**.

This property can be applied to the IIsWebService, IIsWebServer, IIsWebVirtualDir, and IIsWebDirectory IIS Admin Objects.

AspMemFreeFactor

When an ASP application is no longer running, it can be unloaded from memory by clicking the Unload button for the application's virtual directory, as described above. However, IIS does not automatically release all the memory blocks used by the application to the virtual memory pool. Some of the memory blocks are reserved by IIS for use with all ASP applications, improving the performance of the applications by having preallocated memory set aside for running the ASP applications. How many of these memory blocks are reserved for use by ASP applications is determined by the AspMemFreeFactor property.

AspMemFreeFactor specifies a ratio of used to free memory blocks that are reserved for ASP use. If the value is 50, the default, IIS will start releasing free memory blocks when the free memory list is equal to half of the used memory list. A value of 200 means that IIS will release free memory blocks when the free memory list is equal to two times the size of the used memory list.

If the machine used for the ASP application is reserved primarily for ASP processing, this value should be set high. However, if the machine on which the ASP application is hosted also has many other tasks, such as database-related tasks, this value should be low.

This property can be applied to the IIsWebService, IIsWebServer, IIsWebVirtualDir, and IIsWebDirectory IIS Admin Objects.

AspQueueTimeout

AspQueueTimeout specifies the amount of time an ASP script will wait to be executed in a queue. If you have ever received a message from an ASP-based server that the server is too busy or the request has expired, what has happened is that the time the script waited to run exceeded the time allowed for it to run.

This property can be applied to the IIsWebService, IIsWebServer, IIsWebVirtualDir, and IIsWebDirectory IIS Admin Objects.

AspScriptEngineCacheMax

More than one scripting language can be supported for use with ASP. Engines can be loaded and cached in memory for Perl, Tcl, REXX, and other scripting languages. The AspScriptEngineCacheMax property is used to specify the number of scripting engines cached in memory; it is set to 30 by default.

This property can be applied to the IIsWebService, IIsWebServer, IIsWebVirtualDir, and IIsWebDirectory IIS Admin Objects.

AspScriptErrorMessage

If debugging error messages are not sent to the client, a default error message can be set using the AspScriptErrorMessage property. Example 2-10 illustrates setting this property.

Example 2-10. Setting the AspScriptErrorMessage Property

```
Sub MyIISProperties()
    Dim objContext As ObjectContext
    Set objContext = GetObjectContext()
    Set objResponse = objContext("Response")
    Dim myObject
    Set myObject = GetObject("IIS://LocalHost/W3SVC/1/Root/test")
    Dim disableError
    disableError = False
    myObject.Put "AspScriptErrorSentToBrowser", disableError
    Dim strErrormessage
    strErrormessage = "Something broke"
    myObject.Put "AspScriptErrorMessage", strErrormessage
    myObject.SetInfo
End Sub
```

This property can be applied to the IIsWebService, IIsWebServer, IIsWebVirtualDir, and IIsWebDirectory IIS Admin Objects.

AspScriptErrorSentToBrowser

As shown in the code block in Example 2-10, if debugging information such as the filename, line number, and description of an error is not sent to the client, a static error message is sent. To prevent sending the debugging error information, set the AspScriptErrorSentToBrowser property to **False**. This property is **True** by default.

This property can be applied to the IIsWebService, IIsWebServer, IIsWebVirtualDir, and IIsWebDirectory IIS Admin Objects.

AspScriptFileCacheSize

IIS has the ability to cache ASP scripts. Changing this value can change how much caching occurs. Setting AspScriptFileCacheSize to -1, the default, caches all scripts.

Setting the property to 0 turns caching off. A value other than these two will cache that number of scripts. For instance, the Visual Basic component code in Example 2-11 lets the cache store 10 scripts only.

Example 2-11. Setting the AspScriptFileCacheSize Property to Cache 10 Scripts

```
Sub MyIISProperties()
    Dim myObject
    Set myObject = GetObject("IIS://LocalHost/W3SVC/1/Root/test")
    myObject.AspScriptFileCacheSize = 10
    myObject.SetInfo
End Sub
```

Adjusting this value dynamically is an effective technique to fine-tune the performance of a web site based on current usage.

This property can be applied to the IIsWebService, IIsWebServer, IIsWebVirtualDir, and IIsWebDirectory IIS Admin Objects.

AspScriptLanguage

VBScript is the default scripting language used for an ASP application. Setting the AspScriptLanguage property can alter this default scripting language. The following code sets the default scripting language to JScript:

```
myObject.AspScriptLanguage="JScript"
```

This property can be overridden with the use of a directive, such as the following:

```
<%@LANGUAGE = "JScript"%>
```

This property can be applied to the IIsWebService, IIsWebServer, IIsWebVirtualDir, and IIsWebDirectory IIS Admin Objects.

AspScriptTimeout

By default, scripts have 90 seconds until a timeout occurs and the script is terminated. This timeout value can be changed either by using the ScriptTimeout method for the built-in Server object or by setting the AspScriptTimeout property to a different value.

If an ASP application has components that can take considerable time, such as components that access a database, the AspScriptTimeout property should be changed to prevent the script accessing the component from timing out.

AspSessionTimeout

Each request to an ASP application from a single web page reader resets the timer for the Session object timeout. If another request from the same reader exceeds this timeout time, an error message is returned to the reader. The Session timeout time can be reset using the AspSessionTimeout property.

This property can be applied to the IIsWebService, IIsWebServer, IIsWebVirtualDir, and IIsWebDirectory IIS Admin Objects.

The ADSI Container Object Properties and Methods

The sample program discussed in the last section makes use of the fact that IIS Admin Objects that contain other objects support the **IADSContainer** interface. This means that the object can support certain container functionality such as a count of contained objects and a method of enumerating through these objects.

The ADSI Container Object properties are:

_NewEnum

For automation languages such as Visual Basic, this property returns an enumerator that allows the language to retrieve the contained objects. An enumerator in Visual Basic is an object that provides built-in functionality to iterate or enumerate the objects in a collection. Visual Basic Collection objects automatically have this enumerator capability built in. This means that each object can be accessed using the following syntax:

```
For each obj in ObjectCollection
    ...do something
Next
```

Count

Returns a count of contained objects

In the sample program provided by Microsoft that outputs information about the local IIS installation, discussed at the beginning of the section "The IIS Metabase," the properties of specific objects were listed using an enumerator. The following code taken from this sample application demonstrates an enumerator:

```
For Each PropName in OptPropList
    Response.Write Indent & PropName
    If ShowInh = "T" Then
        Response.Write Space(35-Len(PropName))
        Response.Write InhList(IsInheritable(PropName))
    End If
    If ShowType = "T" Then
        If ShowInh = "T" Then
        ' Already vertically aligned - just move on a little
        Response.Write Space(4)
    Else
        ' Pad out to align vertically
        Response.Write Space(35-Len(PropName))
```

```
      End If
      Set PropSchemaObj = GetObject("IIS://" & MachName & "/Schema/" & PropName)
      Response.Write PropSchemaObj.Syntax End If Response.Write "<BR>"
   Next
```

In this code, each property in the schema object's optional properties is accessed.

The ADSI Container Object methods are:

CopyHere
    Copies an object into a container and returns a pointer to the object

Create
    Creates a new object within the container given the type and name of the object

Delete
    Removes an object of a given type and name from a container

GetObject
    Returns the ADSI object given the class and name of the object

MoveHere
    Removes an object from its source and places it in the container

These container methods and properties allow you to add or remove new virtual web sites, or to access information about any aspect of an IIS installation.

The IIS Base Admin Object

The IIS Admin object works directly from an ASP script, or it can be accessed in Visual Basic or from Java. However, to administer IIS from a C++ application requires accessing the **IMSAdminBase** interface, found in the IIS Base Admin Object.

The IIS Base Object has several structures used by the Base object methods. Covering these structures and the associated object methods and the IIS Base Object errors requires understanding the C++ language, which goes beyond the scope of this chapter. Instead, this object is covered in more detail in Chapter 12, *The C++ ASP Built-In Interfaces*.

For Further Reading

For additional reading about the topics covered in this chapter, check out the following:

*   The documentation installed with IIS 4.0 for more information about the IIS Administration Objects.

- You can also access information about the IIS Admin objects at Microsoft's web site. Specifically, search for the keywords "ASP IIS Admin" at *http://search.microsoft.com/*.

- You can access more information about IIS, including articles and an overview, at *http://www.microsoft.com/ntserver/web/default.asp*.

3

ASP Components and COM

ASP components are dependent on an architecture being in place to support component communication, and COM, or the Component Object Model, is the approach Microsoft has taken for this type of communication. In actuality, ASP components, or for that matter MTS components, are also known as OLE automation servers, or just plain automation servers. This chapter and most of the book refers to the objects simply as "components."

COM is based on a binary and network standard that transcends any dependence on computer language. By using machine-level communication, a component written in Visual C++ can invoke functions exposed by a component written in Java, and a Java component can invoke a function within a C++ object. All that is required is that the underlying COM implementation be installed for the operating system where the components reside.

This chapter does not provide an in-depth description of how COM works, since entire books have been written about COM alone. However, it does cover some of the information that component developers should understand about COM before beginning to write components. At the end of the chapter is a list of articles and books that provide more in-depth discussions of COM.

The chapter begins with a brief overview of how COM works and how it is implemented, and then progresses into those features of COM that are incorporated into COM-compliant components. Lastly a simple ASP component is created at the end of the chapter using Visual C++, Visual Basic, and Visual J++ to demonstrate how each language/tool creates a COM-based component, and how each implements the required functionality necessary to access the component.

A Very Brief Overview of COM

One important aspect you should know about COM is that implementation details are hidden, and COM components are usually seen as black boxes with no exposure at all of the component internals. A component exposes its functionality through interfaces, which can be considered "strongly typed semantic contracts between the client and the object," according to the documentation on the COM specification provided by Microsoft. When a COM developer provides an interface, he or she is saying that the interface will perform in the same manner throughout all time, or at least for the life of the component. What this means is that an application developer can create a client that accesses the component's functionality, and the developer does not need to know how the functionality is implemented. Moreover, by saying that an interface is a "semantic" contract, there is a defined behavior for each interface, a behavior that is guaranteed to exist regardless of future changes to the component.

To ensure that one component's interfaces are unique to that component, regardless of the interface names used, each component is assigned a unique identifier; hence the term "strongly typed."

The COM specification provides for:

- Binary communication between components

- A unique class identifier to represent a unique component

- Functionality accessible through interfaces

- Interfaces that are never changed and are considered immutable

- A method to query for interfaces if a component contains more than one interface

- A method to track references to an object, to determine when an object is no longer being referenced, and to remove a reference to an object

There are other aspects to COM, but at a minimum this list captures the fundamentals, which are covered in more detail in the following sections.

Binary Communication

The COM specification is a binary and network specification, which means that the components are not language-dependent. They are, however, dependent on the implementation of the COM infrastructure, an implementation that is at this time primarily limited to Windows 95/98 and Windows NT. However, as IIS is limited to this same environmental constraint, this should not pose a problem unless you want to create a remote component on some operating system other than a Windows 32-bit operating system.

Actually, companies such as Software AG have provided programmatic support for COM/DCOM within Unix environments. In addition, the company Chili!Soft has provided software support for ASP
from web servers such as Netscape's Enterprise Server. Based on
these, one can't assume that an ASP application will be running
within a Windows 32-bit environment. However, the majority of ASP
applications and ASP components are created for NT, so we'll concentrate on this in this book.

One of the most powerful features of COM is that when a client accesses a COM
component, the actual location of that component is transparent to the client. This
means that the component can exist locally, on the same machine as the client, or
remotely, on some other machine. This location independence makes a COM-
based application highly scalable, since components can be moved to separate
machines to decrease the load on one machine for better performance, without
requiring changes within the application using the component.

If the component is an in-process component, it runs within the same process as
the client; this type of component is created as a dynamic link library, or DLL. An
out-of-process component is one that runs in its own process space, and COM further specifies two versions of out-process components, those that run locally and
those that run remotely. A local out-of-process component is created as a separate
executable with an *.exe* extension. A remote component can be created as either
an executable or as a DLL. If it is created as a DLL, accessing the component
remotely actually creates a surrogate client on the remote machine in order to load
the component.

ASP components are rarely created as executables, and extra effort
must be taken to use such components, including modification of IIS
metabase attributes. Additionally, out-of-process components cannot
be created as MTS components. The chapter on creating simple components for Visual Basic (Chapter 7, *Creating a Simple Visual Basic
ASP Component*) discusses the creation of in-process and out-of-process components. The examples in this book are created as in-process components.

How does the operating system know which component is being accessed? Each
component is registered on the machine containing the client and on the machine
containing the component if the component is accessed remotely. The most common tool used to register COM components is the utility *regsvr32.exe*. Other tools
used to view the registry information for a component are *oleview.exe*, included

with Visual Studio or downloadable from Microsoft, and *dcomcnfg.exe*, which is used to manage remote components and which can be found in the Windows subdirectory—usually *c:\windows* or *c:\winnt*. Other utilities or tools are used for a specific purpose, such as registering components with MTS, and are discussed more fully in Chapter 5, *Components, Transactions, and the Microsoft Transaction Server.*

Since more than one component can be used within an application, and components can have the same interface names, how does the application and the operating system know which specific component is being accessed? The use of class identifiers ensures access to a specific component, and they are discussed next.

Strong Typing Through Unique Identifiers

Each COM component has an identifier, called a *class identifier* (CLSID), also known as a *globally unique identifier* (GUID). Because of this, no two components with the same object or interface names can be mistakenly used for each other, since each is identified by its own unique CLSID. The concept of the unique identifier first arose in the Open Software Foundation (OSF) Distributed Computing Environment (DCE) specification. The DCE has a concept called the *universally unique identifier* (UUID), which is a 128-bit integer guaranteed to be unique (at least, virtually guaranteed to be unique) across time and space.

The COM CLSID can be generated using a variety of tools, or is created as part of building a COM component using Visual C++, Visual Basic, and Visual J++. In fact, with these tools you won't have to perform any special activities in order to access and include the CLSID within the component: the tool handles this for you. For objects created with other tools or versions of these tools that don't support automatic handling of the CLSID, the utilities *UUIDGEN.EXE* and *GUIDGEN.EXE* can be run separately to create unique identifiers. These utilities can usually be found in the */bin* subdirectory of one of the Visual Studio tools, or can be downloaded from the Microsoft web site.

A real key to the power of COM is the use of interfaces, which is detailed in the next section.

If this is your first exposure to working with COM, you should take the time to read at least chapters one and two of the Component Object Model Specification, accessible from the web at *http://www.microsoft.com/com/*, in addition to reading this chapter.

Interfaces

By using interfaces, COM provides support for objects that can be accessed externally, but without having to publish the object's implementation. The interface itself never changes and basically does nothing more than provide a pointer to the actual implementation. However, by providing this layer of separation between the client of the component and the component implementation, the component developer can make changes internally to the component without requiring any changes at all to the client. The client doesn't even need to be recompiled, since all of its access to the component occurs through the interface.

This separation of interface and implementation provides support for true object-oriented encapsulation, or implementation hiding, though COM itself is not object-oriented in the purest sense. Based on this, the COM component developer can implement the object using any technique or even any programming language, as long as the technique and language support COM.

In the last paragraph, I stated that COM is not object-oriented in the purest sense. What I meant by this is that COM is not based on code source reusability, with a new object derived by inheritance from an existing object. It is based on binary reusability, with a component or application using the existing functionality of a component by including a reference to the component within code, rather than inheriting from the component.

One aspect of COM that can be difficult to work with at first is the fact that COM interfaces are not mutable, which means that different versions of an interface cannot be created. For example, I can create an interface called `IAddress`, with a method called AddAddress. In the beginning, I could have four parameters for the AddAddress method: street address, city, state, and zip code. However, let's say that I open up the interface for international use. In this case, I would want an address to consist of items such as street address, city, region, country, and postal code. I couldn't just modify `IAddress`'s existing AddAddress method and redistribute it as version 2.0, since this would cause havoc with existing customers using the original address interface. What I would do instead is create a new interface—let's call it `IInternationalAddress`—to support international customers, which inherits from my existing interface and expands on it as needed. By doing this I "keep the faith" with my existing clients, so to speak, as well as providing the necessary new functionality for my new clients.

When I first worked with COM, I was not used to this concept of multiple interfaces. Like most developers, I had spent considerable time creating different versions of the same software, going from revision 1.0 to revision 2.0 and so on. I was not comfortable at first with the concept of creating a whole new interface whenever a change was needed. However, it is this quality that is absolutely essential for the success of COM.

First, components are not applications, but instead are grouped functions and data created for a specific purpose and with methods that are guaranteed to work in a specified manner. Based on this, whenever an application developer has need of the same behavior in more than one application, the same component can be used again and again. If the component creators decided to support a new set of behaviors and altered the component methods as well as added new methods, the applications developers would have to upgrade all applications using the component to use the newer version, even if they only wanted to use the new functionality for some of the applications.

However, if the component developers added a new interface to the component that contained the new functionality, then the applications developer could access the new interface only when needing to use the new functionality. The applications that didn't need the new functionality would continue to use the same, unchanged, interface.

In order to support multiple interfaces, applications need to have some method of querying a component's interfaces to see what it supports and what it doesn't. A basic COM feature is the ability to return a pointer to an interface based on a request, discussed next.

Referencing an Interface

To return a reference to an interface, each COM object must implement a function that allows the client to query for a specific interface. In the COM system, this function is called *QueryInterface*. *QueryInterface* takes a unique identifier of the interface as the first argument, and an interface pointer as the second argument. If the *QueryInterface* call is successful, this second argument will contain the pointer to the interface when the method returns.

Rather than adding to the complexity and size of a component by adding automated garbage collection routines, COM utilizes a manual process of freeing component resources. When a component interface is first accessed, the component is loaded into memory and remains in memory as long as at least one interface is accessed. However, when the last interface is released, the component can then be unloaded.

A component can provide pointers to the same interface to more than one application, so how does COM know when there are no longer any references to any component interfaces so that it can unload the component from memory? The answer is that, in addition to having to implement the *QueryInterface* function, each component must also implement a method to increment some form of a counter when an interface is accessed. When a pointer to an interface is success-fully accessed, a counter associated with the interface is incremented by one. This counter is then used by COM to determine when all references to an interface have been released so that the component can be released from memory. So, in addition to the function to query for the interface, another function, *addRef,* adds to the reference count, and a third function, *release,* decrements this reference count. When the component's reference count reaches zero (0), the component is marked for removal from memory.

If a COM-based component—ASP or otherwise—supports no other methods, it must support the ability to query for a specific interface, to increment the count when an interface reference is returned, and to decrement the interface reference count when an interface reference is released. However, as you will see in the sec-tion on COM implementation, much of this functionality is added to a component automatically, just by inheriting from one specific interface. Other aspects of COM functionality are discussed next.

Additional COM Functionality

In addition to the major COM specifications for immutable interfaces that can be queried, and for maintaining reference counts for interfaces, other basic COM functionality has to do with maintaining state for a component, known as persis-tent storage, as well as the use of *Monikers. Persistent storage* is the ability of an object to write state information about itself to storage and later retrieve this state information from storage.

Monikers are an interesting concept. Without going into too much detail, a Moni-ker can be thought of as an intelligent name. By this I mean that not only does a Moniker maintain a reference to some object, it also has information about how to access the object. For example, consider an application that accesses a compo-nent on a remote server using a Moniker to maintain a reference to the pointer to the component interface. While the application was off doing other things, the connection to the server component was lost. However, the Moniker would not only know what component interface to access, it would have enough informa-tion to reinitialize the reference to the component interface if the interface pointer were no longer valid.

Since a Moniker must have enough information about the component interface to recreate the interface pointer, Monikers are actually created by the interface instance itself and are made available to clients.

In addition to persistence and Monikers, COM also contains processes for dealing with data transfer through its Uniform Data Transfer (UDT) specification. This specification provides for an interface that separates the transfer protocol from the actual data itself, and also provides definitions for the transfer medium, and a mechanism to determine what data is being transferred and whether the data of interest has changed. UDT serves to provide a standard for data transfer regardless of the medium used to make the transfer.

How COM Is Implemented

COM is a specification and an implementation. It consists of interfaces that separate client access from component implementation, a defining language to describe these interfaces in a tool- and language-neutral manner, and a predefined set of interfaces that are used to derive all other COM interfaces.

What Is an Interface?

Interfaces are abstract base classes. As such, they are not implemented, but instead contain virtual functions that are themselves pointers to the actual functions that implement this functionality. The actual functions are contained in what is known as the virtual function table, or *vtbl* for short.

The concept of virtual functions arose in C++ object-based programming, not with COM. When a C++ compiler finds a reference to a virtual function, it generates an entry into an array that contains a function pointer for every virtual function. For example, if the C++ compiler finds the following definition in a C++ source code file:

```
class someclass {
public:
    virtual void somefunction();
};
```

it creates an entry into the **vtbl** for *somefunction*. How does a client access the function pointer to invoke the actual implemented function? The answer is that each time an instance of the class **someclass** is created, a pointer is also created within the instance that points to the first entry of the **vtbl** for the class. The C++ compiler implements this pointer for every instance derived from a class that contains virtual functions. The C++ compiler also handles all of the details for the virtual to real function call, which makes this type of functionality doubly attractive. Additionally, the overhead for this functionality is equivalent to an indirect function call—in other words, it is minor at most.

So for the example class just shown, if I write client code that calls the function *somefunction*, the C++ compiler generates the code that accesses the pointer to the class **vtbl**. The C++ compiler also generates the code to access the index for the function—again with no intervention by the C++ class developer—which then returns the function pointer to the *real* function, as shown in Figure 3-1.

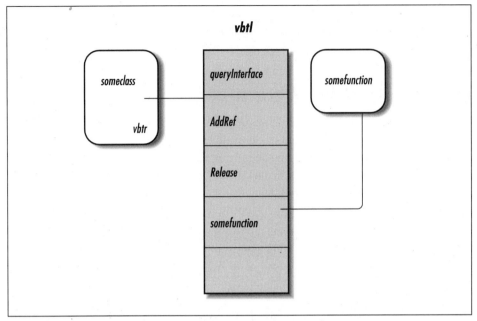

Figure 3-1. Pointer to vtbl, and on to the actual somefunction function

This use of virtual functions enables polymorphism within C++, and this same concept of virtual functions is used to separate the interface from the implementation within COM. However, what happens when you use some programming language other than C++ to create the COM component or the client? You can't use C++ programming language data types directly, since these might not map cleanly between the client and the component.

What is needed is a language-neutral method to define objects, methods, method parameters, and return types; for this task, Microsoft uses *Interface Definition Language* (IDL) for COM.

Using IDL to Define the Interfaces

Interfaces are usually, but not always and not required to be, defined in a separate file using a language called Interface Definition Language (IDL). IDL is itself a subset of the Object Definition Language (ODL) used in OLE, which in turn is derived from the Open Software Foundation's (OSF) Distributed Computing Environment (DCE) Remote Procedure Call (RPC) IDL.

IDL provides a neutral language to describe interfaces, their parameters, and their results. The IDL Microsoft supports for COM is similar to the IDL the OMG group supports for CORBA, though not identical. As an example of a fairly neutral IDL, the following is the definition of a method that takes two long values and returns a short value:

```
short somefunction (in long lParamOne,
                    in long lParamTwo);
```

The modifier **in** is used to denote a parameter that is passed by value only. Another modifier is **out** to denote a parameter passed by reference.

As stated, Microsoft has its own version of IDL that has COM-specific *annotation* or *decoration*. The Microsoft-specific version of the IDL for the function shown previously is:

```
HRESULT somefunction([in] long lParamOne, [in] long lParamTwo,
        [out,retval]short retVal);
```

To explain this example, Microsoft requires that the return type of all COM methods be **HRESULT**, a macro for an OLE data value that returns the success or failure of the method call. However, you can actually return, literally, a different data type to the calling program by using the modifier **[retval]**. For the method somefunction, the parameters are two long values passed in by value, and one return value of type short.

Though the IDL defines three parameters, and the function within the COM component would code for three parameters, you would actually only code for two parameters and a short result in the client, as the VBScript shows in the next block:

```
Dim retValue
Dim lParam1, lParam2
lParam1 = 2
lParam2 = 3
retValue = somefunction(lParam1,lParam2)
```

If the method were coded in Visual Basic, the return value parameter would be listed as the actual return for the method instead of one of the parameters, as shown in the following Visual Basic code fragment:

```
Public Function somefunction(ByVal lParam1 As Long, ByVal lParam2 As Long) _
                As Integer
```

How IDL is used to handle parameter typing and method description within COM is discussed in the next two sections, beginning with the base COM interface, IUnknown.

IUnknown

In order to support a multiple immutable interface approach, COM has provided an interface, IUnknown, and all component interfaces must be derived, directly or indirectly, from it. IUnknown has three abstract methods, QueryInterface, AddRef, and Release, which provide references to the necessary functionality for querying for a specific interface, adding a reference to the interface from within an application, and releasing the reference when the interface pointer is no longer needed.

IUnknown is an *abstract base class*, which means it contains nothing but virtual functions and has no implementation itself. You cannot directly create an instance of IUnknown. In addition, each of the IUnknown functions is a pure virtual function, which means that each of these functions *must* be implemented within any interface that inherits from IUnknown.

IUnknown provides the methods to access an interface and update the interface reference counter, but a problem with runtime access of an interface and its methods is determining the structure of a particular method call, including the number and types of parameters passed in the call. To address this problem, Microsoft also provides another standard interface, itself derived from IUnknown, called IDispatch. IDispatch is also known as the COM *automation* object.

IDispatch

As mentioned earlier, interfaces can be defined in IDL to provide a language-independent description of the interface. However, IDL doesn't just define the interface and its methods as an esoteric exercise. An IDL file can be used to generate a *type library*. A type library contains information about a COM object, such as the interface object's methods and parameters. This information can then be used whenever an interface method is invoked.

If the client does not have access to the type library, does it mean it can't access the component? No, but extra effort is necessary to allow access to a component's methods. If the client does not have information about the component interface method, it must first call a method to get identifiers for the method and each of the method's parameters, then pass this information along on each call to the method. The functionality to make this call resides with another basic COM interface, IDispatch.

The earliest implementations of IDispatch performed two function calls for every method called on the interface that was derived from IDispatch. The first call was to a function called *GetIDsOfNames*, which returned a special id, called the DISPID, for the method. The DISPID is passed as the first parameter of another IDispatch method, invoke, which is used to actually invoke the derived interface method. So if you had a component with a method called getTestScores, calling this method from an application or another component resulted in two method calls on IDispatch: one to *GetIDsOfNames* to get the DISPID of getTestScores, and one to invoke with the DISPID to actually call the method. In addition to the DISPID passed to the IDispatch invoke method, a structure containing the parameters for getTestScores is also passed to invoke. This structure is of type DISPPARAMS and is generated by default using a standard proxy/stub Microsoft implemented specifically for default marshaling.

As you can imagine, having to call two functions for every interface method call, a process known as *late binding*, could become a bit of a performance issue, particularly if that component exists across a network. In answer to performance concerns, Microsoft provided the type library, discussed earlier. What was not discussed earlier was how the type library can be used in place of the IDispatch *GetIDsOfNames* function.

Instead of having to call *GetIDsOfNames* to get the DISPID of the method, the type library provides the DISPIDs for each of the interface methods; IDispatch can use these to pass to the invoke method, rather than having to call *GetIDsOfNames*. Because the binding information is retrieved early on, it is known as—what else?—*early binding*.

However, using IDispatch is not the only technique that can be used to access an interface method. Another technique to invoke a method on an interface is to access the vtbl entry for the method directly, rather than accessing it through IDispatch. Accessing the vtbl directly is supported for most programming languages, including Visual Basic, Visual C++, and Java (with help from the Microsoft COM Java wrapping), but it is not supported for scripting languages such as VBScript and JScript. Because of this, vtable binding is not supported in ASP scripting blocks. Since not all COM clients support vtbl binding, most COM-based components, including ones created specifically for use in ASP applications, use a method known as the *dual interface*. A dual interface component is one that has support both for vtable binding as well as IDispatch in cases where vtbl binding is not supported. The components in this book all use the dual interface.

At a minimum, a COM-based component can be created using just IUnknown and, usually, IDispatch, and in a later section we'll use Visual C++ to create just such a simple component. However, for the client to access a reference to a class instance through an interface, the instance must be created, and this is where IClassFactory enters the picture.

IClassFactory

IUnknown defines a method that can be used to query for an interface, and IDispatch can be used to invoke a method on the interface, but we are missing something here. Something, somewhere, has to create the instance of the class associated with the interface.

When a client wants to create an instance of a component and query for an interface on that component, it must do two things. First, it must initialize COM—call it waking COM up—by calling a function named *CoInitialize* or *CoInitializeEx*. *CoInitialize* takes one parameter, a value of NULL, and *CoInitializeEx* takes two parameters, the first again being NULL and the second containing a flag describing the thread's concurrency model. Either of these functions is only called once on a thread and basically initializes the COM library on that thread.

Threads are discussed in more detail in Chapter 4, *ASP Components and Threads*.

After the function call to kick COM awake, so to speak, the next function the client must call is either *CoCreateInstance* or *CoCreateInstanceEx*. *CoCreateInstance* takes as parameters the CLSID for the object, either a pointer to an object for aggregation or NULL, the context of the component (whether the component is in process or not, or running remotely or locally), the identifier of the interface reference used to communicate with the object, and, lastly, the pointer to hold this interface reference. The more modern version of *CoCreateInstance*, *CoCreateInstanceEx*, takes the same first three parameters, but then it takes the name of the component server as a fourth parameter (or NULL if the component is local), a number for the number of query interface structures passed in the last parameter, and an array of query interface structures in the last parameter. *CoCreateInstance* can return only one interface on the local machine. *CoCreateInstanceEx* can return an array of interfaces on either the local or a remote machine.

As *CoCreateInstance* implies, the purpose of this method is to create an instance of the object identified by the CLSID. For this to work, the component must have some associated technique to provide for class construction, and this technique is implemented through the IClassFactory interface. Internally, with either *CoCreateInstance* or *CoCreateInstanceEx*, each method invokes the IClass-Factory interface method *CreateInstance*.

When a call to *CreateInstance* is made for an interface, it is the component's implementation of the IClassFactory interface that generates the new instance of the component, becoming literally the component's class factory, hence the name.

IClassFactory, as well as *CoInitilize* and *CoCreateInstance*, is implemented in the background when working with Java and Visual Basic, and is usually hidden within the templates when using ATL with Visual C++.

So what happens when a client creates an instance of a COM object and calls one of its methods? The client first initializes COM (*CoInitialize*), then creates an instance of the component (*CoCreateInstance*), which in turn creates an instance of the component (through IClassFactory's *CreateInstance*). Next, it queries the component for a specific interface (IUnknown's *QueryInterface*), and once the interface is returned, it invokes a method on the interface (the IDispatch method invoke). If the client does not have a type library associated with the interface, COM must obtain the dispatch identifiers for the method (IDispatch *GetIDsOfName*). If a dual interface is supported, the client may make a call to get the function pointer for the method directly.

Other Pertinent COM Interfaces

A couple of the interfaces commonly used in components are IConnectionPointer and IConnectionPointerContainer, which implement *connection points.* Connection points are equivalent to callback functions; they are communication points in the client that allow the server component to communicate with the client in addition to the usual communication from the client to the server. Consider push technology, which requires that the client "subscribe" to a push service for regular updates or updates when data changes. What is happening with this type of technology is that the client has provided a point of communication that the server can use to send information to the client. Chapter 13, *Integrating Data Access in C++ ASP Components with OLE DB*, has an example that demonstrates the use of connection points.

Another interface that is commonly used is IProvideClassInfo, which provides a method that returns type information for a COM object. This information is the "coclass" entry in the type library, and can also be seen in the IDL file for the component. An additional interface is IExternalConnection, used with DLLs to ensure the appropriate shutdown of links to embedded objects.

ISupportErrorInfo ensures the proper handling of errors and that error information is returned to the client. The interface **IMarshal** is used when an application invokes an interface method across threads, processes, or even machines, and custom marshaling is used to move method parameters between the two different objects. COM has a default implementation to handle cross-process parameter movement.

Reusability

If you are just learning about COM and writing COM-based components, you are probably concerned first of all with creating a component that doesn't break, and second with creating one that actually works. Your component's reusability is probably a distant concern at this time. Eventually, though, you may want to extend an existing component, and reusability is the key to doing this.

COM provides not just one but two mechanisms for reusability. The first is known as *containment/delegation*; the second is known as *aggregation*.

Containment/delegation basically wraps one component around another, with the outer component intercepting all of its own interface method calls and those of the contained object. The outer component then uses whatever interfaces of the contained component it needs to create its own implementation.

Aggregation is used when the outer component exposes an inner component's interfaces as if they were its own. The advantage of this approach is that the outer component only implements extended functionality, rather than having to implement its own functionality and that of its contained component. However, problems occur with the handling of IUnknown calls to the inner component interface. IUnknown calls increment or decrement a reference count, and, when made by the client, should go to the outer component, not to the inner component. Yet with exposure of the inner component directly to the client, IUnknown calls are being made to the inner component.

To prevent this, COM provides a mechanism so that when the outer component creates the inner component, it passes its own IUnknown interface to the inner component. As you may remember from the section on IClassFactory, the inner component is created with *CoCreateInstance* or *CoCreateInstanceEx*, but instead of passing in NULL as the second parameter, the pointer to the outer component is passed. Sending a non-NULL value serves as a signal to the inner component that it is being aggregated. If the inner component supports this, it creates two IUnknown interfaces, one that is non-delegating and one that is delegating. When the client makes IUnknown calls, these are made on the delegating IUnknown interface and are delegated to the outer component. When the outer component itself, though, makes a request for the IUnknown interface from the inner component, the component knows to return the non-delegating IUnknown interface. With this, the IUnknown calls from the client are correctly routed to the outer component, and the outer component can control the lifetime of the inner component by its own IUnknown calls.

Each of the language sections in the book contains examples of each type of component reusability.

Implementing COM in Visual C++, Visual Basic, and Visual J++

This book contains sections devoted to creating ASP components using Visual C++, Visual Basic, and Visual J++, but this section provides an early demonstration of creating a simple example in all three of these tools. The purpose of these demonstrations is to show how a COM-based component is implemented in all three environments, how the environments differ, and how similar the components implemented in each environment are.

We'll use all three languages/tools to create an example component that contains one class, with one interface and only one method. The class is a conversion object, taking a string containing some content and returning the content formatted with HTML tags. The single method we'll create is ConvertH1, which takes a string and returns the same string formatted as an <H1> HTML header (HTML headers are created with different tags, each representing a different size header and sometimes a different font).

Once each of the components is created and installed, we'll use a simple ASP page to test the component. Additionally, we can view each component using the OLE/COM viewer, *oleview.exe*, which is installed with any of the visual tools or with the Platform SDK.

How COM Is Implemented with Visual C++

Creating a COM component with Visual C++ has actually gotten to be fairly easy, thanks to the ActiveX Template Library (ATL), provided with Visual C++ 5.0 and up. In addition, other tools such as C++ Builder from Inprise, Inc. (formerly Borland) also support ATL.

 The demonstration in this section does not go into any detail on creating an ASP component using Visual C++. Part III, *Developing ASP Components with Visual C++*, covers the details that are left out of this demonstration. The demonstration in this section is concerned primarily with the COM aspects of a Visual C++ ASP component.

To create the demonstration component in Visual C++, start a new project using the ATL COM AppWizard. Set the project name to ConvertCPP and accept the project defaults, which means that the component is compiled as a dynamic link library, and the proxy, MTS, and MFC options are not checked.

Once the project is created, add an ATL object to the project by selecting the New
ATL Object option from the Insert menu. From the ATL Object Wizard dialog that
opens, choose ActiveX Server Component as the type of ATL object to create and
then press Next. The Names tab of the ATL Object Wizard Properties dialog opens
to add the object names and to choose object options. For the first page of the dialog, set the short name for the object to DHTMLConvertCPP and accept the generated defaults for all other values but Prog ID, which should be set to
`ConvertCPP.DHTMLConvertCPP`. Figure 3-2 shows the dialog after the additions
and changes have been made.

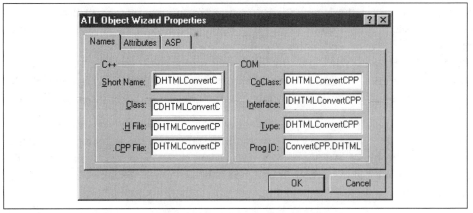

Figure 3-2. The first tab page in the dialog used to create first ATL object

In the dialog's Attributes tab, set the threading model to Both and turn off Aggregation for the component. Accept all of the other default values, including using
the dual interface (which was discussed in the previous section, "How COM Is
Implemented"). In the dialog's ASP tab, uncheck the OnStartPage/OnEndPage
checkbox, since the built-in scripting objects and event handlers are not used in
this simple test case.

> Accessing the built-in objects when creating a Visual C++ ASP com-
> ponent is covered in detail in Chapter 12, *The C++ ASP Built-In
> Interfaces*. Working with IDL syntax is covered in detail in
> Chapter 11, *Creating a Simple C++ ASP Component*.

An interface is created automatically using the ATL Object Wizard. The interface is
called `IDHTMLConvertCPP`, the same name as the class that's created except for
the addition of the "I" preceding its name.

Next, add the one and only method for the component interface by right-clicking on the interface in the ClassView window and selecting Add Method from the context menu. In the dialog that opens, assign a name of `ConvertH1` to the new method and indicate the method's parameters. These parameters are given using IDL syntax, because a new interface method is being added, and the IDL defines the interface. For the demonstration, give the method an input parameter of type `BSTR`, and an output return value parameter of a `BSTR` pointer, as shown in Figure 3-3.

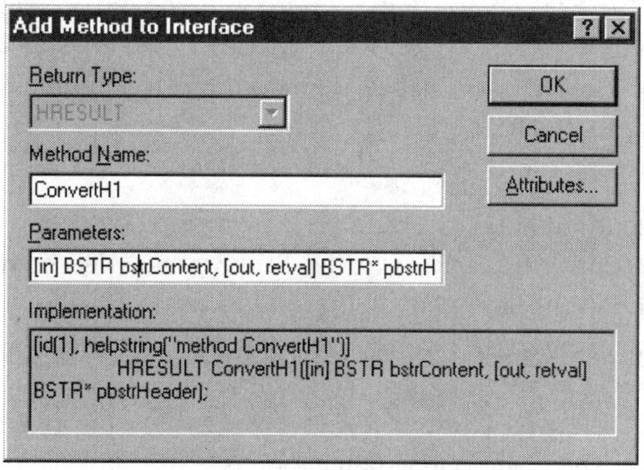

Figure 3-3. The interface method for the demonstration component

When creating a new COM component, Visual C++ actually creates an associated IDL file and adds to this file for every interface and object added to the component. The Visual C++ build process also includes the calls to the MIDL compiler, which creates a type library when the project is compiled.

Adding a new method to the interface adds a definition of the method to the interface in the IDL file, and adds a method stub to the underlying class in the class CPP file, *DHTMLConvertCPP.cpp*. Next, add the code for the ConvertH1 method shown in Example 3-1 to the interface to modify the string passed to the method and turn it into an HTML header.

Example 3-1. C++ Code for Class Method Created for Simple ASP Component

```
STDMETHODIMP CDHTMLConvertCPP::ConvertH1(BSTR bstrContent, BSTR * pbstrHeader)
{
    // Create instance of CComBSTR wrapper class
    // to work with header
    CComBSTR bstrHeader("<H1>");
    if (!bstrHeader)
        return E_OUTOFMEMORY;

    // add BSTR and ending HTML tag
```

Example 3-1. C++ Code for Class Method Created for Simple ASP Component (continued)

```
    bstrHeader+=bstrContent;
    bstrHeader+="</H1>";

    // assign to return variable, set CComBSTR to null
    *pbstrHeader = bstrHeader.Detach();

    return S_OK;
}
```

The method uses the **CComBSTR** wrapper class, which has useful methods for working with **BSTR**. For demonstration purposes, no error handling is implemented for the method except to test if the **CComBSTR** object was instantiated. The method uses the **CComBSTR** overloaded operator "+=" to append the **BSTR** content and the ending tag to create the header string. The header is then assigned to the returning variable using the **CComBSTR** Detach method.

Once the component method is written, your next step is to build the component, by selecting Build ConvertCPP.dll from the Build menu. The component is registered automatically as the last part of the build operation, though it could have been registered using *regsvr32* directly, or using MTS. To ensure that the component was successfully registered, use the OLE/COM Object Viewer to view the new component; it should be found in the Automation objects section within the viewer. Clicking on the component name opens a window with information on the component, as shown in Figure 3-4.

Note from Figure 3-4 that the component has three interfaces: the one created manually for the component, **IDHTMLConvertCPP**, and two others, **IDispatch** and **IUnknown**. The **IDispatch** interface is created because the Dual Interface option was accepted by default when the ATL object was created. Choosing the custom interface option would have created only the **IUnknown** interface, but this option is not available when creating an ASP ATL component (it is available when creating an MTS and other component types).

As stated earlier in the chapter, all COM-compatible components must implement the **IUnknown** interface, since this is the only way to access the query interface and reference counting methods. In fact, clicking on the **IUnknown** interface in the OLE/COM viewer shows that the interface has three methods. The three methods are, as you can guess, QueryInterface, AddRef, and Release. Fortunately, with ATL, the **IUnknown** implementation, as well as the implementation of **IClassFactory**, is handled by the templates and does not have to be implemented directly by the component developer.

The component can be accessed from the following ASP page:

```
    <HTML>
    <BODY>
```

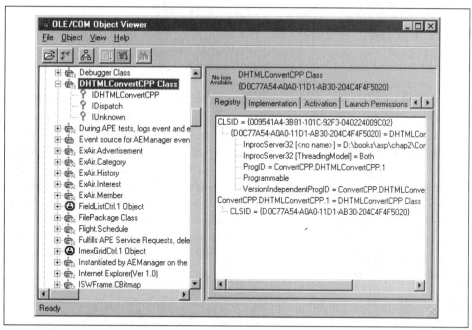

Figure 3-4. View of component using OLE/COM Object Viewer utility

```
<%
Dim tst
Set tst = Server.CreateObject("ConvertCPP.DHTMLConvertCPP.1")
Dim tmp
tmp = "first"
Dim tstr
tstr = tst.ConvertH1(tmp)
Response.Write(tstr)
%>
</BODY>
</HTML>
```

Though the simple component created in this section is a perfectly acceptable ASP component, it really isn't a production-level component. It doesn't provide error handling, nor does it provide connection points for two-way communication between the client and the component, and it doesn't provide aggregation support for reusability. However, it does demonstrate the smallest type of ASP component that can be created. An ASP component created in Visual Basic, covered in the next section, by default utilizes far more of the COM interfaces.

A COM Component Implemented with Visual Basic

The easiest approach to take to creating a component is to use Visual Basic. Virtually all aspects of the underlying COM implementation are hidden from the component developer. However, there are also limitations with VB components, one of the most important being that VB components only support the apartment threading model. As will be explained in more detail in Chapter 4, COM objects are implemented on certain threads based on the type of threading model selected. For an apartment-threaded model, the in-process component is implemented on the thread that created the component instance, and all communication between code on this thread and the component occurs without the use of marshaling. However, any multithreaded communication between the client application and the component needs to occur through this thread, ensuring that the component is thread-safe, but also ensuring that all communication between the application and the component has to be serialized.

 The example in this section does not go into any detail on creating an ASP component using Visual Basic. Part II, *Developing ASP Components with Visual Basic*, covers the details that are omitted.

Creating a simple ASP component in Visual Basic is mostly a matter of picking the right wizard and VB application type. Open Visual Basic and select the ActiveX DLL application type in the New Project dialog to create a new project that will generate an in-process component. Visual Basic generates a new project complete with one class module. Rename the project to ConvertVB, and rename the class to DHTMLConvertVB. Open the Project Properties dialog by right-clicking on the project in the Project Explorer and selecting the Project Properties option. Then, in the General tab of the Project Properties dialog, select the ApartmentThreaded threading model.

Next, add the *ConvertH1* function to the class. The source code for the function, which takes an input string, adds the HTML header tags, and then returns the modified string, is shown in Example 3-2.

Example 3-2. Simple Method for VB Component Class

```
Public Function ConvertH1(strInput As String) As String
    Dim strOutput
    strOutput = "<H1>" + strInput + "</H1>"
    ConvertH1 = strOutput
End Function
```

After the function is finished, create the DLL by selecting Make ConvertVB.dll from the File menu. While the DLL is being built, the component is automatically registered on the build machine. You can also register it using *regsvr32.exe*, as follows:

```
regsvr32 ConvertVB.dll
```

After the component is successfully registered, opening the OLE/COM viewer displays information about the new Visual Basic component, as shown in Figure 3-5.

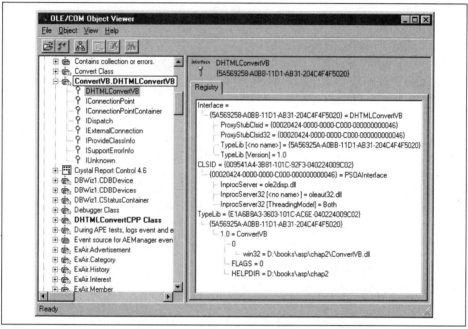

Figure 3-5. View of Visual Basic component using OLE/COM Object Viewer utility

There are actually more interfaces created for the Visual Basic component than for the Visual C++ component. First, the Visual Basic component was implemented, by default, to take advantage of connection points (which were discussed earlier in the section on COM implementation).

Both the Visual C++ and the VB components are similar in that both inherit from the IDispatch and IUnknown interfaces, the latter again being a requirement for all COM objects.

Other interfaces the VB component uses are IExternalConnection, to support the correct shutdown of embedded DLLs, and IProvideClassInfo, to provide run-time information about the component. Connection points are also supported with the IConnectionPoint and IConnectionPointContainer interfaces. Finally, error handling is facilitated with the use of ISupportErrorInfo. Note, though, that all of these interfaces are added and implemented automatically when creating the ActiveX DLL, rather than being implemented manually by the component developer.

Once the component is compiled and registered, it is tested using virtually the same ASP test page, as shown in the following code block:

```
<HTML>
<BODY>
<%
Dim tst
Set tst = Server.CreateObject("ConvertVB.DHTMLConvertVB")
Dim tstr
tstr = tst.ConvertH1("first")
Response.Write(tstr)
%>
</BODY>
</HTML>
```

As can be seen, a COM component that can be accessed in an ASP page is created using two widely different techniques with two different tools, but the underlying implementation is the same. Both components have interfaces that are derived from **IDispatch**, which is itself derived from **IUnknown**, and both components support dual interfaces. To further highlight these different implementation techniques and similar results, let's create the component in Java using Visual J++.

A COM Component Created with Visual J++

Java presents a unique challenge for building COM components, because Java does not support the concept of a pointer, yet earlier in the chapter I mentioned that clients access component methods through pointers to functions. However, one workaround to this problem in Java is to use one-dimensional, one-element arrays to contain all data passed by pointer, since Java passes arrays by reference. However, this is mainly a concern when Java uses a COM interface directly. Creating a COM-based Java component can actually be pretty simple.

An automation server such as an ASP component can be considered equivalent to a JavaBean, which is a Java component that can be used by many different applications. To enable the Java class to be treated as a COM component, Microsoft implemented a JavaBean-to-COM bridge in the Microsoft Virtual Machine (VM), which makes converting the Java class to a COM-accessible object as simple as running one command.

The demonstration in this section does not go into any detail on creating an ASP component using Visual J++. Part IV, *Developing ASP Components with Visual J++*, covers the details that are left out of this demonstration.

In addition, Microsoft also provides for automatic implementation of a COM interface for a Java class within Visual J++. To use this, create a new Java project using Visual J++, select the Components project types, and then select the COM DLL project option. This creates a project with one class, `Class1.java`. Rename the project to ConvertJPP and the class to `DHTMLConvertJPP.java`.

The **public** modifier is added to the class by default. Also by default, a COM directive is included in the comments just before the class declaration, as shown in the following code block:

```
/**
 * This class is designed to be packaged with a COM DLL output format.
 * The class has no standard entry points, other than the constructor.
 * Public methods will be exposed as methods on the default COM interface.
@com.register ( clsid=9EBAF530-5C6E-11D2-874B-204C4F4F5020,
                typelib=9EBAF531-5C6E-11D2-874B-204C4F4F5020 )
 */
```

This block provides the COM directive, including the reference for the COM CLSID and the type library, necessary to expose the component as a COM-based DLL when the component is compiled. It is essential that no code comes between the COM directive and the class definition. All imports and package information should be placed in the component before the comments.

The class will become part of a package called `ConvertJPP`, so add the following line to the Java source code just before the COM directive:

```
package ConvertJPP;
```

Next, add the ConvertH1 method to the class. This is the same method name used in the Visual Basic component and the Visual C++ component. The method has a String return type and has a parameter that is also a String. Once the method stub is generated, add the rest of the code. Example 3-3 shows the entire code for the Java class.

Example 3-3. Simple Java Component with One Class and One Method

```
//
// DHTMLConvertJPP
//
package ConvertJPP;
/**
```

Example 3-3. Simple Java Component with One Class and One Method (continued)

```
 * This class is designed to be packaged with a COM DLL output format.
 * The class has no standard entry points, other than the constructor.
 * Public methods will be exposed as methods on the default COM interface.
@com.register ( clsid=361584F4-8631-11D2-8768-204C4F4F5020,
typelib=361584F5-8631-11D2-8768-204C4F4F5020 )
 */

public class DHTMLConvertJPP
{
        // Component method
        public String ConvertH1 (String strContents)
        {
            // create conversion string
            String strOutput;
            strOutput = "<H1>" + strContents + "</H1>";
            return(strOutput);
        }
}
```

Once you add the code to the Java class and compile it by selecting the Build option from the Build menu, both a Java class file and a DLL are created. The DLL is automatically registered during the compilation process. The Java class file does not need to be moved to the Java **CLASSPATH** location, since the DLL assumes the class is located in the same location as the DLL. However, when moving the DLL, the component will need to be reregistered.

 Chapter 15, *Creating a Simple Java Component*, also contains instructions for creating a COM object of an existing Java class using a set of utilities that can be used with other Java tools or for existing Java classes.

Once the class is successfully compiled and registered, it can be accessed from an ASP page like the following:

```
<HTML>
<BODY>
<%
Dim tst
Set tst = Server.CreateObject("ConvertJPP.DHTMLConvertJPP")
Dim tstr
tstr = tst.ConvertH1("first")
Response.Write(tstr)
%>
</BODY>
</HTML>
```

Opening the OLE/COM utility, the new "component" can be found in the main listing, "Java Classes." Figure 3-6 shows the entry for the Java class.

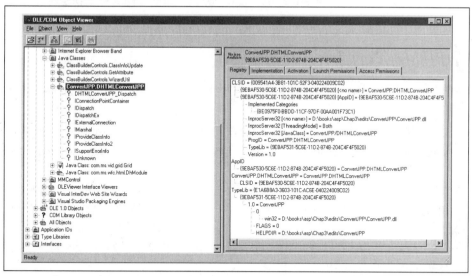

Figure 3-6. View of Java component using OLE/COM Object Viewer utility

Note that a COM wrapper is created for the class, and it, as with Visual VB and Visual C++, uses the **IDispatch** interface. **IDispatch** is derived from **IUnknown**, also shown in the component listing. In addition, as with the VB component, the component uses the connection point interfaces, **IConnectionPointContainer** and **IConnectionPoint**, for event handling and communication between the client and the component. The Java component COM wrapper also uses the **IExternalConnection** interface for tracking an external connection; the **IProvideClassInfo** interface, which contains type information and is required for runtime controls; and the **ISupportErrorInfo** interface, providing safe propagation of error information. In addition, the component also utilizes **IMarshal** to provide custom marshaling. Two additional interfaces shown are **IDispatchEx** and **IProvideClassInfo2**. The **IDispatchEx** interface is an extension to **IDispatch** and was created specifically for scripting languages that support late binding. The **IProvideClassInfo2** interface is a later variation of **IProvideClassInfo** and can be used to get the class identifier for the component as well as type information. The **IDispatchEx** interface is covered in more detail in Part IV.

The technique just shown creates a Java ASP component and demonstrates the underlying similarity between COM-based components created in Visual Basic, Visual C++, and Visual J++, but does not create an actual DLL for the Java component. If a DLL is needed, steps can be taken to actually create a DLL from the Java class. In addition, accessing other COM components such as the built-in ASP objects requires some readjustment of the Java class, as well as generating Java classes from the type libraries for the COM objects. Both of these types of efforts are covered in detail in Chapter 15.

Further Reading

For additional reading about the topics covered in this chapter, check out the following:

- "The COM+ Programming Model Makes It Easy to Write Components in Any Language," by Mary Kirtland, at *http://www.microsoft.com/msj/1297/complus2/complus2.htm*.

- "How Microsoft Transaction Server Changes the COM Programming Model," by David Chappell, located at *http://www.microsoft.com/msj/0198/mtscom/mtscomtop.htm*.

- The definitive book on COM is *Essential COM,* by Don Box, Addison Wesley Longman, Inc., published in 1998.

- A nicely written book that provides one of the clearest overviews of COM and DCOM is *Inside Distributed COM*, by Guy and Henry Eddon, Microsoft Press, published in 1998.

- Microsoft derived its IDL from the OSF DCE IDL. You can read more about DCE and the associated IDL online, at *http://www.transarc.com/Library/documentation/dce/1.1/index.html*.

4

ASP Components and Threads

I first had a chance to really learn about threads and NT when I attended a Boston University WinDev conference outside of Boston years ago. The big story at the conference was Microsoft's brand-new operating system, which many of us had not seen yet. The operating system later became NT, and though I didn't necessarily realize it at the time, I was learning about NT from the masters.

I have never attended another conference that had so many well-known Windows development people. I attended one session given by Charles Petzold, probably the undisputed father of Windows API programming, who invited the whole group to join him for beers at the end of the day. I also attended sessions on OLE given by Kraig Brockschmidt. All the sessions were terrific, but one of my favorites was on threads and was given by none other than Jeffrey Richter, author of the well-known book *Advanced Windows NT*. If you are going to learn about something, there's nothing like learning from the best.

When I mention threads in this chapter, I mean the threads that are defined as "units of execution in a process," as Richter defines it. I don't mean threads of communication between client browser and web server. Multithreaded applications are ones that take advantage of a threaded environment to split off part of their functionality into separate executable chunks. On a multiple CPU system, these can run simultaneously. On a single CPU system, the operating system kernel gives each thread a period of time to run, and then cycles through each thread in a round robin fashion.

ASP components are first and foremost COM components. This means that whatever works and doesn't work with COM components will and won't work with ASP components. One aspect of COM that can either speed up performance or bring your application crashing to the ground is the use of threads. Because of this, this chapter provides an overview of threads, threading models, and the impact each of the models has on ASP components.

 O'Reilly publishes a book, *Win32 Multithreaded Programming*, by Aaron Cohen and Mike Woodring, that discusses programming issues in a multithreaded environment.

What Are Threads?

Threads are the smallest unit of execution, and a process (or an application) can execute its functionality using one thread or many threads executing at the same time.

Threads can enhance the performance of an application by assigning I/O intensive operations such as file or database access to one thread while other threads continue with other processing. These types of operations are ideal for creation on separate threads because most of the time in I/O operations is spent waiting and listening for a response, whether from you or from the printer. While these operations are waiting, other operations can continue with their work.

In Windows 95 or 98 and Windows NT, if you run a process in the background, chances are good that the application has been programmed to create a new thread for the background process. By assigning the process to a background thread, the user can continue to work with the application and do other tasks while waiting for the background process to complete. For example, if you are out browsing the Internet using a browser such as IE or Navigator, and you find a file to download, this downloading process is actually performed in the background on a separate thread. Because the download occurs separately from the main browser thread, you can continue browsing other pages while the download occurs. As each new page is downloaded to the browser, synchronization occurs between the thread handling the file download and the thread handling the download of a page to the browser. The thread performing the file download shares bandwidth and CPU with the browser thread, and both actions seem to be occurring simultaneously. If this didn't happen, you would not be able to see the new page until the file finished downloading.

You can actually see something like this happening. To demonstrate, go to the Microsoft web site and select a file for downloading. An excellent place to get such files is the COM web site at *http://www.microsoft.com/com/*. Pick a larger file. Once the file starts to download, browse through the rest of the site, but always bring the download dialog up after clicking on a new URL. You can actually see the download progress "hesitate" each time the browser page receives content, and vice versa. When the file is finished downloading, depending on the browser, a message may open that states the download is finished, or the download dialog may be removed. This is a preemptive action on the part of the new thread that passes control to this thread so it may inform you that the action is finished, and perform any cleanup necessary after the action is complete.

On a single-processor system, multiple threads can only work one at a time, but the system provides a bit of time for each thread to work and then gives each thread a turn running its task. This "round robin" approach of assigning time to each process running on a separate thread in turn prevents one operation from holding up all the others. It is this type of process that allows you to continue typing into a Word document while another document is printing, or that allows a file to be downloaded form the Internet while you continue to browse. This activity occurs even in a single-processor system, and with an operating system such as Windows 95 or 98 that only allows single processors.

Using multiple threads in a single-processor system can improve performance with I/O bound operations, such as printing or opening a document. However, using multiple threads with a single processor for an operation that is CPU-intensive can actually degrade the performance of the operation. This type of thread, also called a compute-bound thread, competes for scarce system resources and, unlike I/O operations, does not normally have periods of time awaiting responses. If the system contains only one CPU, a context switch must occur to allow each compute-bound thread its opportunity at the CPU. This effort adds a small measure of activity to the load on the CPU that would normally be offset by the advantages of using multiple threads. If the compute-bound thread's activities are short and over quickly, the overhead for managing the different threads is not offset by the overall result, and the performance can actually degrade in comparison to serial requests to the CPU.

In a multiprocessor system, a thread can be running in the background by actually using a different CPU than the thread currently handling interactive commands. If a system has multiple processors, and an application uses threads to take advantage of them, the application can be very fast. That is, up until a point of diminishing returns is reached, and the overhead of maintaining all the different processors and threads actually diminishes performance. Other unexpected results from using multiple threads occur when threads access the same resource, discussed in the next section.

Of Deadlocks, Odd Results, and Thread Synchronization

When threads access the same resource, their activity must be synchronized. When synchronization is used correctly, the results are definitely an improvement over serial access of the resource. However, the lack of synchronization can lead to problems. When two threads compete for the same resource at the same time, a deadlock condition may result, and both threads can become suspended, each waiting for access to the resource. Or worse, if multiple threads access the same resource and modify the resource in some way, the results may be unwanted.

For instance, imagine that a file contains a string with a value of 10. One thread accesses this file and increments its value by 5, and another thread accesses the same file and increments its value by 10. But in the meantime, the first thread has already written a value of 15. What is the result? The file now contains a value of 20, not the value of 25 that you'd expect by incrementing the original value by 5 and then by 10. Why is this? Because the first thread modified the value between the time the second thread accessed the original value of 10 and the time the second thread wrote the new value of 20. In the process of doing this, the second thread overwrote the value of 15 that the first thread wrote. I know this may sound as clear as mud, but an actual demonstration of something like this occurring within an ASP application is given later in this chapter.

In order to ensure reliable and consistent results and to prevent deadlock, there are certain synchronization mechanisms that can be used, some of which are beyond the scope of a book on writing ASP components. However, there are measures that can be taken—such as obtaining an exclusive lock on a file before allowing the contents to be modified and releasing that lock as soon as possible, and using caution with global data—that can prevent problems.

 The summary at the end of the chapter has some references to online articles that discuss synchronization techniques within Visual C++, Java, and Visual Basic.

One other consideration with the use of multiple threads, or multiple processes for that matter, is that communication between components that exist on different threads or processes requires some special handling. This is discussed in the next section, which covers marshaling.

Marshaling

When a component and a client reside on the same process and on the same thread, both share the same address space, which means that both share the same address space stack. This means that when a client calls a component's method and passes parameters with the method call, the component can access these values directly from the stack. When the method finishes, if it returns a value or if the parameters are passed by reference, the client can also access the values directly from the stack. This is an efficient and fast way to access parameter data. However, if a client and a component execute on different threads or in different processes, the two no longer share the same address space stack. Instead, the parameters passed to and returned from the method must be *marshaled*. Marshaling is the process whereby values passed as parameters are accessed on the client stack, placed into a stream, and pushed onto the component stack.

When a client calls a component method on a different thread or process, it is a client *proxy* that pulls the values for the parameters from the client's address space stack and creates a stream of data that is sent to the component. On the component side, a *stub* function then accesses this stream and pulls the separate parameter values from the stream, pushing these values on the component's stack. The component method then accesses the parameters from the stack.

Marshaling can occur when a client and a component are on different threads, known as *cross-thread marshaling*, or when a client and a component are on different processes, known as *cross-process marshaling*. Even if the component resides on a separate machine, the same type of process occurs, it's just that other players become involved, such as the DCOM runtime and the Service Control Manager (SCM). In addition, information about the component's methods must be installed on the client, usually by installing the component's type library.

The process of cross-process or cross-threaded local communication can be improved with the use of *aggregation*, which uses a free-threaded marshaler to allow direct access to an object, rather than having to go through marshaling. When using the free-threaded marshaler, a pointer to the actual component is passed to the client rather than a pointer to the proxy, even if the component resides on a different thread. Aggregation provides the best overall performance because the component can be created on a separate thread, but can still be accessed directly. Of course, the cost of using the free-threaded marshaler is that the component must be made thread-safe, something that does add a burden to the component developer.

The concept of aggregation and free-threaded marshaling is covered in more detail in the next section, where the different threading models are discussed from an ASP perspective.

The Threading Models and Component Type

There are actually four threading models:

- The *single-threaded* model. IIS creates each instance of a component on a single main thread.

- The *apartment-threaded* model. In this model, an instance of the component is created in the same thread of the client that created the instance. Thread safety is guaranteed, since all calls to the component are serialized through the client thread.

- The *free-threaded* model. This is the least constrained of all the threading models and is not recommended for ASP. When an instance of a component is created, COM creates the instance on a different thread than the one that created the instance, and then marshals all calls to this thread.

- The *both-threaded* model. This is actually the most highly recommended threading model for ASP components. A both-threaded component is treated as both an apartment-threaded component and a free-threaded component, and, as seen later, is accessed directly by clients created using either threading model.

 ASP has now been implemented in Windows 95 on the Personal Web Server, so when mention is made of IIS, this also includes the Personal Web Server (PWS) where applicable. PWS, unlike IIS, was created more for people to test their web pages before posting to a more robust web server or for individuals who simply want to put up their own web page. It does not implement some of the multi-user functionality that IIS does, and, because of this, the examples in this chapter specifically may not work the same way they would with IIS.

When a client application such as a browser window is created, the system creates one main thread, which becomes the apartment the process resides in. It may create additional threads to handle other tasks within the process, or, if the application is single-threaded, all tasks of the process are run within this main thread.

Threads work differently depending on whether the component is created as an in-process component or an out-of-process component. An in-process component is created as a DLL and marks the type of threading model it uses in its `InProcServer32` key in the registry. An out-of-process component calls one of the COM initialization methods (CoInitialize, CoInitializeEx, or OleInitialize) in order to initialize the COM library, and all calls to the component occur as cross-process calls and are marshaled.

If the component is in-process, its interaction with the client depends on both the client and the component's threading models. If both the component and the client are single-threaded, the component is created on the client's main thread. If, however, the client is multithreaded and the component is single-threaded, the component is created on the client's main thread, and all calls to the component from the client occur through the client proxy.

If the client is free-threaded and the component is apartment-threaded, a single apartment thread is created to house the component and an interface pointer is returned to the client. All calls to the component then occur through this pointer. The same is true, but in an opposite manner, if the client is single-threaded and the component is multithreaded; in this case, a free-threaded apartment thread is created and returned to the client. In all of these cases, calls to methods are marshaled.

If the component and client use the same threading model, the client has direct access to the component and can call the component's methods directly. Based on this, components created as both-threaded can be accessed directly by a client regardless of which threading model the client implements. The reason is that both-threaded components support both the single-threaded as well as the free-threaded threading models. If the component is accessed from a single-threaded client, it is created in the single-threaded client's thread. If a multithreaded client accesses the component, it is created in the multithreaded client's main thread. However, access to the component must occur within the apartment in which the component is created, even though other threads within the same process may try to access that component.

To speed access to both-threaded components, aggregation can be implemented using a special function (*CoCreateFreeThreadedMarshaler*), which basically allows all threads of one process to access the component directly. This and the results of implementing in-process components using the different threading models are demonstrated in the following sections.

 The components demonstrated in the rest of this chapter are all in-process components. Which threading model is used is particularly significant with in-process components, and less significant with out-of-process components. Access to out-of-process components must be marshaled regardless of what type of threading model the component is based on. However, the performance of an in-process component can differ dramatically based on the threading model of the client and the threading model of the component.

Are Single-Threaded or Multithreaded Components Better?

I have one word for you if you are considering creating a single-threaded component: don't. By their very nature, web applications are multiuser, and a single-
threaded ASP component basically restricts all access to the component to one
main thread, the one started when the first call to *CoInitialize* or *CoInitializeEx* is
made. If an application wants to access a COM object, a call must be made to the
CoInitialize or *CoInitializeEx* function before the application can make use of
COM features. With ASP, IIS creates a thread that calls *CoInitialize* and then directs
all object calls to this thread. When an application accesses an ASP component, IIS
must marshal all calls to the component through this single, main thread. So if one
page is accessing the component, another access to the component from within
the same page or from another page has to wait until the component is finished
processing the earlier page request. All requests to the component are queued, a
situation quickly leading to a condition known as bottleneck.

To demonstrate this, the code in Example 4-1 contains a simple component created using Visual Basic that contains one loop containing another loop. The outer
loop cycles 32,000 times, and the inner loop cycles 10,000 times, basically forcing
the component to take a visually noticeable amount of time to run.

Example 4-1. Testing Queuing of Requests with Single-Threaded Component

```
' global data
Public count2 As Integer

' test method
Public Sub threadTest()
   Dim count As Integer
   count2 = 0

   ' outer loop
   For count = 1 To 32000
      count2 = count2 + 1
      Dim count3

      ' inner loop
      For count3 = 1 To 1000
         '
      Next
   Next count
End Sub
```

Compile the component as an in-process, single-threaded component by selecting
the Single Threaded option from the Project Properties dialog. Then create an ASP
page that contains the ASP scripting block shown in Example 4-2. This script cre-

ates an instance of the component shown in Example 4-1, writes out the time, runs the component method, and then writes out the time again.

Example 4-2. ASP Code Block to Test threadComp.tstThread

```
<%
Dim tst
Set tst = Server.CreateObject("threadComp.tstThread")
Response.Write Time
tst.threadTest()
Response.Write Time
%>
```

Open two different browser windows and call the test ASP page from both. Open the page first in one browser and then immediately switch over to the second browser and open the test page in it without waiting for the first browser to finish. Figure 4-1 shows the result of running the same ASP page in both browsers at the same time, with both accessing the same single-threaded component. As you can see from the figure, the process takes seven microseconds to run, and the process in the second browser window does not begin until the first process is finished, no matter how quickly you access the page.

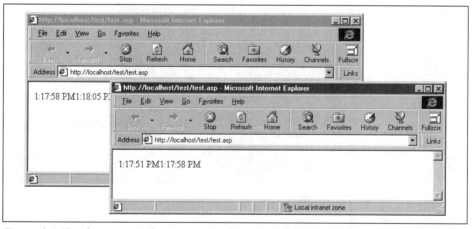

Figure 4-1. Two browser windows accessing the same single-threaded ASP component

No matter how many times the same test is run, the effect is the same: the second ASP page cannot run until the first is finished. The reason for this is that the ASP component created from the code in Example 4-1 is first instantiated by the ASP application based on the call to the CreateObject method in the page for the first browser, and the component's only method is called. Since the component is single-threaded, all other requests to this component are queued until the current request is finished processing, which does not occur until after the method is finished. This means that the request to create the new object using CreateObject in the same ASP page accessed in the second browser is queued until the ASP page in the first browser is finished being processed. Since the first time in the page is written after the component is created, this value is not accessed and added to the page until the second browser's CreateObject request is finally processed.

Next, recompile the component, except this time as an apartment-threaded in-process component, using the Apartment Threaded option in the Project Properties dialog. This means that the component is created within each thread that creates the object, and that the two separate browser windows create separate instances of the ASP component.

Running the same test by accessing the ASP page that instantiates the component in two separate browser windows at the same time has a different result when the component is based on the apartment-threaded model. Figure 4-2 shows the two browsers with the results of running this new version of the component. Notice from the figure that the first time value in the second browser window appears during the time that the first browser's ASP page is being processed, rather than after the component has finished in the first page. Running the test several times has virtually the same results. The reason is that the component in the second page is created before the first page is finished because the two requests are being handled by two different components on two different threads.

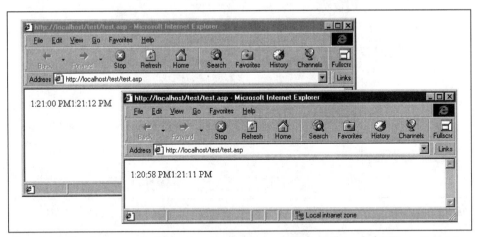

Figure 4-2. Two browser windows accessing the same apartment-threaded ASP component

As a comparison of Figure 4-1 and Figure 4-2 show, the accumulated time for both processes to run is about the same as each running separately, one after the other. That's because, in this case, the machine running the ASP component has only a single processor. However, if the machine had multiple processors, each thread would run on a different processor and the component's run time should be correspondingly less.

Even with a single-processor machine, if a component method invoked in one ASP page is involved in an I/O-intensive operation such as accessing a database, component methods invoked in other ASP pages, even those belonging to the same component object, can be processed while waiting for the IO operation to complete. Additionally, if the component method is itself accessing another component method that resides on a remote machine, the process can continue without waiting for the remote method to finish.

Note that single-threaded components run with the same permissions as the SYSTEM account, something you don't want an ASP component to do. Considering that on NT, the SYSTEM account can start and stop services, allowing anonymous access to this capability through an ASP component is not a very good idea.

In summary, ASP components should not be created as single-threaded components.

The Single-Threaded and Multiple-Threaded Apartment Schemes

A form of thread classification builds on the concept of apartment threading and classifies threading into Single-Threaded Apartment (STA) and Multiple-Threaded Apartment (MTA) schemes. STA is equivalent to the original classification of single-threaded and apartment-threaded models, and MTA contains the free-threaded model. When a combination of STA and MTA models is used, the threading scheme encompasses the threading model known as both-threading or mixed-model threading.

The single-threaded model is considered an STA, main thread only, as all instances of the component are created on the same main thread. As stated in the last section, this type of threading model is not appropriate for use with ASP components. The other threading models are discussed in the next three sections.

The Apartment-Threading Model

The apartment-threading model is the only multiple threading model Visual Basic 5.x or 6.x supports. The concept is fairly straightforward. IIS creates an instance of the component on the thread that issues the call to create the component, if the client is multithreaded. All calls to the component on this thread are not marshaled, and all calls outside this thread are marshaled. (Again, marshaling is the process of pulling the parameters for the called function from the client's stack, then sending this data to the server, which unmarshals the data and adds these parameters to the component's own stack.)

The apartment-threading model is recommended for ASP components for one reason: the chance of a bottleneck occurring is less likely because each component instance created within a session is created in a separate thread. It is also a relatively safe model to use, since any global data for the component is created in its own global data area within the thread containing it, and is protected from corruption from processes running on any other thread. The only potential problem with global data for a component built using the apartment-threading model occurs when a call is made to the component from within the same session, and the component is created as a session-level element.

To demonstrate why global data needs to be protected within a session, Example 4-3 shows a modified version of the Visual Basic component used for testing single threading in the last section. The loops have been removed, as timing is not really a factor for this test. What is a factor is the global variable *count2*, which is modified and printed in two methods and just printed in the third method.

Example 4-3. Testing Impact on Global Data with Apartment-Threaded Component

```
' create global value
Public count2 As Integer

' Set global value to 100
Public Sub threadTest()
    Dim objResponse As Response
    Set objResponse = GetObjectContext()("Response")
    count2 = 100
    objResponse.Write ("thread is " + CStr(App.ThreadID))
    objResponse.Write ("<br>count2 is " + CStr(count2))
End Sub

' Set global value to 5443
Public Sub threadTest1()
    Dim objResponse As Response
    Set objResponse = GetObjectContext()("Response")
    count2 = 5443
    objResponse.Write ("thread is " + CStr(App.ThreadID))
    objResponse.Write ("<br>count2 is " + CStr(count2))
End Sub

' just print out global value
Public Sub threadTest2()
    Dim objResponse As Response
    Set objResponse = GetObjectContext()("Response")
    objResponse.Write ("thread is " + CStr(App.ThreadID))
    objResponse.Write ("<br>count2 is " + CStr(count2))
End Sub
```

In addition to altering and printing out the value of the global variable, each of the methods also prints out the ID of the thread the component is currently running in. Compile the component as an apartment-threaded component using the Project Properties dialog.

To test the component, create three separate web pages, each containing one of the three small ASP scripting blocks shown in Example 4-4. Each block calls one of the methods created for the test component.

Example 4-4. ASP Scripting Blocks to Test Apartment-Threaded Component

```
<%
' first web page ASP block
Dim tst
Set Session("tst") = Server.CreateObject("threadComp.tstThread")
Response.Write Time
Response.Write "<p>"
Set tst = Session("tst")
tst.threadTest()
Response.Write "<p>"
Response.Write Time
%>

<%
' second web page ASP block
Dim tst
Set tst = Session("tst")
Response.Write Time
Response.Write "<p>"
tst.threadTest1
Response.Write "<p>"
Response.Write Time
%>

<%
' third web page ASP block
Dim tst
Set tst = Session("tst")
Response.Write Time
Response.Write "<p>"
tst.threadTest2
Response.Write "<p>"
Response.Write Time
%>
```

Open a browser window and load the first ASP page, which makes a call to the first method, threadTest. As would be expected, the page displays the time before the method is called, the thread identifier of the component (a long value), the value of the global variable *count2* (which is 100), and the time the method finished. Next, open a new browser window using the File → New → Window menu option. Opening a new browser window this way places the window in the same session as the parent window. Then use this browser to open the second ASP page, the one that contains the script block that calls the threadTest1 method. This second page again prints out the before and after times, but also prints out the same thread ID that was shown in the first page results and the new global *count2* value of 5443.

Next, switch to the first browser again and open the third ASP test page. This page contains the third test script block, which invokes the third component method. The third component method just prints out the thread ID and the value of the global variable, and does not modify the value of the global variable. Again, the same thread number and the current value of *count2*, which is 5443, are displayed, as shown in Figure 4-3.

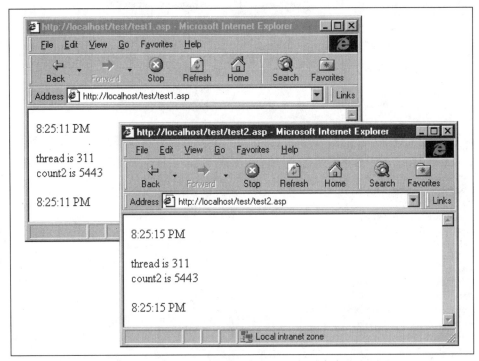

Figure 4-3. Browser windows accessing same apartment-threaded ASP component

Even if both of the browser windows were to run the first page with the script block that assigns the reference to the component to the Session object, both browsers would still show the same thread ID and would still access the same global variable. The actual thread the component is being instantiated on is the thread that was created when the first browser window was opened, and it is this thread that is used throughout the entire session. The same thread will continue being used until both same-session browser windows are closed.

Finally, open a new browser window using the browser icon or by selecting the browser from the Start menu. This opens the browser on a different session and thread. When this browser accesses the first script block, the results show a different thread ID. Regardless of which method the ASP page invokes, it has no effect on the value of the global variable accessed by the same-session browser windows, as shown in Figure 4-4.

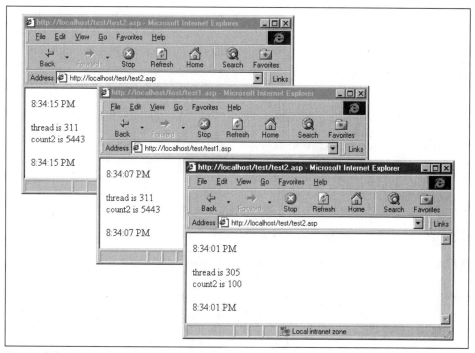

Figure 4-4. Browser windows accessing the same apartment-threaded component

Having to protect global data can be considered a disadvantage to using the apartment-threaded model, unless the global data is meant to be accessible from all components and ASP pages within a session. However, a better approach is to store the global data directly into the ASP Session object, since the alternative—depending on correct access to a global variable—is most likely to break at some point.

A second disadvantage to the apartment-threaded model is that all accesses to a component within the same session are processed on the same thread, which means that component method calls are queued. If one method gets involved in intensive I/O, the person waiting for the ASP page to return with a result could be waiting a long time. In addition, based on the length of time for timeouts, the ASP script could actually time out before the page is returned.

Another disadvantage to the apartment-threading model is that components created using this model cannot be stored in the ASP Application object, since this results in an error. The component can be forced to be an Application object using the <OBJECT> tag in the *global.asa* file, but, as Microsoft states in the documentation it provides with IIS, doing so locks the Application object to a single thread. The reason why is the same as when the Session object is locked down to a single thread of execution if an apartment-threaded component is added to it: the component is created on the same thread of the client that created it, and all calls to the component must occur on this thread. As you will see in the next section, the free-threaded model can be used to create an Application object, but not without generating its own set of problems.

Unlike the single-threaded model, the apartment-threaded component runs in a thread that has the same permissions as the user and not as the SYSTEM account, so it is a much safer model to use. As long as the object is not assigned to the Session or Application object, it is a recommended model for ASP components.

The Free-Threaded Model

When IIS receives a new ASP request, it creates a new thread to handle the request. If the requested page instantiates an ASP component built based on the free-threaded model, the component is created in the IIS multithreaded apartment. Each application can have, at most, one multithreaded apartment, and free-threaded components must be created within a multithreaded apartment. This means that the component will reside on a different thread than the client thread that created it. Because of this, all calls to the component's methods must be marshaled, reducing the overall performance of the object.

If a free-threaded component is created as an application-level element, all accesses to this object from any ASP page are locked down to this single thread. This also means that all ASP application pages accessing the same component basically share the same global data. A free-threaded component must ensure that its data is safe, since threads accessing any one of the component's methods can change global data, even while one thread is processing one of the method calls. The component can be accessed by multiple threads, and there are no controls about which thread accesses the component or when. Based on this, the component developer must ensure that the component is thread-safe.

To demonstrate the problems that can occur with a free-threaded component that has global data, Example 4-5 contains the source code for a simple C++ component generated using the Visual C++ ATL AppWizard. This component has three methods. Two of the methods modify a value created as a member of the C++ class, basically creating a data value global to all the components in the class. The third method returns this value to the client.

 If you don't work with Visual C++, you can skip the following section, which details creating the component, and continue following the code shown in Example 4-5.

You can create the component by generating a default DLL project using the ATL COM AppWizard. Then use the ATL Object Wizard by selecting the New ATL Object option from the Insert menu and choosing the ActiveX Server Component object from the choices the Wizard presents. In the Name tab of the ATL Object Wizard Properties dialog, assign the component *thrdTest* as a short name; this is used to derive both file names and class and interface names. In the dialog's Attributes tab, select the free-threading model, and change the Aggregation option to No not to use aggregation. On the ASP tab, turn support for onStartPage and onEndPage off by unchecking this option.

When you finish with the dialog, the ATL Object Wizard generates the necessary support files and creates both the component class `CthrdTest` and the component interface `IthrdTest`. As Example 4-5 shows, the component has three methods; you add each of them to the component by right-clicking on `IthrdTest` in Class View and selecting Add Method from the resulting popup menu. Two of these methods set a data member, one, setValue, to a constant value, and the other, testLongThread, to a value derived from running a large loop. Additionally, for this latter method, an inner loop is created within the outer loop to add enough of a time delay to test the potential problem. Neither of the two methods takes a parameter, so only the method names, setValue and testLongThread, need be provided in the Add Method to Interface dialog.

Example 4-5. Visual C++ Component with Three Methods

```
// thrdTest.cpp : Implementation of CthrdTest
#include "stdafx.h"
#include "CPPThread.h"
#include "thrdTest.h"

/////////////////////////////////////////////////////////////////////////////
// CthrdTest

// return global data member
STDMETHODIMP CthrdTest::testThread(int * intReturn)
{
    // return tstValue
```

Example 4-5. Visual C++ Component with Three Methods (continued)

```
   *intReturn = tstValue;
   return S_OK;
}

// set global value to constant
STDMETHODIMP CthrdTest::setValue()
{
   // set tstValue
   tstValue = 4334;
   return S_OK;
}

// set global value to derived value
// after long loop
STDMETHODIMP CthrdTest::testLongThread()
{
   // set tstValue, but after long loop
   int count2;
   tstValue = 0;
   count2 = 0;
   while (count2 < 32000) {
      count2++;
      int tst = 0;
      while (tst < 10000)
         tst++;
   }

   // set value - should be 32,000
   tstValue=tstValue + count2;
   return S_OK;
}
```

The third method created for the component, testThread, takes one parameter; the following should be entered in the Parameters text box of the Add Method to Interface dialog:

```
   [out, retval] int * intReturn
```

This creates a method that takes one parameter, a pointer to an integer, and returns this value to the client.

Next, add the data member referenced in the methods to the class by opening the header file generated for the component, *thrdTest.h*, and adding the following to the public members for the new class:

```
   int * tstValue;
```

Finally, add the code for the three component methods shown in Example 4-5 to the class file, *thrdTest.cpp*.

To test the component, create two ASP pages, each containing one of the script blocks shown in Example 4-6. Each script block calls methods of the new component. The first page calls the testLongThread method to set the public data variable and then calls the testThread method to output its value. The second page calls the setValue method to set the public data member and then calls testThread to print out the results.

Example 4-6. Script Blocks to Test the Free-Threaded Component in Example 4-5

```
<%
' first page
Dim tst
Set Application("tst") = Server.CreateObject("thrdTest.thrdTest.1")
Set tst = Application("tst")
tst.testLongThread
Dim iValue
iValue = tst.testThread
Response.Write CStr(iValue)
%>

<%
' second page
Dim tst
Set tst = Application("tst")
tst.setValue
Dim iValue
iValue = tst.testThread
Response.Write CStr(iValue)
%>
```

Running both pages at the same time using two separate browsers results in one browser showing the value of 32000 in its page and the second showing the value of 4334 in its page. Though the two components ran virtually at the same time, each component was created on a new thread. The free-threaded component was created in a separate multithreaded apartment, and the global data area for both component instances was kept separate.

Next, modify the ASP pages to create an instance of the component as an application-level element in the first page, which is then accessed in the second page. The code for the modified ASP page is shown in Example 4-7.

Example 4-7. Scripting Block for the Modified ASP Page

```
<%
' first page
Dim tst
Set Application("tst") = Server.CreateObject("thrdTest.thrdTest.1")
Set tst = Application("tst")
Response.Write CStr(Time) + "<p>"
tst.testLongThread
Dim iValue
iValue = tst.testThread
Response.Write CStr(iValue)
```

Example 4-7. Scripting Block for the Modified ASP Page (continued)

```
Response.Write "<p>" + CStr(Time)
%>

<%
' second page
Dim tst
Set tst = Application("tst")
Response.Write CStr(Time) + "<p>"
tst.setValue
Dim iValue
iValue = tst.testThread
Response.Write CStr(iValue)
Response.Write "<p>" + CStr(Time)
%>
```

By showing beginning and ending times, the time taken for each script block to run is also displayed on the web page.

Again, open each ASP page in a separate browser, and start each browser as an independent session by accessing the browser icon on the desktop, or by accessing the browser from the Start menu. The first browser should run the first scripting block, which sets the application-level object and runs the longer method, testLongThread. The second browser runs the page containing the block that accesses the application-level object and then runs the short method, the one that just assigns the global data member a constant value. Unlike the results when the component was instantiated by two different browsers, the results of this test are definitely unexpected. Instead of a value of 32000 showing in the first browser page, it shows a value of 36334, as shown in Figure 4-5.

The first page shows an "incorrect" value because the components run on totally separate threads, which means that the calls to the component's methods are not serialized, and happen asynchronously. However, both browsers are accessing the same instance of the component, which is created as an application-level component. The method calls from both ASP pages are made directly to this application-level component, and methods in both pages share the same global data area. The result is that the component data member *tstValue* is set to 0 in the testLong-Thread method called in the first page, but while the loop is being performed in this method, a second ASP page calls the setValue method on this same component, which sets *tstValue* to 4334. As you can see from the timestamps in Figure 4-5, the second ASP page method has a chance to finish before the first ASP page finishes. When the long loop in the first method finally does finish, it sets *tstValue* to the sum of *tstValue* and the counter. Instead of *tstValue* having a beginning value of zero, which it received when the method first started, it has been changed to 4334 based on the results of the method call from the second ASP page.

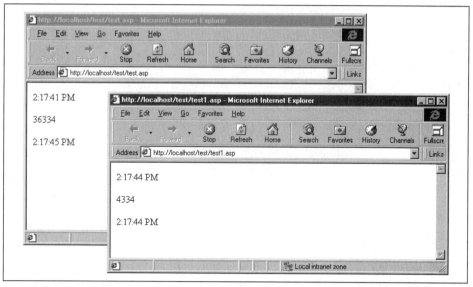

Figure 4-5. Browser windows accessing methods of the same free-threaded ASP component

For a further test, open a browser page and then open a second one using File →
New → Window, which effectively places both pages in the same session. This
means that both browsers are accessing the same component from the same client thread. Running the first ASP page in the first browser window and the
second ASP page in the second browser window does not have any unexpected
consequences. The reason is that both browsers run in the same session, and
effectively on the same thread, and method calls to the same component for both
browsers are serialized. The method calls to the component for the first ASP page
have a chance to finish before the method calls from the second ASP page are run.

Aside from the shared data area, which requires protection in a production-level
component, there are a couple of other disadvantages to using the free-threaded
model with ASP components. The first is that free-threaded models cannot access
the built-in MTS ObjectContext object unless they are specifically registered as MTS
components. Apartment-threaded and both-threaded components can access
ObjectContext without having to be registered in MTS. The second reason is that a
free-threaded component, like a single-threaded component, performs all of its
work within the context of the SYSTEM user account. Since SYSTEM can also shut
down and start system processes, having anonymous access to a component running in SYSTEM via an ASP application is not a great idea.

This leads us to the last threading model, the both-threading model.

The Both-Threading Model

The best threading model to use with ASP components is the both-threading model. Components created with this threading model actually adapt to the type of thread creating the component. If the client is running as a single-threaded apartment, the component is created in that same apartment and all accesses to the component from the client are direct. If the client is a free-threaded component, the component is created in the client's main thread and can support multiple thread requests from the same client process, with all accesses to the component from the same client thread occurring directly. The one disadvantage to the both-threaded model, though, is that requests to the component occurring from the same client process but from other threads have to be marshaled, which can impact access performance.

There is a solution to this, though: the use of aggregation through the special function *CoCreateFreeThreadedMarshaler*. Fortunately, when creating a component in C++ using the ATL wizard, the use of aggregation and this function can be added to the component just by checking two boxes.

To demonstrate this, create two components that are very similar to the single component created in the last section, but this time set the threading model to both-threaded for both.

> Actually, the two test "components" created in this section are created in the same ActiveX DLL created in the last section. One DLL can support more than one ASP component, and the components can even have different threading models. Again, if you are unfamiliar with C++ or Visual C++, you can skip the paragraphs until after Example 4-8. Just know that one component is created with aggregation support and one is created without aggregation support.

When creating the first component, set it to both-threaded and turn off support for aggregation by selecting the No radio button in the Attributes tab of the ATL Object Wizard Properties dialog. The ATL component Attributes tab options are shown in Figure 4-6.

The second component is also set to the both-threaded model, but support for aggregation and the Free Threaded Marshaler are added to the component, as shown in Figure 4-7.

Again, add global data member to the class header file using the syntax shown in the previous section. Give each component the same two methods, testLong-Thread and testThread, one that runs the long process to set the global data value and one that accesses this value and returns it to the script block that accessed the

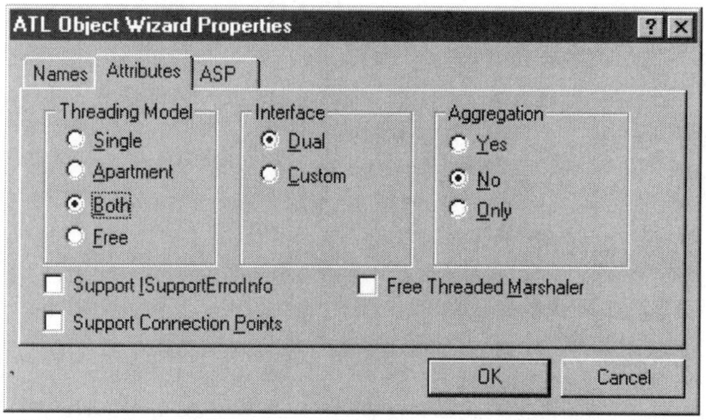

Figure 4-6. ATL component Attributes tab settings for the first component

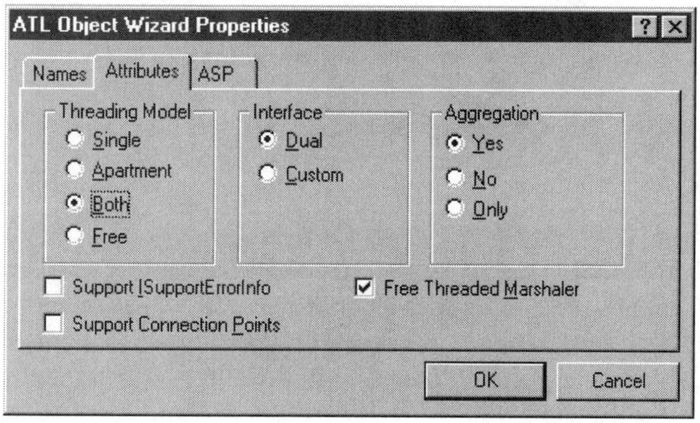

Figure 4-7. ATL component Attributes tab settings for the second component

component. Add the methods by clicking with the right mouse button on the interface in Class View and selecting Add Method. The method testLongThread does not contain parameters, and the method testThread has one method which returns a pointer to an integer. Example 4-8 shows the manually created code representation of each component.

Example 4-8. Source Code for Free-Threaded Components

```
// again.cpp : Implementation of Cagain
#include "stdafx.h"
#include "CPPThread2.h"
#include "again.h"

/////////////////////////////////////////////////////////////////////
// Cagain
```

Example 4-8. Source Code for Free-Threaded Components (continued)

```
STDMETHODIMP Cagain::testLongThread()
{
    // create counter and add to value of global data
        // member and set global data member
    int count2;
    returnValue = 0;
    count2 = 0;
    while (count2 < 32000) {
        count2++;
        int tst = 0;
        while (tst < 10000)
            tst++;
    }

    // set value - should be 32,000
    returnValue=returnValue + count2;
    return S_OK;
}

STDMETHODIMP Cagain::testThread(int * intReturn)
{
    // access global data and return value
    *intReturn = returnValue;
    return S_OK;
}
```

To test the components, create two identical ASP pages, one to access each component. Each page's ASP scripting block calls both component methods. The results are timed by printing out a timestamp before and after the methods are run, as shown in the following code, representative of the scripting block in both pages:

```
<%
Dim tst
Set tst = Server.CreateObject("again.again.1")
Response.Write CStr(Time) + "<p>"
tst.testLongThread
Dim iValue
iValue = tst.testThread
Response.Write CStr(iValue)
Response.Write "<p>" + CStr(Time)
%>
```

Run both pages in the same browser. On the machine where I ran the test, the time to invoke both methods for the component not using the free-threaded marshaling object was seven seconds, and the time to do the same for the component that did use the free-threaded marshaling object was four seconds. The results were consistent through several tests. The improvement in times between the tests occurs because using aggregation with the free-threaded marshaler means that all component method calls are passed directly to the component, even though the component resides in a different thread from the client. Without aggregation support, all component method calls must be handled through the proxy-stub pair.

 Note that using the free-threaded marshaling object with a both-threaded component means the component can respond to calls from more than one thread. Based on this, the component must be thread-safe, with protection provided for the global data.

Other advantages to using the both-threading model are that the component always runs within the context of the user security account, never the SYSTEM security account, and the component can be added to the Application or Session objects without locking down either object to serialized requests. The only consideration with using the both-threading model, particularly when using it with aggregation, is that global data needs to be protected, since no requests to the component are serialized.

Further Reading

For additional reading about the topics discussed in this chapter, check out the following:

- To find out more about threading in general, I recommend the book *Advanced Windows*, published by Microsoft Press and authored by Jeffrey Richter.

- For information about writing multithreaded applications, the book *Win32 Multithreaded Programming*, mentioned earlier in the chapter, is a good choice.

- An article that covers synchronization classes provided in the Visual C++ MFC can be found at *http://premium.microsoft.com/msdn/library/devprods/devdoc/F1/F6/D8/S22CA6.HTM.*

- An article, "Threads and Locks," that talks about synchronization and locks within the Java language can be found at *http://premium.microsoft.com/msdn/library/devprods/vj++/vjlang/chap17.htm.*

- An article titled "Designing Thread-Safe DLLs," which contains an explanation of why apartment-threading provides for thread safety with Visual Basic, can be found at *http://premium.microsoft.com/msdn/library/devprods/vb/vb50docs/f1/d5/s1af22.htm.*

- In addition to the above articles, one of the best articles on threading, DCOM, and threading models is "DCOM Architecture," by Markus Horstmann and Mary Kirtland, located on the MSDN library CD, or at *http://premium.microsoft. com/msdn/library/bkgrnd/html/dcomarch.htm.* If you have not worked with threads before, you should take time to read this article in addition to this chapter.

5

Components, Transactions, and the Microsoft Transaction Server

In a distributed system, client applications call methods in components that can reside on the same machine as the application or on some remote machine, and the client application should not know or care where the component resides. The COM/DCOM (Component Object Model/Distributed Component Object Model) specification was created specifically to handle distributed component-based systems.

One of the problems with COM/DCOM is that creating components to participate in this type of system is not trivial, and considering that the components or applications may have to handle multiple threads as well as distance adds to the complexity of the development process.

ASP components are based on the COM/DCOM specification, as outlined in Chapter 3, *ASP Components and COM*, except that instead of being accessed directly from a custom-built interface, they are accessed from a web server through ASP scripting blocks. Since ASP components are a form of COM component and definitely participate in distributed processing, they are also candidates for creation and management as transaction-based components through the Microsoft Transaction Server (MTS).

With the release of Internet Information Server (IIS) 4.0 and of MTS 2.0, Microsoft has tightly integrated the use of transactions with existing ASP applications, an integration that impacts heavily on creating ASP components in at least two major ways. First, accessing the built-in ASP objects, covered in Chapter 6, *Overview of the Intrinsic (Built-in) Objects*, is no longer dependent on capturing the component's load events and accessing the objects from the ScriptingContext object. Now, the built-in objects are accessed from ObjectContext, an object that is an MTS object rather than an ASP object. Based on this, ASP components are no longer as page-scope–dependent as they were before the MTS integration.

Secondly, an ASP component can be created within the context of a transaction, and the results of method calls to that component can be marked as successfully completed or aborted as failures. The methods can signal whether they succeed, and if all components succeed, the entire transaction is committed. However, if any of the components fail, the entire transaction can be failed.

This chapter covers component-based systems, transactions, and how ASP components can also be MTS components and can participate in transactions.

Developing Component-Based Systems

A component-based system is one that separates out individual processes into reusable chunks of code and data, then uses one or more of these components to build a complete application. Among the different types of applications that can be built are client-server, distributed, and n-tier systems. A *client-server system* is one in which processing is split between the client and the server, with the client handling all user interaction, display, and client-side validation, and the server handling most database access, server-side validation, and business rule enforcement. A *distributed system* is one in which the components of the application can exist on different machines and may exist in different geographical locations. In addition, more than one instance of a component can be created in order to handle multiple requests and provide the same service to multiple clients. An *n-tier system* combines elements of the client-server systems and elements of the distributed systems; there is a hierarchy of components, as with a client-server system, but the components themselves can be duplicated to distribute processing load and can be distributed across many machines and locations, as with a distributed system. The traditional n-tier system can consist of the client, which handles all user interaction, client-side validation, and display; the business layer, which enforces all business rules and performs overall transaction management and validation; and the data layer, which handles all the direct data access.

The use of components facilitates distributed systems, primarily because components are small, compact, and portable (as long as the host machine provides the framework the component needs). If an access load on one server begins to impact the machine, and the machine's overall performance starts to degrade, the component or group of components is easily moved to another server with no impact to the code accessing the component. Additionally, because the components are components, one or more can be moved to one new server and others moved to other servers until the balance of processing of all servers is balanced. Applications created as complete applications and that can't be split apart also cannot be broken apart to be placed on different machines.

Another advantage of components is that more generic functions can be split into separate components and used throughout the system. Additionally, the use of components facilitates the design and construction of an n-tier system. An example of an n-tier system is one where an interface component accesses and validates address information. The validation is generic and confirms that all the necessary fields such as city and zip code are filled in. The business layer can then process the address information based on the type of business for the application. It can do things such as perform lookups based on the address information, such as finding shipping zones for a component used in a shipping application or delivery zones for a online ordering system that delivers. The component can then access the data layer to store the address information, retrieve additional information, or even trigger other online business components to perform additional work on the information. The data layer can itself be split over separate machines, separate databases, or even different types of data stores, with some information going into long-term storage and some going into short-term storage to be used for a specific task and then discarded.

However the components perform their task, the concept is to separate more generic functions, such as accessing and validating address information necessary for many applications, from the more business specific functions, such as finding shipping zones for a shipping application. In addition, an n-tier application also looks to separate the user interface components, which should only contain enough processing to successfully acquire the information needed, from the business layer, which understands how the information relates to other information in order to perform a business function. The business layer is separate from the data layer, which only concerns itself with having enough information to successfully make a data transaction and does not care how the information is acquired or the purpose for the information being acquired.

ASP components participate in this type of system by providing functionality at either the business level or the data level, with the interface handled in the browser that is accessing the ASP application.

MTS, MTS Components, and Transactions

One of the problems with components based on COM/DCOM is that component communication, especially remote communication, is not trivial. Compound that with having to be concerned about tracking whether a component successfully completes its processing, and what to do and how to recover if one component fails to accomplish its task while others succeed, and a distributed system can soon become very difficult to create and maintain.

MTS was created to simplify this process by taking care of much of the administration of a distributed system. It ensures that a transaction completes successfully as a whole or fails in its entirety. It also manages processing and threads for an application, something that becomes very critical when one component calls methods on another which calls methods on another, and so on.

MTS also provides Resource Managers and Dispensers that actually control stored data, such as database data. If fact, any database system that supports OLE transactions, such as SQL Server, can participate in transactions controlled by MTS. This means that if a component that participates in a transaction fails, not only can the action of the component and other components be rolled back (reversed), any database activity can also be rolled back.

What Are Transactions?

If you have had experience with commercial database systems such as Oracle, Sybase, and Microsoft SQL Server, you are probably aware of what transactions are. A *transaction* is one or more tasks, grouped in some logical manner and meant to succeed together or fail together if any one task within the transaction fails. If a transaction fails, no changes are made to any of the data associated with the transaction. If the transaction succeeds, changes made to the data are committed. An example of a transaction containing more than one task is the transfer of money from your savings account to your checking account. Though it seems like one transaction, two are actually happening. The first is that the money must be taken from the savings account (or debited to the account). The second is that the money must then be added to your checking account (or credited to your account). If the debit operation on your savings account succeeds but the credit to your checking account doesn't, you will want the entire transaction to be reversed and start over again. Transactions are essential in a system that updates more than one data structure, such as database tables based on one action, and updates must succeed for all of the data structures in order for the one action to successfully complete.

MTS expands on this by introducing the concept of transaction management to component development. It also simplifies the process of developing distributed component-based applications by handling most of the transaction success/failure communication.

How Components Participate in Transactions

A component can be an MTS component if it meets certain criteria. First, the component must be an in-process server (that is, a DLL). Second, the component must not be free-threaded. Further, if the component is implemented in Visual C++, it must implement a class factory and use standard marshaling. A type library must be created for the component.

Microsoft provides libraries exposing MTS objects for use in Visual Basic, C++, and Java. Incorporating MTS components into Java and Visual Basic is no more difficult than incorporating any other in-process component. It is also actually very simple to create a C++ MTS component; the ActiveX Template Library (ATL) Wizard can create an MTS component as easily as it can create an ASP component. If the component needs to work in both environments, it is probably best to implement it as an MTS component, since MTS is more restrictive than ASP.

Once a component meets the minimum requirements to participate as an MTS component, it needs to be registered with MTS for MTS to provide transaction support for it. During the registration process, the type of transaction in which the component participates is set as a property of the component. Though no other coding needs to occur to allow a component to participate in a transaction, it can assist MTS in doing a better job with component management by creating an instance of an MTS object called ObjectContext, which is then used to implement the SetComplete and SetAbort transaction methods. Components that are registered in MTS should implement these methods. However, components can participate in transactions without being registered as MTS components by being created using ObjectContext's CreateInstance method.

An example of creating an MTS-aware component is given in the next section.

Creating MTS-Aware ASP Components

Most ASP components can also be MTS components with no change as long as they are in-process components. Additionally, if the component is created as free-threaded, access to the MTS built-in ObjectContext object requires that the component be registered with MTS. Components do not have to be registered with MTS to do such things as access the built-in ASP objects, discussed in other chapters. However, a component will perform more effectively in an MTS environment if it is created as an MTS component or converted to an MTS component and registered with MTS. This section demonstrates creating two very simple MTS components, with one component also implementing ASP functionality. The components are created using Visual Basic, primarily because VB hides many of the language implementation details and frees us to concentrate on the MTS-specific details.

Building an MTS component is not that different from building an ASP component, except that the component must be created as an in-process or ActiveX DLL. (While out-of-process components are discouraged in ASP applications and require modifications of the IIS environment to access them, they are nevertheless supported.) A reference to an additional library, the Microsoft Transaction Server Type Library, must be added to the Visual Basic project using the Project → References menu option. (This is in addition to the Microsoft Active Server Pages Object Library, which contains references to the five built-in ASP objects and which must still be added to the project in order to make these objects accessible.)

Adding the MTS library adds references to four objects to the component. These objects, which are viewable using the Object Browser within Visual Basic, are:

AppServer object

Exposes two methods to direct access within the application: GetObjectContext and SafeRef. The GetObjectContext method is used to obtain a reference to the ObjectContext object, discussed later. The SafeRef method is used to create a safe self-reference to an object to be passed to other objects such as the client. This method is used only when an instance of the current component is passed to other methods for callback purposes and is used in place of the object-specific `this` pronoun. Using `this` would pass a reference to the object that will become invalid once the reference passes from the object context of the current object.

ObjectContext object

Represents the current object's context in an MTS and ASP environment. It returns references to the ASP built-in objects, which are accessible using the Item property and passing in a string containing the name of the built-in object, such as "Response", to access the Response object. Additionally, other components can be created on the same transaction as the current object by using the CreateInstance method. Information about the context of the object and its transaction and security setting can be found using IsCallerInRole to determine if the calling client is of a certain role, IsInTransaction to determine if the component is participating in a transaction, and IsSecurityEnabled to determine if security is enabled for the component (security is always enabled for an ASP component, since security is enabled by default for all server components). To prevent a component from being committed until it is finished with all its processing, the DisableCommit method can be used to disable the ability to commit the component. The EnableCommit method turns the commit capability back on. Finally, the component can mark that it has finished its processing and its changes are ready to be committed using the SetComplete method, or it can use the SetAbort method to roll back changes.

ObjectControl object

Handles component activation and cleanup activities. It can also be used to determine whether a component is destroyed when it is no longer active, or whether it is returned to a pool and can be used again. The Activate event handler is automatically called when the component is loaded into memory by MTS, and can be used to perform component activation activities. When the component is unloaded from memory by MTS, the Deactivate method is automatically called, and the component developer can include component cleanup activities in this event handler. The CanBePooled method returns a Boolean that indicates to MTS whether the component can be pooled (object pooling is discussed later). Implementing CanBePooled as an event and returning a value of **False** prevents the component from being pooled, while returning **True** allows the object to be pooled.

SecurityProperty object

Used to get the caller's or creator's name. In this context, a creator is the identity that created the component instance, not the person who developed the component. This object has four methods: GetDirectCallerName, GetDirectCreatorName, GetOriginalCallerName, and GetOriginalCreatorName.

The ASP library exposes the standard built-in objects—Response, Request, Server, Session, and Application—as well as the now obsolete ScriptingContext object.

The sample application that uses MTS and ASP together includes two components; one is created directly within an ASP page, while the other is created within the first component. We'll begin by building the latter component first.

Create the component by starting Visual Basic and selecting ActiveX DLL as the project type. Rename the project to mtsObject, and rename the class that is generated by Visual Basic for the component from **Class1** to **tstMTSObject**. Keep the component's class properties at their default values, including a value of **NotAnMTSObject** for the MTSTransactionMode property. This property will be set when the component is registered with MTS, a topic discussed in "Installing and Monitoring an MTS Component in an ASP Environment" later in this chapter. Set the project properties to the apartment threading model, and to unattended execution. Finally, add a reference to the MTS type library.

More detailed information on creating a Visual Basic ASP component can be found in Chapter 7, *Creating a Simple Visual Basic ASP Component*. For non-Visual Basic programmers reading this section, the actions just performed will result in a COM DLL marked with the apartment-threading model that can directly access the MTS type library.

As the source code in Example 5-1 shows, the component has one primary method, tstLoop, that executes a loop that itself contains another loop. The first executes a number of times determined by an argument passed to the method; the second executes for a fixed number of iterations. The effect of this code is to create a method that has a perceptible execution time. This will be important for trying out MTS tracking, discussed later. The method also performs error processing; if the value passed in is greater than a coded value of 30,000, an error is raised.

In addition to the component's primary method, support for the MTS ObjectControl object is also added to component class by adding the following line to the top of the component:

```
Implements ObjectControl
```

The **Implements** statement tells Visual Basic to map the methods of a class to the methods contained in the current component's code, where they appear as events. In addition, an ObjectContext object is created as a global class variable. This object is instantiated in the Activate method, which is coded as an event handler of the ObjectControl object by using the standard "noun-event handler" syntax, as shown in Example 5-1. The same is true of the Deactivate method, where the reference to ObjectContext is released, and the CanBePooled event handler, which returns **True** and therefore allows the component to be pooled.

Example 5-1. MTS Component Instantiated Within Another Component

```
Implements ObjectControl
Dim objContext As ObjectContext
Option Explicit

' pull in object context
Private Sub ObjectControl_Activate()
    Set objContext = GetObjectContext()
End Sub

' reset context object
Private Sub ObjectControl_Deactivate()
    Set objContext = Nothing
End Sub

' pool object
Private Function ObjectControl_CanBePooled() As Boolean
    ObjectControl_CanBePooled = True
End Function

Public Sub tstLoop(intCount As Integer)

' setup error handling
    On Error GoTo ErrorProcess

' generate error condition
```

Example 5-1. MTS Component Instantiated Within Another Component (continued)

```
    If intCount > 30000 Then
      Err.Raise vbObjectError + 1, "mtsObject.tstMTS", _
      "Value too large"
    End If

' perform sub loop
    Dim i As Integer
    For i = 1 To intCount
      Dim j As Integer
        For j = 1 To 10000
          '
        Next
    Next i

' finish successful task
    objContext.SetComplete
    Exit Sub

' process unsuccessful task
ErrorProcess:
  objContext.SetAbort
  Set objContext = Nothing
  Err.Raise Err.Number, Err.Source, Err.Description
  Exit Sub

End Sub
```

Although GetObjectContext is a method of the MTS AppServer object, because we've added a reference to the MTS type library to our project, a reference to the AppServer object is implicit; in other words, it does not need to be explicitly specified in the call to GetContextObject in the ObjectControl_Activate event handler. This call retrieves the ObjectContext reference, which is used for transaction support. If no error occurs in the main component method, tstLoop, the component marks a successful completion of the transaction by calling the ObjectContext object's SetComplete method. If an error occurs, the SetAbort method is called instead, and the error is raised to the calling application.

Once you successfully compile the first component, you can begin work on the second. The second component, which creates an instance of the component that you just created, is called directly from an ASP page. It too is an ActiveX DLL. Rename the project to aspobj, and rename its associated class to **objASP**. The project's properties should also be changed to support the apartment-threading model and unattended execution. Finally, add references to the MTS and Active Server Page Object type libraries to the new project.

The new component does not code the ObjectControl event handlers, and creates a new instance of ObjectContext within the component's single method, Test-Method, as shown in Example 5-2. This method tests the value of an integer passed to the component and issues an error if the value is too small; otherwise, it instantiates the MTS component created in Example 5-1. The new component uses the ObjectContext object's CreateInstance method to create the MTS component, which effectively adds the object instance to the same transaction as that used with the current component, depending on the transaction property settings, which will be explained in detail in the section of the chapter on registering the component with MTS.

Error handling is also incorporated into this component, and the SetComplete and SetAbort methods are invoked depending on whether an error occurred or not, as shown in Example 5-2.

Example 5-2. ASP Component That Instantiates MTS Component

```
Public Sub TestMethod(intCounter As Integer)

    ' define variables
    Dim objContext As ObjectContext
    Dim objResponse As Response
    Dim objMTS

    ' get object context, set error
    Set objContext = GetObjectContext()
    Set objMTS = objContext.CreateInstance("mtsObject.tstMTSObject")
    Set objResponse = objContext("Response")

    On Error GoTo ErrProcess

    If intCounter < 5000 Then
      Err.Raise vbObjectError + 2, "aspobject.objASP", _
          "Value too small"
    End If

    ' call component method
    objMTS.tstLoop (intCounter)

    ' successful finish
    objContext.SetComplete

    objResponse.Write ("Successful completion of task")
    Exit Sub

ErrProcess:
    objResponse.Write (Err.Description)
    objContext.SetAbort
    objResponse.Write ("<p>Failure of Task<p>")
    Exit Sub

End Sub
```

If an error occurs in either component, the transaction is aborted. In addition, an error in the inner component raises an error in its event handler, which triggers the error handler in the outer component. The purpose for this is to write the error message to the web page returned to the user. Since the inner component does not instantiate its own Response object, and in fact can be used by non-ASP applications, it returns any errors to the component or application that created it. The outer component or application can then process the error as appropriate for the circumstances.

Both of the components are compiled into DLLs, but neither should be registered using the *regsvr32.exe* utility. Registration will occur when the components are added to MTS, demonstrated in the next section.

Creating an MTS Test Environment

Creating an MTS test environment can occur on the computer where MTS is installed or on a remote computer. The rest of this section makes an assumption that the test environment is created on the computer where MTS is installed and that this computer is local to the development effort.

Setting up a test environment involves creating an *MTS package* (a group of components that share the same MTS process and security), adding one or more components to the package, and defining at least one role for the package. Before running a test, actual users are assigned to the role.

First, open the Transaction Server Explorer application, where online management of MTS components occurs. Once the Explorer is opened, clicking on the *Microsoft Transaction Server* folder and then the *Computers* folder should expose the computers managed by the MTS installation. One computer, My Computer, is added to MTS when it is installed, and this is where you should create the test environment.

To create an MTS test environment, a new package is created on the computer by clicking on the *Packages Installed* folder in the left window, then selecting New from the Action drop-down, or right-clicking on *Packages Installed* and selecting New from the popup menu. A dialog then opens asking whether a pre-built package is being installed or an empty package is being created. To create the test environment, select the "Create an empty package" option. A second dialog opens that asks for the name of the package; name the package test. Another dialog opens to set the package identity. This defines whose account the package will run in. For the test environment, the package will run under Interactive User, or the person currently logged in. Click the Finish button, and the new package will be created and appear in the right window, as shown in Figure 5-1.

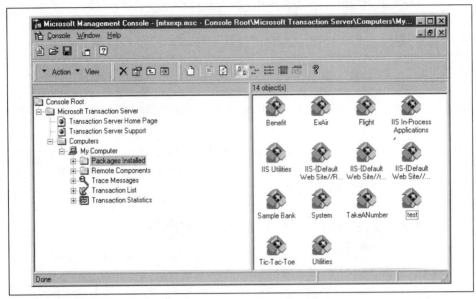

Figure 5-1. MTS Explorer Window showing new test package

Right-clicking on the new package and selecting Properties from the popup menu opens the package Properties dialog, where items such as the package's security and identity are set. In addition, how the package is activated can also be set from this dialog. MTS supports two forms of activation: library and server. *Library activation* causes the package to run within the client process, and *server activation* runs in a separate process. By default, the package is set to server activation, and this setting shouldn't be changed for the test environment. An advantage to server activation is that process isolation is maintained for the package, definitely of value for a test environment. If a problem occurs during a test, the specific package can be shut down without affecting any other package or the client that activates a component within the package.

Once the package is created, two new folders are automatically created for the package: *Components* and *Roles*. This example will use a new role, so to create a role for the component, right-click on the *Roles* folder and select New from the popup menu, or click on *Roles* and select New from the Action drop-down menu. A small dialog opens that asks for the name of the role; give a name of "developer." When the role is created, a new folder labeled *Users* is added to the role. To add users to the role, again click on the folder and select the New option from the Action drop-down menu or the right mouse menu. A group of defined users is shown in the dialog that opens next. In my case, I added two users to the role, a default one of Administrator and one created using the NT Administration tools called "shelleyp." Figure 5-2 shows the dialog after these two users were added to the role.

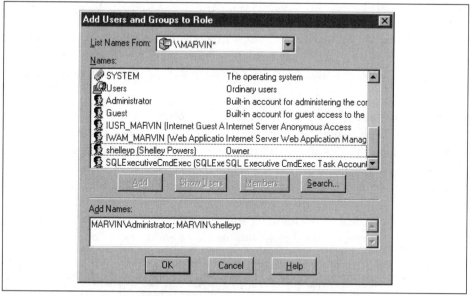

Figure 5-2. Adding users to defined role

Properties for any one of the MTS objects can be viewed and modified just by right-clicking on the object, then selecting Properties from the popup menu, if shown.

Once the test package is created and a role and its associated users are added, all that is left is to add components. This is covered in the next section.

A detailed explanation of the installation and setup of MTS on a machine goes beyond the scope of this book. For additional information on setting up the MTS/ASP test environment, check with your MTS or NT administrator, or check the documentation that is installed with MTS.

Installing and Monitoring an MTS Component in an ASP Environment

First and foremost, this is a book on creating ASP components. However, with the tight integration of ASP and MTS, it is important to see how to install an ASP component into the MTS environment, and then how to monitor that component in both an ASP and MTS environment.

I installed the MTS and ASP components created in the section "Creating MTS-Aware ASP Components" in the Test package created in the last section. Components are added by right-clicking on the *Components* folder under the package and selecting New → Component from the popup menu, or clicking on the component folder and selecting New → Component from the Action drop-down menu.

A dialog opens asking whether to install a new component or import a component that is already registered. The components have not been registered previously, so click on the "Install new component(s)" button. The Install Components dialog opens, containing two windows and a button that can be used to add files, in addition to the standard dialog navigation buttons. Click the "Add files..." button. An Explorer window opens and you can navigate to the subdirectory that contains *aspobject.dll* and *mtsObject.dll* and select the two components. Figure 5-3 shows the Install Components dialog with the two components to be installed.

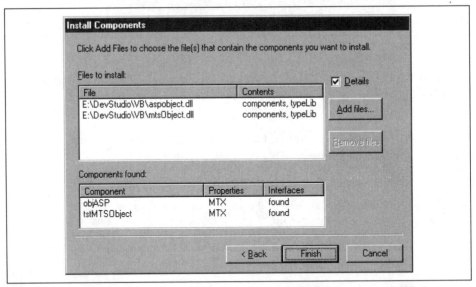

Figure 5-3. The Install Components dialog with the two ASP/MTS components added

Once the two components are added, clicking on either of them shows that two folders have been created for each component: *Interfaces* and *Role Membership*. Clicking on the *Interfaces* folder shows the interfaces that have been generated for the component class and the methods accessible from those interfaces. Several methods are shown in addition to the ones created manually for the component.

These methods are generated automatically by Visual Basic in order for the component to be a COM object.

To complete the registration of each component, right-click on the top-level component, select Properties from the popup menu, choose the Transaction tab, and set the transaction requirements for each. The transaction options are:

Requires a Transaction
> The component requires a transaction, which means that a new transaction will be started if the component is not created on a transaction; otherwise, the component uses the existing transaction.

Requires a New Transaction
> MTS will create a new transaction for the component regardless of how the component is created, even if the component is created using the ObjectContext object's CreateInstance method, which is used to create a component on an existing transaction. If the component is created within an existing transaction, the new transaction is nested within the existing transaction.

Supports Transactions
> The component will be created within an existing transaction, but if one is not present, the component is created without a transaction.

Does not Support Transactions
> The component will be created without a transaction, and any transaction management within the component will result in an error.

For *aspobj.objASP*, the component accessed within a web page, the Transaction property is set to "Requires a New Transaction". For *mtsObject.tstMTSObject*, the component accessed within the component we've just registered, set the transaction property to "Requires a Transaction". Accept the default values of all other properties for both components. Setting the first component to require a new transaction forces the component into a new transaction. The setting on the second component just requires that the component run in some transaction.

Once the components are added to the package, they are ready to be tested and monitored. The simple ASP page shown in Example 5-3 does nothing more than create the ASP specific component and call its only method.

Example 5-3. ASP Page to Test ASP and MTS Components

```
<HTML>
<BODY>
<%
Dim tst
Set tst = Server.CreateObject("aspobject.objASP")
tst.TestMethod(29000)
```

Example 5-3. ASP Page to Test ASP and MTS Components (continued)

```
%>
</BODY>
</HTML>
```

In Example 5-3, the call to TestMethod passes a value of 29,000, which is larger than the value of 1000 required by the first component, but less than the 30,000 required by the second component, so the processing should complete success-fully, provided that MTS and ASP can access the components and no environmen-tal issues arise.

To see how MTS has handled this test, open the MTS Explorer and select the com-puter with the Test package. Then select the Transaction Statistics page. This page shows the current activity of all components currently active, aborted, or commit-ted, and whether any transactions are in doubt because of some communication failure. Figure 5-4 shows the statistics page with no activity.

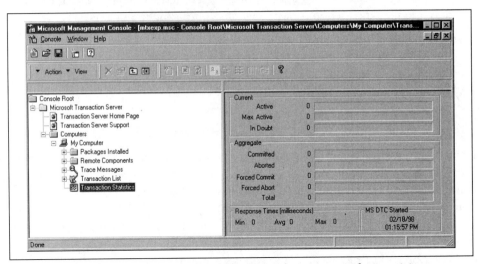

Figure 5-4. MTS Transaction Statistics page for the local computer, with no activity

After you access the test page four times from your browser, the MTS Transaction Statistics monitor shows that one component is active at any time, the maximum number of components running at a time is one, and that the total of committed transactions is equivalent to the total times the ASP page is run.

Try changing the test page to set the value passed to TestMethod to 31,000. This is okay for the outer ASP/MTS component, but too large for the inner one. As expected when running this page, a message that the value is too large is written out to the web page, and the monitor shows that one transaction has been aborted.

Finally, change the test page yet again, this time using a value of 500, which is too small for the outer ASP/MTS component in the call to TestMethod. When the page is accessed again, an error again occurs, except this time the error message indicates that the value is too small. The monitor now shows that the number of aborted transactions is two, the number of successful transactions is four, and the total number of transactions is six, as shown in Figure 5-5.

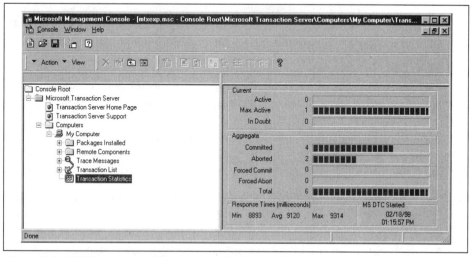

Figure 5-5. MTS Transaction Statistics page for the local compute

 In addition to adding components to packages and monitoring the component activities, MTS also provides thread management for the components (no small task) as well as the ability to terminate badly behaving components. It can also terminate a transaction manually if necessary. Before creating ASP/MTS components, read the section of the MTS documentation labeled *Microsoft Transaction Server Programmer's Guide.*

MTS as a Component Management Tool

MTS goes way beyond transaction management as its only purpose and goal. It is actually a very effective component management and distribution tool as well as a transaction server. For instance, if the package created in the previous sections were to be moved to a different machine, MTS also provides the ability to export the package to a single installation file, which can automate the installation in the new environment not only of the package, but of the associated components as well. In addition, MTS provides for thread support for a component, as well as resource pooling and component activation management.

Exporting and Importing an MTS Server Package

To create an installation file for an MTS package, right-click on the package in the MTS Console and select Export from the popup menu. This opens a dialog that allows you to specify a path as well as a package name for the package file, as well as whether to add the associated roles and NT user IDs to the exported package. Once the package is exported, the generated file, with an extension of *.PAK*, can be moved to any other computer on which MTS is installed.

To install the file, click on the *Packages Installed* folder in MTS and then select New from the Action menu to open the dialog for creating a new MTS package, as described earlier in the chapter. However, instead of creating a new, blank package, select the "Install pre-built packages" option instead. This opens a dialog that allows us to access the package that was created using the Export facility earlier. The other options for the package creation are the same as those discussed earlier.

By using the package export and import facilities, not only is the package, along with its associated roles, moved to the new machine, but the NT IDs associated with the roles as well as the MTS components are also added to the package. This export and import process also works with MTS components that are also ASP components, as long as IIS is installed in the target environment.

For MTS components that are accessed directly in a multi-tier development environment, MTS also provides the ability to create an installation program to install the necessary type library and registry information for a client program to access a component on the server remotely. Though the client in an ASP application is usually considered the browser, a client could also be the ASP application itself, with one or more of the ASP/MTS components distributed on remote machines. To provide support to access components that are installed remotely, when the installation package is created for the server installation, a client-side installation package is also created as a standalone executable. This file has the same root filename as the package file, but has an *.EXE* extension. The file is created in a subdirectory named *clients* in the same location where the exported package was created.

The client installation provides the type library or proxy/stub DLL for the component and registry information in order to access the component. Java and Visual Basic components usually have a type library, while C++ components can have a type library or a proxy/stub DLL. To access a component remotely, the registration must contain the name of the remote server. This name will be the name of the server where the exportation occurred, unless the properties for the current computer (known as My Computer) are changed to name a remote server. You can change the properties by right-clicking the *My Computer* folder, selecting the Properties option, and then selecting the Options tab. In the Options tab, type the name of the remote server that will host the ASP/MTS components into the Remote Server Name field. Each component within the MTS package is registered on the client machine, and each is registered as remotely accessible from the server given in the remote server name.

Component Activation

The components created in this chapter made use of the ObjectContext object's SetComplete and SetAbort methods. These methods don't just mark whether the component successfully completed its process or not; they also mark when the component can be released from memory.

Normally with COM, when a client accesses a component, the component is activated and loaded into memory and stays in memory until the client is itself finished, the component's object reference is no longer in scope, or the client specifically releases the component. This also means that the component holds all of its resources, including threads, database connections, and other resources, until the client releases the component. This is not the most efficient or scalable approach to distributed application development.

With the use of MTS, a component's call to the SetComplete or SetAbort method informs MTS that the component is finished with its processing and can be released from memory. MTS then releases the component from memory *regardless of whether the client still maintains a reference to the component or not.* Then, when the client again calls a method on the component, MTS loads a new instance of the component into memory without the client ever being aware that it is referencing a new component. This whole process is known as *just-in-time activation.*

MTS implements just-in-time activation as follows: when a client creates an reference to a new instance of a component, what it really receives is a reference created by MTS for the component. It is this reference, and not the one actually returned by the component when it is instantiated, that the client uses in all of its operations. Therefore, when MTS releases the component from memory, the reference to the component that the client has is still valid, since it is an MTS reference and not a direct component reference. When the client again calls the component, MTS creates a new instance of the component, but the reference the client has works with the new instance of the component as well as the previous instance.

In addition, when a component provides support for the MTS ObjectControl object, the component can participate in resource or object pooling. This means that when the object is marked for release from memory, it isn't totally released from memory, but instead is returned to an object pool that MTS creates and maintains. The impact of object pooling is that when the client accesses a new instance of the object, it is already created and is quickly activated for use with the new client request.

Resource pooling has been widely used with database connectivity as well as thread management for controlling the number of instances of these expensive resources, yet allowing fast access to a resource when a client application has need of it.

All of these component management facilities, such as just-in-time activation and resource pooling, work together to make the component, whether it is an ASP component or not, highly scalable. Because of this, I strongly recommend the use of MTS with ASP components.

Further Reading

For additional reading about the topics covered in this chapter, check out the following:

- For more information on MTS, Microsoft has provided an online MTS summary page that contains links to several articles on MTS. This page can be accessed at *http://msdn.microsoft.com/developer/news/feature/010598/mts/mts-summary.htm.*

- More MTS resources and articles can be found at the Microsoft COM web site at *http://www.microsoft.com/com/default.asp.*

- For more specific information about MTS and just-in-time activation, try the article "Employing Microsoft Transaction Server in Multitier Applications," found at *http://premium.microsoft.com/msdn/library/periodic/period97/html/viper.htm.*

- For more information about MTS and resource dispensers, the article "Writing Transaction Server Resource Dispensers" at *http://premium.microsoft.com/msdn/library/techart/msdn_resdispr.htm* should be interesting.

6

Overview of the Intrinsic (Built-in) Objects

An ASP COM component is differentiated from another COM component primarily by its use within an ASP application. However, an ASP component can be used within any type of application unless specific use is made of several built-in objects available only from an ASP page or to a component used within an ASP application. These objects, known as the ASP intrinsic or built-in objects, are provided by Microsoft as a means of communicating back and forth between the client and the application, as well as for providing techniques to access environmental and other information.

Consider this: an ASP component, or even an ASP page, for that matter, does not exist independently, but instead exists as part of an integrated whole with the entire ASP application. Breaking an ASP application down into five basic activities, the application itself begins when the first page of the application is accessed after the web server supporting the application is started, and continues until the web server is shut down or the application is itself shut down. The ASP server manages loading and unloading ASP pages, as well creating new server components to support the application. A client accessing a page within the ASP application for the first time triggers the beginning of a session, which lasts until the client logs off, its connection terminates, or the session itself is terminated. The client accessing the ASP page may or may not send information to the ASP application, and the application usually sends information back to the client.

To facilitate the integration of all of these basic activities, Microsoft created five built-in objects that match the five major activities of an ASP application, and that are part of the ASP application without any additional effort on the part of the web application or component developer. The objects are the Application, Session, Server, Request, and Response objects.

Briefly, the Server object is responsible for access to server components just like the ones you will create in the remainder of this book. The object also provides methods to encode a string using both HTML and URL encoding. The Session object is created automatically when the user logs into the ASP application, and remains until the user leaves the application or the session times out. The Application object, on the other hand, is created for the ASP application as a whole; its single instance is available from all ASP pages and to all application users. The Request and Response objects, however, are created for each specific ASP application page access, either from the user, which generates a Request object, or to the user via the Response object.

These built-in objects have methods, properties, and events that are accessible using server-side scripting, or through an interface created in the target language of your component. This means that each of the objects has a Java, Visual Basic, and C++ interface, in addition to the scripting interface.

ASP Scripting Syntax and Application Scope

This chapter assumes that you are familiar with ASP scripting syntax and notation. If you have not had a chance to work with ASP prior to reading this chapter, you might want to review the documentation that is installed with IIS on ASP development.

Additionally, Chapter 4, *ASP Components and Threads*, discusses application-, session-, and page-level scoping and how the different threading models work, or don't work, with each specific scoping level. You may wish to review that chapter before reading this chapter, and consult *ASP in a Nutshell*, written by A. Keyton Weissinger and published by O'Reilly & Associates.

Rather than repeating detailed information about what each object is and what it can do in all three of the language-specific sections of this book, this chapter provides a reference for the built-in objects, including a description of object properties and an explanation of object methods. It also provides demonstrations of some of the methods using server-side scripting. Specific programmatic access of the objects in C++, Visual Basic, and Java are explored in more detail in each of the respective interface chapters: Chapter 8, *The Visual Basic Built-in Object Interfaces*; Chapter 12, *The C++ ASP Built-in Interfaces*; and Chapter 16, *The Java Interfaces*.

The Application Object

The Application object is used to create variables and values that are accessible by all sessions and users of a common ASP application. Remember that an ASP application is all the ASP files within a virtual ASP directory and all subdirectories contained within this same directory, whereas a session is created for each ASP application client.

An Application object is created when the first page of the ASP application is accessed by a client after the web server for the application is started. The Application object lasts until the web server is shut down. As the Application object's sole purpose is to provide a common area for sharing information, it has two methods, Lock and Unlock, which are used to lock the Application object while one of the object's data values is being modified and to free it so that it can be accessed by other processes. The Application object also has two collections, Contents and StaticObjects, which contain values that are declared within server-side scripts and within the *Global.asa* file, respectively.[*]

The Application object also has two events, `Application_OnEnd` and `Application_OnStart`. Code can be created to provide event handling whenever the ASP application is started or at the application's end. Again, these events can be coded using script within the *Global.asa* file.

The Global.asa file and StaticObjects

Each ASP application has one, and only one, *Global.asa* file, and it is located in the root directory for the application. Your application can use it to add scripted events at the application or session level, and to add application- and session-level component instances to the ASP application.

An *application component* is an instance of an ASP object that exists for the life of the application and is shared by all sessions accessing the same application. An example of such a component is a counter, which is incremented each time a particular page is accessed or some other activity occurs. This component is not reset for each person, but once for the application itself or for some other significant event. When all pages within the application access the component, they are accessing the same component and the same value. Additionally, the component can be persisted, with the value periodically saved to a file in case some problem occurs and the ASP application or the web server hosting the application is

---

[*] If you are not familiar with the term *collection*, it is a predefined array structure used to hold known types of data structures, both complex and simple.

stopped. When the application is restarted, the saved value is accessed and the counting process begins from that point.

 Note that an ASP application is started when a page within the application is accessed, not when the web server hosting the application is started.

To follow through on the counter example and to demonstrate how to create an application-level component, Microsoft has created an ASP Counters component that can be used any time some form of counter is needed. The syntax to use to add this component to the application is:

```
<OBJECT RUNAT=Server Scope=Application ID=PgCounter PROGID="MSWC.Counters">
</OBJECT>
```

The **Scope** attribute can take two values, **Application** or **Session**, depending on whether the component is available for the entire application or only the specific session. The **ID** is the identifier for the component instance, and is the name used to access the component from the Application object at runtime. The **PROGID** is the program ID for the component class. Either a program ID or a specific CLSID must be specified for the component. The format for the program ID is *vendor.component.version*, with the vendor and version parts being optional, as long as the values correspond to the registry entry for the component. A class ID follows the format for an OLE class identifier, explained in more detail in Chapter 3, *ASP Components and COM*. The value for RUNAT is fixed at this time, and only takes the value of **Server**.

Once a component, in this case the Counter object instance, has been created within the *Global.asa* file, any page within the entire ASP application can access it using syntax similar to the following:

```
<% PgCounter.Set("ItemRF45",0) %>
There have been <%= PgCounter.Increment("ItemRF45") %>
copies of Item RF45 sold
```

In the example, the first line of server-side script sets the value of the counter to zero (0). The second line increments the existing counter and then prints out the results. Regardless of which ASP application page accessed the *PgCounter* counter, the value set for the counter item *ItemRF45* will be the same for all the pages.

The StaticObjects collection of the Application object contains references to all object instances created using the <OBJECT> tag within the *Global.asa* file. It is provided as a means to iterate through all component instances created within *Global.asa*, and to check for the existence of component instances, perhaps in an application administration page that lets an administrator quickly see what component instances have been added. Code for this display might be similar to:

```
<%
Dim obj
For Each obj in Application.StaticObjects %>
  Object Instance : <%= obj %> <p>
<% Next %>
```

In this example, each object is printed out to the web page returned to the client.

The advantage of using the <OBJECT> tag to create application-level components is that all of the components are declared and maintained in one place. Also, the component instance can be referenced directly, rather than having to be prefaced with the Session or Application object, as will be demonstrated in the next section. Finally, there is an improvement in application performance when a component instance is defined with the <OBJECT> tag, since this type of component is not instantiated until it is accessed. A component instance created using the CreateObject method, discussed next, is created instantly. This has little impact on an application-level component, but it can make a difference with session-level components.

Application Variables and Objects and the Contents Collection

To create a variable that is available to all sessions of a specific application, you can use the following syntax:

```
<% Application("counter1") = 0 %>
<% Set Application("PageCounter") = Server.CreateObject("MSWC.PageCounter")
%>
```

The first line of code shows how to create a scalar variable that is available throughout the application. The second line of code creates a reference to an object instance that is available for application-wide access. Both statements create an entry within the Application object's Contents collection, unlike objects created in the *global.asa* file, which adds entries to the StaticObjects collection. However, code can access the values in this collection in the same manner as values are accessed in StaticObjects, as the following code demonstrates.

```
The counter is <%= Application.Contents("counter1") %>
<% Set tmp = Application.Contents("PageCounter") %>
The page has been visited <%= tmp %> times
```

Application components created using CreateObject can also be accessed directly from the Application object, as the following code fragment demonstrates.

```
The counter is <%= Application.("counter1") %>
<% Set tmp = Application.("PageCounter") %>
The page has been visited <%= tmp %> times
```

The Application object reference must be used with objects created using CreateObject.

A handy technique to use to set initial values when an application starts is to code for the **Application_OnStart** event within *Global.asa*, and then access the application global values throughout the application, as shown in the following short scripting block:

```
<SCRIPT LANGUAGE=VBscript RUNAT=Server>
Sub Application_OnStart
    Application("tst") = "value1"
    Application("second") = "value2"
End Sub

</SCRIPT>
```

The Application object's **Application_OnEnd** event can also be trapped to code for handling of Application-level values, perhaps by storing the values in files in order to maintain some form of persistence for the item.

Using the Lock and Unlock Methods

One problem with variables or objects that can be modified by different people at the same time is that one person may access a variable and modify it at the exact same time another person accesses the same variable and performs the same modification. The following scenario demonstrates the unexpected results:

1. Person A accesses the page with Application counter *itemRF8*, which tracks the number of RF8 items that have been ordered. There are only 9 of these items for sale, and 8 have been sold, so Person A can safely order item RF8. The person places an order for the item.

2. In the meantime, Person B accesses the same page and wants to order the same item. As the Application counter is not locked, she accesses this counter and sees, as did Person A, that there is still one RF8 item for sale. This person, too, places an order for the item.

3. Person A's order has incremented the RF8 item counter as a part of the order process, effectively blocking any other order from going through for the item, since the total available is compared to the total sold for any item before an order is allowed. However, Person B's order has been allowed, since the number of items sold when Person B accessed the data was 8.

4. During order processing for Person B, the item counter is incremented, meaning that the item counter is now set to a value of 10, and Person B has effectively ordered something that doesn't exist. Needless to say, person B is not happy when she doesn't receive her item.

An ASP developer does not want an updateable value to be accessed at the same time that an update occurs. To prevent this, the Application methods Lock and Unlock are used to lock out all access to the Application item until the update has occurred. For the scenario just demonstrated, the code to perform this action is the following:

```
<%
If (Application("itemRF8") < 9 Then
  Application.Lock
  Application("itemRF8") = Application("itemRF8") + 1
  Application.Unlock
End If
%>
```

A note of warning with the use of Lock and Unlock: when you lock the Application object, you lock the object for all Application variables for all sessions. You will want to lock and unlock the Application object quickly and minimize the amount of code to run while the Application object is locked. Ideally, the only code that should be run while the Application object is locked is the code to modify the Application variable value.

As stated earlier, Application components and variables last the lifetime of the Application object. Session components and variables last for a specific session, and are detailed next.

The Session Object

While the Application object manages object instances and variables at the ASP application level, the Session object manages object instances and variables at the session level. Session-level variables can be created for such uses as maintaining a running balance for an online store, maintaining a connection to a client through many ASP application pages, or even tracking the flow of a transaction to determine if all the transaction's actions have completed successfully or not.

Unlike the Application object, a Session object is unique to a session, and thus is uniquely accessed by one client. Because of this, the Session object does not need to be locked and unlocked during updates: only one client accesses any one session variable or object at a time. Instead of the Lock and Unlock methods, the Session object has a method called Abandon that can be used to destroy all Session objects and release Session resources. Normally, the Session objects would be freed when the session timed out, but if the ASP developer has an explicit logout page, the Abandon method could be called to free up Session resources prior to a timeout.

Another difference between the Session object and the Application object is how object information is maintained. Application information is maintained by the application web server, and is not affected by any client-side setting. Session state, however, is maintained using client-side cookies, and works only if the client accessing the ASP application supports cookies and allows cookies to be set.* The SessionID that identifies the particular session is stored as a cookie and maintains a connection between the client and the session variables stored on the web server. If cookies are not supported or allowed, this SessionID property cannot be maintained.

 ASP server-side scripting sets certain properties, such as the CODEPAGE property (which is discussed in this section), using directives. Directives being with "@" and are usually the first line within the ASP page or the first line of a server-side scripting block. An example of setting a directive that changes the scripting language is the following, which changes the scripting language from the default VBScript to JScript:

```
<%@LANGUAGE=Jscript %>
```

Properties that can be set with directives are CODEPAGE, ENABLESESSIONSTATE, LANGUAGE, LCID, and TRANSACTION. If the directive is not set, a default value is provided.

In addition to the SessionID property, other Session properties are:

CodePage

Sets the code page to be used for the ASP file. A code page is for support of internationalization and includes characters and glyphs specific to a language and a locale. A default code page can be set in the @CODEPAGE directive.

---

* If you haven't worked with web development, a *cookie* is a small bit of information that is stored for a set period of time on the client machine, and is stored as a named value and keyed by the ASP application path.

LCID

>   The locale identifier. This identifier is a standard locale identifier used to display locale-specific content.

Timeout

>   The specific time period that determines when the session ends. If the client has not accessed a page within the ASP application before the time period ends, the session is ended. The default time period is 20 minutes.

Internationalization

As you can see, two of the Session properties have to do with support for internationalization, a concept to keep in mind when creating your own components. Consider whether they are to be accessed by English-speaking people only, or whether they must support a broader audience base. If they must support a multilingual audience, check out the internationalization topics for ASP applications at Microsoft's online Microsoft Developer Network pages, at *http:/ /www.microsoft.com/msdn/.*

Like the Application object, the Session object has both a StaticObjects collection, containing all objects defined using the <OBJECT> tag in *Global.asa*, and a Contents collection. As both collections behave identically for the Session object as for the Application object, the only difference being application scope, I won't go into detail on these objects, except to demonstrate how the Session object variables and object instances are created.

To create a Session-level component in the *Global.asa* file, use the following syntax:

```
<OBJECT RUNAT=Server Scope=Session ID=PgCounter PROGID="MSWC.Counters">
</OBJECT>
```

This actually creates a counter that is available for the session only.

To create a Session variable using a script block, use syntax similar to the following:

```
<% Session("variable1") = "somevalue" %>
<% Set Session("object1") = Server.CreateObject("MSWC.Counters") %>
```

Finally, to access objects created using the <OBJECT> tag, you can use the StaticObjects collection. To access objects and variables created using scripts, you can use the Contents collection or access the value directly from the Session object, as shown in the following code block.

```
<%
Dim obj
For Each obj in Session.StaticObjects %>
  Object Instance : <%= obj %> <p>
<% Next %>
...

<% Session("itemRF8") = 1 %>
<% Session.Contents("itemRF8") = 1 %>
...
There have been <%= Session("itemRF8") %> items sold
```

As with the Application object, there are restrictions on which threading model can be used with session-level variables; you can read about this in Chapter 4.

> Again, whether to create session component instances using <OBJECT> tags or CreateObject is up to you, but there is a performance improvement to using the <OBJECT> tags when creating session-level components. Additionally, application maintenance can be easier, since all application and session component instances are created in the same place. A good choice is to use the <OBJECT> tags to create both application and session component instances.

The Server Object

The Server object is used to create instances of server component objects, which can then be used within another component or within an ASP page. This includes any of the ASP components demonstrated in this book. Components must be instantiated before any of the component's properties or methods are accessed.

There are actually two different techniques that can be used to create an ASP component instance, as was demonstrated in the previous two sections. The first is to use the <OBJECT> tag in the *Global.asa* file. The second uses the CreateObject method of the Server object and assigns the results to a variable, as the following code demonstrates:

```
<% Set PageCounter = Server.CreateObject("MSWC.PageCounter") %>
```

The ASP PageCounter component counts the number of times a web page is accessed. This count is maintained within a file, and the file path and name are stored as part of a registry key. Once a local *page-level* reference to the Page-Counter object is created, it can then be used to access the methods for this object, in this case Hits, to access the number of page hits, and Reset, to set the counter back to zero. The value returned from the Hits method can then be displayed within the page, as the following code shows, or used for other purposes:

```
You are visitor <strong>#<%= PageCounter.Hits %></strong> to
access this Web page. I bet you really wanted to know this,
didn't you?
```

When the PageCounter component instance was created, it was defined to be of local page scope only, meaning that the variable is destroyed when the web page is unloaded.

The other methods for the Server object, in addition to CreateObject, are:

HTMLEncode

Takes a string as a parameter and returns the same string with HTML encoding

MapPath

Maps a virtual or relative path to a path relative to the directory of the ASP file being accessed

URLEncode

Takes a string as a parameter and returns the same string with URL encoding

Both HTTP and HTML have reserved characters, such as the angle brackets for HTML and the plus sign (+) for HTTP. When these characters are used in a text stream, such as name-value pairs appended to a URL to be sent to an application, or within a web page, the reserved characters need to be "encoded." This ensures that the web server does not process the characters in the URL stream, and the browser does not process the HTML reserved characters contained within the web document. The characters are encoded as their hexadecimal equivalent, or they can be encoded using predefined alias values. For instance, the HTMLEncode method applied to a string such as:

```
<%= Server.HTMLEncode("<H1>This is a header</H1>") %>
```

would print out a line in the web document as follows:

```
&lt;H1&gt;This is a header&lt;/H1&gt;
```

but it would appear to the user viewing the web page in a browser as:

```
<H1>This is a header</H1>
```

rather than being processed as a header element and displaying the text as larger, bolder script.

URL encoding relates to the text appended to a URL. Certain characters in the text string have special meaning, such as the ampersand (&), which indicates an additional name-value pair, or the equals sign (=), which separates the name-value pair. Even spaces are encoded using the plus sign, meaning that a literal plus sign within the text must itself be encoded.

An example of using the Server object URLEncode method to encode a string to attach to a URL is shown in Example 6-1. This small ASP page uses URLEncode to create a set of name-value pairs, which are then attached to a URL within a link in the page. The URL calls another ASP page that prints out the name-value pairs in a table.

Example 6-1. Creating a String to Attach to a Hypertext Reference

```
<%@ LANGUAGE = javascript %>
<HTML>
<HEAD>
<TITLE>URL Encoding</TITLE>
</HEAD>
<BODY>
<%
value = Server.URLEncode("last name") + "=powers&" +
        Server.URLEncode("special characters")+"=" +
        Server.URLEncode("+% &/!=#") + "&address=" +
        Server.URLEncode("1243 Some Avenue North, Some City, VT, 00000") +
                    "&" +
        Server.URLEncode("Some other special characters:")+"=" + _
        Server.URLEncode("%/.. . ! = && .. \/#");
%>

<a href="test1.asp?<% = value %>">Test</a>
</BODY>
</HTML>
```

This URL-encoded string contains four name-value pairs. The target ASP file, *test1. asp*, then parses the name-value pairs and displays the results, as shown in Figure 6-1. Note the URL in the browser's Location text box. It shows the strings as they are encoded. However, when the string is accessed as a query string in the receiving application, the ASP built-in Request object decodes the string before parsing the name-value pairs.

Figure 6-1. Parsed name-value pairs after URL-encoded string has been decoded by Request

The only property the Server object has is ScriptTimeout. This property can be set to the number of seconds any one script can run within the application page, a useful technique to handle overly long scripting runs. If the script runs longer than the allocated time, it is terminated and an error message is written to the log file.

The IIS Metabase Values

A general attribute, `AspScriptTimeout`, is used to set the script timeouts for the web server. This attribute is one of the IIS Metabase values, which replace the need for registry entries. Metabase values, unlike registry values, are preloaded into memory and have faster access times. To read more about the metabase, consult the documentation that comes with IIS 4.0.

The Request Object

When a web page returns information to the server by appending it to a link or posting it from a form, the information is collected in the Request object. The only method the Request object has at this time is BinaryRead, which accesses the data passed with the Request object as bytes, and stores the value in a *SafeArray*—an array that includes dimension information, such as bounds and the number of dimensions of an array. The only property for the Request object, aside from several collections which will be detailed in a moment, is TotalBytes. This property gives the total number of bytes sent in the client request.

The Request object includes references to the query string, form field values, digital certificate information, and predefined environment variables, and each of these values can be accessed as a collection. Which type of collection to access depends on what type of information is needed within the ASP application, and how the information was sent from the client. The collections that have been defined for the Request object are:

QueryString

Contains name-value pairs sent using the form's GET posting method or appended to the end of the URL used to reference the ASP page. Each name-value pair becomes one entry in the QueryString collection.

Form

Contains name-value pairs sent from a form using the POST form posting method. Each form element becomes one entry in the Form collection.

ClientCertificate

> Contains information about the client certificate, if a client certificate is requested by the server.

Cookies

> Contains Netscape-style cookies sent as part of the HTTP request. A cookie can contain multiple keys, each of which can be accessed as a group or individually.

ServerVariables

> Contains certain pre-selected environment variables, such as QUERY_STRING, REMOTE_ADDR, and REQUEST_METHOD.

The collections are stored as name-value pairs, and to access the value, you enter the name. For example, the following code will set a variable to a query string value with a given name of "lastname":

```
Dim Lastname
Lastname = Request.QueryString("lastname");
```

If the ASP page is opened using a hypertext link similar to the following, the value of "lastname" would be set to "Powers":

```
<A href="file.asp?lastname=powers&firstname=shelley">Open</a>
```

Each of the collections is discussed and demonstrated in detail in the following sections.

The QueryString Collection

The QueryString collection is an array containing name-value pairs and is parsed from the QUERY_STRING environment variable. Each specific entry within the collection is accessible by its position as it occurs in the collection or by its name. This collection has entries only if the ASP page is opened as a result of a form request sent using the default GET method, or if name-value pairs have been added to the URL to access the page.

 To add name-value pairs to a URL, the values must be URL-encoded, as discussed earlier in the Server section.

As an example of accessing a value from the QueryString collection, if one page in the ASP application contains a form with a field named "name" and the form was posted using the GET method, accessing the specific field values can be done using the following:

```
<% name = Request.QueryString("name");
    address = Request.QueryString("address");
%>
```

As stated, another way the QueryString collection gets name-value pairs is if the values are appended to the end of a URL, as was demonstrated in Example 6-1. This example showed how to encode strings to append to the URL. The code in Example 6-2 shows how the name-value pairs are accessed using the QueryString collection and then displayed in an HTML table.

Example 6-2. ASP Page That Displays the Name-Value Pairs Appended to the URL

```
<HTML>
<HEAD>
<TITLE>QueryString</TITLE>
<STYLE type="text/css">
    BODY { margin: 0.5in }
</STYLE>
<BODY>
<H1> QueryString name-value pairs </H1>
<TABLE border=0 width=90% cellspacing=5>

   <% For Each name In Request.QueryString %>
   <TR><TD> <% = name %></TD><TD> <% =Request.QueryString(name) %></TD></TR>
   <% Next %>

</TABLE>
</BODY>
</HTML>
```

In this example, the page returned displays both the name of the name-value pair as well as its associated value.

If the same name is given more than one value within a query string, the ASP application creates an array of objects for a specific name within the QueryString collection. So if I use the following string within a hypertext link URL, I end up with a named array instead of a scalar value for the name "test":

```
<a href="test.asp?test=one&test=two&test=three">Test</a>
```

Accessing the individual values for test requires code similar to the following:

```
<%
  test1 = Request.QueryString("test")(1);
  test2 = Request.QueryString("test")(2);
  test3 = Request.QueryString("test")(3);
%>
```

Notice that, unlike standard VBScript arrays, the first index for a collection array begins with the value of 1 instead of a value of 0 (zero). Also, the QueryString collection object and array index references use parentheses instead of square brackets regardless of the scripting language used. The same holds true for all built-in object collections.

To find out if a specific element within the QueryString collection is an array object, you can access the Count property for the element, which returns the number of elements that make up the object. In the previous example, the following would print out the value 3:

```
The number of text objects is <%= Request.QueryString("test").Count %>
```

You can also access all of the values for a collection array element at once by accessing it without using an index. The value returned is a list of the values separated by commas. Additionally, if you want to access all of the QueryString data without parsing it, access the QueryString collection name directly without specifying a name, as follows.

```
The data sent is <%= Request.QueryString %>
```

Again, the result returned is the name-value pairs as sent with the original request.

The Form Collection

If a form is posted using the POST method, the form field name-value pairs are added to the Form collection rather than the QueryString collection. You will usually want to use the POST method rather than the GET method because there is a limit on the length of the string that can be appended to a URL in a GET request. This length can easily be exceeded with a larger form. Additionally, it can be a bit intimidating to the client to see the long, encoded string attached to the URL.

There is absolutely no difference in how the Form name-value pairs are accessed compared to the QueryString pairs. The following code is how the values used earlier in Example 6-2 would be accessed if the form had been posted instead of submitted with GET:

```
<% name = Request.Form("name");
   address = Request.Form("address");
%>
```

A form field that can return multiple values can also have each value accessed individually using the index value, just as with QueryString:

```
<% street_address1 = Request.Form("streetaddr")(1) %>
```

Additionally, the entire form contents can be accessed by referencing the Form collection without providing a name with the Form collection. For collection arrays, the entire array can be returned as a comma-delimited string by referencing the array name without providing an array index:

```
<% street_address1 = Request.Form("streetaddr") %>
```

The ClientCertificate Collection

Server digital certificates are used to verify that a server application being accessed is from the originating server, has not been improperly modified, and is safe. Client certificates verify that the client is who it claims to be. When a client accesses a secure application located on a secure server, the web server may then transmit the server digital certificate and request that the client submit its digital certificate. Once the client's certificate information is transmitted back to the server, a secure communication channel is established between the client and the server.

When the server requests a digital certificate, the Request object returns digital certificate information in the ClientCertificate collection. Instead of generic data, the ClientCertificate contains very specific information, detailed in the following list:

Subject
> Contains subject values that can be accessed independently using the different subject field names; among these subject field names are "C" for company name and "L" for locality

Issuer
> Contains subject values for the digital certificate issuer that can be accessed independently, just as with the Subject collection item

ValidFrom
> Date specifying the start date for the certificate

ValidUntil
> Date specifying when the certificate ends

SerialNumber
> Certificate serial number

Certificate
> All of the certificate as a binary string

Flags
> A set of flags that contain additional certificate information

Before working with digital certificates, I suggest that you read the information on the certificate process that Microsoft has at its Developer Network web site, at *http://www.microsoft.com/msdn/*.

The Cookies Collection

As stated earlier, the ASP Session object makes use of client-side cookies. In addition, the ASP developer can also use client-side cookies to store persistent information that relates to the specific client. The information can then be accessed the next time the client accesses the ASP application.

Cookie information is accessed by the browser and by using the path of the document being loaded as a key to finding whether any cookies exist for the specific page within the client's cookie file or directory. If so, the cookie name-value pairs are added to the HTTP request for the page.

This same cookie information can be pulled from an HTTP request using the Cookies collection. The cookie can be a scalar value, accessible by name for the name-value cookie pair. Or the cookie can be part of a more complex cookie dictionary, with the value itself being another name-value pair.

To access a cookie, use the following syntax:

```
<% tmp = Request.Cookies("first") %>
```

In this example, if the cookie named "first" existed, the value for "first" would be returned; otherwise, an empty string would be returned. If the cookie itself contained a name-value pair, or *key*, the key value could be accessed using the following syntax:

```
<% tmp = Request.Cookies("first")("second") %>
```

Unlike array elements in the other collections, the Cookies collection assumes a named index for the second level of values. In addition, no other levels of values are supported. An attribute, **HasKeys**, can be used to determine if a cookie is a dictionary object or a scalar value. A value of **True** is returned if the cookie is a more complex object; a value of **False** is returned if the cookie is not a complex object.

Cookies can be created using client-side scripting, and this technique is explained in detail at both Netscape's and Microsoft's web sites. Cookies can also be created using server-side scripting and the Response object, discussed later in this chapter.

The ServerVariables Collection

There are certain environment variables available with any HTTP client-server transaction. Some of the variables have been discussed already, such as QUERY_ STRING, which contains the query string sent with an HTTP request. Other values include cookies, the type of browser making the request, client certificate information, information about the remote connection, the client language, and a host of other information. All of these environment variables can be accessed via the ServerVariables collection.

Figure 6-2 shows an ASP page that is called from another page and that prints out the server variables. Note that not all variables have an associated value, but all variables do have an entry within the collection. The code to create this display is shown in Example 6-3. I would suggest copying this code and trying this ASP page from your own server to see how the values differ in your own environment based on different types of requests.

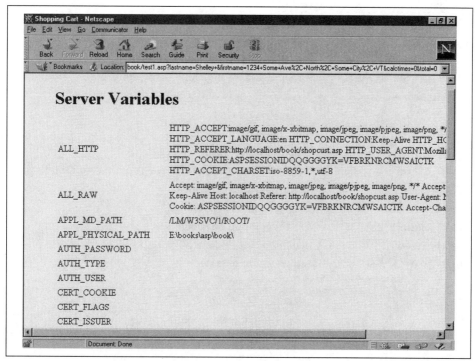

Figure 6-2. Request object ServerVariables collection elements

Example 6-3. ASP Page That Displays the ServerVariables Collection

```
<HTML>
<HEAD>
<TITLE>Server Variables</TITLE>
<STYLE type="text/css">
    BODY { margin: 0.5in }
</STYLE>
<BODY>
<H1> Server Variables </H1>
<TABLE border=0 width=90% align=center cellspacing=5>
<% For Each name In Request.ServerVariables %>
<TR><TD> <% = name %></TD><TD> <% =Request.ServerVariables(name) %></TD></TR>
<% Next %>
</TABLE>
</BODY>
</HTML>
```

The environment variables accessible via the Request object are shown in Table 6-1.

Table 6-1. Members of the Request Object's ServerVariables Collection

Variable	Description
ALL_HTTP - HTTP	All HTTP headers sent by the client
ALL_RAW	All data sent in raw form by the client
APPL_MD_PATH	Metabase path for the application
APPL_PHYSICAL_PATH	Actual physical path name for the application
AUTH_PASSWORD	Contains the password if Basic authentication is used
AUTH_TYPE	Authentication type
AUTH_USER	Authenticated user
CERT_COOKIE	Unique ID for a client certificate
CERT_FLAGS	Flags to determine if a certificate is present and valid
CERT_ISSUER	Client certificate issuer field
CERT_KEYSIZE	Secure Sockets Layer bit key size
CERT_SECRETKEYSIZE	Server certificate private bit key size
CERT_SERIALNUMBER	Certificate serial number
CERT_SERVER_ISSUER	Server certificate issuer
CERT_SERVER_SUBJECT	Server certificate subject
CERT_SUBJECT	Client certificate subject
CONTENT_LENGTH	Client content length, defined by the client
CONTENT_TYPE	Content data type, used with attached data only
GATEWAY_INTERFACE	The CGI revision
HTTPS	Set to "on" if request is from a secure server; otherwise, set to "off"
HTTPS_KEYSIZE	SSL connection key size
HTTPS_ SECRETKEYSIZE	Size of secure server certificate key size
HTTPS_SERVER_ISSUER	Secure server certificate issuer
HTTPS_SERVER_SUBJECT	Secure server certificate subject
INSTANCE_ID	IIS instance ID
INSTANCE_META_PATH	IIS instance Metabase path
LOCAL_ADDR	Server address of request
LOGON_USER	NT account user is logged into
PATH_INFO	Path information of ASP application page
PATH_TRANSLATED	A virtual to physical path translation
QUERY_STRING	The query string
REMOTE_ADDR	IP address of remote host
REMOTE_USER	Name supplied by user without any filter being applied

Table 6-1. Members of the Request Object's ServerVariables Collection (continued)

Variable	Description
REQUEST_METHOD	Method of request, such as GET or POST
SCRIPT_NAME	Virtual path of script
SERVER_NAME	IP or DNS alias of server; `localhost` is the loopback address of 127.0.0.1
SERVER_PORT	Name and revision of request port
SERVER_PORT_SECURE	Set to 0 if request is not through secure port; otherwise, set to 1
SERVER_PROTOCOL	Request information protocol, such as HTTP/1.0
SERVER_SOFTWARE	The web server; the examples in this book were run against "Microsoft-IIS/4.0 Beta 2," which is the second beta release for IIS, version 4.0
URL	Base URL

There are several variables that appear in the ServerVariables collection when the code from Example 6-3 is run, but that are not documented in the ASP documentation. These all have to do with the HTTP request, such as the HTTP cookie, the HTTP host, and the language. As undocumented variables can be dropped or altered without advance notice from Microsoft, I won't document them here in this book.

Accessing a Value Without a Collection

Values can be accessed directly from the Request object, rather than having to use any of the collections. The web server searches through the collections in a specific order, and returns the first value for the given name that it finds. So, if you enter a name request as follows:

```
<% tmp = Request("temp") %>
```

the server first searches through the QueryString collection, then the Form collection, the Cookies collection, the ClientCertificate collection, and finally through ServerVariables. As the same name can be used for an object listed in more than one collection, it might be safer to use the collection name whenever the duplicate use of a name is possible.

The Response Object

If a *request* is information sent from the client to the server, a *response* is output to a client from the server, and the Response object is used to send this information. This can include HTTP header information, as well as output used to create the HTML web page. Because some of this information is part of the document header, some calls to Response object methods have to be made before any other HTML is written for the document page, unless Response buffering (discussed in the next section) is enabled.

Unlike the Request object, the Response object only has one collection, the Cookies collection. This collection allows for creating and setting the value of cookies on the client machine. An additional dissimilarity between the Response object and the Request object is that the Response object has several properties and methods, whereas the Request object only has two methods and one property.

The Response object properties are:

Buffer
> A flag to determine whether Response output is buffered until the server script is finished processing or until a forced buffer output

CacheControl
> A flag to determine whether proxy servers can cache ASP-generated output

ContentType
> The HTTP content type; `text/HTML` by default

Expires
> Minutes before the ASP page content is expired

ExpiresAbsolute
> A specific date and time when the cached page contents are expired

Status
> Three digit status line, such as 404 for file not found, returned by the server

IsClientConnected
> Whether the client is still connected after the last Response.Write method call

Charset
> HTTP response character set

PICS
> PICS label field; PICS is a rating system used voluntarily by sites to rate the adult nature of content within the site

The Response object methods are:

AddHeader
> Adds an HTML header to the response

AppendToLog
> Appends a string of up to 80 characters, not including any commas, to the log file for the response

BinaryWrite

Writes data to output without any character conversion

Clear

Clears the current buffered contents

End

Ends server script processing and forces output of buffered contents

Flush

Forces output of buffered contents and ends keep-alive requests for the page

Redirect

Redirects the connection to a different URL

Write

Writes output to the HTTP output; can be used within server scripting blocks

The following sections take a closer look at some of the more interesting properties and methods. The Cookies collection is also detailed in its own section.

Redirection

An HTTP header is always written first for any web page returned to a browser. Certain object methods can be used to alter this HTTP header, such as the Response object's Redirect method. The method takes a URL as a parameter and redirects the browser to another page:

```
Response.Redirect "http://www.yasd.com/plus.htm"
```

In addition to redirecting the browser to a different page, an HTTP status of "302" is also returned, which tells the browser that redirection is occurring since the object has moved.

When altering the header response, the code that makes the modification must be included before any other HTML for the ASP page, or an error occurs. This includes calling an ASP component that itself contains a method call that makes the modification. The only exception to this is through the use of buffering, discussed in the next section.

The Buffer Property and the Use of Clear, End, and Flush

One of the more important Response object properties is Buffer. The Buffer property is set to **True** when no response is sent to the client until all of the server-side scripting has been processed or until either the Flush or End methods have been called to output the buffer. Buffering output offers a number of advantages.

- Based on some script activity, different content can be displayed, or even an entirely different page can be opened, without any perceptible page flickering that can occur with normal page redirection.

- Buffering maintains a "keep-alive" connection between the server and the client, which means that any client requests are made in the same connection, thus eliminating the overhead from the server having to create multiple connections. Keep-alive requests are basically pings between the two ends of the connection that keep the connection open.

- Buffering allows modifications to the HTTP header from script blocks that are located throughout the page, without having to place the script blocks as the first content of the page. As stated earlier, modifications to the HTTP response must be made before the response is sent or an error occurs.

The disadvantage of page buffering is that no contents are displayed until the scripts are finished processing—and if the script processing takes a considerable amount of time, the client is going to be faced with a blank browser for longer than might be considered wise.

The Buffer property must be set before any other output is sent to the client, so it should be the first line within the HTML document:

```
<% Response.Buffer = True %>
```

The buffer contents can be controlled by using three methods: End, Clear, and Flush. The End method forces the web server to stop processing the server script and output the buffered results immediately. This is effective if you want to display the results up to a point in the script, but no further. The Clear method, on the other hand, does not force an end to buffering, but will clear whatever contents are in the buffer when the method is called. The Flush method does not prevent scripts from processing, but does force an output of the buffer contents, and the server no longer maintains keep-alive requests for the page.

A handy use of these buffer control methods is to process a script until an error occurs, clear the buffer contents so that they do not output to the page, and then call End to stop script processing. The Response headers are output, but not the Response body:

```
<% Response.Clear
   Response.End
%>
```

Altering Output Using ContentType and Status

The simplest change to output can be setting the ContentType property to a different value. For example, if an HTML document normally has a ContentType of text/html, setting this value to text/plain causes most browsers to display HTML as text, including the markup tags, rather than interpreting the tags directly. This is a handy technique to use for links labeled "show source." The link would contain:

```
<a href="test.asp?source=1">Show Source</a>
```

The top of the document being opened could have logic to test whether source should be shown, and the content type set accordingly:

```
<%
If Request.QueryString("source") = 1 Then
    Response.ContentType = "text/plain"
Else
    Response.ContentType = "text/html"
End If
%>
```

Since the content type is part of the header, this block of server code must precede any other block, unless the Buffer property is set to **True** to allow for output buffering.

The Status property can be used to return any HTTP response status code, such as "404 file not found" or "302" for file redirected. Using a value of "401 Unauthorized" can literally trigger a dialog for the user to enter a username and password. However, canceling the dialog allows access to the page, since security really has not been implemented; only the status returned to the browser has been modified.

The Response.Write Method and IsClientConnected Property

Probably one of the most effective Response methods is Write. In previous examples within this chapter, document output is created using a combination of script blocks interspersed with regular HTML output. The advantage of the Write method is that the ASP developer does not have to "chop" up the scripting block in such a way that can make the code difficult to read.

To demonstrate the improvement to readability that Write can make, the document shown in Example 6-3 is rewritten to use the Write method, and is shown in Example 6-4.

Example 6-4. Displaying ServerVariables Collection Using Response.Write

```
<HTML>
<HEAD>
<TITLE>Server Variables</TITLE>
<STYLE type="text/css">
        BODY { margin: 0.5in }
</STYLE>
```

Example 6-4. Displaying ServerVariables Collection Using Response.Write (continued)

```
<BODY>
<H1> Server Variables </H1>
<TABLE border=0 width=90% align=center cellspacing=5>
<%
For Each name In Request.ServerVariables
    Response.Write "<TR><TD>"
    Response.Write name
    Response.Write "</TD><TD>"
    Response.Write Request.ServerVariables(name)
    Response.Write "</TD></TR>"
Next
%>
</TABLE>
</BODY>
</HTML>
```

The page output is less choppy, with distinct separation between direct HTML output and server script-generated output. Additionally, the FOR loop is more distinct, making it clear what output is controlled by the loop and what output is located outside the loop. An improvement—and this is only a simple case.

A good rule of thumb to use when determining whether to use embedded script output or the Response object's Write method is that if the output must be controlled by some conditional or looping statement or traverses multiple lines, use the Write method. For simple variable assignment and one-statement outputs, use embedded script instead.

One last note before leaving the Response.Write method. If the script generating the output is time-consuming, the client may actually disconnect between one Response.Write method call and another. In order to prevent a write to a disconnected client, use the IsClientConnected property to test if the client is still connected, and then issue the Write method call if the property is set to True:

```
<%
If Response.IsClientConnected Then
    Response.Write ...
```

The Response Cookies Collection

The Response object's Cookies collection is used to send a cookie to the client, rather than pulling cookie information from the client request. Cookies can be created as scalar values, consisting only of one name-value pair, or a cookie can be a dictionary, with the value component being made up of other name-value pairs. If the cookie does not exist when it is set with the Response object, it is created.

As an example, the following sets the value of a cookie called "test" to 1. In addition, it uses several Cookies collection attributes to determine how the cookie is created:

```
<%
Response.Cookies("test") = 1
Response.Cookies("test").Expires = "March 1, 1998"
Response.Cookies("test").Path = "/book/"
Response.Cookies("test").HasKeys = FALSE
%>
```

This code creates a cookie named "test" that has an initial value of 1. It expires on March 1, 1998, and has a relative path of */book/*, which means that it is sent with the HTTP request only when a page is accessed on this particular path. The cookie is a simple scalar value and does not have a key, so the HasKeys attribute is set to False. Other properties that could have been used with this cookie are Domain, which sets the domain (such as "yasd.com") of the cookie, and Secure, which sets whether this cookie is secure.

To create a more complex cookie, one that has keys, I could use the following:

```
<%
Response.Cookies("test")("value1") = 1
Response.Cookies("test")("value2") = 2
%>
```

In this case, the expiration is set to the default, which means the cookie will expire when the client closes the browser. The cookie attribute HasKeys is set to a value of True by the fact that the cookie is created with key values.

Further Reading

For additional reading about the topics covered in this chapter, check out the following:

- A good reference on general ASP programming is *ASP in a Nutshell*, written by A. Keyton Weissinger and published by O'Reilly & Associates, 1999.

- An article about the ASP built-in objects titled "Built-In ASP Objects Reference" can found at *http://msdn.microsoft.com/library/sdkdoc/iisref/iiwaobb. htm.*

- Included with the installation of IIS 4.0 is excellent online documentation about all of the NT Option Package tools. If you are sharing an IIS installation, check with the webmaster for the location of this documentation.

II

Developing ASP Components with Visual Basic

7

Creating a Simple Visual Basic ASP Component

Visual Basic offers the simplest approach to creating an ASP component. At a minimum, the ASP component developer only needs to create a new project for the component, add in the class methods and properties, compile the component, and register it with the OLE registration server. However, there are a number of decisions that can impact how the component works with the ASP application. Among these are whether the component is an in-process or out-of-process component; whether the component is multiple- or single-use; whether the component is multithreaded and, if so, how many threads it has and when a new thread is created; and what instancing type is used. Some decisions are made for you based on other decisions. Many you make yourself, and the decision can literally mean the difference between a component that assists in the smooth operation of the ASP application and a component that becomes the worst bottleneck within the application.

In the next sections, a simple ASP component is created, and each section explores the different options faced in the component creation process. The component is named *dhtml* and includes methods to return browser-specific scripting code to perform certain dynamic HTML techniques. Among some of these techniques are moving an HTML element, hiding it, and showing it. This useful component can then be used to create browser-specific dynamic HTML pages without having to create duplicate web pages or add in different scripting sections. Creating the component is also an effective technique to demonstrate how each aspect of the component is implemented using Visual Basic 6.0. By the end of the chapter, you will know the advantages and disadvantages of creating an in-process component compared to an out-of-process component; the advantages and disadvantages of a multiple-use compared to a single-use and even a global-use component; what Visual Basic does to ensure a thread-safe component; what factors can influence parameter passing when creating component methods; how to register the component; and how to add error handling and debug the component.

Creating an In-Process or Out-Of-Process Component

An ASP component in Visual Basic is really an ActiveX object, either a dynamic link library (DLL) or an executable. An ActiveX DLL is an in-process component, which means that the component shares the same address space (memory, resources) and threads as the application that creates the component. An ActiveX executable is an out-of-process component, which means that this type of component has its own threads and resources.

The most common and simplest component to create is the ActiveX DLL, the in-process component. This type of component shares the same address space as the client, which can lead to performance gains when the client interacts with the component. For instance, when a client calls a component method, and the component and client share the same threading model, as will be discussed, the method's arguments are loaded into the client's own stack. For an out-of-process component, the method arguments are moved between the two processes through a process called *marshaling*—pulling arguments from a stack via a proxy on the client and putting the arguments onto the component's stack through a stub. This extra effort slows the communication process.

A second advantage to in-process components is that if the component is set to use the *apartment threading* model, it will work safely with a multithreaded client. The component is created as thread-safe using a technique discussed later in the chapter.

A third advantage to in-process components—or I should say another disadvantage to using an out-of-process component?—is that extra measures must be taken to allow ASP page access to out-of-process components. These types of components cannot normally be called from within ASP pages. To enable IIS version 3.0 to handle such calls, a value of 1 must be added to the `AllowOutOfProcCmpnts` value entry of the `HKEY_LOCAL_MACHINE\SYSTEM\CurrentControlSet\Services\W3SVC\ASP\Parameters` registry key. For IIS 4.0, the value is changed in the IIS metabase.

In spite of the problems with out-of-process components, there are also advantages to using these types of ASP components. First, the component itself can assign a different thread to each process begun for each client request. Secondly, out-of-process components do not require either Microsoft Transaction Server (MTS) or some form of DLL surrogate when accessed on a remote system.

An in-process component must be implemented in the address space of a client. If the client is remote from the component, the component must then be instantiated on some form of surrogate application that acts as the component's client. MTS can act as this surrogate, and Microsoft provides *DLLHOST.exe* as a remote in-process component surrogate.

Regardless of the advantages of an out-of-process component, the component in this chapter is created as an in-process or ActiveX DLL component, since most ASP components are created in this format.

The component created supplies client-side Dynamic HTML (DHTML) depending on the browser accessing the ASP page. To create the example component *dhtml*, start Visual Basic 6.0 and create a new project. When Visual Basic is first started, you are presented with several options for the type of project to create, including a standard executable, an ActiveX control, an ActiveX exe, an ActiveX DLL, whether to use the VB Application Wizard, and other choices. For *dhtml*, the choice is the ActiveX DLL.

Once a choice is made, Visual Basic creates the VB project and adds a class to it. Rename the project by clicking on the project in the Project window, double-clicking its only property, Name, in the Properties window, and changing the project name from Project1 to dhtml. The *dhtml* component has only one class, named `Positioning`, that includes methods to generate script to position HTML elements. A class named `Class1` is created automatically when the ActiveX DLL project type is chosen. Change the class name from `Class1` to `Positioning` by clicking on the class in the Project window, double-clicking on the class Name property in the Properties window, and typing in the new name. The ASP component and its associated object class have now been created.

Creating an ASP component with Visual Basic 5.0 is very similar to creating one for Visual Basic 6.0. Where differences occur, they will be noted in the text.

Component Instancing

Another property of the `Positioning` class is *instancing*. By default, the component is set to an instancing value of 5 – Multiuse. This means that each request to the component generates a new instance of the Positioning object. This type of instancing enables the component to process more than one request to the Positioning object at any one time by providing a different object instance for each object request, a behavior that is essential for any component accessed via a web page, as any ASP component is.

There are six different options for the Instancing property; they may or may not be available, depending on the type of component the project creates. The six different options are:

Private

Access to the class is limited to the component itself; no other application can access the class.

PublicNotCreatable

A class with this instancing type must first be created by the component, usually as a result of calling a method on a publicly creatable object instance, and a reference to the instance passed to the client.

MultiUse

Probably the most commonly used instancing type, multiuse means that the component can be instantiated by the client and can provide more than one new object instance for a specific client, or multiple object instances for multiple clients.

SingleUse

Creates a new instance of the component, which then provides access to a single instance of the component class.

GlobalMultiUse

Creates an object instance whose methods and properties can be accessed by the client without having to create the object, and without having to precede the object's properties and methods with an object reference. The methods and properties are treated as if they were global values.

GlobalSingleUse

A new component instance is generated for each component class request, and the properties and methods of the class are treated as if they are globally accessible values.

The type of component can determine which instancing types are available for the component classes. An in-process component (an ActiveX DLL) cannot have a class that uses SingleUse or GlobalSingleUse instancing, because a component must be able to supply multiple instances of its classes to the client the component shares its address space with. Because of this, when assigning a value to the Instancing property in the Properties window, these two instancing types are not even displayed in the drop-down list box when an ActiveX DLL is being created.

The global instance types GlobalMultiUse and GlobalSingleUse can be used with a component to allow for global access to methods and properties. *Global access* means that a new object instance does not need to be expressly created, and the methods and properties are accessed as if they are part of global data. To use this approach, however, the component must be added as a Reference to the client at design time. This is accomplished through the Project menu and the References dialog. The component is found within the list of available, registered components. Checking the box next to the component adds the component into the project.

Because the client needs a way to attach a reference to a component at design time, in effect accessing the component's *type library*, this also means that the global instance types can be used within a Visual Basic project, but not directly within an ASP page.

The PublicNotCreatable instancing type can be used to create a *dependent object*. A dependent object is one that is created from within a different object, usually via an Add method. For example, a component can contain a reference to a collection, and each collection member can actually be another class instance rather than a scalar value. The collection Add method then creates the dependent instance, adds it to the collection, and returns a reference to the collection element. Access to the dependent object's methods and properties occurs through the collection element rather than through direct access to the object. This use of dependent objects works within ASP pages, as is demonstrated more fully in this chapter.

The Private instance type is used primarily for classes that are only created and accessed internally.

 For the sample component, the other properties, such as DataBindingBehavior and Persistable, are kept at their default values. This includes the MTSTransactionMode property, which, when the component is used within MTS, controls whether the objects run within an existing transaction, a new transaction, or can't be run within a transaction. This can also be set when the component is registered with MTS, as discussed in Chapter 5, *Components, Transactions, and the Microsoft Transaction Server*. For now, set the value to 0 – NotAnMTSObject. Visual Basic 5.0 does not have this property, nor does it have the other two just mentioned.

Component Execution and Threads

Visual Basic supports single-threaded ActiveX in-process components, but this is not an option you are going to want to use with an ASP component. If a component is single-threaded, accessing the component locks the client to that component, and all requests to the component are serialized. Within an ASP application, the *client* is the web server, and you won't want to lock the web server down to a single instance of one component. A preferred choice for ASP in-process components is the apartment threading model. This model enforces thread safety because each thread has its own global data area, which prevents objects on one thread from contaminating global data for objects on another thread.

 Chapter 4, *ASP Components and Threads*, discusses the different threading models.

In the apartment model, objects can be created on the same thread as the calling application if the models between the two—the client and component—are compatible. If the object cannot be created on the calling application's thread, all arguments passed during method calls must be marshaled. In addition, apartment-threaded objects cannot share global data, and any communication between different objects also occurs through cross-thread marshaling. With marshaling, method arguments passed to objects across process or thread boundaries have to pass from a proxy on the client side to a stub on the component side, and the arguments have to be copied into the address space of the component. If the argument is passed by reference, it then has to be sent from the component back to the client and copied on the client's side. This process of passing arguments from proxy to stub and back again can slow the performance of the component.

Out-of-process components also support the apartment-threading model. In order to create a multithreaded out-of-process component (that is, an ActiveX exe) within Visual Basic version 5.0, the Unattended Execution box should be checked.* At that time, other options become available, including whether to create a new thread for each object or whether to create a thread pool with a fixed number of threads. (These options only become available with an out-of-process component that sets the Unattended Execution flag.) In Visual Basic 6.0, the threading and thread number options are available whether Unattended Execution is checked or

---

* The Unattended Execution property of an ActiveX exe is not accessible in the Properties window. To access it, right-click on the project in the Project window and select the <Project> Properties option. This opens the Project Properties dialog; Unattended Execution is a checkbox in the lower right corner.

not. Built-in thread safety, the advantage that in-process components have with apartment threading, is also an advantage of using this threading approach with out-of-process components.

In addition to the apartment-threading option, the developer can also choose to create the out-of-process component with a fixed pool of threads. With this approach, the number of threads available for the component is predetermined at design time rather than at runtime. Creating a fixed pool of threads and setting the thread count to greater than 1 uses a *round robin* method of assigning the next object created to the next thread up for assignment. This means that if three clients create a total of five objects from a single component, and the component has a fixed pool of three threads, the first two threads have two objects each, and the last has one. The next object created goes into the last thread. Which object was assigned to what thread depends only on the order in which the object was created and which thread was next up for assignment.

An advantage of a fixed thread pool is that the number of threads can be created to equal the number of processors on a system, if the operating system supports multiple processors, as Windows NT does.* Assigning a fixed pool of threads can maximize the overall performance of the application utilizing the component. However, there are also two disadvantages to this threading technique. The first is that if one object is processing a call, it blocks the thread of execution from any other object within the thread. If another object also receives a call, it cannot process that call until the first object releases the thread after it has finished its own processing. A second disadvantage to this technique is that load balancing does not occur. In the previous example, with three clients and five objects, if the two objects on the first thread are destroyed, the thread no longer has any objects. However, if a client requests a new object, it is placed on the third thread, the next one up for assignment. This means that the first thread now has no objects, the second and third have two objects, and the process load is not balanced evenly across the threads. Combine that with the blocking nature of multiple objects on one thread, and you have some potential degradation in performance.

A second thread pooling approach is to assign one thread to each new object created by selecting the Thread per Object option in the Project Properties dialog. When the object is destroyed, the thread is ended. This same thread is also used for dependent objects that are created using an instancing type of PublicNotCreatable. Unfortunately, dependent objects using their parents' threads is actually a major disadvantage to using this threading approach. With dependent objects, the

---

* Assuming, of course, that you're an in-house developer who knows how many processors are available on the system on which your out-of-process component will run.

thread is not ended until all objects with a reference to the thread have released their reference, meaning that the thread is active until the dependent object is destroyed. Additionally, without any control over the number of threads, more threads can be created than processors exist to handle them, and the performance of the application can actually degrade as the operating system spends too much time trying to handle thread maintenance in addition to application processes.

The explicit use of threads is available only with an ActiveX exe component. If the machine the application runs on has only a single processor, creating a fixed pool of one thread is the best approach to take for performance reasons, as well as the most backward-compatible approach.

Setting a DLL to be apartment-threaded doesn't mean it can create its own threads. It just means that when a client creates a component object, that object is created on the same thread used for the client call. Based on this, no cross-thread marshaling is required. If the client has four threads, each creating a component object, four object instances are created on four different threads. The thread on which each object is created is the thread that initiated the object creation. If one client calls a method on an object that exists in another thread, cross-thread marshaling is used to ensure that the data is not corrupted by the external call. If multiple objects are created on the same client thread, the calls to the objects are serialized, which means that one object blocks other objects from receiving and processing calls until it is finished performing its own process and releases the thread of execution.

Note that some actions can force a component to yield control over the thread of execution before the component is finished performing its processing. These actions are using a DoEvent, invoking a process or method in an object in another thread, and raising an event in an object in another thread. You will want to avoid using DoEvent or any other method that passes execution control to an object on another thread.

In the case of *dhtml*, the example ActiveX DLL component created for this chapter, change the project's properties to use the apartment-threaded model as shown in Figure 7-1. (You should already have assigned the project and class new names and set the Positioning class's Instancing property to MultiUse.) Setting *dhtml* to be an apartment-threaded ActiveX DLL should ensure the fastest communication between the client and the component object the client creates as long as the client is also using apartment threading. This occurs, however, at a loss of performance between calls to objects created on different threads. Since *dhtml* does not make any calls to objects, this is not a performance consideration.

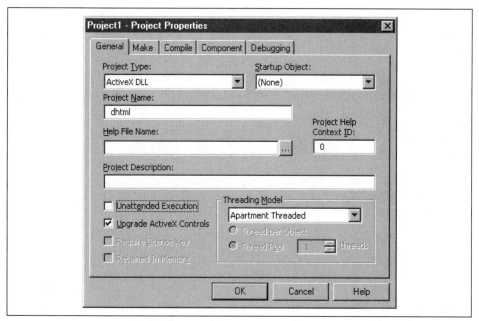

Figure 7-1. Selecting the Apartment Threaded threading option

One final note when discussing threads and object creation: if an object is created publicly that in turn creates a dependent object using the Private instancing type and then provides a reference to the private object to the client, the private object reference becomes invalid when the publicly-created object is released by the client. If this invalid reference is accessed, a page fault occurs. To avoid this, use PublicNotCreatable for any dependent objects that have methods accessible by the client.

Additionally, if a component object maintains a global reference to another object, the internally referenced object is not released when the externally referenced object, the object held by the client, is released. This internally held object is no longer accessible, but continues to occupy memory and use resources, effectively creating a memory leak. To avoid this, do not maintain global variable references to any object internally within a component object.

Creating the Component Methods

Now that the *dhtml* component has been created, set to allow for multiple instances of the component's objects, and set to be multithreaded, it is time to create the component's four class methods, which are as follows.

MoveLeft

> Generates the browser-specific JavaScript to move a positioned and named HTML element to the left at the given position

MoveTop

> Generates the browser-specific JavaScript to move a positioned and named HTML element to the top at the given position

Hide

> Generates the browser-specific JavaScript to hide a positioned and named HTML element

Show

> Generates the browser-specific JavaScript to show a positioned and named HTML element

Now that the *dhtml* component has been created, has been set to allow for multiple instances of the component's objects, and has been set to be multithreaded, create the component's four class methods. These are shown in Example 7-1.

Example 7-1. The Four Methods Implemented for the dhtml.Positioning Class

```
Option Explicit
' Generate browser-specific string to set left value
Public Function MoveLeft(objid As String, byVal browser As Integer, _
                    byVal left As Integer)
    If browser = 1 Then
        MoveLeft = objid + ".style.left=" + CStr(left)
    Else
        MoveLeft = "document." + objid + ".left=" + CStr(left)
    End If
End Function


' Generate browser-specific string to set top value
Public Function MoveTop(objid As String, byVal browser As Integer, _
                    byVal top As Integer)
    If browser = 1 Then
        MoveTop = objid + ".style.top=" + CStr(top)
    Else
        MoveTop = "document." + objid + ".top=" + CStr(top)
    End If
End Function


' Generate browser-specific string to set visibility to hidden
Public Function Hide(objid As String, byVal browser As Integer)
    If browser = 1 Then
        Hide = objid + ".style.visibility='hidden'"
    Else
        Hide = "document." + objid + ".visibility='hidden'"
    End If
End Function
```

Example 7-1. The Four Methods Implemented for the dhtml.Positioning Class (continued)

```
' Generate browser-specific string to set visibility to show
Public Function Show(objid As String, byVal browser As Integer)
    If browser = 1 Then
        Show = objid + ".style.visibility='inherit'"
    Else
        Show = "document." + objid + ".visibility='inherit'"
    End If
End Function
```

There are two optional argument modifiers, **byVal** and **byRef**, that indicate whether the argument is passed by value or by reference. If the argument is passed by value, a copy of the argument is made and sent to the function. If the argument is passed by reference, the address to the argument is passed rather than the value. By default, all parameters are passed **byRef** unless explicitly set to **byVal**. Since no modifier is used with some of the arguments to the **dhtml. Positioning** methods, those arguments are passed by reference by default.

How arguments are passed to a method can impact the performance of the object method, depending on whether the component created is in-process or out-of-process. For an out-of-process component, any object that is passed as an argument by reference won't work if the client and the component don't share the same address space. To allow this type of functionality, the object is copied into the component's address space and a pointer to it is then sent as the argument. This overhead makes this process much slower than if the object is passed by value. From an opposite perspective, passing an argument by reference can actually improve performance when passing a reference to larger data, such as a large string, rather than passing the data itself. However, this performance "gain" actually degrades in cross-process and cross-thread marshaling, since the data must be copied via the marshaling process *and* a pointer created and sent to the method.

For an in-process method call, passing larger strings and arrays by reference benefits from a performance improvement because a pointer for the argument, which is four bytes in size, is sent, rather than the actual data, which is larger than four bytes. However, for passing data such as an Integer, which is only two bytes in size, or a Long, which is four bytes in size, it is more efficient to pass the argument by value. In the **dhtml.Positioning** methods, the integer arguments are passed by value and the strings are passed by reference.

You can create a *main* subroutine, which is called when the component is loaded. This subroutine could be used for component setup tasks. If you use a *main* subroutine, set the startup object to Sub Main in the Project Properties dialog. Otherwise, leave the startup object set to **none**, which is the default. The *main* subroutine should be simple in order to expedite the loading of the component. Additional object class initialization can be included within the Class_Initialize event handler, which is run when the object is first initialized. Cleanup code for the object can be included within the Class_Terminate event handler. The object dhtml.Positioning hasn't any initialization or termination functionality, so the event handler methods are not coded.

With the creation of the *main* subroutine, the coding for the component is complete. The next step is to generate the component DLL, register it, and test it. This is covered in the next section.

Generating, Registering, Installing, and Testing the Component

Generating the ActiveX DLL is actually fairly simple. Once you create the class(es) and their associated methods and properties for the component, save the project. After saving the project, selecting the "Make dhtml.dll" option from the File menu opens a dialog to generate the DLL. The actual name shown matches the name given to the project.

This Make Project dialog can be used to name the DLL that is generated, and to find the location where the DLL is placed. In the case of *dhtml*, since it is an IIS ASP component, the DLL could be stored in the IIS virtual or actual server directory; the actual server directory can usually be found at *C:\Winnt\System32\Inetsrv*. More likely, a separate subdirectory with more stringent security precautions will be used to house ASP components.

The Make Project dialog also has a button labeled Options. This opens a dialog tab labeled Make, which provides a way to add information to the DLL such as a company name, a title, a version number, and whether there are any command-line arguments or constants for the DLL. Figure 7-2 shows the Make tab with the information entered for *dhtml*.

Returning to the original dialog, clicking the OK button generates the DLL.

Once the DLL is generated, it needs to be registered with the OLE Server. Open a command window, change to the subdirectory where the DLL is contained, and then run the RegSvr32 application on the DLL as follows to accomplish this:

```
regsvr32 dhtml.dll
```

The RegSvr32 application returns a message stating "DLLRegisterServer in dhtml.dll succeeded" if the registration is successful.

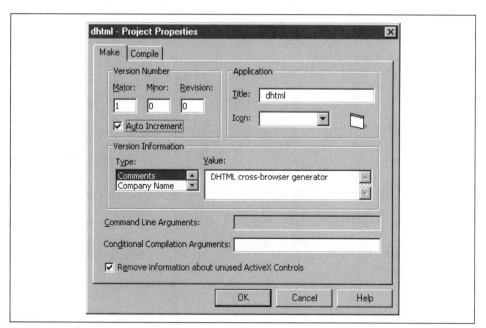

Figure 7-2. The Make tab with the information for dhtml

 You don't have to manually register the component on the build machine; Visual Basic automatically registers the component for you during the build process.

That's it for creating and registering the DLL. The next step is to test the component to make sure the methods work and the object can be safely created.

An ASP test page that creates an instance of dhtml.Positioning that uses two of the class object's methods, MoveLeft and MoveTop, is shown in Example 7-2. The Positioning instance is created using the CreateObject method of the built-in ASP Server object. In addition, the ServerVariables method of the ASP built-in Request object is used to find the value for HTTP_USER_AGENT, which contains information about the browser requesting the page. This value is used to derive the browser parameter passed to the dhtml.Positioning methods. The built-in Response object's Write method is then used to write out the result of calling the component's two methods. These results are written within a JavaScript block function that is invoked when the page is loaded.

Example 7-2. ASP Page Created to Test New dhtml.Positioning Object

```
<!DOCTYPE HTML PUBLIC "-//W3C//DTD HTML 4.0//EN">
<HTML>
```

Example 7-2. ASP Page Created to Test New dhtml.Positioning Object (continued)

```
<HEAD>
<TITLE>DHTML Positioning Object Test</TITLE>
<STYLE type="text/css">
   BODY { margin: 0.5in }
</STYLE>
<SCRIPT>
<!--

// function test moves paragraph object to
// the left and down
function test() {
<%
  ' find the browser using server variable
  Dim ua
  ua = ""
  Dim brwsr
  ua = Request.ServerVariables("HTTP_USER_AGENT")
  If Instr(1,ua, "MSIE",1) Then
      brwsr = 1
  Else
      brwsr = 0
  End If

  ' create the component instance
  Dim tmp
  Set tmp = Server.CreateObject("dhtml.Positioning")

  ' create the DHTML JavaScript string using a call to MoveLeft
  ' and MoveTop
  ' write out the strings
  Dim strng
  strng = tmp.MoveLeft("para1",brwsr,200)
  Response.write(strng & ";")
  strng = tmp.MoveTop("para1",brwsr,200)
  Response.write(strng & ";")
%>
//-->
}
</SCRIPT>
<BODY onload="test()">
<H1> Testing Positioning Component</H1>
<DIV id="para1" style="position:absolute; left: 10; top: 10">
<p style="font-family: Arial; color: red; font-style: italic">
This is the paragraph
</p>
</DIV>
</BODY>
</HTML>
```

The Request and Response objects are built-in ASP objects and don't need to be created, as will be discussed in Chapter 8, *The Visual Basic Built-in Object Interfaces*; the *dhtml* component object does need to be created, however. Note also that both the component owner name, which is the same name as the DLL by default for Visual Basic, and the component name must be provided with the CreateObject method call. An alternate approach for creating the object is to use the <OBJECT> tag within the *Global.asa* file, as discussed in Chapter 6, *Overview of the Intrinsic (Built-in) Objects.*

Figure 7-3 shows the test page when run within Internet Explorer 4.0.

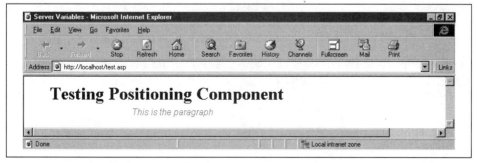

Figure 7-3. Results of running the dhtml test ASP page within IE 4.0

The JavaScript code block created with the use of the dhtml.Positioning object is as follows:

```
<SCRIPT>
<!--

// function test moves paragraph object to
// the left and down
function test() {
para1.style.left=200;para1.style.top=200;
//-->
}
</SCRIPT>
```

Since the test page was accessed from an IE 4.0 browser, the DHTML used to move the paragraph <DIV> block uses IE-specific techniques only.

This combination of component owner name, followed by a dot (.) followed by the component name, is the component's *programmatic identifier*, or *ProgId*. The Visual Studio tools, such as Visual Basic, use the DLL name as the component owner by default, and the class name as the component name, again by default.

Figure 7-4 shows the same test page, this time run within Netscape Navigator 4.0.

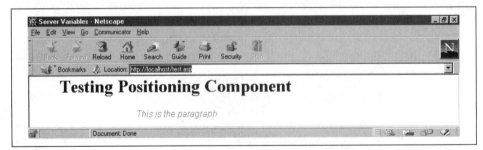

Figure 7-4. Results of running the dhtml test ASP page within Navigator 4.0

The JavaScript code block is created with the use of the dhtml.Positioning object and run within Navigator as follows:

```
<SCRIPT>
<!--
// function test moves paragraph object to // the left and downfunction
test() {document.para1.left=200;document.para1.top=200;//-->}</SCRIPT>
```

Note that this time the scripting block uses Navigator-specific DHTML techniques.

Be careful when using an untested component within a scripting block for an ASP page. If the object has problems and error handling is not used, the ASP scripting block terminates, which also prevents the output of the ending script tag, `</SCRIPT>`. Without this tag, the entire document, including any error messages generated for the ASP block, does not display.

The *dhtml* component has been successfully created and had a preliminary testing. The next section covers how error handling can be added to the component.

Adding Error Handling

The primary purpose of formal error handling using techniques such as raising errors is to prevent ASP applications from having fatal errors, and, if errors occur, to provide information that can be used to prevent or fix the error.

You and I know that we never create bugs, and errors can never occur with any code we create, but the powers that be need reassurance to that effect, so this section mentions how to provide error handling for the ASP component.

Handling errors within the component follows the standard Visual Basic practices of trapping errors that are raised (also known as exception handling) or using inline techniques to test return values for errors. The same two techniques can be used to return error information to the clients that access the component object's methods. As a good general practice, raising an error is preferred, especially since returning error information as a result of a function call means that the function result has to be created as a parameter passed by reference.

The downside to using exception-raising techniques for error handling is that only VBScript in the ASP page can handle errors that are raised within the component. This error-handling capability is not available with JavaScript or JScript.

Raising errors uses an error data structure, Err, with members such as Number, Source, and Description. The error numbers and descriptive text are created by the component developer(s), and the error numbers are communicated to the users who will use the components within ASP pages. Usually, error-handling codes are included with whatever documentation is included with the component.

For the `dhtml.Positioning` class, an exception is created and an error is raised if the browser number that is sent to the functions is not 0 or 1. The Err object's Raise method is called to raise the error condition.

For component class-to-Visual Basic application communication, the error number is usually handled by a Public constant that is used as the base for deriving all developer-defined error numbers. This constant is called **vbObjectError**, and it returns the correct error number to the class that traps the error, as shown in the following:

```
Err.Raise Number:=INVALID_BROWSER + vbObjectError, _
          Description:="Invalid Browser Number"
```

Unfortunately, this doesn't translate well into use with ASP pages, since the **vbObjectError** constant is not available with VBScript. Another approach must then be used. An error number that is not used in VBScript should be picked as the base value. I start my error numbers at 40,000, and then increment each error number by 1. At the time this book was written, these values had not caused any problems.

 You can use **vbObjectError** to raise an error in the VB code, and then check to see if Err.Number is not equal to zero (0) in the script assessing the component. However, you won't be able to trap for specific user-defined errors with this approach.

To return an error number and description, the number must be between 0 and 65,535, and the description can be any bit of text. The code to provide the error handling for the browser number in the MoveLeft method can be similar to the following:

```
' Generate browser-specific string to set left value
```

```
Public Function MoveLeft(objid As String, ByVal browser As Integer,
              ByVal left As Integer)
    If browser > 1 Or browser < 0 Then
        Err.Raise Number:=40000, Description:="Invalid Browser Number"
    End If
    If browser = 1 Then
        MoveLeft = objid + ".style.left=" + CStr(left)
    Else
        MoveLeft = "document." + objid + ".left=" + CStr(left)
    End If
End Function
```

In the ASP page, this particular error can be trapped, and an error message printed out internally as a JavaScript comment, as shown in the following VBScript code:

```
strng = tmp.MoveLeft("para1",4,200)
  If Err.Number > 0  Then
      Response.write("//Error Number: " & Err.Number)
      Response.write("; Error Source: " & Err.Source)
      Response.write("; Error Description: " & Err.Description)
      Err.Clear
  Else
      Response.write(strng & ";")
      strng = tmp.MoveTop("para1",4,200)
      Response.write(strng & ";")
  End If
```

Instead of sending an acceptable value of 0 for IE or 1 for Navigator, values normally derived using the built-in ASP objects, this code sends through a hardcoded value of 4 for the browser number, triggering the error. The error-handling code is included right after the method call, and it prints out the comment containing the error message and number:

```
// function test moves paragraph object to
// the left and down
function test() {
//Error Number: 40000; Error Source: dhtml3;
        Error Description: Invalid Browser Number
}
```

Based on what action should be taken and who should be informed of an error, the error message can be generated for the page developer as comments, as the previous example showed, or it can be displayed as an external message to the person accessing the page. The Clear method for the Err object is called to clear the error.

Error handling can also occur within the component by using an error handler, or the error can be passed through to the client without any error handling. To use an error handler within the component, add in a handler using an **On Error Goto** statement similar to the following:

```
On Error Goto HandleError
```

The error handler can then handle the error itself, pass the error through to the client, or raise a different error number:

```
HandleError:
    If Err.Number = 11 Then
      ' division by zero
      Err.Raise Number := Err.Number, Description := "some text"
    ...
```

In this example, the same error number is returned, but the descriptive text can expand on the error and why it occurred (such as "A division by zero occurred within an ASP component used...") so that it's more descriptive then just "Divide by zero."

Error handling can be also be especially helpful when debugging complex ASP applications that include more than one component or components that themselves create other objects, as discussed in the next section.

Further Testing and Debugging Techniques

In the previous section, raising and handling errors was examined. This is one technique for debugging an application, though it is meant more for error handling in released products than as a development debugging technique.

As was discussed earlier in the chapter, using an ASP component directly within ASP pages is an effective testing mechanism. However, a downside to testing and debugging a component within an ASP page is that compiling and reinstalling the component, particularly an ActiveX DLL component, requires that the ASP application accessing the component be shut down in order for the component to be released from memory. Until this occurs, a new copy of the DLL cannot replace the older version. If you are developing in your own environment, with your own version of both IIS and the ASP application, this isn't a problem. If you are using another web server, such as PWS, you may need to shut the server down to unload the object from memory. Additionally, if you are sharing a development environment with other developers, having to shut down the ASP application could itself become an issue.

Another approach is to use a small Visual Basic application to test the components. As long as none of the built-in ASP objects, such as Request, Response, Application, Server, ObjectContext, and Session, are used, an ASP component can be tested within a standard executable as well as an ASP page.

Components using the ASP built-in objects can be tested using a standard VB executable as long as the functionality being tested is not dependent on the built-in objects containing data. The built-in objects get their data in the context of being used within an ASP page. Chapter 8 contains examples of testing components that reference built-in objects using a standard VB executable.

To create a test application for an in-process component such as *dhtml*, create a new VB project and choose a standard executable as the type of project. In the form that is opened, add buttons that can be clicked to run each component test. For example, if the component has two objects with a total of six methods, you can add six buttons, one to test each method. Also add a button that unloads the form.

In the Click event for each button, create the instance of the object whose method is being tested using code similar to that shown in Example 7-3. In this code, different types of method calls are used for dhtml.Positioning, each testing a different browser, and one, MoveTop, testing the error condition for the component (the browser number must be 0 or 1). The values used with the method calls are changed to match different testing conditions, and the message box displays the string that is returned to the calling application.

Example 7-3. Using a Standard VB Executable to Test In-Process Component

```
Private Sub MoveLeft_Click()
    Dim tmp as Object
    Set tmp = CreateObject("dhtml.Positioning")
    Dim strng
    strng = tmp.MoveLeft("opt", 1, 200)
    MsgBox (strng)
    Set tmp = Nothing
End Sub

Private Sub MoveTop_Click()
    Dim tmp as Object
    Set tmp = CreateObject("dhtml.Positioning")
    Dim strng
    strng = tmp.MoveTop("opt", 4, 200)
    MsgBox (strng)
    Set tmp = Nothing
End Sub

Private Sub Show_Click()
    Dim tmp as Object
    Set tmp = CreateObject("dhtml.Positioning")
    Dim strng
    strng = tmp.Show("opt", 0)
```

Example 7-3. Using a Standard VB Executable to Test In-Process Component (continued)

```
    MsgBox (strng)
    Set tmp = Nothing
End Sub

Private Sub Quit_Click()
    Unload Form1
End Sub
```

By being able to test the ASP in-process component using a Visual Basic application, it's a simple matter to switch quickly to the component VB project, make a change, recompile the DLL, and then switch back to the test program. In addition, debugging can be used by running the in-process component in Visual Basic and accessing the component from the application either loaded into another copy of Visual Basic or run outside of Visual Basic. Visual Basic debugging can also be used to test an out-of-process component. Again, a test program needs to be created that includes a reference to the component objects being tested. For either in-process or out-of-process components, the component project itself is loaded into Visual Basic, and breaks and watchpoints are added into the code where appropriate. The component is started (loaded into memory) by clicking on the Run → Start menu command. A second version of Visual Basic is started, the test program is loaded, and breaks are set in the test program. The test program is then run. When the debugger enters break mode for the component, pressing the Switch To button switches focus to the component code, if the focus doesn't switch automatically. At that point the developer can step through the component code.

This technique of using two versions of Visual Basic to debug the component won't work with in-process components for Visual Basic 5.0, and is a bit excessive if the component method code is fairly simple. The approach should probably be used only with more complex ASP components.

Further Reading

For additional reading about the topics covered in this chapter, check out the following:

- The article "Performance of Visual Basic Multithreaded ActiveX Servers" at *http://premium.microsoft.com/msdn/library/techart/msdn_multinvb.htm.*

- The article "The Script Debugging Process" at *http://premium.microsoft.com/ msdn/library/devprods/vs6/vinterdev/vidue/html/viconthescriptdebugging-process.htm.*

- The article "Designing ASP Files within Visual Basic" at *http://www.microsoft. com/mind/0498/aspvb.htm.*

- The article "Build MTS Components with Visual Basic for Deployment in your ASP-Based Files" at *http://www.microsoft.com/mind/0498/mts.htm.*

- The article "Creating Components for ASP" at *http://premium.microsoft.com/ msdn/library/sdkdoc/iishelp/iis/htm/sdk/crtcomp_88c0.htm.*

8

The Visual Basic Built-in Object Interfaces

Visual Basic ASP components sometimes need to have information about the environment they are operating in, and they may need to communicate with the application user. The ASP built-in objects provide information about the environment and a means with which the ASP component can get information from and return information to the user. To support the ASP built-in objects within Visual Basic and other development tools, Microsoft has provided COM-based interfaces for the ASP built-in objects.

There are several ASP built-in objects, each created to provide specific information for a specific purpose. For instance, the Application object is used to retrieve and set application-level information. The Session object is used to retrieve and set session-level information as well as change the character set mapping and locale for applications supporting internationalization. The Request object handles communication from the user, including information such as the HTTP request containing form and query string data, as well as client-side certificates and cookies. Communication to the user occurs through the Response object. The Server object is used for character conversion as well as to create instances of other COM-based components.

The built-in objects are accessed through the ScriptingContext object for IIS 3.0 applications using a technique that is based on specific page-level events. Access to the built-in objects for IIS 4.0 is dependent on the ObjectContext object, a Microsoft Transaction Server (MTS) object, but not dependent on any particular event. In addition to providing access to the built-in ASP objects, ObjectContext also adds transaction control to the Visual Basic component, and can be used to create references to other ASP components.

This chapter covers how to access the built-in ASP objects using both Scripting-Context and ObjectContext, reviews each of the built-in objects, and demonstrates their use in building a Visual Basic ASP component.

Each of the built-in objects and its properties and methods are discussed in detail in Chapter 6, *Overview of the Intrinsic (Built-in) Objects*. The rest of this chapter demonstrates the Visual Basic interfaces for these objects, but assumes the reader has read Chapter 6 or is familiar with these objects. Additionally, Chapter 7, *Creating a Simple Visual Basic ASP Component*, covers the steps to take to compile and register a VB ASP component. If you have never created an ASP component using Visual Basic, you should read Chapter 7 before proceeding with this chapter.

Accessing the Built-in Objects in IIS 3.0

ASP components created for use with Internet Information Server 3.0 use a built-in object called *ScriptingContext* and specific page-level events to access the other built-in objects. Though you should consider using ObjectContext for new development, the ScriptingContext object is still supported in IIS 4.0 for backward compatibility. Because there are existing IIS 3.0 components and there are developers porting existing ASP components from IIS 3.0 to IIS 4.0, this section covers the use of ScriptingContext for completeness.

To support ASP built-in objects, ScriptingContext has five methods, one for each of the built-in objects, each of which returns a reference to the object:

- Response as `IResponse` returns a reference to the Response object.
- Request as `IRequest` returns a reference to the Request object.
- Session as `ISession` returns a reference to the Session object.
- Application as `IApplication` returns a reference to the Application object.
- Server as `IServer` returns a reference to the Server object.

Each of the respective object's collections, properties, or methods can then be accessed once the object reference is returned to the calling application.

In addition to the methods handling the object reference requests, ASP also supports ScriptingContext with two page-level events, `OnStartPage` and `OnEndPage`, that are associated with page loading and unloading, respectively. The

OnStartPage event is called when the ASP page containing the object reference is loaded, and passes a reference to the ScriptingContext object as its only parameter. The OnEndPage event is called when the ASP page is unloaded, and dereferences ScriptingContext.

> The OnStartPage and OnEndPage methods are not required within an ASP component. Use them when performing page loading and unloading activities or accessing the built-in objects within a component using ScriptingContext.

When a component is loaded, ASP looks for the OnStartPage event and invokes it if it finds it. Within this event-handler function, any of the built-in objects can be accessed from the ScriptingContext interface and processed locally within the function or assigned to component properties or global variables for access outside of the page-level events.

As an example of accessing a built-in component using the OnStartPage event handler and the ScriptingContext object, we'll create an ASP component that accesses the Response built-in object and calls its Redirect method.

In order to access the built-in objects, begin by creating a new ActiveX DLL project and adding a reference to the ASP object library to the project. You can do this by selecting the References option from the Project menu and finding and checking the Microsoft Active Server Pages Object Library. By attaching this reference, Visual Basic has access to the type library associated with the ASP objects.

> Instead of attaching the ASP object library to the Visual Basic project, you could use CreateObject to create a runtime reference to the object. If you use this approach, though, you will need to define all your objects as Object, rather than as the specific object type, or a compile error will occur.
>
> However, without attaching a reference to the library, the Auto List Member capability, which completes the typing of methods and properties and ensures their correct implementation, can't be used. More importantly, performance with accessing a component using late binding (which is what you get with CreateObject) is worse than the performance you would get using early binding (accessing the object's type information at design time).

After ensuring that the ASP object library is attached to the project, add the event-handler function in Example 8-1 to the class code module generated automatically for this project.

Example 8-1. The OnStartPage Event Handler

```
Public Function OnStartPage(myScriptingContext As Object)
   Dim rspnseObj As Object
   Set rspnseObj = myScriptingContext.Response()
   rspnseObj.Redirect ("temp.htm")
   Set rspnseObj = Nothing
End Function
```

This function uses the ScriptingContext object to obtain a reference to the ASP Response object. Once the reference to the Response object is obtained, the object's Redirect method is called and passed a new URL as a parameter.

After the OnStartPage event handler is coded, name the class module test and the project tstresponse. Select the "Make tstresponse.dll" option from the File menu to generate the server component DLL. All that's left to do is register the DLL using the *regsvr32.exe* utility:

```
regsvr32.exe tstresponse.dll
```

Next, instantiate the new component in an ASP test page. Since HTTP response information, such as an URL redirection, must occur before any HTML content is sent to the browser or an error occurs, and because our ASP component redirects the page URL, the following script block that instantiates the object must be placed before any HTML content in the page:

```
<%
Dim objTest
Set objTest = Server.CreateObject("tstresponse.test")
%>
<HEAD>
...
```

When the page is loaded, the component is instantiated, and its OnStartPage event handler is called. The component in turn accesses the built-in Response object from the ScriptingContext object, and invokes the Redirect method. The result is that the redirected URL is opened into the browser.

Not all accesses to the built-in objects must occur within the OnStartPage event handler. For instance, the built-in object can be stored within a variable and accessed by another method within the class. Example 8-2 shows the entire code for a class that stores a reference to the Response object to a private variable and then uses this variable within another method.

Example 8-2. ASP Component Using ScriptingContext to Access Response Built-in Object

```
Option Explicit
Private rspnseObj As Response

' OnStartPage event handler
' access Response object
Public Function OnStartPage(myScriptingContext As Object)
  Set rspnseObj = myScriptingContext.Response()
End Function

' Use Response object to write out new header
Public Sub objWriteHeader(myHeader As String)
  rspnseObj.Write (myHeader)
End Sub
```

The component's objWriteHeader method then uses the Response object reference contained in the private variable to write out a header to the web page. A test page for this ASP component is shown in Example 8-3. Note that the ASP component is created in one scripting block and its objWriteHeader method referenced in another.

Example 8-3. Creating an ASP Component and Invoking Its Method in Different Blocks

```
<HTML>
<HEAD>
<TITLE>Response Test</TITLE>
<BODY>
<%
  Dim myObject
  set myObject = Server.CreateObject("tstresponse.test")
  myObject.objWriteHeader("<H1>test</H1>")
%>

<H1> Server Variables </H1>

<%
  myObject.objWriteHeader("<H1>test 2</H1>")
%>

</BODY>
</HTML>
```

By assigning the object reference to the private variable, the Response object is now available to the class code, including each of the class methods. If the object had been assigned to a public reference, it would be available to all of the components within the project.

More than one built-in object can be accessed from the ScriptingContext object, and any one of the built-in objects can be accessed at the same time.

There are two limitations to using the ScriptingContext object to reference the ASP intrinsic objects:

- The objects can only be referenced when the component is first loaded, because the ScriptingContext object, which serves as the access path to the ASP built-in objects, is passed to the component only in the OnStartPage event.

- The component cannot be stored as an ASP application-level object. An application-level object is one that is declared to have scope across the application rather than having page-level or session-level scope. When a component is instantiated as an application-level object, the necessary OnStartPage event only occurs when the object is created for the first time. If a reference to a built-in ASP object such as Request or Result is stored in a component variable, the reference is valid only for the ASP page where the OnStartPage event occurs. When the component is accessed through the Application object on another ASP page and a component method is called that expects to have a valid reference to one of the built-in objects, an error occurs.

To demonstrate this, if a component is created from the class shown in Example 8-2, and a reference to the component is stored as an application-level object, as shown in Example 8-4, accessing the Application object and the objWriteHeader method does not cause an error.

Example 8-4. Accessing a Method Containing a Reference to a Built-in Object

```
<HTML>
<HEAD>
<TITLE>Response Test</TITLE>
</HEAD>
<BODY>
<%
  Dim myObj
  set myObj = Server.CreateObject("tstresponse.test")
  Set Application("myObject") = MyObj
  myObj.objWriteHeader("<H1>test</H1>")
%>
<H1> Server Variables </H1>
<%
  Set tmpObject = Application.Contents("myObject")
  tmpObject.objWriteHeader("<H1>test 2</H1>")
%>
</BODY>
</HTML>
```

No error occurs because the Response object stored as a component variable is still valid as long as the component methods are invoked within the same page that created the object. However, invoking the method from another page does result in an error, since the reference to the Response object is no longer valid. For instance, accessing the component created in Example 8-2 within a second ASP page, as shown in the code block in Example 8-5, *will* result in an error:

Example 8-5. An Invalid Reference to an Application-Level Object

```
<HTML>
<HEAD>
<TITLE>Response Test</TITLE>
</HEAD>
<BODY>
<H1> Server Variables </H1>
<%
  Set tmpObject = Application.Contents("myObject")
  tmpObject.objWriteHeader("<H1>test 2</H1>")
%>
</BODY>
</HTML>
```

The error occurs not because the application-level object is accessed, but because the objWriteHeader method references an object that is ScriptingContext-specific. Because ScriptingContext is *page*-dependent, a new ScriptingContext reference exists for the new page, and the reference to the Response object from the previous ScriptingContext object is no longer valid. If the object method called had not tried to use a reference to a ScriptingContext built-in object based on another page, no error would have occurred.

Initializing a component as session-level, however, has different results. First, referencing a session-level component on any ASP page invokes the `OnStartPage` event. This, in turn, calls the OnStartPage event handler, which creates a new reference to the Response object. Because of this, invoking the objWriteHeader method on the second page uses the new Response object reference associated with the ScriptingContext for the new ASP page, rather than the previous page, and no error occurs. The Application object, on the other hand, does not fire the `OnStartPage` event, and does not trigger the OnStartPage event handler within the component. Because of this, the variable holding the Response object is never instantiated, and an error results when it is used.

Having event-level creation for the ASP built-in objects was not a concept that Microsoft decided to support with version 4.0 of IIS. The company, rightfully so, incorporated transaction support into IIS with MTS, and decided that support for objects should be transaction-specific rather than page-specific. Based on this decision, the ScriptingContext object was dropped with IIS 4.0, and its use is supported only for backward compatibility.

The new method for accessing the ASP built-in objects is through the use of the MTS ObjectContext, discussed next.

The ObjectContext Interface

The ObjectContext object is not specific to use within IIS, but is instead an MTS object. By adding support of ObjectContext to an ASP component, that component can be marked for release when it is finished with its work, and its effort can be marked as a success or failure. When the component is participating in a transaction with other components, all the components can mark their efforts as either a success or a failure. Based on any one component failing, the changes all the components made can be rolled back. If all components signal successful completion of their work, then the transaction can be committed as a whole.

The ASP built-in objects are accessed by ObjectContext so that they may be created within the context of the existing MTS transaction, and can then participate within the transaction. In addition, by creating these components with the use of ObjectContext, MTS can control when the ASP built-in object is loaded into memory or released from memory.

 The use of MTS and the concepts of object state and just-in-time activation are discussed in Chapter 5, *Components, Transactions, and the Microsoft Transaction Server.*

Auto List Member support in addition to support for early binding for ObjectContext can be added to the project by adding a reference to the MTS object library (listed as the Microsoft Transaction Server Type Library; its filename is *mtxas.dll*) in addition to the Microsoft ASP Library.

A constraint to using ObjectContext is that MTS is multithreaded, which means that the ASP component must be thread-safe and must be created using the apartment threading model. To create a thread-safe Visual Basic component, the Unattended Execution checkbox, found in the Project Properties dialog, must be checked in VB5 only. Not setting this property results in an error when your code uses ObjectContext to access the built-in objects.

Once a component is marked as thread-safe and using the apartment threading model, it can no longer be assigned as an application-level component, since the Application object does not support storage of apartment-threaded objects.

The Application object does not support the apartment-threading model but does support the both-threading model. Visual Basic only uses the apartment-threading model. If your component uses the ObjectContext object, provide documentation for the users of the component that they cannot assign this object to the scripting Application object. See Chapter 4, *ASP Components and Threads*, for more information on the different threading models.

The MTS library has a function, *GetObjectContext*, that returns the ObjectContext method, as shown in the following code:

```
Dim objContext As ObjectContext
Set objContext = GetObjectContext()
```

ObjectContext supports several different methods and properties. Two methods handle transaction support: SetAbort, which aborts the current transaction, and Set-Complete, which overrides any call to SetAbort and commits the transaction. Additional methods are:

Count

Returns a count of the number of ObjectContext properties

CreateInstance

Instantiates an object that has been registered with MTS

DisableCommit

Prevents the transaction from being committed

EnableCommit

Allows the transaction to be committed

IsCallerInRole

Determines whether the process calling the server process (the component method) is within a specific role

IsInTransaction

Indicates whether a component is within a transaction

IsSecurityEnabled

Indicates whether security is enabled for all components except those running in the client's process

Item

Returns one of the built-in objects (Request, Response, Application, Session, and Server)

Security

Returns the Security property for the object

The next section demonstrates how an ObjectContext object accesses the built-in objects, and what some of the ObjectContext methods and properties do.

Accessing the Built-In Objects with ObjectContext

 MTS support for a component can be added in a couple of different ways. For Visual Basic 6.0, you can set the MTSTransactionMode property to any value other than 0 – NotAnMTSObject. You can also define the MTS property by registering the component using MTS, covered in this section. Regardless of the approach used, you can access ObjectContext without having to use MTS transactions.

Accessing the built-in objects from ObjectContext is fairly simple. First, a function called *GetObjectContext* returns a reference to the ObjectContext interface. This is then used to obtain references to the ASP built-in objects. For instance, the code shown in Example 8-6 creates a component similar to that shown in Example 8-2, except that it uses the ObjectContext object to access the ASP built-in Response object.

Example 8-6. Using ObjectContext to Access the Built-in Response Object

```
Option Explicit

Private objResponse As Response
Private objContext As ObjectContext

' create ObjectContext object and access Response object
' set to class variable and use Response to write out content
' to page
Public Sub objResponseMethod()

  Set objContext = GetObjectContext()
  Set objResponse = objContext("Response")
  objResponse.Write ("<H1>test One</H1>")

End Sub

' write out header using existing Response object reference
Public Sub objWriteHeader(strHeader As String)

  objResponse.Write ("<H1>" + strHeader + "</H1>")

End Sub
```

Both the ObjectContext and Response object references are assigned to private variables. If this new ASP component is created and stored as a Session object, the component methods can be accessed across several pages if each page is accessed during the same user session and from the same ASP application. For instance, the component is created as a Session object within an ASP page using the following script:

```
<%
  Set Session("MyObject") = Server.CreateObject("tstobjcntx.tstcntxt")
  Dim MyObject
  Set MyObject = Session("MyObject")
  MyObject.objResponseMethod()
%>
```

This script results in creating an instance of the component defined in Example 8-6, which in turn writes out a header with the words "test One." A second ASP page accesses the session-level object reference with the following script block:

```
<%
  Dim MyObject
  Set MyObject = Session("MyObject")
  MyObject.objWriteHeader("Testing ObjectContext")
%>
```

This script invokes the component's objWriteHeader method, which results in a page with a header containing the words "Testing ObjectContext."

 Note that you can also replace the objResponseMethod method with the component's Class_Initialize event handler. This event handler is invoked when the component is initialized—in this case, when the component is created with the CreateObject method in the ASP page. Using this approach, you can drop the objResponseMethod method call from the testing ASP script.

There is one important difference between using ObjectContext and ScriptingContext. With ScriptingContext, the example discussed in the previous section required an OnStartPage event handler to instantiate the Response object, and this event handler is called for every page that accesses the Session component. With Object-Context, the OnStartPage event handler is not required, though it is still supported, and the built-in object reference is valid throughout the life of the component. As the component is created as a Session object, the built-in object reference is then valid throughout all pages within the application that are accessed within the user session.

If the class variable maintains a reference to an ASP built-in object that contains page-level information, such as the Request object, the global reference will not change from page to page. This means that the Request object reference contained within the global variable remains the same even though the page differs.

Accessing MTS Components with ObjectContext

Though the ObjectContext object can be used to access the ASP built-in objects within an ASP component, it can also be used to control a transaction and add other objects to the same transaction as the current ObjectContext object. This section will demonstrate both.

With ObjectContext, an ASP component can control the transaction and determine whether enough of the functions within a transaction have been successfully completed in order to complete the entire transaction or whether the transaction should be aborted.

Chapter 5 goes into detail on creating MTS packages and adding roles and components. It also covers transaction processing, particularly as it applies to ASP components and components being accessed by ASP components. If you are not familiar with working with the Transaction Server Explorer, you can skip the rest of this section and continue to rest of the chapter.

To demonstrate using ObjectContext within an ASP component that is also part of a transaction, we'll create a simple MTS component that has two methods, each of which takes a string as a parameter and returns a modified string. Both methods create HTML statements out of a string of text, one creating an <H1> header, the other creating an <H2> header (the header types determine the size of the header and sometimes which font is used as well). The component for the demonstration is shown in Example 8-7.

Example 8-7. Component with Two Functions

```
Option Explicit
' add H1 HTML tags
Function First(strHeader As String) As String
   First = "<H1>" + strHeader + "</H1>"
End Function

' add H2 HTML tags
Function Second(strHeader As String) As String
   Second = "<H2>" + strHeader + "</H2>"
End Function
```

Name the component project *testmts*, and name the class `mtstest`. Then generate the ActiveX DLL after making sure the object is created as thread-safe by checking the Apartment threading model checkbox.

Once the component DLL has been generated, it must be registered with the Transaction Server in order to participate in an MTS transaction. However, before this can happen, an MTS package must be created to hold the component.

Since the component is not running as part of any other ASP application, you should create a new package. Call the package Test and add it to the MTS computer labeled My Computer, which is also the computer MTS is installed on. After the new package is created, a default role of Interactive User (the person currently logged into the computer where the package is running) is automatically given to the package. Add an additional role to the package, and map the user Everyone to this role. This means that all users, regardless of their login domain and group membership, have permissions to access the MTS component assigned to the Test role.

Once the package is created, add the newly-generated *testmts* component to the package. This is accomplished by opening the package, clicking on the *Components* folder that is generated automatically for the package, and then right-clicking on the folder and choosing New → Component. Selecting the button labeled "Install New Components" opens a dialog to add the specific component. The DLL is added by clicking on the Add Files button and locating *testmts.dll* using the Explorer window that opens.

After the component is added to the package, two folders are automatically created for it, one with the component interfaces and one for role membership. You can view the methods created for the MTS component by double-clicking on the *Interfaces* folder in the right pane, double-clicking on the derived interface object, and then double-clicking on the *Methods* folder. The first and second methods created for the MTS component are shown, but so are several methods that actually belong to the underlying `IUnknown` and `IDispatch` interfaces, as shown in Figure 8-1.

Next, add a new method, shown in Example 8-8, to the ASP component shown earlier in Example 8-6. This new method uses the predefined objContext and objResponse objects in addition to using the ObjectContext object's CreateInstance method to create an instance of `testmts.mtstest` on the same transaction as the existing ASP component. (Note that you also have to use the References dialog to add a reference to *testmts* for the project to compile successfully.)

Additionally, an error handler is added to process any errors within the method. This error handler, shown at the bottom of the method, uses the module-level Response object to write out the error number and message for any errors that occur.

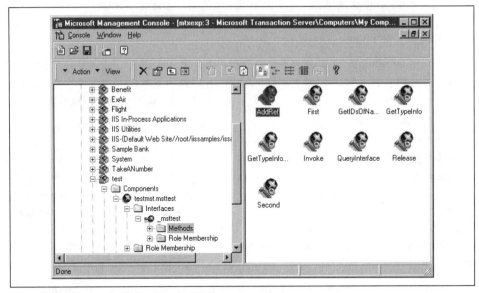

Figure 8-1. The methods for the new MTS component

Example 8-8. Creating an Instance of an MTS Object

```
' Using ObjectContext to pull in another MTS object
Public Sub objTestMTS(strHeader As String)

' define objects
 Dim objTest As mtstest
 Dim strHdr As String

On Error GoTo HandleError

  ' access MTS object
  Set objTest = objContext.CreateInstance("testmts.mtstest")

  ' call MTS object functions, and use
  ' predefined Response object to write results
  strHdr = objTest.First(strHeader)
  objResponse.Write (strHdr)
  strHdr = objTest.Second(strHeader)
  objResponse.Write (strHdr)

 ' write out ObjectContext information
 objResponse.Write ("<strong>")

  ' write out security info
  If objContext.IsSecurityEnabled() Then
    objResponse.Write ("Security for component is enabled")
  Else
    objResponse.Write ("Security is not enabled")
  End If
```

Example 8-8. Creating an Instance of an MTS Object (continued)

```
' write out transaction info
objResponse.Write ("<p>")
If objContext.IsInTransaction() Then
   objResponse.Write ("object is within transaction")
Else
   objResponse.Write ("object is not within transaction")
End If
objResponse.Write ("<p>")

' write out if contained in role
If objContext.IsCallerInRole("test") Then
   objResponse.Write ("caller is in roll 'test'")
End If

' write out count of properties
objResponse.Write ("<p>")
objResponse.Write ("count of properties is " + CStr(objContext.Count))

objResponse.Write ("</strong>")

Exit Sub

' handle errors
HandleError:
 objResponse.Write ("<p>")
   objResponse.Write ("Err number: " + " " + CStr(Err.Number) + _
                Err.Description)

End Sub
```

Once the MTS component object is instantiated within the ASP component, its two publicly accessible methods are called and the results of these methods are written to the web page. In addition, several of the functions and properties of the ObjectContext object are accessed and their associated values are printed out to the web page.

The first of the ObjectContext methods called that returns information about the current component is *IsInTransaction*. This method returns **False** because the ObjectContext object is not within a transaction, since the current ASP component has not been registered with the Transaction Server. The security for the component is enabled because the component is running within a server process (IIS), not a client process, and security is enabled by default for server processes.

A test page is created to invoke the new ASP component, as shown in the following code block:

```
<HTML>
<HEAD>
<TITLE>MTS tests</TITLE>
```

```
<BODY>
<%
  Dim MyObject
  Set MyObject = Server.CreateObject("cntxt.test")
  MyObject.objTestMTS("TEST")
%>

</BODY>
</HTML>
```

An error is also displayed on the page, as Figure 8-2 shows. When the role is accessed with the ObjectContext object's IsCallerInRole method, an error occurs because no roles have been defined for the ASP component. This is understandable, since the ASP component is itself not an MTS component.

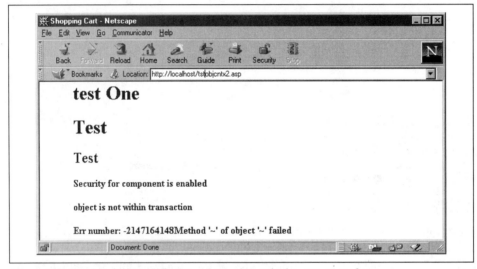

Figure 8-2. Results of testing the MTS component and ObjectContext object

To prevent the error from occurring when the IsCallerInRole method is invoked, you must add the ASP *tstobjcntxt* component to the MTS test package created earlier. By adding the ASP component to the same package as the previously registered MTS component, you assign both components to run within the same process. Additionally, to turn on transaction processing for both components, open the Transactions tab from the Properties dialog for the *tstobjcntxt* component, and check the Requires a Transaction option. Also change the Transaction Support option for the *testmts* component from the default of Does Not Support Transactions to Supports Transactions.

Additionally, add a role to the MTS package and name it test. A role is added by right-clicking on the Roles tree item and then selecting New from the context menu. After adding the role, add users to the role by selecting the new role, selecting the Users tree item, and right-clicking on it. Then select New from this menu. A list of available users for the machine opens, and you can add as many users as you want. For the example, adding "Everyone" should add everyone to the test role.

Finally, start a transaction for the component by adding the transaction directive to the ASP page:

```
<%@ TRANSACTION=Required LANGUAGE="VBScript" %>
```

This directive, created as the first line within the ASP document, starts a transaction and sets the scripting language to VBScript. Another way to start a transaction is to set the transaction support for the components to require a transaction or require a new transaction, as discussed earlier.

When you run the ASP test page again after adding the ASP component to the MTS server, the generated web page no longer shows an error, and the rest of the page contents are displayed. The object is now within a transaction, since tstobjcntxt requires a transaction, and a new transaction is created for the component as soon as it loads. In addition, when the ASP component creates the new instance of the MTS component, the instance is created in the same transaction as the ASP component. As a result, note that now the caller is within the role of test. In addition, the ObjectContext object returns a value of 5 when the Count method is called. The Count method returns the number of properties defined for the object; the five properties are the built-in objects: Response, Request, Application, Session, and Server.

Running a component within a transaction and creating an instance of another ASP and/or MTS component is great, but the transaction still needs to be controlled; this is covered next.

Controlling Transactions with ObjectContext

Another use for the MTS ObjectContext object is controlling transactions. ObjectContext has two methods, SetAbort and SetComplete, which are used to do two things. The first is to signal that the component is finished with its processing and can be unloaded from memory at any time. The second purpose is to signal the success or failure of the process. If SetAbort is called from within an error-handling block, such as in the following code:

```
' handle errors
HandleError:
 objResponse.Write ("<p>")
   objResponse.Write ("Err number: " + " " + CStr(Err.Number) + _
             Err.Description)
 objContext.SetAbort
```

the component is set for unloading with a status of failure. If transaction processing is being maintained for this component and others, all of the components involved within the transaction are considered to fail, and any changes are rolled back. However, using the SetComplete method call not only marks the component as ready for unloading, but does so with a successful processing status.

Again, for a more in-depth discussion of MTS, see Chapter 5. The ASP built-in objects are detailed more fully in the next several sections.

The Application Object Interface

This section provides an overview of the Application object, including demonstrations of its methods and properties.

An ASP application begins when the first ASP page for the application is accessed after the web server is started, and continues until the web server is shut down, or the application times out after the last person to reference the application logs out. The ASP built-in Application object can be used to access objects and values that are defined as application-level objects.

An application-level element can be added using an `<OBJECT>` tag within the *global.asa* file, by using script, or from within a component. Each ASP application has one *global.asa* file, located in the root directory of the application, which contains definitions for both application and session level objects. An example of an entry within *global.asa* is:

```
<OBJECT RUNAT=Server SCOPE=Application ID=MyInfo
    ProgID = "testmts.mtstest">
</OBJECT>
```

The value created in the *global.asa* file can be a scalar value, such as an integer or a string, or it can be a COM object. Either type of value can then be accessed from the Application object using the StaticObjects collection, as shown in Example 8-9.

Example 8-9. Accessing a COM Object from the StaticObjects Collection

```
Public Sub OnAccessObj()
  Dim objContext As ObjectContext
  Dim objApplication As Application
  Dim applApplicationObject As Object

  ' get objects
  Set objContext = GetObjectContext()
  Set objApplication = objContext("Application")

  ' get object from Contents
  Set applApplicationObject = objApplication.StaticObjects("MyInfo")
  applApplicationObject.objWriteHeader ("test")
End Sub
```

You can alter the *global.asa* file by removing the definition of an object using the
<OBJECT> tag and replacing it with a scripting block to trap the Application start
event and assign the tstresponse.ResponseTest object to the Application object, as
shown in the following code block:

```
<SCRIPT LANGUAGE=VBScript RUNAT=Server>
' setup Application level constants and variables
Sub Application_OnStart
  Dim tmpObject
  Set tmpObject = Server.CreateObject("tstresponse.responsetest")
  Set Application("MyInfo") = tmpObject
End Sub
</SCRIPT>
```

With this scripting block, the component reference is assigned to the Application
object's Contents collection, rather than the StaticObjects collection. In addition,
the **OnStartPage** event for tstsresponse.ResponseTest is fired when the object is
created with the Server.CreateObject method. You can then access the new application-level object by name from the Contents collection, as shown in
Example 8-10.

Example 8-10. Accessing Object from the Contents Collection

```
Public Sub OnAccessObj()
  Dim objContext As ObjectContext
  Dim objApplication As Application
  Dim applApplicationObject As Object

  ' get objects
  Set objContext = GetObjectContext()
  Set objApplication = objContext("Application")

  ' get object from Contents
  Set applApplicationObject = objApplication.Contents("MyInfo")
  applApplicationObject.objWriteHeader ("test")
End Sub
```

The difference between the two code blocks is that the first accesses the *MyInfo*
component through the Application object's StaticObjects collection, the second
through the Contents collection.

You can access a value from either the StaticObjects or the Contents collection by
referencing the item directly off the Application object:

```
Set applApplicationObject = ObjApplication("MyInfo")
```

Note that accessing the object identified as `MyInfo` in either Example 8-9 or Example 8-10 using the technique shown does not use the component's type library and therefore uses late binding. As stated earlier in the chapter, late binding or runtime binding is not the most efficient technique to use to access a COM component.

An application-level variable can be accessed and updated using the Application object. For instance, within the *global.asa* file, a script block can be created that accesses the application's `OnStart` event. Within this block, a variable can be added to the Application object's Contents collection. Then, the variable's value can be accessed within a script or by a component.

To demonstrate this, adding the following script block to the *global.asa* file creates an Application-level variable called *intCounter*:

```
<SCRIPT LANGUAGE=VBScript RUNAT=Server>
' setup Application level constants and variables
Sub Application_OnStart
  Application("intCounter") = 0
End Sub
</SCRIPT>
```

The variable *intCounter* can be accessed within a script, but it can also be accessed from within an ASP component using the Application object and accessing the value from the Contents collection. The code in Example 8-11 does this, and also uses the Response object to print out the next value.

Example 8-11. Incrementing a Value from the Application Contents Collection

```
Public Sub OnAccessValue()
  Dim intCounter As Integer
  Dim applicationObj As Application
  Dim rspnseObj As Response

  ' access built-in objects
  Dim objContext As ObjectContext
  Set objContext = GetObjectContext()
  Set rspnseObj = objContext("Response")
  Set applicationObj = objContext("Application")

  ' lock, access counter and change value, and unlock
  applicationObj.Lock
  intCounter = applicationObj.Contents("intCounter")
  intCounter = intCounter + 1
  applicationObj("intCounter") = intCounter
  applicationObj.UnLock

  ' print out new value
```

Example 8-11. Incrementing a Value from the Application Contents Collection (continued)

```
   rspnseObj.Write (CStr(intCounter))
End Sub
```

The code also uses the Application object's Lock and UnLock methods to prevent any changes to the Application object until the object is unlocked. This prevents multiple simultaneous accesses and modifications to the counter object, which could result in unwanted side effects.

 After locking the Application object, it should be unlocked as soon as possible, since no other application component can access the Application object until then. Chapter 6 contains a more detailed explanation of this, and examines why the locking mechanism is necessary.

Application-level objects and values can also be accessed directly using the Application object's Value method and passing in the name of the object:

```
   applicationObj.Value("intCounter")
```

To summarize, the Application object has three collections (the StaticObject, Contents, and Value collections) and two methods (Lock and UnLock).

The Application object maintains references to elements at the application level, but the Session object maintains references to elements for each user session. The Session object is covered next.

The Session Object Interface

This section provides an overview of the ASP Session object, including demonstrations of its methods and properties.

The Session object maintains references to elements for each user session. An ASP session begins when a user accesses an ASP application page for the first time since opening a browser or logging into the application, and continues until the user exits the application (if the application provides this functionality), closes the browser, or times out.

All of the Session properties, methods, and collections are accessible via scripting and from within an ASP component; they are:

Abandon method
    Destroys the Session object

CodePage property
    The character set for pages, including characters that can be locale-specific

LCID property

　　The international abbreviation used to identify the locale

SessionID property

　　An ID unique to the session that identifies the user

TimeOut property

　　The number of minutes a session can be idle before it terminates

Contents collection

　　All elements added to the Session object using script or from within components

StaticObjects collection

　　All elements added to the Session object using the *global.asa* file

Many of the Session properties—such as CodePage and LCID—are used specifically for internationalization. Others have to do with the Session itself, such as its timeout value and the session identifier used to track the user throughout the current session. In fact, a limitation of the Session object is that the SessionID is actually stored as a cookie, which requires that the client browser must support the use of Netscape-style cookies. Cookies are discussed in more detail in Chapter 6.

As with the Application object, objects can be added to the Session object and accessed throughout all application pages. An object can be added statically with an <OBJECT> tag in *global.asa* even if the object has an OnStartPage event handler, because the OnStartPage event is fired when the object is referenced for the first time in a session. In one of our examples in the previous section, "The Application Object Interface," the *tstreponse.ResponseTest* component could not be added as a static object, since the OnStartPage event handler was not invoked. However, the *tstresponse.ResponseTest* component can be added to the session's static objects using the following <OBJECT> tag:

```
<OBJECT RUNAT=Server SCOPE=Session ID=MyInfo
PROGID="tstResponse.ResponseTest">
</OBJECT>
```

A component can then access the session-level static object MyInfo using the Session object's StaticObjects collection, as shown in Example 8-12.

Example 8-12. Accessing a Component from the StaticObjects Collection

```
' OnStartPage event handler
Public Sub objSessionTest()

  ' define variables
  Dim sessnObject As Session
  Dim objContext As ObjectContext
  Dim sessnTestObject As test
```

Example 8-12. Accessing a Component from the StaticObjects Collection (continued)

```
  ' access objects
  Set objContext = GetObjectContext()
  Set sessnObject = objContext("Session")
  Set sessnTestObject = sessnObject.StaticObjects("MyInfo")

  ' invoke method
  sessnTestObject.objWriteHeader ("test")
End Sub
```

The *tstResponse.ResponseTest* component's `OnStartPage` event is fired when the new component is created for the first time. Because the `OnStartPage` event is fired, the Response object is created within the component. Accessing the objWriteHeader method from the page, or even from a different page, does not result in an error.

As with the Application object, objects can be added to the Session object dynamically and then accessed from the Contents collection. The Session object also has its own start and end events, which can be trapped by event handlers within the *global.asa* file. The Session_OnStart event handler can be used to set constant values accessible from throughout the session, as shown in the following code block:

```
<SCRIPT LANGUAGE=VBScript RUNAT=Server>
' setup Session level constants and variables
Sub Session_OnStart
  Session("intCounter") = 0
End Sub
</SCRIPT>
```

The Session object can actually be abandoned and the resources it contains released. As an example, the following code abandons the Session object and then accesses the object to invoke the ResponseTest method objWriteHeader:

```
Set sessnObject = objContext("Session")
sessnObject.Abandon
Set sessnTestObject = sessnObject.StaticObjects("MyInfo")
sessnTestObject.objWriteHeader ("test")
```

When the Abandon method is called, the Session object is queued for destruction, but only after the current script is finished. Since the component is invoked within the script, the component method is finished before the object is destroyed.

Use caution when destroying any object that can be accessed by scripts or other components, since they might expect values to be present, and errors can result.

In addition to abandoning the Session object, a timeout can be set for the session to ensure that a session is not left idle for too long a period of time. Maintaining an open session uses server resources, and a timer can be used to prevent a user from logging onto a session and then leaving their computer, and the session, running. Using timers can also prevent a breach of security for the session, preventing someone else from accessing the client computer when the user is not present, and in turn accessing session information that may be confidential. The timeout is set through the TimeOut property, as follows:

```
sessnObject.Timeout = 20          ' 20 minute timeout
```

Once the session has timed out, any of the objects contained within the Session object are destroyed. Accessing any of the members of a Session object results in an error, an event component developers should plan for when creating components that depend on Session variables and constants.

Session information can be used to internationalize the application. A user may select an option to view the ASP application using Russian, and the Session LCID and CodePage properties reflect the types of strings used in the application, and the type of character set used for the ASP pages. The LCID property is used to identify specific information, such as how dates and times are formatted, how strings are sorted, and other information. The CodePage properties determine how symbols map to a character set. For the Russian example, the CodePage property is set as follows:

```
sessnObject.CodePage= 866
```

Of course the client would have to be set up to use the specific CodePage and LCID value; information on this can be found in the operating-system help for Windows NT and 95/98.

 The Session object also contains a reference to the Session identifier, SessionID, which should never be used directly by the component developer as a database or any other identifier. Its only purpose is to serve as a session identifier between the client browser and the web server application.

The Request Object Interface

The Request object contains information about the user request to the web server, including general browser and client information, as well as specific query string and form data.

The Request object's methods and properties are:

ClientCertificate collection
   Used to retrieve client certificate information

Cookies collection
   Used to retrieve cookie information

Form collection
   Used to retrieve form element data

QueryString collection
   Used to retrieve query string data

ServerVariables collection
   Used to access server and client environment information

BinaryRead method
   Retrieves posted data in binary form and stores it in a safe array

TotalBytes property
   The number of bytes sent with the client request

Unlike the Session and Application objects, the Request object has a short life-time. A specific instance of a Request object is valid from the time a web page request is submitted until a response is made from the server back to the browser. Based on this, component developers should store information that should be persisted beyond a specific page request into component-level variables.

As stated, the Form and QueryString collections contain information passed from a web page to the application, usually from an HTML form or by concatenating the information to the URL invoking the ASP application. Which collection is used depends on how the data is sent.

The Form collection contains all values from a form that has been submitted using the POST method. The QueryString collection contains all values from a form that has been submitted using the GET method or by appending values directly onto the URL that invokes the ASP application. One characteristic of this latter type of data transmittal is that you can actually see the data appended to the URL as key-value pairs. Regardless of which approach is used and which collection is accessed, the data is transmitted in key-value pairs.

The Request information contained within the Form and QueryString collections can be accessed by name or by an index number representing the value's location within the data set. As an example, the code block in Example 8-13 contains an HTML form with three input fields.

Example 8-13. HTML Form Submitted Using the POST Method

```
<FORM action="testrspnse.asp" method=post>
<INPUT type="text" name="field1">
<INPUT type="text" name="field2">
<INPUT type="text" name="field3">
<INPUT type="submit">
</FORM>
```

The form posting method is POST rather than the default of GET. Using the POST method results in the field values being added to the Form collection rather than to the QueryString collection, as stated earlier.

To demonstrate the use of the request collections, we'll create a component that accesses the Request object from the ObjectContext object and iterates through the Form collection, printing out the names and values for each field within the form. The code to do this is shown in Example 8-14.

Example 8-14. Accessing Field Names and Values with the Request Object's Form Collection

```
' write out Request Form Value
Public Sub wrtRequest()
  Dim objContext As ObjectContext
  Dim rqstObject As Request
  Dim rspnseObject As Response
  Dim x As Variant

  ' Access the built-in components
  Set objContext = GetObjectContext
  Set rqstObject = objContext.Item("Request")
  Set rspnseObject = objContext("Response")

  ' for each collection member, print out name
  ' and value
  For Each x In rqstObject.Form
      rspnseObject.Write (x + "=" + rqstObject.Form(x))
      rspnseObject.Write ("<br>")
  Next

End Sub
```

Each form element is accessed and its name and value are displayed. The result of running this application is a page with the field names, an equals sign (=), and the field values, if any, listed one after another. Figure 8-3, for example, shows the web page displayed on the browser when data input into the HTML form in Example 8-14 is processed by the wrtRequest method.

The values could also have been submitted as attachments to the URL, using syntax similar to the following:

```
<a href="test.asp?test=one&test2=two&test3=three">Test</a>
```

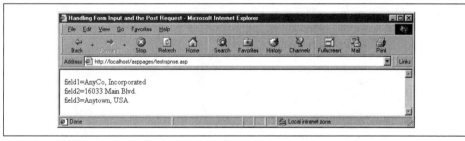

Figure 8-3. Processing the Request object's Form collection

Regardless of which collection is accessed, the approach is the same as that demonstrated in Example 8-13.

Another technique to access the posted data is to use the BinaryRead method, which takes a single parameter, *count*, that represents the number of bytes of the client's posted data to be read, and returns the posted information as raw data assigned to a SafeArray. A SafeArray is a structure that contains the array entries, but also contains information about the array, such as the number of dimensions and bounds for the dimensions.

When BinaryRead returns, *count* is updated to reflect the number of bytes actually read. Note, though, that using this method precludes the use of the Form collection, and using the Form collection precludes the use of BinaryRead. If using this method, the TotalBytes method provides the size of the data in bytes. An example of using the BinaryRead method is shown in the following code:

```
Dim binData As Variant
Dim varCount As Variant

varCount = rqstObject.TotalBytes
binData = rqstObject.BinaryRead(varCount)
```

The BinaryRead method can be used to access non-text-based data, or to process the data using some other process or technique, or even to store the raw data for later access.

When searching through all collections of the Request object using an implicit search, such as `objRequest("somevalue")`, if the Form collection is used within the Search, BinaryRead will no longer function, and vice versa.

The Request object also maintains collections for client certificate fields and for any cookie information sent with the request. The client certificate properties are defined as key fields; these are the following.

Certificate
> The complete certificate as a binary stream

Flags
> The certificate's flags

Issuer
> The certificate's issuer

SerialNumber
> The certificate's serial number

Subject
> The certificate's subject

ValidFrom
> The valid beginning date for the certificate

ValidUntil
> The valid ending date for the certificate

To access a client certificate value, use the key name to retrieve the value from the ClientCertificate collection, as shown in the following code fragment:

```
subj = rqstObject.ClientCertificate("Subject")
```

Test to see if the certificate values are present using the IsEmpty method.

The cookies collection contains individual cookies sent with the request. Each cookie can be a discrete bit of data or can itself contain a hierarchy of cookie information, stored by keys, and known as a cookie dictionary. The HasKeys method is used to determine if the cookie information is a single unit (its value is **False**) or a cookie dictionary (its value is **True**). The *IIS Programmer's Guide* installed with IIS 4.0 has a script routine for iterating through any cookie dictionaries included in the Request object. Source code converting this to using Visual Basic within a component is shown in Example 8-15.

Example 8-15. VB Code to Print the Values of All Cookies Sent with a Request

```
Dim cookie As Variant
Dim Key As Variant
For Each cookie In rqstObject.Cookies
   If cookie.HasKeys Then
      For Each Key In rqstObject.Cookies(cookie)
         rspnseObject.Write (cookie + "=" + Key + "=" + _
         rqstObject.Cookies(cookie)(Key))
      Next
   End If
Next
```

Cookies are stored on the client and are referenced by the URL of the web page matching the page being accessed in the current request. The browser searches the list of cookies for a matching URL and, if found, returns all cookie name/value pairs as part of the request. It is these name/value pairs that are stored in the Request object. If there is a cookie reference at the URL *http://www.somecompany. com/first/* and a cookie reference for the relative URL (relative to the main web page) */first*, the browser returns the cookies that match the lowest level URL, which would be the one at */first/*.

Complete documentation on cookies can be found at Netscape's site, *http://developer.netscape.com/library/documentation/communicator/ jsguide4/index.htm.*

The Request object contains references to cookies that have already been created. The Response object can (among other things) actually set the values of cookies; it is discussed next.

The Response Object Interface

The Response object has been used throughout this chapter to write output to the web page; it controls the output returned to the browser after a request.

Of all the built-in objects, the Response object has the most methods and properties; they are:

AddHeader method
    Adds an HTTP header to the response

AppendToLog method
    Appends a string to the web server log

BinaryWrite method
    Writes the content as raw data without any character conversion

Buffer property
    Defines whether page output is buffered

CacheControl property
    Indicates whether proxy servers can cache output

Charset property
    Appends the character set name to the content type header

Clear method
    Erases buffered output

ContentType property

Specifies the type of HTTP content; its default is `text/html`

Cookies collection

The cookies sent with the response

End method

Forces ASP to stop processing and return any buffered output

Expires property

Indicates the time until the response expires

ExpiresAbsolute property

Indicates the absolute date and time when the response expires

Flush method

Sends buffered output immediately

IsClientConnected property

Indicates whether the client is still connected

PICS property

The PICS rating

Redirect method

Sends a 302 redirect status to the browser

Status property

The HTTP status line

Write method

Writes output with character conversion to the client browser

The Write method has been used throughout this chapter to output results to a web page. However, the Response object's BinaryWrite method could also have been used to write output without any character conversion.

Buffering can be controlled from within a component. One limitation, though, is that the buffering must be turned on before any other output is sent to the page. Based on this, buffering is usually controlled through scripting by including the following as the first line in an ASP file:

```
<% Response.Buffer = True %>
```

When buffering is enabled, the Response object's End method stops any further buffering and forces an output of the buffer, the Clear method clears the buffer, and the Flush method forces an output of the buffer.

Should buffering be controlled from within an ASP component? Buffering can control whether any other output is sent to an ASP page or whether the output is cleared. The buffering methods and properties should be used sparingly within a component, and their use should be communicated to the component users. A better approach is to provide error messages and return values and to let the ASP application developer control buffering from the page.

The ContentType property can be used to specify the type of content being returned to the client. One use of this property could be for a component that determines whether a person wants to see a web page as it is normally displayed within a browser, or if they want to see the actual HTML source. The decision would be sent as a parameter to the component method, as shown in Example 8-16.

Example 8-16. VB Component Subroutine to Change How Page Contents Are Displayed

```
Public Sub ChangeDisplay(intDisplayFlag As Integer)
  Dim objContext As ObjectContext
  Dim rspnseObject As Response

  ' access objects
  Set objContext = GetObjectContext()
  Set rspnseObject = objContext("Response")

  ' write content type
  If intDisplayFlag = 1 Then
    rspnseObject.ContentType = "text/HTML"
  Else
    rspnseObject.ContentType = "text/plain"
  End If
End Sub
```

The ContentType property can also be used with binary content stored in databases to display the content in a meaningful format, such as **image/JPEG** for a JPEG image.

Most browsers support page caching in some manner, which means that the next time the page is accessed, the page is pulled from the client cache, not the server, if the server page has not changed. This can cut down on download times as well as decreasing the load on the web server. However, if an ASP component makes regular queries to a database and updates a page's contents at a specified interval, the component developer can set the page cache to expire in that same interval to ensure that the most current page is shown to the reader. The Response object has two methods to control page cache expiration: the Expires property, which sets the expiration to a specific number of minutes, and ExpiresAbsolute, which sets the expiration to a specific date and time.

You can add an absolute expiration for an ASP page from within a component by using a line similar to the following:

```
rspnseObject.ExpiresAbsolute = #5/1/98 11:00:15 AM#
```

This tells the browser to add an expiration date to the page of May 1, 1988, at a little after eleven in the morning. When you use the Explorer to view the browser's cached pages, you can see the expiration date added to the ASP page, as shown in Figure 8-4.

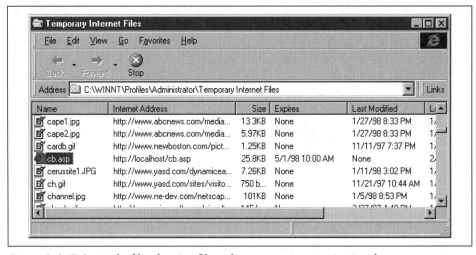

Figure 8-4. IE 4.x cache files showing file with component-set expiration date

In addition to controlling the cache expiration date for a page, the Response object can set or create a cookie. For example, the following code block adds a cookie named temp that has two key values, "one" and "two":

```
rspnseObject.Cookies("temp")("one") = "one"
rspnseObject.Cookies("temp")("two") = "two"
rspnseObject.Cookies("temp").Expires = #5/1/98#
```

The same string is used for both the key name and key value. In addition, an expiration date is given for the cookie. If a cookie with the name temp did not exist, it would be created. Otherwise, a new value and expiration date would be assigned to the cookie. Accessing this component from an ASP page displayed by Netscape Navigator would generate the following line in Navigator's cookies file, *cookies.txt*:

```
localhost    FALSE    FALSE    893995200    temp    TWO=two&ONE=one
```

If no date is used, the cookie is assumed to expire at the end of the session.

If you try setting a cookie using the Response object, and then can't see the cookie in the *cookies.txt* file, note that the cookie is not actually written until the browser is closed. The cookie is actually maintained in memory until some event forces an output to persist the information.

The AppendToLog method is a great way to record information about the use of an ASP component. One use of this method is to record information about an error if one occurs in the component. Based on this approach, an error handler for a component could have the following code:

```
ErrorHandler:
' write out error to log
rspnseObject.AppendToLog ("Error in rspnseTest: " + CStr(Err.Number) + _
                    " " + Err.Description)
```

When an error occurs within the component, a line containing the error number and error description is written to the server log.

Another Response method is AddHeader, which adds to an HTTP header and should be used with caution. This method could be used to ask the client (the browser) to provide additional authentication for the request, but could also result in the page being undeliverable if the header is malformed as a result of using the AddHeader method. As with other functions that generate header output, the output must occur before any other page contents, including the opening <HTML> tag.

Additional information about authentication can be found at the W3C web site, listed in the "Further Reading" section at the end of this chapter.

The Response object's IsClientConnected method checks to see if the client is still connected. This could be used to make sure the client is still connected before running a process-intensive calculation or accessing a database. Don't put the server through work no one will be receiving.

The Response object's Redirect method sends a status of 302 with the HTTP response and redirects the browser to another specified URL. Again, this method must be used before any HTML content is written to a page. This method is particularly helpful to direct the browser based on browser information extracted from the client's request, such as the name or version of the browser, and can be used to prevent older browsers from accessing web pages created with newer technologies. For instance, the code in Example 8-17 checks for type of browser and opens another page if the browser is IE. Otherwise, IsClientConnected is used to make a check to see if the client is still connected and a message is written that IE is necessary to view the page.

Example 8-17. Using Redirect to Redirect Output from One Page to Another

```
Public Sub ChangePage()
   Dim objContext As ObjectContext
   Dim rspnseObject As Response
   Dim rqstObject As Request

   ' access objects
   Set objContext = GetObjectContext()
   Set rspnseObject = objContext("Response")
   Set rqstObject = objContext("Request")

   Dim ua As String
   ua = rqstObject.ServerVariables("HTTP_USER_AGENT")
   If InStr(1, ua, "MSIE", 1) Then
       rspnseObject.Redirect ("temp.htm")
   Else
     If rspnseObject.IsClientConnected Then
         rspnseObject.Write ("You are using another browser" + _
           " and this page requires IE")
     End If
   End If
End Sub
```

This example uses IsClientConnected to test whether the client is still connected. A connection can be lost between the time a request is made and the response is returned, especially if database access occurs in the component. Because of this, it is always a good idea to test whether the client is still connected before outputting a response.

The Server Object Interface

The built-in Server object is mainly used to create object instances, as demonstrated throughout this chapter. In addition, it has some methods that can perform HTML and URL encoding, as well as map a logical location to a physical location.

The Server object's properties and methods are:

CreateObject method
   Creates an instance of a server component

HTMLEncode method
   Applies HTML encoding

MapPath method
   Maps a relative or virtual path to a physical one

ScriptTimeout property

  Defines the timeout interval for a script

URLEncode method

  Applies URL encoding

Along with instantiating components from ASP pages, the Server object's Create-Object method can also be used to instantiate a component from within a component. With this, applications can be broken down into reusable chunks of code, each chunk coded as a component yet each able to invoke the methods of other components if necessary.

To see how the Server object can be used to foster component-based development, compile the component with the public ChangePage method shown in Example 8-17 into a component named *rspnseTest.responseObject*. It is accessed by a new ASP component using its ServerOpen method, which is shown in Example 8-18.

Example 8-18. Instantiating One ASP Component Within Another

```
Option Explicit
Public Sub ServerOpen()
   ' create objects
   Dim objContext As ObjectContext
   Dim srvrObject As Server
   Dim rspnseObject As Object

   ' set objects
   Set objContext = GetObjectContext()
   Set srvrObject = objContext.Item("Server")

   ' create ASP component and access method
   Set rspnseObject = srvrObject.CreateObject("rspnseTest.responseObject")
   rspnseObject.ChangePage
End Sub
```

In addition to creating **rspnseObject** as a generic Object data type, a reference to the Visual Basic component's type library can also be added to the new ASP component. In that case, **rspnseObject** can be defined as follows:

```
Dim rspnseObject As rspnseTest.ResponseObject
```

The Server encoding methods provide ways to convert a string for passing as part of a URL, or for displaying as part of an HTML page. The ASP component code in Example 8-19 shows a component using the Server methods to create various strings, and then using the Response object to output the strings to a web page.

Example 8-19. Encoding Strings Using URL and HTML Encoding

```
Option Explicit
Public Sub ServerOpen()
```

Example 8-19. Encoding Strings Using URL and HTML Encoding (continued)

```
' create objects
Dim objContext As ObjectContext
Dim srvrObject As Server
Dim rspnseObject As Response
Dim strURL As String
Dim strHTML As String
Dim strURLPath As String
Dim strMapPath As String

' set objects
Set objContext = GetObjectContext()
Set srvrObject = objContext("Server")
Set rspnseObject = objContext("Response")

strURL = srvrObject.URLEncode("% this is a test % ++")
strHTML = srvrObject.HTMLEncode("<H1>This is a test</H1>")
strURLPath = srvrObject.URLPathEncode("test/test2/this is a test")
strMapPath = srvrObject.MapPath("/test/test2/")

If rspnseObject.IsClientConnected Then
  rspnseObject.Write (strURL)
  rspnseObject.Write ("<p>")
  rspnseObject.Write (strHTML)
  rspnseObject.Write ("<p>")
  rspnseObject.Write (strURLPath)
  rspnseObject.Write ("<p>")
  rspnseObject.Write (strMapPath)
End If

End Sub
```

The URLEncode method uses URL encoding on the string, which does such things as redefine a space as a plus sign (+). The HTMLEncode method uses HTML encoding on the string passed to it, which redefines angle brackets such as the left angle bracket (<) into a HTML-safe string, "<", which allows the actual printing of the value. The URLPathEncode method uses URL path encoding to convert characters, unlike the URLEncode method, which is primarily used for converting a query string. The MapPath method maps a path to the relative location of the page.

Add the component to a web page surrounded by the <STRONG> tag to highlight the results, and call the ASP component's ServerOpen method, as shown in Example 8-20.

Example 8-20. ASP Page for Example 8-18

```
<HTML>
<HEAD>
<TITLE>Test</TITLE>
</HEAD>
```

Example 8-20. ASP Page for Example 8-18 (continued)

```
<BODY>
<strong>
<%
  Dim tmp
  Set tmp = Server.CreateObject("tstServer.ServerTest")
  tmp.ServerOpen
%>
</strong>
</BODY>
</HTML>
```

The results of accessing this file can be seen in Figure 8-5. Notice from the figure that the space is converted to "+" in the URL encoding, but to "%20" in the URL path encoding. The space is left alone with the HTML encoding.

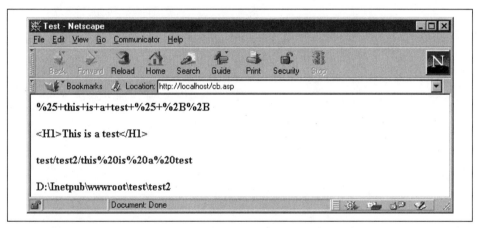

Figure 8-5. Results of different encoding and mapping methods of the Server object

The MapPath method is an effective way to map the logical path of the ASP page to an actual physical location. This physical location can be necessary for file or even database access.

The only Server property is ScriptTimeout, which can be set to the number of seconds the script containing the component can run before the script times out. This is primarily used to cancel processing that is taking too long.

Further Reading

For additional reading about the topics covered in this chapter, check out the following:

- Read more about HTTP response headers and authentication at *http://www. w3.org/*.

- Read a tutorial all about basic authentication at *http://www.aspalliance.com/ flicks/*.

- A good general all-about-ASP web site is located at *http://www. activeserverpages.com/*. In particular, check out the Components section.

- Microsoft has a reference page on ASP objects located at *http://premium. microsoft.com/msdn/library/sdkdoc/iishelp/iis/htm/asp/introbj_1orp.htm*.

9

Creating VB Data Access Components

Ask most people interested in building an Internet or an Intranet applications what would be one of the main uses for the application, and chances are the person you ask is going to respond that they want some form of data access. The type of data access can change, encompassing such applications as online catalogs, transaction systems, or most forms of information lookup. The key component, however, is that the system must provide some form of data access on the server.

Microsoft supports a couple of different techniques to access data, including Remote Data Service (RDS) to access data directly from a client page, as well as the more traditional Data Access Objects (DAO) to connect to a data source on the server using the Jet database engine. However, to increase the ease with which data is accessed from any application, including an ASP one, Microsoft provides OLE DB, a set of COM interfaces that supports any type of data format as long as the data source implements an OLE DB *provider*. To support OLE DB with existing applications, Microsoft has already supplied an OLE DB provider for ODBC, which means any data source accessed via an ODBC driver can be accessed using OLE DB.

One of the problems with OLE DB is that it is a relatively complicated technology to use to access data. To facilitate the use of OLE DB, Microsoft also created ActiveX Data Objects, a set of objects built on OLE DB, but hiding most of the complexity of OLE DB. ADO can be used to access data in multiple formats, including relational as well as ISAM databases, and even straight text.

As for ASP applications, ADO was created originally for use from Internet applications, and can be used directly in server-side scripts as well as within ASP components. ADO is used throughout this chapter, and the first section of this chapter provides a quick overview.

Using ADO, data can be accessed directly within the ASP pages, but if the data changes—for example, if a column is added or removed from a table, or a column data type changes—each and every instance where the changed data item is accessed has to be altered. One very useful implementation of ASP components is to build a database access layer between the ASP pages and an actual database. So, instead of having several ASP pages making the same direct database access to perform a recurring operation, such as a customer search, you can create an ASP component and have it perform the search and return the results. With this approach, changes to the underlying data structure, such as the customer table, results in changes just to the component rather than to all the pages that use this functionality.

An additional reason to encapsulate data access within ASP components is that each component can be used many times, from many different ASP pages, without having to recode the same data access mechanics each and every time. This increases the maintainability of the application, as well as making it easier to alter the access characteristics for the data.

This chapter covers using ADO from within Visual Basic ASP components in order to encapsulate data actions meant to be used from different ASP pages.

 To use ADO, you must define a data source using the ODBC administrator first, and the ODBC driver for the data source must be version 3.0 and up. If you haven't used the ODBC administrator before, the "Further Reading" section at the end of the chapter contains a reference to a web page Microsoft provides that has a nice overview of ODBC, including how to use the Administrator.

Using ActiveX Data Objects (ADO)

ADO provides a simplified technique to access data, regardless of how the data is formatted. This means that ADO can access data stored in a relational database, in an ISAM file, in a generic text file, or in some other supported format. Support for this flexibility occurs through the connection string and the values you use to connect to the source, create a record set, and issue a database command. These actions can, and do, differ based on the provider.

At the time this was written, all ADO access occurred through three OLE DB providers from Microsoft:

• Microsoft OLE DB Provider for ODBC

• Microsoft OLE DB Provider for Microsoft Index Server

• Microsoft OLE DB Provider for Microsoft Active Directory Service

This chapter concentrates on using ADO to access ODBC data sources.

As stated, the OLE DB Provider for ODBC allows ADO to connect to most ODBC drivers that support ODBC version 3.0 and above. But there are differences from driver to driver. One thing that may differ is the connection string. In addition, each driver can provide differing levels of transaction support. For example, Microsoft Access supports up to five nested transactions, while the ODBC driver for SQL Server provides support for eight.

Another difference is the number of ADO properties and methods that are supported. For SQL Server 6.5 and above, all ADO properties and methods are supported. For other databases, such as Oracle, not all aspects of ADO may be supported, and you will need to read the documentation included with the database system to find out the connection information and to map between the ADO methods and the ODBC driver support for the database.

 The examples in this chapter were created to run against a SQL Server 7.0 database. The database is the *pubs* database installed as a sample with SQL Server. The ODBC connection to this database is set to the name of the server containing both the database and IIS, the DSN for the database is set to **books**, and the default login is "sa" with no password. For more information on creating an ODBC entry, access the ODBC Administrator from the Control Panel, and access Help from any of the tabs. To run the examples in this chapter, you will need to adjust the example to use your own ODBC data sources, or create an ODBC entry for the *pubs* database that comes with SQL Server.

To support the constants used with some of the methods or properties, there are also special files created specifically for use with certain scripting or programming languages. For instance, the file for VBScript is included in the ASP page using the following directive as the first line of an ASP page:

```
<!-- #Include file="adovbs.inc" -->
```

The directive for JScript is:

```
<!-- #Include file="adojavas.inc" -->
```

Visual C++ adds support for ADO with two libraries that are automatically added with the use of the OLE DB templates. For Visual Basic, all the constants in addition to the ADO objects can be accessed at design time when a reference to the "Microsoft ActiveX Data Objects 2.0 Library" or "Microsoft ActiveX Data Objects Recordset 2.0 Library" is added to the VB project. For Visual J++, Microsoft provides a set of classes for ADO as part of the Windows Foundation Class (WFC) library. Chapter 17, *Integrating Java ASP Components with ADO and MTS,* provides an example of using ADO with Visual J++, ASP, and the Microsoft Transaction Server (MTS); and Chapter 13, *Integrating Data Access in C++ ASP Components with OLE DB*, covers using the OLE DB templates from Visual C++.

The ADO object model is actually quite simple, with seven objects and four collections. The seven objects are:

Connection
Makes a data source connection and contains connection information

Command
Contains a data source data modification or query

Recordset
Manages rows returned from a query

Error
Contains information about any error that happens with the data source action

Property
Represents a specific property contained within a Properties collection for any of the ADO objects

Field
Represents information and data from a specific column within a Recordset

Parameter
Manages mapping between values being passed to and from the data source and some programmatic value or variable

Accessing ADO objects directly from an ASP scripting block offers a quick introduction to ADO; the rest of this section provides such an introduction.

Normally, the first action taken when accessing a data source is to make a connection to it. The ADO Connection object can be used for this. The first steps involve creating an instance of the object by passing its PROGID, **ADODB.Connection**, as a parameter to the CreateObject method:

```
Set cn = Server.CreateObject("ADODB.Connection")
cn.Open "driver={SQL Server};server=MARVIN;uid=sa;pwd=;database=pubs"
```

The Open method establishes the database connection, in this case to the database named *pubs* on the server MARVIN using the SQL Server ODBC driver.

The Connection object also provides transaction-processing support with the BeginTrans, CommitTrans, and RollbackTrans methods. However, not all data sources or OLE DB providers provide transaction support. To see whether a particular data source driver supports transactions, Microsoft suggests checking for the Transaction DDL property within the Connection object's Properties collection. Example 9-1 lists all of the Connection object's properties.

To access the Properties collection (which contains one Property object for each property belonging to an object) and to see what each property is set to, Example 9-1 contains an ASP page that lists the properties of the Connection object for the *pubs* data source. In order to understand what your data source will and will not support, I suggest that you copy this code and run the example yourself after changing the connection string to reflect your own data source.

Example 9-1. Printing out Connection Object Properties for SQL Server Data Source

```
<!-- #Include file="adovbs.inc" -->
<HTML>
<BODY>
<%

Dim cn
Dim rs

Dim thestring
Response.Write("connecting...<p>")

On Error Resume Next
Set cn = Server.CreateObject("ADODB.Connection")
cn.Open "driver={SQL Server};server=FLAME;uid=sa;pwd=;database=pubs"

If Err.Number <> 0 Then
   Response.write("//Error Number: " & Err.Number)
   Response.write("; Error Source: " & Err.Source)
   Response.write("; Error Description: " & Err.Description)
   Err.Clear
Else

   Response.Write("Writing out Connection Properties<p>")
   Response.Write("<table>")
   For each prop in cn.properties
     Response.write("<tr><td>" & prop.Name & "</td><td>")
     Response.Write(prop.Value)
     Response.write("</tr>")
   Next
   Response.write("</table>")
   End If
    rs.Close
' End If


cn.Close
%>
</BODY>
</HTML>
```

When running against the SQL Server 7.0 database, the Transaction DDL property had a value of 8, meaning that the database supports a depth of 8 nested transactions, as stated earlier. Other useful information was the Extended Properties property, which contained the connection information:

```
Extended Properties    DRIVER=SQL Server;SERVER=MARVIN;UID=sa;PWD=;
                       WSID=MARVIN;DATABASE=pubs
```

Additional properties provided information about whether the database supports stored procedures, ordering, outer joins, the name of the OLE DB provider, whether multiple table updates are supported, and other useful information that's handy to know before creating the ASP/ADO component.

Connection object methods aside from Open and transaction processing methods are:

Execute

Executes a query, stored procedure, or some provider-specific text.

OpenSchema

Provides information about the database metadata, or schema.

One of the most commonly accessed of the ADO objects is the Recordset object. The Recordset object is used to access a set of records returned from a query, a stored procedure call, or as the result of an executed command.

A Recordset object can be created from an existing Connection or Command object, or it can be used to create the data source connection (that is, you don't need to explicitly work with the Connection object) as well as run the data query. This object also has an Open method, as shown in the following VBScript code:

```
Set rs = Server.CreateObject("ADODB.Recordset")
rs.Open "select * from authors", cn, adOpenStatic, adLockReadOnly
```

The parameters passed with Recordset.Open are:

- A string containing a command, a table name, or a SQL query (as shown in the example).

- The Connection object.

- A constant to define the cursor type. These are listed in Table 9-1.

- A constant to define the lock type. These are listed in Table 9-2.

Table 9-1. Cursor Types Supported by the Recordset.Open Method

adOpenForwardOnly	Creates forward-only cursor; this allows you to do a single pass through the record set, navigating forward only
adOpenKeyset	Data changes by other users are made viewable
adOpenDynamic	Deletions, insertions, and updates made by others are made available
adOpenStatic	Any changes made by others are not visible; creates a static copy of the records

Table 9-2. Lock Types Supported by the Recordset.Open Method

`adLockReadOnly`	Read only lock: data cannot be changed
`adLockPessimistic`	Pessimistic locking: records are usually locked just after edits are made. This varies by provider
`adLockOptimistic`	Optimistic locking: records are locked when an Update call is made
`adLockBatchOptimistic`	For batch modes, locks all records for update just before an update is made

A final parameter can include information about how the source should be evaluated. For this example, the Recordset is opened with a static cursor, as a read-only query, and without any information about the source object, which then defaults to "unknown."

The Recordset object also has a Properties collection containing useful information about the data query, stored procedure, or other data source items. The script in Example 9-2 prints them to a web page. Again, I recommend you copy and run the ASP page contained in this example in order to find out information about the Recordset object returned in response to your request or query. To run the example, change the Connection object and the source for the Recordset to reflect your data source.

Example 9-2. Outputting the Properties for the ADO Recordset Object

```
<!-- #Include file="adovbs.inc" -->
<HTML>
<BODY>
<%

Dim cn
Dim rs

Dim thestring
Response.Write("connecting...")

On Error Resume Next
Set cn = Server.CreateObject("ADODB.Connection")
cn.Open "driver={SQL Server};server=MARVIN;uid=sa;pwd=;database=pubs"

If Err.Number <> 0 Then
   Response.write("//Error Number: " & Err.Number)
   Response.write("; Error Source: " & Err.Source)
   Response.write("; Error Description: " & Err.Description)
   Err.Clear
Else
   Response.Write("accessing data...")

   Set rs = Server.CreateObject("ADODB.Recordset")
   rs.Open "authors", cn,  adOpenDynamic , adLockPessimistic
```

Example 9-2. Outputting the Properties for the ADO Recordset Object (continued)

```
    If Err.Number <> 0 Then
       Response.write("//Error Number: " & Err.Number)
       Response.write("; Error Source: " & Err.Source)
       Response.write("; Error Description: " & Err.Description)
       Err.Clear
    Else
    Response.Write("<table>")
    For each prop in rs.properties
       Response.write("<tr><td>" & prop.Name & "</td><td>")
       Response.Write(prop.Value)
       Response.write("</tr>")
    Next
    Response.write("</table>")
End If
    rs.Close
End If


cn.Close
%>
</BODY>
</HTML>
```

Among the type of information contained in the Recordset properties is whether other people's database changes are visible to the user running the page that creates the Recordset, and whether the user's own updates are visible. Additional information includes whether the object is part of a pending transaction and whether the client has update privileges. Unlike the Connection object, whose properties are determined by the data provider, the Recordset properties change based on how the Recordset is defined and the security enforced on the data source.

Aside from the Open method, the Recordset object also has several methods that are demonstrated in later examples. The object also has several properties other than those specified in the Properties collection. Many of them, such as Absolute-Page, PageSize, PageCount, and AbsolutePosition, have to do with splitting the records into pages and accessing the contents based on which page the record is in and its position relative to the other pages. Other properties such as BOF and EOF indicate the cursor's position within the record set. The status of a record—whether it has been changed or deleted—can be determined using the Status property. These and other properties are demonstrated more fully in the rest of this chapter and in Chapter 18, *Java ASP Components and J/Direct, Native Code, and Marshaling.*

It's handy to know what information can be found about a Recordset object, but the real purpose of the object is to access and manipulate data from the source. For instance, the following code prints out the authors' first and last names, cities,

and phone numbers from the AUTHORS table using the same Recordset created in
Example 9-2:

```
Response.Write "<TABLE border=2 cellpadding=3>"
Do While rs.EOF = False
    Response.Write "<TR><TD>"
            Response.Write rs("au_lname") & ", " & rs("au_fname")
            Response.Write "</TD><TD>"
            Response.Write rs("city")
            Response.Write "</TD><TD>"
            Response.Write rs("phone")
            Response.Write "</TD></TR>"
            rs.MoveNext
Loop
Response.Write "</TABLE>"
```

As the code shows, the fields of the Recordset form another collection. Each
Recordset field can be accessed directly by specifying the field name. The Field
object has two methods, AppendChunk and GetChunk, used to get and set binary
large objects, otherwise known as BLOBs. These can be particularly effective
when accessing a graphic stored in the database and then outputting it as a viewable image to the client browser.

Instead of storing an image within a database, consider storing the
relative path and the name of an image file, and use this to return an
image to the browser. This may actually improve performance,
since the image does not have to be "built" with many accesses to
the database. This approach, though, can be more difficult to maintain because information must be stored in more than one location.

The Field object has several properties, including the Value property, which can
be used to set or get the current value for the field. You can also access other
information about the field, such as its numeric scale (NumericScale), precision
(Precision), its defined and actual size (DefinedSize, ActualSize), as well as the
field's original value if the value is altered (OriginalValue, which contains the
field's value before an update occurred).

The Error object is actually a member of another collection of the Connection
object, the Errors collection. This object is used to hold error information provided by the OLE DB provider and can include the error number and any descriptive text. This does not include ADO errors, which are handled as regular error
processing.

The remaining two objects in the ADO object model are the Command and the
Parameter objects. The Command object allows you to execute a provider command, a stored procedure, or some other action, and to assign the result set to a

Recordset object. The Parameter object can be used to create parameters to be passed to the Command object, though simple parameters can be sent directly with an Execute method. As a demonstration, Example 9-3 creates a new Command object that invokes a stored procedure. This stored procedure returns the author ID for all authors who earn a royalty of 100% (which, unfortunately, does not include yours truly).

Example 9-3. Executing Stored Procedure and Assigning Results to Recordset Object

```
Dim cn
Set cn = Server.CreateObject("ADODB.Connection")
cn.Open "driver={SQL Server};server=MARVIN;uid=sa;pwd=;database=pubs"

Dim conn
Set conn = Server.CreateObject("ADODB.Command")

conn.ActiveConnection = cn
conn.CommandText = "byroyalty"
Dim returnvalue
Set rs = conn.Execute(returnvalue, 100)
If Err.Number <> 0 Then
    Response.write("//Error Number: " & Err.Number)
    Response.write("; Error Source: " & Err.Source)
    Response.write("; Error Description: " & Err.Description)
    Err.Clear
Else

    Response.Write "<TABLE border=2 cellpadding=3>"
        Do While rs.EOF = False
      Response.Write "<TR><TD>"
      Response.Write rs("au_id")
      Response.Write "</TD><TR>"
      rs.MoveNext
    Loop
    Response.Write "</TABLE>"
End If
```

Though not complete, I hope this section has provided enough of an overview of the ADO objects to make the examples in the next sections more comprehensible. For a detailed description of all the ADO objects, methods, collections, and properties, check out the documentation included with IIS 4.0 or with Visual Basic 6.0.

Accessing Data from a VB ASP Component

The last section provided an overview of the ADO objects; this section uses these objects from within Visual Basic ASP components.

When creating a component using ADO, the first task is to attach the ADO type library to the component. By doing this, you can take advantage of auto completion and verification Visual Basic provides, as well as using early binding, discussed in more detail in Chapter 3, *ASP Components and COM.*

There are actually three different ADO libraries you can attach to your project. The Microsoft ActiveX Data Objects 2.0 Library (ADODB) contains the standard ADO objects. The Microsoft ActiveX Data Objects Recordset 2.0 Library (ADOR) contains the objects used in conjunction with Remote Data Service, discussed briefly in the next section. The Microsoft ActiveX Data Objects (Multidimensional) (ADOM) actually contains new objects that provide for multidimensional access of data.

 Though not covered in this book, ADOM is an interesting look at querying data using a three-dimensional structure. To find out more about ADOM, check the documentation that comes with the Data Access SDK, downloadable at *http://www.microsoft.com/data/.*

To attach any of the ADO libraries, select the References menu option from the Project menu and check the box next to the appropriate library. From the list that opens look for the following library:

```
Microsoft ActiveX Data Objects 2.0 Library
```

If this library isn't currently checked, check it; that's all you have to do to attach a reference to the ADO type libraries within the ASP component.

ADO and Remote Data Server Applications

The differences between ADODB and ADOR have to do with where the component resides. ADOR is used to implement RDS, to marshal record sets between the client and the middleware server in an n-tier application. RDS is a data bound control that can be embedded directly within a web page and then used to cache data on the client. Caching the data on the client allows for direct manipulation and detailed examination of the data without having to return to the server. No other server access needs to occur until the data cache is changed or needs to be refreshed.

With RDS, if the reader updates the data in some way, such as inserting or deleting rows or altering existing values, the changes are cached until the reader is ready to commit the changes to the database. When the changes are committed, the records are marshaled from the client to the server through an ADOR record. In other words, the records are not sent to the ASP component, the ADOR object is. The ASP object is created using the standard ADO library and its purpose is to then process the record set, saving the changes to the data source.

Breaking this out into a sequence of events, and without getting into too much detail on RDS, when changes are pending with RDS.DataControl, the RDS control, an ADOR.Recordset object is created. On the server, an ASP component contains some method used to actually commit the changes. It is this method that receives the passed ADOR.Recordset object. The client component instantiates a new ADODB Recordset object and passes the ADOR.Recordset object as the data source for the server component. The server ADODB Recordset object then invokes the UpdateBatch method, which writes all pending updates to the data source.

The ability to create an n-tier system consisting of a client, a business layer, and a data layer in such a simple manner is an attractive concept. However, there is one limitation: this approach works only with Internet Explorer as the client browser. Since this book covers server-based scripting components that should work equally well with IE, Netscape Navigator, or any other browser, I won't go into any more detail on RDS.

If you are creating an application for your company Intranet, and your company has chosen IE as the browser, read the documentation that comes with IIS on using RDS and consider using data-bound controls with your data access applications.

That's not to say you can't have an n-tier system using ASP for the business layer for an Internet application that supports more than one browser. This is discussed in more detail in Chapter 10, *Creating N-Tier ASP Components Using Visual Basic.*

Creating a Simple ASP Component That Uses ADO

After adding a reference to the ADODB library to your project, you can create instances of ADO objects. The following syntax, for example, creates instances of a Connection and a Recordset object:

```
Dim cn As New ADODB.Connection
Dim rs As New ADODB.Recordset
```

Once the object instances are created, you can use them in virtually the same manner as was demonstrated in the previous section using VBScript. Example 9-4 shows a complete VB component that accesses the AUTHORS table from the *pubs* database in SQL Server, and writes out the authors' names, cities, and phone numbers.

Example 9-4. Accessing a Method Containing a Reference to a Built-in Object

```
Public Sub AuthorList()

    'Declare object variables for the database connection and recordset
    Dim cn As New ADODB.Connection
    Dim rs As New ADODB.Recordset

    Dim objContext As ObjectContext
    Dim objResponse As Response
    Set objContext = GetObjectContext()
    Set objResponse = objContext("Response")

    cn.ConnectionString = "driver={SQL Server};server=MARVIN;uid=sa; " & _
                    "pwd=;database=pubs"
    cn.Open
    rs.Open "select * from authors", cn, adOpenStatic, adLockReadOnly

    'Write resulting information to a table
    With objResponse
        .Write "<TABLE border=2 cellpadding=3>"
        Do While rs.EOF = False
            .Write "<TR><TD>"
            .Write rs("au_lname") & ", " & rs("au_fname")
            .Write "</TD><TD>"
            .Write rs("city")
            .Write "</TD><TD>"
            .Write rs("phone")
            .Write "</TD></TR>"
            rs.MoveNext
        Loop
        .Write "</TABLE>"

    End With

    'Close the recordset and the database connection
    rs.Close
    cn.Close

End Sub
```

Note that the connection string is the same as that used within the script block in the previous examples in this chapter, and that the Recordset object's Open method is exactly the same, including the defined constants passed to control the cursor and locking. One difference between the scripting example and this Visual Basic example is that, with this component, the Response object must be accessed first, and once accessed, can be used within a With statement block, to avoid having to repeat the objResponse object.

The With statement attaches all method calls to the object specified in the block header.

Once compiled into a DLL, the new ASP component can be created within an ASP page and the AuthorList method called.

There are some performance issues to be aware of when using ADO from within ASP components. First, the ADO library objects are created as both-threaded objects, but are registered as apartment-threaded objects. This means that if you create an instance of an ADO object that you store as an application- or session-level object, you are locking that object down to a specific thread. This can limit the overall performance of the application.

You should not assign an ADO object, and particularly the Connection object, as an application-level object regardless, since this maintains an open connection to the database. If you assign an ADO object as a session-level object, you can run a registry file, which is included with the installation of ADO, that sets the threading model in the registry for the ADODB objects to both-threaded. These registry files are usually found in the *C:\Program Files\Common Files\System\ado* subdirectory, though this and the batch file names can vary based on installation. However, you can look for a file beginning with "ado" and with an extension type of ".reg" to find the registry files.

Microsoft does not recommend storing the ADO Connection object even as a session-level object, which keeps the connection to the database open for as long as it takes the reader to respond to page content. Instead, the company recommends that the *string* used to make the connection be stored as a session-level object and then used to create any new data source connection. Since this string can contain userid and password information, as well as data source location information that can change, storing this string as a Session object means that the web page reader gets the same type of connection for each data access he makes, resulting in a consistent data interface.

Releasing the database connection quickly allows database connection pooling to be used, particularly if MTS is used with the ASP components. Releasing the database connection allows it to be returned to the pool and be available for the next application that needs a database connection.

Another performance consideration is limiting the number of rows returned with each query. For example, you don't want to allow users to submit queries that generate overwhelming amounts of data (such as results, for example, when someone tries to find all customers whose last name begins with "S" in a database with several million records). Limiting the number of rows returned will at least prevent serious problems with queries that return too large a result set. However, if you do limit the number of rows returned, the ASP page may contain buttons to scroll through a set of rows and display a set number of rows with each movement. For this type of access, storing the ADO Connection and Recordset objects as session-level objects that transcend one-page access may make sense.

Creating Interactive Database Query ASP Components

The examples of using ADO from within an ASP application have demonstrated full table retrievals. In most cases, your application wouldn't want to return all of the data, but only some relevant subset. To determine which data is pertinent, your application should query the user to see what specific information she is interested in.

Creating an interactive data query is usually a multiple–ASP page operation. First, one page is created to get the query information from the web page reader. A second page accesses this information, makes the retrieval and returns the result. In more sophisticated applications, this second page may have buttons to allow the reader to scroll through sets of records when a larger number is returned.

To demonstrate an ASP interactive query application using an ASP component to make the data retrieval, Example 9-5 contains the code for a VB component that accesses the AUTHORS, TITLES, and AUTHORTITLE tables from the *pubs* SQL Server database. The query will return the full name and all book titles of any author that matches the search criterion. To keep things simple, the same method that makes the retrieval also makes the database connection, queries for and returns all rows matching the search criteria, and then closes the database connection. The search criterion is the author's last name, entered into a simple text field contained in a form.

Example 9-5. AP Page to Access the Data Store Based on a User Query

```
Public Sub SimpleQuery()

    'Declare object variables for the database connection and recordset
    Dim cn As New ADODB.Connection
    Dim rs As New ADODB.Recordset

    ' create ASP Response object
    Dim objContext As ObjectContext
    Dim objResponse As Response
    Dim objRequest As Request

    On Error GoTo HandleError
```

Example 9-5. AP Page to Access the Data Store Based on a User Query (continued)

```
' create ASP objects
Set objContext = GetObjectContext()
Set objResponse = objContext("Response")
Set objRequest = objContext("Request")

Dim strLastName As String
strLastName = objRequest.Form("lastname")

' connect to database
cn.ConnectionString = "driver={SQL Server};" _
                    & "server=MARVIN;uid=sa;pwd=;database=pubs"
cn.Open

' create Recordset
rs.ActiveConnection = cn
rs.CursorType = adOpenForwardOnly
rs.LockType = adLockReadOnly
rs.Source = _
"select au_lname, au_fname, title from " _
& "authors,titles,titleauthor where au_lname = '" & strLastName _
& "' and authors.au_id = titleauthor.au_id and " & _
"titles.title_id = titleauthor.title_id"
objResponse.Write ("For query: " & rs.Source & "<p>")
rs.Open

' output results
'Write resulting information to a table, record by record
With objResponse
    .Write "<TABLE border=2 cellpadding=3>"
    Do While rs.EOF = False
        .Write "<TR><TD>"
        .Write rs("au_lname") & ", " & rs("au_fname")
        .Write "</TD><TD>"
        .Write rs("title")
        .Write "</TD><TR>"
        rs.MoveNext
    Loop
    .Write "</TABLE>"
End With

' close record set, connection
rs.Close
cn.Close

' print out any error message
HandleError:
    If Err.Number <> 0 Then
        objResponse.Write (Err.Description)
    End If
End Sub
```

The component retrieves the author's name from the Form collection of the Request object. This value is then concatenated to the Recordset source property as part of the query. The actual query itself is output to the page along with a table containing the Recordset rows, if any. Outputting the actual query is a handy debugging technique to use while in development.

Remember from Chapter 8, *The Visual Basic Built-in Object Interfaces*, that the POST method adds in the form name-value pairs to the Form collection, and the default GET method puts these values into the QueryString collection.

An obvious limitation with this example is that the web page reader must guess what the last name of the author might be. Additionally, there is nothing to check whether the reader even entered the last name. To improve this application, a couple of modifications are possible. First, client-side scripting can be used to verify that the last name is entered before the form can be posted. As an additional check, though, the component itself can also make sure a value is entered before opening the record set.

A better approach to ensuring the reader enters a name is to use a list box containing all of the authors in the database and have the reader choose one of the names. To implement this, create another component in the same DLL as the one started in Example 9-5. This new component accesses all existing last names from the database and uses them to populate a list box. The list box itself opens with one name already selected, the first one on the list.

Instead of creating a separate component, you can also add a new method to the existing component. However, creating a separate component for something that can prove to be generally useful by itself makes more sense. The query for the title information may be run once, but the query to access the authors' names can be run many times. Instead of loading one large component containing many methods into memory, a small "utility" component can be loaded for generalized use.

To access the names, a couple of techniques could be used. First, a query that returns the full names and all the book titles can be used to provide the authors' last names and then maintained as a session-level object. The second component can then access this data from the Session object, filter it to the criteria, and return it. This implements a form of server-side data caching.

There are, however, a few disadvantages to this server-side caching technique:

- A multiple table join is run against all the authors just to return the author names. This is not an efficient query and will slow the ASP process. If several people access the application at a single time, the whole system can bog down.

- It's not efficient to maintain several records for each person accessing the application, especially a web-based application.

- Between the time the reader chooses a last name and gets the result set, new titles for the same author could be added to the database. The reader is seeing an old "snapshot" of the data, rather than the most up-to-date data matching the criteria. For the author query, this is unfortunate. In the case of an application such as a catalog app, which maintains a running stock count, the effect of working from an older snapshot of data can mean that an item is oversold. Companies that oversell items and can't fulfill existing orders don't remain in business very long.

In contrast to this server-side caching scheme, caching data on the client makes sense, since it limits the number of accesses to the database and the server across a network or the Internet. Caching data on the server really only makes sense if the database itself is part of a distributed system and must be accessed across a network. Even then, the faster access of the data must be balanced with the necessity of having access to correct and up-to-date data.

Another, better, approach is to maintain the data connection string in the session-level object, connect to the database and perform a simple query for all authors' last names, and then connect to the database again to perform the multiple table join that returns all of the selected author's books.

The component that returns the author names to be displayed in a form's drop-down list defined by the HTML <SELECT> tag is called from a script block contained within an ASP page. Example 9-6 contains the code for the component, which queries the AUTHORS table and concatenates the first and last names for the visible selector, but returns the last name as the selection item.

Example 9-6. ASP Component to Build a Selection List of Authors

```
Public Sub authors()

    'Declare object variables for the database connection and recordset
    Dim cn As New ADODB.Connection
    Dim rs As New ADODB.Recordset

    ' create ASP Response object
    Dim objContext As ObjectContext
    Dim objResponse As Response
```

Example 9-6. ASP Component to Build a Selection List of Authors (continued)

```
On Error GoTo HandleError

' create ASP objects
Set objContext = GetObjectContext()
Set objResponse = objContext("Response")

' connect to database
cn.ConnectionString = "driver={SQL
Server};server=MARVIN;uid=sa;pwd=;database=pubs"
cn.Open

' create Recordset
rs.ActiveConnection = cn
rs.CursorType = adOpenForwardOnly
rs.LockType = adLockReadOnly
rs.Source = "select au_lname, au_fname from authors"

rs.Open

' output results
'Write resulting information to a table, record by record
Do While rs.EOF = False
        objResponse.Write "<OPTION VALUE='" & rs("au_lname") & "'>"
        objResponse.Write rs("au_lname") & "," & rs("au_fname")
        rs.MoveNext
 Loop

' close record set, connection
rs.Close
cn.Close

' print out any error message
HandleError:
    If Err.Number <> 0 Then
        objResponse.Write (Err.Description)
    End If
End Sub
```

The ASP page that contains the new component and calls its authors method is
displayed in the code block shown in Example 9-7.

Example 9-7. ASP Page to Invoke the authors Method

```
<HTML>
<BODY>
<H1> Search for Authors </H1>
<FORM action="testr.asp" method="post">
Select name of author:<p>
<SELECT NAME="selname">
<%
  Dim myobj
  Set myobj = Server.CreateObject("datadhtml.author")
```

Example 9-7. ASP Page to Invoke the authors Method (continued)

```
  myobj.authors
%>
</SELECT><p>
<input type="submit" value="Find Titles">
</FORM>
</BODY>
</HTML>
```

Figure 9-1 contains a page demonstrating the form's drop-down list prefilled with author names that are returned from the component shown in Example 9-6. Note that now instead of the reader typing in the last name, he just needs to select from the list of available authors.

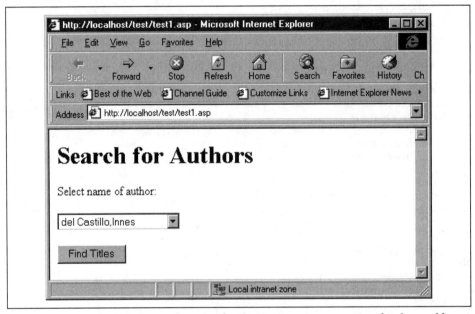

Figure 9-1. Drop-down listbox with entries from ASP component querying database table

The component that processes the request is modified slightly, primarily to pull the value out of the form's author name selection object.

The example could also use a stored procedure for the query and then use the ASP component as a "wrapper" for the stored procedure call. The advantage to this approach is that the data queries can be called from more than one application and are maintained at the database. An additional advantage is that stored procedures are compiled and usually perform more quickly than straight SQL queries. They also increase the simplicity of creating a library of ASP components for data access, discussed in the next section.

Building a Library of Data Access Components

Instead of including data access directly in an ASP page, consider creating a library of data access components that can be used in the ASP pages and by other components. One very real advantage to packaging data access into ASP components is that the data access functionality can be accessed quickly and easily from more than one ASP page. In addition, ASP components that need access to the data and that perform additional functionality can also access these other ASP data access components.

Once a library of data access components has been created, it's a simple matter to use the components whenever certain data needs to be returned or modified. Candidates for common data access are any queries that look up names or products, or any other objects of interest for the business. Another type of candidate is an update statement that can be called when more than one action occurs. An example would be updating the total of items within an online inventory table. The update could occur because of damage found during normal inventory processing and handled via an Intranet inventory application. Or the update could occur because of an order from an online Internet application. Two applications, accessing the same component, accessing the same stored procedure, and performing the same operation equals component reuse.

Another candidate for ASP component encapsulation is complex queries that would be handled more efficiently as stored procedures and accessed more easily if the stored procedure call, including any parameters, is packaged within a component. This is in addition to the performance improvement obtained when using a stored procedure.

To demonstrate the concept of creating a library of data access routines wrapped in ASP components, create a stored procedure in the *pubs* database on SQL Server that joins several tables: AUTHORS, TITLEAUTHOR, TITLES, and PUBLISHERS. The stored procedure takes an author id (AU_ID), and returns the title, author last name, first name, publisher name, price, and the year-to-date sales for each book written by the author whose code is AU_ID. The stored procedure code is shown in the following code block:

```
CREATE PROCEDURE bookinfo @au_id varchar(11)
AS
select title, au_lname, au_fname, pub_name, price, ytd_sales
from titleauthor, titles, authors, publishers
where titleauthor.au_id = @au_id and
titles.title_id = titleauthor.title_id and
authors.au_id = titleauthor.au_id and
publishers.pub_id = titles.pub_id
```

Notice that the author ID parameter must be defined before being used within the stored procedure.

Next, modify the component created from Example 9-6 to assign a value of the author ID instead of the last name when a name is selected. The only change to the component code is the following line:

```
objResponse.Write "<OPTION VALUE='" & rs("au_id") & "'>"
```

Then build a new component, shown in Example 9-8, that creates an ADODB Command object as well as the Connection and Recordset objects. The Command object is used in order to pass the parameter for the stored procedure call. As the stored procedure is receiving a simple parameter, not an array of values, the parameter can be passed directly within the Command object's Execute method, rather than having to create a Parameter object for each parameter.

Example 9-8. ASP Component to Wrap a Stored Procedure Call and Output Results

```
Public Sub WrapBookInfo()
    'Declare object variables for the database connection and recordset
    Dim cn As New ADODB.Connection
    Dim rs As New ADODB.Recordset
    Dim conn As New ADODB.Command

    ' create ASP Response object
    Dim objContext As ObjectContext
    Dim objResponse As Response
    Dim objRequest As Request

    On Error GoTo HandleError

    ' create ASP objects
    Set objContext = GetObjectContext()
    Set objResponse = objContext("Response")
    Set objRequest = objContext("Request")

    ' connect to database
    cn.ConnectionString = "driver={SQL Server};" & _
                          server=MARVIN;uid=sa;pwd=;database=pubs"
    cn.Open

    conn.ActiveConnection = cn
    conn.CommandText = "bookinfo"
    conn.CommandType = adCmdStoredProc

    Dim lng As Long
    Dim strAuthorId As String

    strAuthorId = objRequest.Form("selname")

    Set rs = conn.Execute(lng, strAuthorId)
```

Example 9-8. ASP Component to Wrap a Stored Procedure Call and Output Results (continued)

```
If Not (rs.EOF) Then

    ' output results
    With objResponse
      .Write "<H1>Search Results for " & rs("au_lname") _
             & "," & rs("au_fname") & "</H1>"
      .Write "<TABLE border=2 cellpadding=3>"
      .Write "<tr><th>Title</th><th>Publisher</th>" _
             & "<th>Price</th><th>YTD Sales</th></tr>"
    Do While rs.EOF = False
      .Write "<TR><TD>"
      .Write rs("title")
      .Write "</TD><TD>"
      .Write rs("pub_name")
      .Write "</TD><TD>"
      .Write rs("price")
      .Write "</TD><TD>"
      .Write rs("ytd_sales")
      .Write "</TD></TR>"
    rs.MoveNext
    Loop
    .Write "</TABLE>"
  End With
Else
  objResponse.Write ("<H1>No Titles Found for Author</H1>")
End If
' close record set, connection
rs.Close
cn.Close

' print out any error message
HandleError:
    If Err.Number <> 0 Then
        objResponse.Write (Err.Description)
    End If
End Sub
```

When the Execute method is invoked on the Command object, the command calls
a stored procedure that returns a result set. This is then assigned to the instantiated Recordset object and used to output each of the record's fields. Figure 9-2
shows the results of accessing the database using this component and passing in
the author name of "Anne Ringer."

Notice also from Figure 9-2, and from the code shown in Example 9-8, that the
ASP component actually displays the data in a formatted manner. The problem
with including presentation with the ASP component wrapper is that this limits its
usefulness. Now, if I want to change the presentation of the data, I would have to
create yet another wrapper component. A more efficient approach is to create the
wrapper components for the stored procedure call, create yet more wrapper components that can present data using different techniques, and combine these two

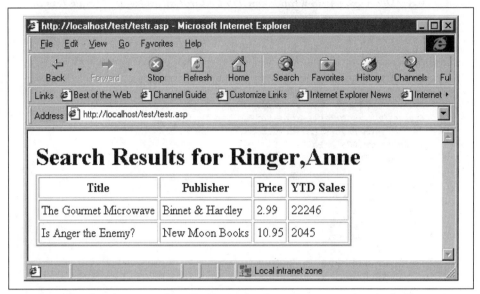

Figure 9-2. Results of running the ASP component that wraps a stored procedure

types of components for various effects. This is actually demonstrated in the next chapter, providing a more in-depth use of data access components to implement the business logic layer of a multitier application.

Further Reading

For additional reading about the topics covered in this chapter, check out the following:

- An overview of using ODBC can be found at *http://www.microsoft.com/data/reference/odbc2/sdkodbcoverview_4vcn.htm*.

- Microsoft has provided a terrific web site covering all of the company's data access techniques, including ADO, at *http://www.microsoft.com/data/*.

- For a fairly extensive example of multitier development, see the Duwamish Book sample at *http://www.microsoft.com/data/duwamish.htm*.

10

Creating N-Tier ASP Components Using Visual Basic

For years, the most commonly used implementation model for new systems was either the mainframe dumb terminal model, with its whisper-thin client, or the client/server model, usually containing fat and chunky clients. With these approaches, the processing tended to congregate totally in the back end of the application, with the mainframe application or with the presentation layer for the client-server model. The problem with both approaches is that presentation, data, and business processes become so intertwined that it is virtually impossible to separate the layers in order to modernize or replace any one of them.

Another approach that is gaining popularity, especially with applications making use of the Internet/Intranet, is the multi-tier or n-tier application model. This model, usually implemented in three tiers, splits the business processing from the presentation and the data layer. The advantage to this is that the presentation can be changed or even moved to a new medium without impacting on the business layer. Additionally, the data access can itself be moved to a different database, database model, or different machine, again with no impact on the business layer. The business layer itself can also be replaced without necessarily impacting on either the presentation or data layers.

This chapter provides a brief overview of an n-tier system, and demonstrates creating one using the *pubs* sample database that Microsoft provides with SQL Server. Different aspects of the application are examined, mainly from the perspective of how ASP components can be used to implement the functionality.

What Is an N-Tier Application, and Why Is It Necessary?

Any application is an n-tier application. Replace the n with a 1 and you have a standalone executable. Replace the n with a 2 and you have the traditional client-server application. Commonly, though, an n-tier application is one that separates the presentation layer from the business layer and the business layer from the data layer to form a three-tier application. Further layering could also include splitting the business layer into yet more layers, or splitting the data access layer into a layer that actually handles the data access method calls to a second layer that makes the actual physical database access.

Why use an n-tier application model? One of the biggest reasons for using this type of architecture is the openness it provides to an application. By openness, I mean the ability to swap one component out of the application and replace it with another without having to alter the components that interface with the replaced component. Including data access directly within a client in a client-server application makes it difficult to change the database schema without having to make several changes within the client. Including business processes within the presentation layer makes it difficult to use a different tool or even a different medium for the front end without having to rewrite all of the business process code. With the increased popularity of the web in business applications, including front ends that reside in browsers, more companies are looking for ways of not having to duplicate the same business rules and logic each time they want to add some new form of front-end access.

Another reason for n-tier applications is that the development process becomes more modularized. With this approach, the developers writing the business processes don't need to become fully intimate with the database design in order to write their code. The data access layer handles the more complex database manipulation. Additionally, the front-end piece can be coded with minimal awareness of the internal characteristics of a business process; they only have to know how to handle successful or failed process logic. Without having to know all aspects of the application, developers of each layer can concentrate more fully on writing the best code possible to control what happens within their layer, and only their layer.

An additional advantage to an n-tier application is that it lends itself to being a distributed application. If the business process layer is made up of separate components, each performing one specific bit of functionality, these components can actually be distributed to different systems if performance for the application degrades. Additionally, the data layer can be implemented in not one, but two, or even three different data sources, each contained on a different machine, and perhaps even maintained with a different type of database engine. The front end can also be created with visual components, which themselves may be embedded into a web page for Internet access, or into an application for other types of access.

Example: An N-Tier Application for the pubs Database

As stated earlier, one reason n-tier applications are gaining popularity is their use within a web-based solution. To demonstrate this, consider the *pubs* database that Microsoft includes as a sample database with SQL Server. This small database contains several tables, including ones for AUTHORS and TITLES and their associative table, TITLEAUTHOR. In addition, the database also includes tables such as EMPLOYEES and STORES, but for now this demonstration centers on the tables that have to do with a book title: AUTHORS, PUBLISHERS, PUB_INFO, ROYSCHED, TITLEAUTHOR, and TITLES.

 If you are creating this example using another database, you can get a description of the tables used in the examples in this chapter from *http://premium.microsoft.com/msdn/library/sdkdoc/sql/tsqlref/src/append_b_8885.htm*. This URL provides a complete description of every table in *pubs*, including data type and keys. The examples use only the AUTHORS, PUBLISHERS, PUB_INFO, ROYSCHED, TITLE-AUTHOR, and TITLES tables. Unfortunately, you will also need to create test data for the tables, but you should need only a few rows in each table to run the examples.

Several of the tables are linked to each other with foreign key references, and each of the tables has a unique, clustered index. Figure 10-1 shows a diagram, created with SQL Server 7.0, that contains the tables of interest for the example in this chapter and their relationship to each other. The database also has three user-defined datatypes: *empid*, *id*, and *tid*, in addition to one view, basically a table join saved as a separate entity, which can then be queried against, and in some cases updated. The database also has several stored procedures.

In this chapter's example we are creating a small application that I call the Books application, which contains front-end web page forms to add, query, or delete an author, publisher, and book title. The application's data access is handled by several stored procedures created for the application that hide some of the database schema details. The stored procedures are called by the business components, which pull in the information from the front end and perform any additional business processing of the information.

The Books application is an MTS-based application, using web pages to update and retrieve information from a database.

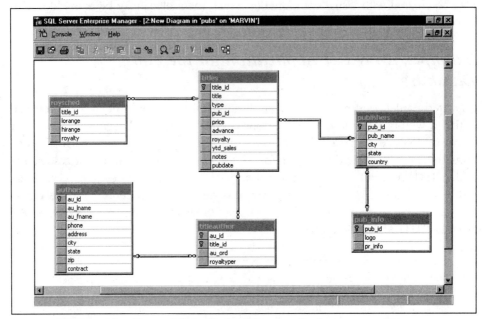

Figure 10-1. Example tables and their relationships to each other

Passing a Result Set to the ASP Page

Data can be accessed and processed and web page contents generated all within an ASP component. However, this is not always the best approach to take. Using ADO, script within an ASP page can also open a direct connection to a database and run a query, but this is not always the best approach to take, either. Sometimes, the best solution is a combination of the two, with an ASP component making the data request to the database but passing the result of the request directly to the client.

As an example, the Books application has a web page that contains three drop-down list boxes and three associated buttons. Each of the list boxes has a different set of data, with one containing a list of available authors, one a list of available publishers, and one a list of all titles in the database. The buttons next to the list boxes represent actions that can be taken, such as Add a title, Delete the selected title, or View the selected title.

The data for the list boxes must reflect what's currently in the database, so hard-coding items in the list box is not acceptable. The solution is to either directly query for this information from the database or use an ASP component to access the data. The Books application chooses to use an ASP component to get the information.

Once the need for an ASP component is decided, the next step is to determine whether one component will return the data for all three list boxes or whether separate components will be created. Considering that the list boxes really contain information about three different types of objects, the best choice is to create three new components: Title, Publisher, and Author, each created in its own DLL.

Each list box item has a value that contains the identifier of the specific object and a descriptive string shown to the web page reader. For authors, the descriptive text is a concatenated string with the author's first and last name, and the identifier is the author's associated identifier, au_id. For titles, the descriptive string is the title, and the identifier is the title_id field. For the publisher, the publisher name is the string, and the pub_id field is the identifier.

Another decision for ASP component development is the database views used to access the information. As an example, the view for the Authors table actually concatenates the first and last names:

```
CREATE VIEW [authors_VIEW]
AS SELECT [authors].[au_id],  [authors].[au_fname] + ' ' + [authors].
    [au_lname] 'author'
FROM [authors]
```

An advantage of a view is that it can be accessed exactly as a table is accessed—including updates for simple one-table views—and the query can be optimized to return a specific result set.

Another component design decision is how the records from each of the queries are added to the HTML form's <SELECT> element. Two approaches are common. The first is for the ASP component to use the ASP built-in Response object to write the option items directly to the page. However, this approach does have disadvantages. First, if the ASP component were to be used for a more traditional client-server application, something that is very possible with component development, the Response object would not be available and the output would be meaningless. Second, the same data could be presented in a web page using different formats, such as options in a list box for one page and cells in an HTML table in the next page. These disadvantages are two good reasons for choosing the second approach, which is to return the data as a result set to the ASP page.

Returning data as a result set is actually pretty easy. You simply create a component method with a return type of ADO.Recordset. At the end of the method, the function returns the results of the query executed by the component. Example 10-1 shows the complete source code for the Author object method, get-Authors.

Example 10-1. Returning a Recordset Object to the ASP Page

```
Public Function getAuthors() As ADODB.Recordset

   'Declare object variables for the database connection and recordset
   Dim cn As New Connection
   Dim conn As New Command
   Dim rs As New Recordset

   ' add error handler
   On Error GoTo HandleError

   ' connect to database
   cn.ConnectionString = "driver={SQL Server};
         server=MARVIN;uid=sa;pwd=;database=pubs"
   cn.Open

   conn.ActiveConnection = cn
   conn.CommandText = "select * from authors_VIEW"
   conn.CommandType = adCmdText

   Set rs = conn.Execute()

   Set getAuthors = rs

' print out any error message
HandleError:
    If Err.Number <> 0 Then
        Err.Raise Err.Number, Err.Source, Err.Description
    End If

End Function
```

The component method uses the ADO Connection, Command, and Recordset objects, but does not use any ASP-specific components. Error handling is turned on, but instead of writing out the error, it is passed on to the parent application, in this case the ASP page, using the Err object's Raise method. This approach avoids having to use any I/O operations directly within the component, such as writing out error information. Other than that, the method is very simple, with a database connection, a Command object used to perform the query, and the Recordset. At the end of the function, the Recordset object is returned to the client.

Within the ASP page, the ASP script to access the author data is also fairly simple. After the component is instantiated and its getAuthors method called, the Err object is checked to see if an error occurred. If not, the script loops through the returned result set and outputs each value as an <OPTION> tag's VALUE attribute and the descriptive string as the <OPTION> tag's displayed value, as shown in Example 10-2.

Example 10-2. Using a Returned Recordset Object to Populate a Form Selection Listbox

```
<%
  Dim authorsObject
  Set authorsObject = Server.CreateObject("Authors.Author")

  ' get data, add to selection
  Dim mydata

  ' handle error
  On Error Resume Next

  Set mydata = authorsObject.getAuthors

  If Err.Number <> 0 Then
      Response.Write ("<OPTION value='none'>Error: " & Err.Description)
      Err.Clear
  Else
      Do While mydata.EOF = False
        Response.Write ("<OPTION value='" + mydata(0))
        Response.Write ("'> " + mydata(1))
        mydata.MoveNext
      Loop
  End If
%>
```

The resulting page, shown in Figure 10-2, has the three list boxes and buttons for further actions. The ASP components and methods for Publisher and Title are created in a similar manner to Author.

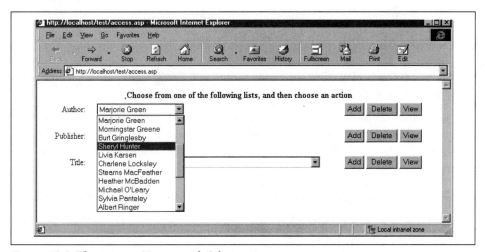

Figure 10-2. The Access ASP page with Select options

Since each list box item has both the descriptive text and an identifier, when an action request, such as adding or deleting a new author, publisher, or title, is submitted, the identifier is already present and can be sent with the request, as is demonstrated in the next section.

Creating a Presentation Layer "Helper" ASP Component

One of the biggest misconceptions about an n-tier system is that all the elements that handle the presentation are located within the presentation layer and on the client, while all of the ASP components specific to the process layer, the data layer, or both, are handled on the server. Well, this just isn't so. The separation between the layers can be more a matter of focus than actual physical location.

As an example of this, the Books application has a web page that contains information about a specific title. This includes information pulled directly from the TITLES table, but can also include 0 or more rows from the royalty schedule (ROYSCHED) table and 0 or more rows from the AUTHORS table, depending on the number of authors for the book. All of this information can't be extracted easily with one query, but all of the information can be returned with three queries contained within one stored procedure. There are three major ways to integrate the query and the presentation of its information:

- Each of the query result sets could be returned to the ASP page that calls the component that runs the query.

- The stored procedure could be invoked directly within the ASP page.

- The presentation can be included within the ASP component itself.

The Books application implements the latter approach for the book title, primarily to demonstrate the usefulness of this approach. Though it is a component residing on the server, it actually operates as part of the presentation layer because it is directly associated with the presentation style.

To create the example, create a stored procedure with information about the title, as shown in Example 10-3. Note that information for the title is actually pulled in from several different sources: TITLES, PUBLISHERS, ROYSCHED, AUTHORS, and TITLEAUTHOR.

Example 10-3. Returning Three Result Sets with One Procedure Call

```
CREATE PROCEDURE [sp_get_title_1]
   (@titleid    tid )


AS
BEGIN
```

Example 10-3. Returning Three Result Sets with One Procedure Call (continued)

```
SELECT title, type, pub_name, price, advance, notes, pubdate
FROM titles, publishers
WHERE publishers.pub_id = titles.pub_id AND titles.title_id = @titleid

SELECT lorange, hirange, royalty
FROM roysched where
title_id = @titleid

SELECT au_fname + ' ' + au_lname
FROM authors
WHERE au_id IN
(SELECT au_id from titleauthor
 WHERE title_id = @titleid)
END
```

Next, create an ASP component that calls the stored procedure and formats the output specifically for web page presentation. For the example, this means that the data is output and formatted using HTML tables.

The new component contains the standard code to create the ADO Connection and Command objects and to create instances of the ASP Request and Response objects. As this is covered elsewhere, I won't repeat it for this example. The component's unique code sets the properties for the Command object and executes the stored procedure shown in Example 10-3. Since the procedure only takes one parameter, only one Parameter object instance is appended to the Command object's Parameters collection, as Example 10-4 shows. A Recordset object is used to capture the data returned from the procedure call.

Example 10-4. Calling a Stored Procedure with One Parameter

```
' set parameters for stored procedure
  cmnd.Parameters.Append cmnd.CreateParameter("titleid", adVarChar, _
            adParamInput, 6, objRequest.Form.Item("titleid"))

  ' set stored procedure
  cmnd.CommandText = "sp_get_title_1"
  cmnd.CommandType = adCmdStoredProc

  ' execute sp
  Set rs = cmnd.Execute
```

The component's next action is to create an HTML table that contains the information from the first data set returned by the procedure. This information is accessed directly from the TITLES and PUBLISHERS tables, and contains most of the general information for a title. Example 10-5 contains the HTML table display output code.

Example 10-5. Writing out the First Record Set Returned from Stored Procedure Call

```
' Write out title info
    objResponse.Write ("<H1>Title</H1>")
    objResponse.Write "<TABLE width=90% align=center cols=2>"

    If Not (rs.EOF) Then
      objResponse.Write "<TR><TD colspan=2>"
      objResponse.Write rs("title")
      objResponse.Write "</TD></TR><TR><TD>"
      objResponse.Write rs("type")
      objResponse.Write "</TD><TD>"
      objResponse.Write rs("pub_name")
      objResponse.Write "</TD></TR><TR><TD>"
      objResponse.Write rs("price")
      objResponse.Write "</TD><TD>"
      objResponse.Write rs("pubdate")
      objResponse.Write "</TD></TR><TR><TD colspan=2>"
      objResponse.Write rs("notes")
    End If
    objResponse.Write "</TABLE>"
```

This code offers a fairly effective technique for outputting information to a web page, but the coding seems a bit laborious. To streamline the code, the functionality to output the next data results, which contain royalty schedule information from the ROYSCHED table, uses the WITH statement to avoid repeating the objResponse object reference. The code also uses the ADO Recordset object's NextRecordset method to get the next record set returned from the stored procedure call, as shown in Example 10-6.

Example 10-6. Writing out the Second Record Set Using the WITH Statement

```
' get next record set, write out royalty schedule
    Set rs = rs.NextRecordset

    objResponse.Write ("<H3>Royality Schedule</H3>")
    objResponse.Write "<TABLE width=90% align=center cols=3>"

    With objResponse
      Do While Not rs.EOF
          .Write "<TR><TD>"
          .Write rs("lorange")
          .Write "</TD><TD>"
          .Write rs("hirange")
          .Write "</TD><TD>"
          .Write rs("royalty")
          .Write "</TR>"
        rs.MoveNext
      Loop

      .Write "</TABLE>"
```

This last bit of code is an improvement over that shown in Example 10-5, but it still seems tedious having to access each individual recordset field to display its value. The final component code fragment, which creates the third HTML table for the Title, shows yet another approach to outputting the data formatted with an HTML table. Instead of specifically accessing each Field, the code uses a collection enumeration procedure to output all of the fields within the Recordset. As you can see in Example 10-7, this technique greatly simplifies outputting of all field values within a row in a recordset.

Example 10-7. Using Fields Collection and Enumeration to Output Record's Fields

```
' get authors
    Set rs = rs.NextRecordset

    .Write "<H3>Author's Name</H3>"
    .Write "<TABLE width=90% align=center>"

    Do While Not rs.EOF
     .Write "<TR>"
     For Each fld In rs.Fields
       .Write "<TD>"
       .Write fld.Value
       .Write "</TD>"
     Next fld
     .Write "</TR>"
     rs.MoveNext
    Loop
    .Write "</TABLE>"

  End With
```

As you can see from Example 10-7, using the **WITH** clause to suppress the repetition of the objResponse object in combination with using enumeration to output the Fields collection creates a much more simplified method to output all returned rows using a formatting code. Additionally, fields can be added and removed from the stored procedure call without having to change the formatting code.

The code shown in Example 10-6 can easily be captured as a separate, generic data display component. All you have to do is pass the result set to the component doing the formatting. With this approach, you can have components that format the data using an HTML table, another that formats it using Dynamic HTML (DHTML) and absolute positioning, and so on.

The result of using the component described in this section with one of the titles in the *pubs* database is similar to that shown in Figure 10-3.

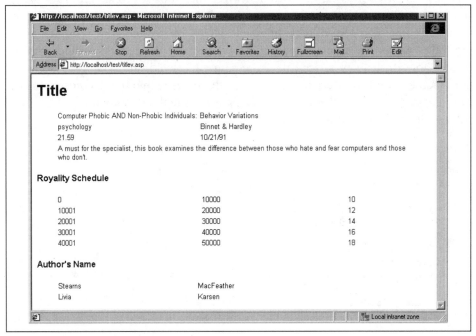

Figure 10-3. Title data formatted as three separate HTML tables

Viewing title information is all well and good, but the data has to be entered into the database first; the ASP component to handle this is discussed next.

Updating Multiple Tables Within One ASP Component

Every system that relies on data has different sets of rules associated with that data. Some rules, referred to as *referential integrity rules*, help maintain the integrity of the data. For example, for every TITLES and AUTHORS association, there is an entry within the TITLEAUTHOR table. This is enforced in the database and is maintained by not allowing an entry from TITLES or AUTHORS to be deleted without first deleting the associated TITLEAUTHOR entry.

Other rules, though, relate to how the business operates and how it manipulates data. For example, a rule driven by a business-processing need is that an entry in the ROYSCHED table is equivalent to the base royalty percentage created within the TITLES table. An additional rule is that this value must be within a standard range of 0 to 10,000 dollars. There is no database rule to enforce this business process, though one could be created. Instead of enforcing this business rule within the database, the ASP component that handles creating a new title is extended to also add an entry for ROYSCHED.

To implement the Books application business rule, create two stored procedures to handle adding both the TITLES as well as the ROYSCHED records; these are shown in Example 10-8.

Example 10-8. Inserting New Rows into TITLES and ROYSCHED

```
CREATE PROCEDURE [sp_insert_roysched_1]
    (@title_id_1  tid,
     @lorange_2   int,
     @hirange_3   int,
     @royalty_4   int)

AS INSERT INTO [pubs].[dbo].[roysched]
    ( [title_id],
     [lorange],
     [hirange],
     [royalty])

VALUES
    ( @title_id_1,
     @lorange_2,
     @hirange_3,
     @royalty_4)
CREATE PROCEDURE [sp_insert_titles_1]
    (@title_id_1  tid,
     @title_2     varchar(80),
     @type_3      char(12),
     @pub_id_4    char(4),
     @price_5     money,
     @advance_6   money,
     @royalty_7   int,
     @ytd_sales_8         int,
     @notes_9     varchar(200),
     @pubdate_10  datetime)

AS INSERT INTO [pubs].[dbo].[titles]
    ( [title_id],
     [title],
     [type],
     [pub_id],
     [price],
     [advance],
     [royalty],
     [ytd_sales],
     [notes],
     [pubdate])

VALUES
    ( @title_id_1,
     @title_2,
```

Example 10-8. Inserting New Rows into TITLES and ROYSCHED (continued)

```
@type_3,
@pub_id_4,
@price_5,
@advance_6,
@royalty_7,
@ytd_sales_8,
@notes_9,
@pubdate_10)
```

Both stored procedures are straightforward, taking input values as parameters. The code to call both stored procedures is also fairly straightforward, as shown in Example 10-9. Note that this code uses two command objects, one for each stored procedure call, and that the Parameter objects are created and stored in the Parameters collection, rather than as distinct objects.

Example 10-9. ASP Component Method to Add a New Title

```
Public Sub addNewTitle()
   'Declare object variables for the database connection and recordset
   Dim cn As New Connection
   Dim cmnd As New Command
   Dim cmnd2 As New Command

   ' create ASP Response object
   Dim objContext As ObjectContext
   Dim objRequest As Request

   Set objContext = GetObjectContext()

   ' create ASP objects
   Set objRequest = objContext.Item("Request")

   On Error GoTo HandleError

   ' connect to database
   cn.ConnectionString = "driver={SQL Server};" & _
                      server=MARVIN;uid=sa;pwd=;database=pubs"
   cn.Open

   ' set connection
   cmnd.ActiveConnection = cn
   cmnd2.ActiveConnection = cn


   ' set parameters for stored procedure
   cmnd.Parameters.Append cmnd.CreateParameter("title_id", adVarChar, _
    adParamInput, 6, objRequest.Form.Item("id"))

   cmnd.Parameters.Append cmnd.CreateParameter("title", adVarChar, _
       adParamInput, 80, objRequest.Form.Item("title"))

   cmnd.Parameters.Append cmnd.CreateParameter("type", adChar, _
```

Example 10-9. ASP Component Method to Add a New Title (continued)

```
      adParamInput, 12, objRequest.Form.Item("booktype"))

  cmnd.Parameters.Append cmnd.CreateParameter("pub_id", adChar, _
    adParamInput, 4, objRequest.Form.Item("publisher"))

  cmnd.Parameters.Append cmnd.CreateParameter("price", adCurrency, _
    adParamInput, 8, objRequest.Form.Item("price"))

  cmnd.Parameters.Append cmnd.CreateParameter("advance", adCurrency, _
    adParamInput, 8, objRequest.Form.Item("advance"))

  cmnd.Parameters.Append cmnd.CreateParameter("royalty", adInteger, _
    adParamInput, 4, objRequest.Form.Item("royalty"))

  cmnd.Parameters.Append cmnd.CreateParameter("ytd", adInteger, _
   adParamInput, 4, objRequest.Form.Item("ytd"))

  cmnd.Parameters.Append cmnd.CreateParameter("notes", adVarChar, _
   adParamInput, 200, objRequest.Form.Item("notes"))

  cmnd.Parameters.Append cmnd.CreateParameter("pubdate", adDBTimeStamp, _
   adParamInput, 8, objRequest.Form.Item("pubdate"))


  ' set stored procedure
  cmnd.CommandText = "sp_insert_titles_1"
  cmnd.CommandType = adCmdStoredProc

  ' execute sp
  cmnd.Execute

  ' add the royalty item, using same transaction
  ' set parameters for stored procedure
  cmnd2.Parameters.Append cmnd2.CreateParameter("title_id", adVarChar, _
   adParamInput, 6, objRequest.Form.Item("id"))

  cmnd2.Parameters.Append cmnd2.CreateParameter("lorange", adInteger, _
   adParamInput, , 0)

  cmnd2.Parameters.Append cmnd2.CreateParameter("type", adInteger, _
   adParamInput, , 10000)

  cmnd2.Parameters.Append cmnd2.CreateParameter("pub_id", adInteger, _
   adParamInput, , objRequest.Form.Item("royalty"))

  ' set stored procedure
  cmnd2.CommandText = "sp_insert_roysched_1"
  cmnd2.CommandType = adCmdStoredProc

  ' start transaction
  cmnd2.Execute
```

Example 10-9. ASP Component Method to Add a New Title (continued)

```
    objContext.SetComplete
HandleError:
    If Err.Number <> 0 Then
        objContext.SetAbort
        Err.Raise Err.Number, Err.Source, Err.Description
    End If

End Sub
```

Notice also from Example 10-9 that the MTS ObjectContent object is used to complete the transaction. Based on this, and using the SetComplete method call, both inserts to the database are committed at the same time. In addition, if an error had occurred within the component, both transactions would have been rolled back with the use of SetAbort in the error-handling code. The use of SetAbort and SetComplete also marks the component as finished with processing and indicates that the component is ready to be unloaded from memory.

If the component were not an MTS component, the Connection object methods BeginTrans, Commit, and Rollback would need to be used to ensure that both inserts either succeed fully or that both are rolled back.

 Instead of calling both stored procedures within one component, each stored procedure could be contained within a separate component method, and one component could call the other, or the ASP page could call both.

The data is gathered using a standard HTML form, as shown in Figure 10-4. Notice that this page has a drop-down list box that contains all the publishers in the database. This information is pulled in using the Publishers component method getPublishers. The book type information is also pulled in using a Titles component, getTypes.

Once the title is successfully added, another page opens that allows the user to add more royalty schedule information or associate the title with the author. Each of these is implemented as a separate form page, and each allows the user to add one royalty schedule item or one author association at a time. The Title identifier is added as a hidden field to both of these forms so that this value is also submitted along with the new information. Neither of these forms or associated ASP components demonstrate new technology, so they aren't repeated here.

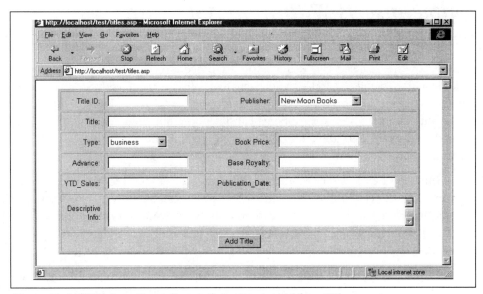

Figure 10-4. HTML form that collects information to add for a Title

 A hidden field is an HTML form element that can be used to contain information but is not visually shown to the web page reader. It is frequently used to pass information such as customer identifier from one web page to the next within a business application.

The Publisher and Author view pages are identical to the Title pages, and the components are very similar. For the Author, all associated titles are also displayed. For the Publisher, all associated titles are displayed, as well as information contained within the PUB_INFO table.

Using a stored procedure to handle inserts is a feasible technique to hide data implementation details from the ASP business process components. However, one of the problems with this technique, as can be seen in Example 10-8, is that stored procedure calls—in fact, any parameterized database call—require a great deal of work to define the parameters passed with the call. Another approach—especially with simple table inserts—that still hides the data implementation details is to create a layer of ASP data implementation components that use techniques such as the AddNew method with an updateable Recordset object. This technique is demonstrated next.

Simple Inserts Within an ASP Data Component Layer

As stated in the last section, using a stored procedure can hide the database's implementation details. Another approach that can be used with stored procedures, or in place of stored procedures, is to create a separate layer of ASP data access components. These components can include embedded SQL, which is SQL embedded directly into the component methods, or the components can use stored procedures, or both.

The advantage of creating a separate data access layer is that recordset manipulation can occur directly within the component, which can simplify development. In addition, the data component layer can actually be moved to a different machine from the IIS installation, and MTS can be used to handle cross-machine transaction processing.

For the Books application, inserting a new entry into the Authors table uses an ASP data access component and adds a row directly with the Recordset object. The code for the method is added to the Authors component, and, as you can see in Example 10-10, makes use of the Recordset object's Fields collection.

Example 10-10. Adding an Author

```
Public Sub addAuthor()

    'Declare object variables for the database connection and recordset
    Dim cn As New Connection
    Dim rs As New Recordset

    ' get object context
    Dim objContext As ObjectContext
    Dim objRequest As Request
    Dim objResponse As Response

    Set objContext = GetObjectContext()
    Set objRequest = objContext("Request")
    Set objResponse = objContext("Response")

    ' add error handler
    On Error GoTo HandleError

     ' connect to database
    cn.ConnectionString = "driver={SQL Server};server=MARVIN;" & _
                          "uid=sa;pwd=;database=pubs"
    cn.Open

    ' setup record set - authors table
    Set rs = New ADODB.Recordset
```

Example 10-10. Adding an Author (continued)

```
    rs.Open "authors", cn, adOpenKeyset, adLockOptimistic

    ' access and set values
    rs.AddNew
    Dim fld As Field
    For Each fld In rs.Fields
        fld.Value = objRequest.Form.Item(fld.Name)
    Next fld

    rs.Update

    objContext.SetComplete

HandleError:
    If Err.Number <> 0 Then
        objContext.SetAbort
        Err.Raise Err.Number, Err.Source, Err.Description
    End If

End Sub
```

The Recordset.Update method updates the database with the new record. If data validation were added to this component and one of the values was inaccurate, the CancelUpdate method would be used to cancel the update process and discard either the updated values or the new record. However, most data entry validation should occur within the web page itself to avoid unnecessary traffic over the network. Database or business processing validation should be the only validation occurring within the ASP components.

The MTS SetComplete method marks the component as finishing successfully, and indicates that the transaction is ready to be committed. If an error had occurred with the update, the MTS SetAbort method would still mark the method as finished, but would indicate that the transaction should not be committed.

The Recordset object's LockType and CursorType properties are set to reflect that the record is updateable. The **adLockPessimistic** LockType indicates that the record is not to be locked until the Update occurs. The **adOpenKeyset** cursor type exposes others changes to the database while the activity is happening within this component, except for deletions.

To avoid having to repeat the field names for every field in the row, the code in Example 10-10 uses enumeration and the Fields collection to pull in the like-named field from the Authors form, shown in Figure 10-5. A new table field could actually be added and only the form and the database would need to be altered. Or, if a new field were added and the value could be null, or would be set with a database trigger, neither the web page form nor the code would need changing, and the value would not be sent with the rest of the record.

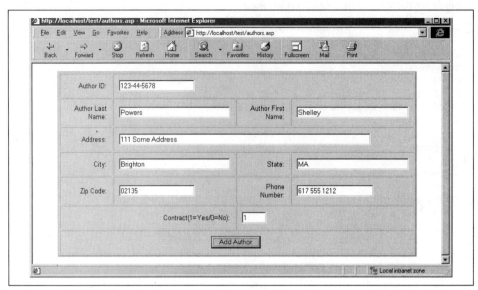

Figure 10-5. HTML form that collects information to add an Author

Using direct inserts into a table from an ASP component is quick and efficient, but should only be used with simple table inserts, where there are no constraints on the table insertion.

Any database system that adds data usually has facilities to delete the data. If there are constraints on adding data, there are usually even more covering data deletion, as shown in the next section.

Deleting Rows and Foreign Key Constraints

The stored procedures for row deletion are a bit more complex than those for insertion. First of all, there is a referential constraint placed on both TITLES and AUTHORS that does not allow rows from these tables to be deleted if there is a matching row in TITLEAUTHOR. This prevents the rows in TITLEAUTHOR from being *orphaned*—rows in a dependent table that no longer have matching rows in the parent tables. Trying to delete the rows in AUTHORS or TITLES will trigger an error with text similar to:

```
DELETE statement conflicted with COLUMN REFERENCE constraint 'FK__titleauth__
au_id__1312E04B'. The conflict occurred in database 'pubs', table
'titleauthor', column 'au_id' error '800a0cae'
```

To prevent this type of error, the delete stored procedures for both authors and titles first delete any associated rows within TITLEAUTHOR, as shown in Example 10-11, before continuing to delete the row in the parent table.

Example 10-11. Stored Procedures to Delete an Author or Title

```
CREATE   PROCEDURE [sp_delete_authors_1]
   (@au_id_1    id)

AS
BEGIN
DELETE [pubs].[dbo].[titleauthor]

WHERE
   ( [au_id]    = @au_id_1)

DELETE [pubs].[dbo].[authors]

WHERE
   ( [au_id]    = @au_id_1)
END

CREATE   PROCEDURE [sp_delete_titles_1]
   (@title_id_1    tid)

AS
BEGIN
DELETE [pubs].[dbo].[titleauthor]

WHERE
   ( [title_id]    = @title_id_1)

DELETE [pubs].[dbo].[titles]

WHERE
   ( [title_id]    = @title_id_1)
END
```

Another approach that could have been taken to handle the constraint between TITLEAUTHOR and TITLES and AUTHORS is for the ASP business process component to delete the associative table row first, and then delete the master record rows. This is the approach taken with TITLES; the title is added with one ASP component method and the association is added with a second method that can be invoked at a different time.

The reason the example application uses a stored procedure to perform both deletions at the same time, when the inserts are kept separate, has to do with the nature of the business. Books has a business rule that basically states that an author can be added to the *pubs* database before any book is published. The reason for this is that the Books application must maintain information about the author, such as author contact information, before any book is published. It is only later, after negotiation, that the proposed title for a book is agreed upon. Even then, the book title is not added to the database until after it is published (though in real life information about the book is usually maintained while the book is being written). Within the *pubs* database, a required field for titles is the publication date timestamp. In addition, a second author can be added for the same book at a later time, requiring yet another row within the author table for an existing book title. For these reasons, the example application requires the ability to add an author, a title, and an association between an author and a title at separate times.

When deleting an author or a title, however, the business has a different set of rules. First of all, if an author is removed from the database, any association between that author and a title must also be removed. This does not mean that the title itself is being removed, since another author or authors may also still be associated with the book. Alternatively, a title can be removed from the database, but the title's author remains with other titles, and only the association between the title and the author is removed with the title.

The method to delete the title is added to the *Titles* component, and isn't very big. Example 10-12 contains the complete example, which again takes advantage of the fact that the component is an MTS as well as ASP component and uses the ObjectContext method SetComplete to commit the database deletion.

Example 10-12. ASP Component Method That Calls a Delete Stored Procedure

```
Public Sub deleteTitle()

    'Declare object variables for the database connection and recordset
    Dim cn As New Connection
    Dim cmnd As New Command
    Dim objRequest As Request
    Dim objResponse As Response

    Set objContext = GetObjectContext()

    ' create ASP objects
    Set objRequest = objContext.Item("Request")

    On Error GoTo HandleError

    ' connect to database
    cn.ConnectionString = "driver={SQL Server};" & _
            server=MARVIN;uid=sa;pwd=;database=pubs"
    cn.Open

    ' set connection
    cmnd.ActiveConnection = cn

    ' set parameters for stored procedure
```

Example 10-12. ASP Component Method That Calls a Delete Stored Procedure (continued)

```
cmnd.Parameters.Append cmnd.CreateParameter("title_id_1", _
adVarChar, adParamInput, 6, objRequest.Form.Item("titleid"))

' set stored procedure
cmnd.CommandText = "sp_delete_titles_1"
cmnd.CommandType = adCmdStoredProc

' execute sp
Set rs = cmnd.Execute

    objContext.SetComplete
HandleError:
    If Err.Number <> 0 Then
        objContext.SetAbort
        Err.Raise Err.Number, Err.Source, Err.Description
    End If

End Sub
```

Unlike the Title delete stored procedure, the stored procedure to delete the publisher information deletes the associated pub_info first. This maintains the child-parent dependency between publisher and pub_info. In addition, since there is a foreign key reference to the publisher ID within the TITLES table, another stored procedure is created that updates the pub_id value within titles. If the publisher is deleted from the database, this procedure is called with the value of **NULL** in order to remove the reference to the publisher. If the publisher changes, the identifier for the new publisher is passed to the stored procedure. These two stored procedures are shown in Example 10-13.

Example 10-13. Delete and Update Stored Procedures for Publishers

```
CREATE  PROCEDURE [sp_delete_publishers_1]
    (@pub_id_1    char(4))

AS
BEGIN
DELETE [pubs].[dbo].[pub_info]
WHERE
    ( [pub_id]    = @pub_id_1)

DELETE [pubs].[dbo].[publishers]

WHERE
    ( [pub_id]    = @pub_id_1)
END

CREATE PROCEDURE [sp_update_titles_1]
    (@pub_id_1    char(4),
    @pub_id_2    char(4))
```

Example 10-13. Delete and Update Stored Procedures for Publishers (continued)

```
AS UPDATE [pubs].[dbo].[titles]

SET  [pub_id]    = @pub_id_2

WHERE
   ( [pub_id]    = @pub_id_1)
```

The ASP component to delete an author is virtually identical to that for deleting the title. The ASP component method to delete the publisher is also identical to that for a title, except that the publisher delete method also calls the title update stored procedure to set the publisher reference to NULL.

Database Updates with ASP Components and ADO

Database activity is sometimes referred to by an acronym of CRUD. This stands for Create, Read, Update, and Delete. So far in this chapter, I have covered Create, Read, and Delete. It's time to finish CRUD by discussing Updates.

Updates can occur via two different techniques. The first method is to delete the existing record and insert a new record with the updated information. This is a fairly simple method to implement and is workable unless—and this is important—an audit trail for the information must be maintained. If a record is deleted and a new one inserted, activity for the item being updated that occurred prior to the new row replacing the old is disconnected from the new row. This means there is no association between information for the new row and that for the old row. In addition, there can be physical database reasons that have to do with storage optimizations that make frequent deletions and insertions unfavorable.

Should you use insert and delete instead of updates for database changes? Your database administrator and database system provider can provide information about which approach is best to use with your database system or configuration.

The second method, which involves replacing the information in individual fields of the existing record, has its own unique challenges. First of all, the original record must be retrieved, and a lock should be maintained on the record until it is released or an update occurs. If the data is to be displayed first to allow the user to review existing information, then an effort should be made to maintain a connection between the record set returned for display and the one used for the update. However, the retrieval and the update are likely to occur in two different

ASP components, and within two different ASP pages. This is where the ASP built-in Session object can come in handy.

For example, the web page reader can retrieve a record for an author specifically to make an update. To support this, a new method called getSpecificAuthor is created in the Authors component. This method returns a recordset to the web page with the author information, as shown in Example 10-14. In addition, though, the component also adds the recordset to the Session object. This maintains a reference to the Recordset object in the Session object's Contents collection.

Example 10-14. Accessing an ADO Recordset

```
Public Function getSpecificAuthor() As Recordset

   'Declare object variables for the database connection and recordset
   Dim cn As New Connection
   Dim rsAuthors As Recordset

   ' get object context
   Dim objContext As ObjectContext
   Dim objRequest As Request
   Dim objSession As Session

   Set objContext = GetObjectContext()
   Set objRequest = objContext("Request")
   Set objSession = objContext("Session")

   ' add error handler
   On Error GoTo HandleError

     ' connect to database
   cn.ConnectionString = "driver={SQL Server};" & _
       server=MARVIN;uid=sa;pwd=;database=pubs"
   cn.Open

   ' setup record set - authors table
   Set rsAuthors = New ADODB.Recordset


   Dim strCommand As String
   strCommand = "select * from authors where au_id = '"
   strCommand = strCommand & objRequest.Form("authors") & "'"

   rsAuthors.ActiveConnection = cn
   rsAuthors.CursorType = adOpenKeyset
   rsAuthors.LockType = adLockPessimistic

   rsAuthors.Open strCommand

   Set objSession.Contents("objauthor") = rsAuthors

   Set getSpecificAuthor = rsAuthors
```

Example 10-14. Accessing an ADO Recordset (continued)

```
HandleError:
    If Err.Number <> 0 Then
        objContext.SetAbort
        Err.Raise Err.Number, Err.Source, Err.Description
    End If

End Function
```

The recordset uses embedded SQL to retrieve the record and attaches the query parameter *au_id* to the end of the query. The LockType for the record is also set to **adPessimisticLock**, the safest technique to ensure a successful update on the record by locking the record directly with the query and not allowing any other changes to occur until the lock is released.

The Recordset object then supplies values for form input fields by using VBScript to write the values out to the form, as shown in the following block of code, which displays the author ID and last name:

```
<%
' get existing values
  Dim authorsObject
  Set authorsObject = Server.CreateObject("Authors.Author")

  ' get data, add to selection
  Dim mydata

  ' handle error
  On Error Resume Next
  Set mydata = authorsObject.getSpecificAuthor

... ' other work happens

<td colspan=3 align=left><input type="text" size=20 name="au_id"
value = '<% = mydata("au_id") %>'>
</td></tr>
<tr>
<td align=right>Author Last Name:</td>
<td><input type="text" size=30 name="au_lname"
value = '<% = mydata("au_lname") %>'>
```

The form is enclosed within an HTML table for formatting. The code fragment:

```
"<% = mydata("au_lname") %>
```

is equivalent to using the following:

```
<%
Response.Write(mydata("au_lname")
%>
```

Figure 10-6 shows the form after the author Stearns MacFeather has been accessed from the *pubs* database. Notice that the BIT data type value for the contract field is set to **True** when a bit value of 1 is used, and to **False** for a bit value of 0. Maintaining the BIT field will actually require a little extra effort when the update occurs, as shown next.

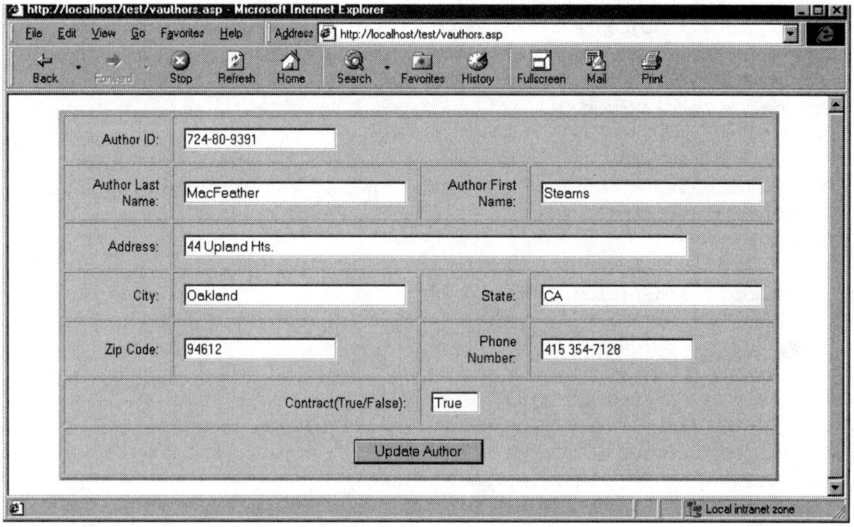

Figure 10-6. Information retrieved about a specific author

Once the web page reader has changed one or more of the fields, clicking on the Update Author button calls another ASP page, which invokes another method on the Authors component, the updateAuthor method.

The updateAuthor method accesses the existing Recordset object stored as a Session object, then checks existing field values against those returned in the Request object's Form collection to see if there are any differences. In order to perform a successful comparison operation with the contract field, the last field in the AUTHORS recordset, the Field object's value property is converted to a string using the Visual Basic *CStr* function, as shown in Example 10-15.

Example 10-15. Update Author ASP Method

```
Public Sub updateAuthor()

    'Declare object variables for the database connection and recordset
    Dim cn As New Connection
    Dim rsAuthors As Recordset

    ' get object context
    Dim objContext As ObjectContext
```

Example 10-15. Update Author ASP Method (continued)

```
Dim objRequest As Request
Dim objSession As Session
Dim objResponse As Response

Set objContext = GetObjectContext()
Set objRequest = objContext("Request")
Set objSession = objContext("Session")
Set objResponse = objContext("Response")

' add error handler
On Error GoTo HandleError

  ' connect to database
cn.ConnectionString = "driver={SQL Server};server=MARVIN;uid=sa;" & _
    "pwd=;database=pubs"
cn.Open

Set rsAuthors = objSession.Contents("objauthor")

' access and set values
Dim fld As Field
For Each fld In rsAuthors.Fields
  If CStr(fld.Value) <> objRequest.Form.Item(fld.Name) Then
    objResponse.Write (fld.Value & " ")
    fld.Value = objRequest.Form.Item(fld.Name)
    objResponse.Write (objRequest.Form.Item(fld.Name) & "<p>")
  End If
Next fld

rsAuthors.Update

Set objSession("objauthor") = Nothing

objContext.SetComplete

HandleError:
  If Err.Number <> 0 Then
    rsAuthors.CancelUpdate
  Set objSession("objauthor") = Nothing
    objContext.SetAbort
    Err.Raise Err.Number, Err.Source, Err.Description
  End If

End Sub
```

Notice that the Session object is set to Nothing whether the record is successfully
updated or not. Setting the object to Nothing releases the Session object's reference count on the Recordset object, allowing it and its resources to be freed from
memory.

The approach of storing the Recordset object within the Session object can also be used for updating multiple rows, and using the UpdateBatch method to make several updates at once. Batch updating can be used when adding, deleting, and updating several rows all based on the same selection criteria, and all through the same Recordset object. However, be forewarned that maintaining locks on several rows for an extended period of time could lead to problems in a multi-user environment. Your best bet is to ensure that record set retrievals are very specific, lessening the possibility of another person wanting to update the same records at the same time. Additionally, limit the length of time a lock remains on a record whenever possible.

 Not covered in this chapter was the use of Remote Data Service to maintain links between a data source embedded within a web page, and associated business and data layers. However, this requires that the web page include the RDS.DataControl, which is specific to Internet Explorer. This book is based on the premise that any browser capable of handling HTML tables and forms can be used as the client for the examples. Because of this, RDS is not covered.

Further Reading

For additional reading about the topics covered in this chapter, check out the following:

- For a description of the PUBS database tables, see *http://premium.microsoft. com/msdn/library/sdkdoc/sql/tsqlref/src/append_b_8885.htm.*

- Microsoft has provided a terrific web site covering all of the company's data access techniques, including ADO, at *http://www.microsoft.com/data/.*

- For a fairly extensive example of multitier development, see the Duwamish Book sample at *http://www.microsoft.com/data/duwamish.htm.*

III

Developing ASP Components with Visual C++

11

Creating a Simple C++ ASP Component

C++ opens the door for efficiency tweaks and more finite control over a component, but at the cost of greater complexity in writing and maintaining the component. For instance, a tool such as Visual Basic allows you to create a component that supports apartment threading or single threading, but C++ allows you to specify the both-threaded model, and even to include access to the free-threaded marshaler to improve performance. However, Visual Basic can cut the time to develop the component in half, since virtually all of the COM implementation details are hidden. With Visual C++, the use of COM is much more exposed. Java, another language used for building ASP components, is simpler to code with, particularly for those with no experience using either C++ or Java. However, Java also relies on wrapper code when accessing other COM-based components and requires the intervention of the Java Virtual Machine, both of which can degrade performance. Coding with C++ does not require the use of wrappers, which means it will perform better overall than Java.

That isn't to say that C++ for ASP development has to be difficult. First, if you are used to coding in C++, particularly Visual C++, the use of VC++ requires very little in the way of a learning curve. In addition, Microsoft also provides a template library known as the Active Template Library (ATL), to help with most of the implementation details. In fact, most ASP components written in C++ for IIS 3.0 and up use the ATL to create the components. This library contains templates that handle much of the default processing necessary for maintaining an ASP component, or for that matter any COM-based component. To make the use of ATL even more attractive there are other advantages to using it, such as the light footprint it adds to any component created using it, detailed in the first section of this chapter.

When using ATL to create the component, Microsoft has provided two ATL wizards to assist in the process. The first is the ATL AppWizard, which generates the project files to maintain the ASP component DLL or EXE, whichever is created. The second is the ATL Object Wizard, used to add an object class (component) and associated interface to the project.

When a project is created, an IDL file is generated, which defines the component's interfaces. Adding a method to the interface generates an entry into the IDL file, as well as creating skeleton C++ code for the method in the C++ component file. This chapter demonstrates all of this, in addition to providing examples of error handling with C++.

ATL or MFC

Creating COM-based ASP components can be accomplished using any C++ library that exposes the necessary COM interfaces such as **IUnknown** and **IDispatch**. Microsoft has provided a couple of different libraries in support of creating COM objects: the Microsoft Foundation Classes (MFC) and the Active Template Library (ATL).

The MFC classes have been around for some time and are used for most Visual C++ application building, component-based or otherwise. The classes provide C++ wrappers for most common data types, and C++ classes to handle many aspects of an application. However, there are reasons not to use MFC to create ASP components.

MFC provides a complete framework, which really is essential when building a stand-alone application. The framework includes document and view objects and an associated frame to hold all of the application sections together. The document objects provide support for the application data, and the view objects are used to provide one or more views/accesses to the application data.

ATL, on the other hand, does not provide a complete framework; instead it provides a lightweight template-based architecture, designed specifically to use for creating COM objects. ATL provides access to all COM implementation objects but little else. This results in the creation of small components that aren't carrying around support for a framework neither used nor needed. Small, optimized components also operate more efficiently as well as more quickly. The major disadvantage to ATL is that it doesn't provide COM transparency—that is, it doesn't hide the COM implementation—as much as the MFC classes do.

ATL is not a replacement for MFC. In fact, you can use both MFC and ATL for a project, particularly a project created as a DLL. Chapter 14, *Persistence with ASP Components Using ATL and MFC*, demonstrates using both to create ASP components that read from and write to files, serialize objects, and start new threads. It's not very difficult to use the two together. For instance, to add an ATL object to an MFC object within the Visual C++ IDE, choose Insert → ATL Object from the menu. Visual C++ then asks whether you want to support ATL within the MFC application. Choosing Yes enables you to add an ATL object and all ATL support templates to the MFC application. Conversely, when you create an ATL application, one of the options you can check is whether to add support for MFC.

ATL provides specific object types all based or dependent on COM, including MTS and ASP objects. Because of this, in addition to the other benefits such as small size and speed, most ASP components created using Visual C++ are created using the ATL project option, and the example described in the rest of the chapter is based on using ATL.

Using ATL AppWizard to Generate the Basic ASP Component Project

Visual C++ has several wizards to assist in building the basic framework of files and code for a certain type of object, and ATL has its own wizard, the ATL App-Wizard. The AppWizard generates the files necessary to provide the basic files for the ASP component, leaving us free to write code specific to the component itself. This section describes the steps involved in using the ATL AppWizard and provides a brief overview of the code and files it generates.

Using the ATL AppWizard to Generate the Project Files

The best way to demonstrate ATL is to create a simple C++ ASP Component; the steps necessary to create the basic component files are detailed in this section. The component is a Dynamic HTML generator that generates the JavaScript necessary to implement functions that will move a web page object based on whether the page is accessed via a Microsoft Internet Explorer browser or a Netscape Navigator browser.

To use ATL, select the ATL COM AppWizard project type when creating a new project. Choose the server type of Dynamic Link Library (DLL) in the second dialog page that opens, and don't check any of the options listed at the bottom of the dialog, as shown in Figure 11-1. When you click the Finish button, Visual C++ generates the project files.

Before proceeding further with the example, some explanation of the options shown in the ATL AppWizard dialog in Figure 11-1 is in order.

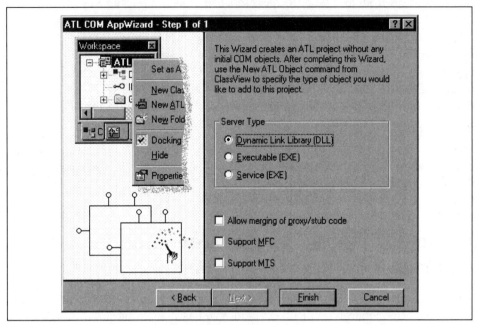

Figure 11-1. Selecting options with ATL AppWizard

Creating an ASP Component as a DLL, an EXE, or a Server

The first option listed in the ATL AppWizard dialog is whether to create the component as a DLL, an EXE, or a Service object. Components created as DLLs are known as in-process components, and components created as EXEs are known as out-of-process components. There are advantages and disadvantages to creating a component using one or the other of these approaches, and these are detailed in the section "Creating an In-Process or Out-Of-Process Component" in Chapter 7, *Creating a Simple Visual Basic ASP Component*. To recap that discussion, an ASP component created as a DLL runs in the same process as the client that invokes the component, and it shares the same address space depending on thread compatibility. An out-of-process ASP component runs as its own process with its own address space.

The advantage to the in-process component is that communication between the client and the component is much faster, primarily because the same stack is used to pass arguments between the client and server. Whenever a method of an object is invoked outside of the same address space for the component, the method's arguments have to be *marshaled* between the client invoking the method and the component. Marshaling is the process of pulling arguments from one address space stack, converting them in to a stream, and then converting them back into arguments on the stack in the component's address space. Threads and C++ components are discussed in greater detail in the section "ATL Object Wizard Properties Attributes Page" later in this chapter.

An advantage to out-of-process components is that the component runs in its own address space, isolated from the client. This tends to make for a more robust environment, where neither the component nor the client can cause too much damage to the other. In addition, if the component is being invoked remotely, it will be treated as an out-of-process component whether it is implemented as a separate executable or not. When a remote component is created as a DLL, a stub executable is generated which handles all marshaling for the component, and any performance advantage to being an in-process component is lost. The advantage, then, to an out-of-process component is that it can be developed to handle remote invocation more efficiently.

Another consideration when deciding what type of ASP component to create is that IIS supports in-process components by default, and you have to actually set an IIS metadata variable to support out-of-process components. This is detailed more fully in Chapter 2, *Setting Up and Maintaining the ASP Development Environment*. If your project also uses MTS for transaction and component management, you must use an in-process component; no other option is supported.

Back to the ATL AppWizard. I mentioned that the second dialog page also allows for a third type of component, a service component. A *service component* is one installed as an NT service, a server that runs in the background when NT starts. Since ASP components should be controlled from IIS (or from MTS, if the component is implemented as part of an MTS package), this third option of creating a Service EXE should not be chosen.

The Other ATL AppWizard Project Options

Other options listed in the dialog shown in Figure 11-1 are those for adding support for MFC and support for MTS, and whether to merge the proxy/stub code directly into the DLL. Support for MFC is not necessary for the simple ASP component created in this chapter, so the option is not checked.

As discussed in Chapter 5, *Components, Transactions, and the Microsoft Transaction Server*, and throughout this book, when a component is accessed across threads, across processes, or remotely, marshaling must occur to pass the method arguments from the client to the object. Marshaling is the process of pulling the arguments from the client stack, converting these arguments into a data stream using a proxy on the client side, and reconverting these arguments back into arguments on the stack via a stub on the server side. Normally when a component is being accessed remotely, you would not want to install the component's implementation DLL on the client, only a separate proxy-stub DLL used to access the remote component. The ATL AppWizard supports this by allowing you to choose whether to include the proxy/stub code in the same DLL as the implementation DLL. If the component is being accessed across threads or processes, such as a component created as a separate executable, you would want to include the proxy/stub code as part of the implementation DLL. If you plan to access the component remotely, you would not want to include the proxy/stub code within the DLL but instead would want to compile this code into a separate DLL to install on the client. As most ASP components are designed to run within the same machine as their client, and in fact are usually designed to run within the same address space of their client, proxy/stub code does not need to be added to the DLL.

The final checkbox option in the ATL AppWizard dialog determines whether to add support for the Microsoft Transaction Server (MTS). Beginning with IIS 4.0, ASP components can also be MTS components, and in fact the ASP built-in objects can now be accessed directly from the MTS ObjectContext object. Adding support for MTS to the project adds in an import to the MTS API and builds in support to launch the MTS runtime, *mtxex.dll*, when the project application is launched. At this time, the example ASP component is created without MTS support.

The files that are generated from the ATL AppWizard are discussed next.

The ATL AppWizard Generated Files

Several files are generated based on the options chosen when using the ATL AppWizard dialog. This section discusses the files that are generated when the simplest ASP component—one that is a DLL, does not include MFC or MTS support, and does not merge in the proxy/stub code—is created.

One of the advantages of using a tool such as Visual C++ to create the ASP component is that the tool generates much of the code to support the DLL, leaving us free to write the code specific to the component itself. As an example of this, the ATL AppWizard generates the C++ code to handle loading and unloading the DLL from memory.

To handle DLL loading/unloading, the DLL's initialization and termination code, which is contained in the DLLMain method, is generated for the component shown in Example 11-1. Since DLLMain serves as an entry point for the DLL when the component is started and is loaded into a process address space, the dwReason code is set to **DLL_PROCESS_ATTACH**, and the initialization code is run.

When the client frees the component, the **dwReason** code is set to **DLL_PROCESS_DETACH**, and the DLL termination code is run.

Example 11-1. The DLLMain Function

```
extern "C"
BOOL WINAPI DllMain(HINSTANCE hInstance, DWORD dwReason, LPVOID /*lpReserved*/)
{
    if (dwReason == DLL_PROCESS_ATTACH)
    {
        _Module.Init(ObjectMap, hInstance, &LIBID_SSPLib);
        DisableThreadLibraryCalls(hInstance);
    }
    else if (dwReason == DLL_PROCESS_DETACH)
        _Module.Term();
    return TRUE;    // ok
}
```

Other code generated by the AppWizard is the DLLCanUnloadNow method, to determine if the DLL can be removed from memory, the DLLGetClassObject method, which returns the class factory to create the object, DLLRegisterServer to register the server, and DLLUnregisterServer to remove the server from the registry.

In addition to generating the C++ code to maintain the DLL and the DEF file, which defines which functions are exported from the DLL, the AppWizard also generates the IDL—or Interface Definition Language—file. This file defines how other COM applications communicate with the component and serves as the placeholder for the component's GUID.

The C++ code to support the DLL is loaded into a file with the same name as the project and can be viewed from the File View tab. The IDL file is also assigned the same name as the project and is initially created with just a few lines of code. Example 11-2 shows the IDL code generated for the example project by VC++ version 6.0.

Example 11-2. IDL Code Generated by the ATL AppWizard

```
import "oaidl.idl";
import "ocidl.idl";

[
        uuid(92918FE8-F323-11D1-ABBC-204C4F4F5020),
        version(1.0),
        helpstring("dhtml2 1.0 Type Library")
]
library DHTML2Lib
{
        importlib("stdole32.tlb");
        importlib("stdole2.tlb");

};
```

First, the import section lists two imported IDL files that contain the interface definitions to handle several data structures, such as **SAFEARRAY**, as well as the **IUnknown** interface. You can actually open and view the contents of these files, but be careful not to make any changes. Following the imports is the interface attribute list. This list includes the UUID, which is the Universally Unique ID, the version number of the interface, and a help string used to describe the object. The latter can be viewed within a tool such as Visual Basic after attaching a direct reference to the object to a Visual Basic project.

Following the interface attribute list is a definition of the type library, including import statements (**importlib**) for two type libraries that have already been compiled. These two type libraries are standard OLE 2.0 type libraries.

In addition to the DEF, IDL, and DLL files, the ATL AppWizard also attaches standard C++ and header files, *StdAfx.cpp* and *StdAfx.h*, which are added by all Visual C++ wizards, and are used to create the precompiled header for the project, as well as the precompiled object file.

After reviewing the AppWizard generated code and files, the next step to creating an ASP component is to add a new ATL object to the project, detailed in the next section.

Adding an ATL Object

In addition to generating support code and files, the ATL AppWizard also adds an option to the Visual C++ Insert menu that is used to add a new ATL object. Clicking on this option opens a dialog that lists categories of objects on the left and types of objects associated with each category on the right. For ASP components, the category to use is Objects, and the type of object to choose is an ActiveX Server Component or an MS Transaction Server Component. For this chapter, the component being created is an ASP component only, so the ActiveX Server Component option is picked, as shown in Figure 11-2.

After clicking on the Next button, the Names tab of the ATL Object Wizard Properties dialog opens; it provides a place to enter the name of the component. The rest of the fields are automatically generated based on this name as it is being typed in, though any of the names can be altered manually. For our example, the component name is *cssp* and the generated names are not modified.

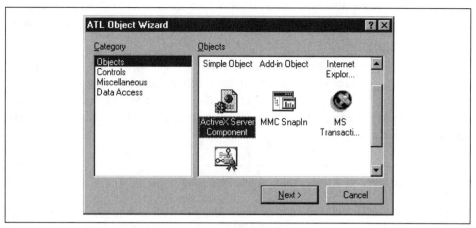

Figure 11-2. Creating a new ATL object as an ActiveX Server Component

After you type "cssp" into the Short Name field, Table 11-1 shows the values generated for the other fields in the dialog.

Table 11-1. Objects Generated for the Component

Element	Name
Class:	Ccssp
.H File:	*cssp.h*
.CPP File:	*cssp.cpp*
CoClass:	Cssp
Interface:	Icssp
Type:	cssp Class
Prog ID:	*cssp.cssp*

Note that the Prog ID field will contain the name used to access the component from within an ASP page or from another ASP component. Again, if you don't care for this ProgID, you can override the generated value and type in your own.

ATL Object Wizard Properties Attributes Page

Once you complete the Names tab, the next step is to click on the dialog's Attributes tab, which defines the component's attributes. These include the threading model used for the component, the interface, and the aggregation, in addition to options to support `ISupportErrorInfo`, `IConnectionPoints`, and the free-threaded marshaler.

The interface option should be set to Dual, which means the component supports late binding with the IDispatch interface, as well as design-time vtable binding. The other interface option—to provide a custom interface—is disabled.

The option to support the ISupportErrorInfo interface allows the component to communicate that it provides support for error reporting to applications using the component. This option should be checked. The support for connection points is necessary only if the component is providing outbound interface connections. This option should not be checked.

 Would you ever want to support connection points within an ASP component? You wouldn't for components accessed directly by an ASP page, but you could for components that access a database such as SQL Server, or that are accessed by other components. Using connection points, a client can then be notified of events that occur within the server.

The next section details the remaining options and the impact of choosing them.

ASP components and threading

Threading is discussed in more detail in Chapter 4, *ASP Components and Threads*, but since Visual C++ allows a more finite control of threading than either Visual Basic or Visual J++, it is worth taking the time to discuss this expanded functionality here.

First of all, you can use Visual C++ to create an ASP component that is single-, apartment-, both-, or free-threaded. Apartment threading is really single-threaded apartment threading, and the both- and free-threading options are treated as multiple-threaded apartment options from the perspective of COM.

You shouldn't select the single-threaded model since this action forces serialized access of the component, meaning that the component handles only one web page access request at a time. However, of the other approaches, apartment, both, or free, each has its own advantages and disadvantages.

In the apartment-threaded model, the component is created in an apartment on the thread that instantiates the component. This means that all calls to the component from that thread are direct and don't have to be marshaled. This approach is also inherently thread-safe, since all global data is isolated, and calls from other client threads are serialized to the thread that created the components. This ensures that all messages to the component are queued and processed one at a time. However, a downside to this approach is that if the component is created from a multithreaded apartment, discussed next, a new single-threaded apartment thread is created to house the component, and all calls between the client and the component must be marshaled.

For the free-threaded component, however, the opposite problem can occur. Applications have at most only one multiple-threaded apartment. Any free-threaded components would then be placed within this apartment. The free-threaded component is created in the multi-threaded apartment for the application, and any thread safety becomes the responsibility of the component developer, since calls to the component are no longer serialized. Additionally, if the client invoking the component is single-threaded, the two threading models are not compatible, and a multi-threaded apartment would need to be created just to house the component. Now, all calls from the client to the component would have to be marshaled, since communication between the two is cross-threaded when the component is created on a different thread from the application.

 In all this discussion, you might be wondering why we should be concerned about threads with ASP components. After all, they are only invoked from within ASP pages, right? Actually, an ASP component can be invoked directly from an ASP page, as well as remotely from another component or application. It is an ASP component primarily because it is part of an Active Server Page application in some way, though not directly called from an ASP page. Based on this, thread awareness is important.

One way to avoid the problems associated with a free-threaded or single-threaded apartment component is to define the ASP component as both-threaded. This means that the component is always created in the same thread of the client, regardless of which threading model the client uses, as long as the client and component live in the same host environment. When the client is STA, the component is created on the client's main STA thread. When the client is MTS, the component is created in the client's only MTA thread. In both cases, no marshaling is necessary, since the client and component share the same address space and the same stack for method parameters.

Aggregation and the free-threaded marshaler

If the component is multiple-threaded, which can occur when it is created as a free-threaded component or as a both-threaded component with a multi-threaded client, performance issues arise if the component is accessed by the same process but from different threads. In this case, the component's methods must be marshaled, and this becomes a performance hit. To compensate for this, aggregation and the free-threaded marshaler can be used.

Aggregation and a free-threaded marshaler are used to supply a direct pointer to an interface, rather than having to marshal calls back and forth between the component and the client. Aggregation is a containment implementation, in that one interface contains another. In order to synchronize the two, the outer object provides for specific implementation of the inner object's IUnknown interface, and then provides for delegation of all other interface methods to the outer object. With this, the client does not need to know that a method is not being handled directly by the object that is called.

With the Aggregation and Free Threaded Marshaler options, the free-threaded marshaler is aggregated with the server component, and enables all calls to the component to occur directly from a client contained within the same process but from a different thread rather than through a proxy/stub pair.

If a component is accessible only by one client and is implemented on one thread within the client process, the use of aggregation and the free-threaded marshaler is not necessary, and the options should not be checked.

Enough of threading issues, back to our test ASP component and the ATL Object Wizard dialogs.

The ASP Page

The ATL Object Wizard's ASP dialog tab page is included to provide backward support for IIS 3.x applications. As you will read in Chapter 12, *The C++ ASP Built-in Interfaces,* IIS 3.0 ASP applications are only allowed access to the built-in ASP objects from specific events: the OnStartPage and OnEndPage events. The objects are then available from an IScriptingContext interface. However, with IIS 4.0, the built-in objects can be available at any time, are not restricted to being accessed from specific events, and are accessed using the MTS ObjectContext object rather than IScriptingContext. As this chapter will not be referencing the built-in ASP objects for the example component, the OnStartPage/OnEndPage option is not checked.

Clicking the OK button generates the files and code to support the new ASP object.

Code Changes Based on Adding a New Object

The ATL Object Wizard creates a new class, Ccssp, and an associated interface, Icssp. Both can be seen from the Class View. In addition, the following new entry is made in the IDL file to define the interface for the new component:

```
[
    object,
    uuid(4DBD05F6-F3D5-11D1-ABBD-204C4F4F5020),
```

```
          dual,
          helpstring("Icssp Interface"),
          pointer_default(unique)
     ]
     interface Icssp : IDispatch
     {
     };
```

Note that one of the IDL attributes is **dual**, which declares that the interface supports both **IDispatch** and **vtable** interface access. Below the interface attributes, a forward declaration for the interface is listed, which shows that the interface implements the **IDispatch** base interface.

In addition to the change in the IDL file, the object map contained within the ATL AppWizard-generated C++ code now has the following new entry to support the new class:

```
BEGIN_OBJECT_MAP(ObjectMap)
OBJECT_ENTRY(CLSID_cssp, Ccssp)
END_OBJECT_MAP()
```

The entry takes the CLSID and the class name for the new interface. The object-mapping macro is used specifically within an ATL application to map between the function pointers to the class constructor and class factory, and the ATL object map. All objects to be registered must be included as entries within the object map. The registration process itself occurs when DLLRegisterServer, another generated method, is invoked.

Once the object has been created, methods can be added, as we will see in the next section.

Adding Methods to the Interface

After an ASP component is added to the project, methods and properties can be added to the component. You can add a new method most easily from the Class View by right-clicking on the interface (not on the class) just added, which opens the Add Method to Interface dialog shown in Figure 11-3. This approach to adding the method to the interface generates the skeleton C++ code for the method in the component class's C++ file, and the method's IDL is added to the IDL file. Adding code directly to the C++ class file does not automatically update the IDL file.

For the sample component, four methods are created:

MoveLeft
> Takes an object, an integer representing the browser type, and a value as parameters, and returns a DHTML string to implement the left movement based on browser type.

MoveTop

> Takes an object, an integer representing the browser type, and a value as parameters, and returns a DHTML string to implement the top movement based on browser type.

Hide

> Takes an object and an integer representing the browser type as parameters, and returns a DHTML string specific to the browser to hide the object.

Show

> Takes an object and an integer representing the browser type as parameters, and returns a DHTML browser-specific string to show the hidden object.

 Though I've indicated that each method returns a string containing browser-specific DHTML, in actuality each method's defined return type is HRESULT. All methods exposed through a dual interface implemented in C++ return this same HRESULT. However, the actual value returned to the client as the result of the function call is the string. The value of HRESULT is accessed through error handling, for example, by accessing the Err object from within a VBScript ASP block.

The first two methods take a string followed by two integers, all of them passed by value only. The second two methods take a string followed by one integer, again passed by value only.

Before these methods are implemented, it's a good idea to take a look at the C++ to IDL data types to see what can and cannot be used with the methods.

ATL Method Interface Data Types

There are several simple data types that are used when defining an interface method. The following is a list of these:

Boolean

> Used to set a value to True or False

Char

> Single character one byte (8 bits) in size

double

> A 64-bit floating point number

Float

> A 32-bit floating pointer number

Int

> For 32-bit environments, a 32-bit integer; for 16-bit, accompanies another keyword, such as small, a 16-bit number; short, an 8-bit number; and long, a 32-bit number. May be signed or not

int64

> A 64-bit integer

Long

> A 32-bit integer

Pointer

> Pointer to type

Short

> A 16-bit integer

Void

> Void

Earlier I mentioned that two IDL files are imported into the newly-generated IDL file for the project. One of these files contains the definitions for the standard interfaces, such as `IUnknown`. The other, *oaidl.idl*, actually contains the definitions for complex data types used in the interface methods. These complex data types are given in the following list:

BSTR

> A length-prefixed string; for C++, BSTR types are wrapped in a COM class, `CComBSTR`

Currency

> A structure; for C++, `Currency` types are wrapped in an OLE class, `COleCurrency`

HRESULT

> An integer

SAFEARRAY

> An array that includes an array element count

VARIANT

> Variant data types are used for any variable/parameter that is not defined as any other type; for C++, they are wrapped in the COM class `CComVariant`

SCODE

> The same as `HRESULT` in a 32-bit environment, or used to derive `HRESULT` in a 16-bit environment; a status code

IUnknown
>   Interface pointer to **IUnknown**

Idispatch
>   Interface pointer to **IDispatch**

 When this book was written, Microsoft did not specifically provide documentation of the IDL data types and their C++ counterparts. The list above has been derived from many sources. You will want to double-check these entries when creating your components.

The methods of all components based on a dual interface must return a data type of **HRESULT**. Because of this, when defining the method, there is no way to specify a return value, since it is generated automatically for you by the Add Method to Interface dialog.

The next section provides details about adding the first interface method, including the code within the class to support the interface.

Adding a Method to the Interface

As stated earlier, instead of adding code for a method directly to the C++ file, the method is defined for the interface. Visual C++, in turn, generates the skeleton C++ code, consisting of the function call, the opening and closing function brackets, and a default **HRESULT** return type of **S_OK**. This skeleton code is added to the interface's implementation class. The developer then manually adds the rest of the code necessary to implement the method.

To demonstrate the code generation and manual implementation process, the first method created for the DHTML component is MoveLeft, which takes as input parameters a string, an integer, another string, and then a return parameter of a pointer to a string. To create this method, click the right mouse button when the focus is on the **Icssp** interface in the Class View window, and select the "Add Method…" option from the context menu. This opens the Add Method to Interface dialog.

The dialog includes a drop-down list box that has been disabled and set by default to **HRESULT**. It also contains two edit fields, one for the method name and one for the parameters, and a disabled multiline text box that shows the current method definition. The name of the method is typed in the first box and the parameters are listed in the second, as shown in Figure 11-3.

As Figure 11-3 shows, there are three input parameters and one output return value. Add the parameters using the following syntax:

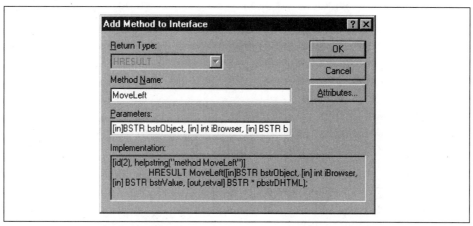

Figure 11-3. Adding a new method to the existing Icssp interface

```
[in]BSTR bstrObject, [in]int iBrowser, [in]BSTR bstrValue, [out,retval]BSTR *
pbstrDHTML
```

The use of the notation [in] is IDL-based and defines an input parameter. [out] is again an IDL-based notation that defines an output variable. The notation [out,retval] defines an output variable that will be returned as a function value through direct assignment in the client.

Clicking on the Attributes button in the Add Method dialog opens a second page containing attributes for the method. By default, the method is given an identifier, in this case a value of one (1), and a help string. The default help string is "method MoveLeft." In the example, this is changed to "method to generate DHTML to control left movement". The main reason to use a more descriptive help string is that this string is displayed from object browsers, such as that included within Visual Basic. Including a more descriptive string makes the component a little more usable.

There are other attributes that can be used with the method, but they aren't used with this ASP component. The documentation that comes with Visual C++ contains more details on these other attributes.

Closing the Add Method dialog and saving the changes generates the IDL for the method:

```
[id(1), helpstring("method to generate DHTML to control left movement")]
HRESULT MoveLeft([in] BSTR bstrObject, [in] int iBrowser, [in] BSTR
bstrValue,
  [out, retval] BSTR * pbstrDHTML);
```

The next task is to provide the rest of the code for this method.

Example 11-3 contains the complete code for MoveLeft. Note that basically all it does is check the browser type and create the appropriate DHTML string based on this type. The BSTR methods are used to build the DHTML string, which is then assigned to the return value.

Example 11-3. The MoveLeft Component Interface Method

```
STDMETHODIMP Ccssp::MoveLeft(BSTR bstrObject, int iBrowser, BSTR bstrValue, BSTR
*pbstrDHTML)
{

    // to work with header
    CComBSTR bstrHeader("");
    if (!bstrHeader)
            return E_OUTOFMEMORY;

    // if browser type of 1 - IE
    if (iBrowser == 1) {
            bstrHeader=bstrObject;
            bstrHeader+=".style.left=";
            bstrHeader+=bstrValue;
    }
    else { // Navigator
            bstrHeader = "document.";
            bstrHeader+=bstrObject;
            bstrHeader+=".left=";
            bstrHeader+=bstrValue;
    }

    // assign to return variable, set CComBSTR m_str to null
    *pbstrDHTML = bstrHeader.Detach();

    // return status code
    return S_OK;
}
```

The BSTR variable used to hold the DHTML string being created is tested to make sure there was enough memory to instantiate the object. The overloaded operator += is used to build the string, though the CComBSTR Append method would work equally well. The Detach method removes the CComBSTR property m_str from the working variable to the one being returned to the calling routine. This also sets the m_str property to null.

At the end, a status of S_OK is returned to show that no errors have occurred. This value is one of the standard, predefined HRESULT code values. Other standard return types, such as E_OUTOFMEMORY, are usually used to denote an error and are discussed more fully in the section titled "Error Handling" later in this chapter.

After the code for the method is added, the DLL is compiled. In the process of being compiled, the ASP component is also registered as a COM component, a process that occurs automatically based on flags and application settings generated by the ATL AppWizard. Once the DLL has been created, the component can then be accessed using HTML similar to that found in Example 11-4.

Example 11-4. Accessing and Testing the New Interface Method

```
<!DOCTYPE HTML PUBLIC "-//W3C//DTD HTML 4.0//EN">
<HTML>
<HEAD>
<TITLE>DHTML Positioning Object Test</TITLE>
<STYLE type="text/css">
   BODY { margin: 0.5in }
</STYLE>
<SCRIPT>
<!--

// function test moves paragraph object to
// the left and down
function test() {
<%
  ' find the browser using server variable
  Dim ua
  ua = ""
  Dim brwsr
  ua = Request.ServerVariables("HTTP_USER_AGENT")
  If Instr(1,ua, "MSIE",1) Then
      brwsr = 1
  Else
   brwsr = 0
  End If

  ' create the component instance
  Dim tmp
  Set tmp = Server.CreateObject("cssp.cssp")

  ' create the DHTML JavaScript string using a call to MoveLeft
  ' and MoveTop
  ' write out the strings
  Dim strng
  strng = tmp.MoveLeft("para1",brwsr,200)
  Response.write(strng & ";")
%>
//-->
}
</SCRIPT>
</HEAD>
<BODY onload="test()">
<DIV id="head1" style="position:absolute; left: 50; top:100">
<H1> Testing Positioning Component</H1>
</DIV>
```

Example 11-4. Accessing and Testing the New Interface Method (continued)

```
<DIV id="para1" style="position:absolute; left: 10; top: 10">
<p style="font-family: Arial; color: red; font-style: italic">
This is the paragraph
</p>
</DIV>
</BODY>
</HTML>
```

The example ASP file is run, and the results show that the component is success-fully instantiated and the correct DHTML function string is returned.

In the C++ component method, the parameter specifier [in] is applied to all of the input parameters. This repetition is not necessary, and one specifier can be used for several parameters in a row. You can try this for yourself: add the other three methods to the component using the same technique as was used to create the first method, except for using only one [in] specifier:

```
[id(2), helpstring("method to generate DHTML to control top movement")]
HRESULT MoveTop([in] BSTR bstrObject, int iBrowser, BSTR bstrValue,
[out,retval] BSTR * pbstrDHTML);
[id(3), helpstring("method to generate DHTML to hide object")] HRESULT Hide(
[in] BSTR bstrObject, int iBrowser, [out,retval] BSTR * pbstrDHTML);
[id(4), helpstring("method to generate DHTML to show object")] HRESULT Show(
[in] BSTR bstrObject, int iBrowser, [out, retval] BSTR * pbstrDHTML);
```

To finish the component, add the code for the other three methods, as shown in Example 11-5.

Example 11-5. The Remaining ASP DHTML Component Methods

```
// MoveTop
STDMETHODIMP Ccssp::MoveTop(BSTR bstrObject, int iBrowser, BSTR bstrValue, BSTR
*pbstrDHTML)
{
    // to work with header
    CComBSTR bstrHeader("");
    if (!bstrHeader)
        return E_OUTOFMEMORY;

    // if browser type of 1 - IE
    if (iBrowser == 1) {
        bstrHeader=bstrObject;
        bstrHeader+=".style.top=";
        bstrHeader+=bstrValue;
    }
    else { // Navigator
        bstrHeader = "document.";
        bstrHeader+=bstrObject;
        bstrHeader+=".top=";
        bstrHeader+=bstrValue;
    }
```

Example 11-5. The Remaining ASP DHTML Component Methods (continued)

```
    // assign to return variable, set CComBSTR m_str to null
    *pbstrDHTML = bstrHeader.Detach();

    return S_OK;
}

// Hide
STDMETHODIMP Ccssp::Hide(BSTR bstrObject, int iBrowser, BSTR *pbstrDHTML)
{
    // to work with header
    CComBSTR bstrHeader("");
    if (!bstrHeader)
        return E_OUTOFMEMORY;

    // if browser type of 1 - IE
    if (iBrowser == 1) {
        bstrHeader=bstrObject;
        bstrHeader+=".style.visibility='hidden'";
    }
    else { // Navigator
        bstrHeader = "document.";
        bstrHeader+=bstrObject;
        bstrHeader+=".visibility='hidden'";
    }

    // assign to return variable, set CComBSTR m_str to null
    *pbstrDHTML = bstrHeader.Detach();

    return S_OK;
}

// Show
STDMETHODIMP Ccssp::Show(BSTR bstrObject, int iBrowser, BSTR *pbstrDHTML)
{
    // to work with header
    CComBSTR bstrHeader("");
    if (!bstrHeader)
        return E_OUTOFMEMORY;

    // if browser type of 1 - IE
    if (iBrowser == 1) {
        bstrHeader=bstrObject;
        bstrHeader+=".style.visibility='inherit'";
    }
    else { // Navigator
        bstrHeader = "document.";
        bstrHeader+=bstrObject;
        bstrHeader+=".visibility='inherit'";
    }

    // assign to return variable, set CComBSTR m_str to null
    *pbstrDHTML = bstrHeader.Detach();
```

Example 11-5. The Remaining ASP DHTML Component Methods (continued)

```
    return S_OK;
}
```

That's all it takes to create a simple component using Microsoft's Visual C++ 6.0 and ATL. However, before we finish the chapter, I want to take some time to talk about error handling.

Error Handling

In the methods just created, you may have noticed that I checked to see if the variable *bstrHeader* was successfully created before using the new variable. If not, the methods returned an HRESULT value representing an error.

The reason for performing checks on newly-created objects is that exception handling is not automatically enabled for components created using ATL. This is because the C runtime library required for exception handling is not automatically included as part of the code generation process, as this can increase the size of the component. However, exception handling can be manually turned on, especially when MFC is added to the project.

 Adding the standard C++ libraries occurs when the /GX switch is added as a compiler option.

If you don't provide exception handling and a new object cannot be instantiated, it is set to NULL. Check to see if any new object is NULL before using it.

One way to safely create an object regardless of whether exception handling is implemented or not is to use the ATL ATLTRY macro. ATLTRY can be used with a new method and actually surrounds the object creation expression. It can also be used when creating a new CComBSTR object:

```
    ATLTRY(CComBSTR bstrHeader(""));
```

The macro is defined within *ATLBASE.H* as:

```
    #if defined (_CPPUNWIND) &
        (defined(_ATL_EXCEPTIONS) | defined(_AFX))
    #define ATLTRY(x) try{x;} catch(...) {}
    #else
    #define ATLTRY(x) x;
    #endif
```

Basically, if ATL exception handling is enabled, the macro wraps the code within a try...catch block. Otherwise, it just processes the code as is. Regardless of which approach is taken, a failure in the instantiation results in the attribute being set to NULL, which can then be tested in the code.

As we saw when discussing basic ATL options when the ASP component was created, choosing the option that adds support for the ISupportErrorInfo interface enables error handling. This option adds the method shown in Example 11-6 to the component:

Example 11-6. Supporting the ISupportErrorInfo Interface

```
STDMETHODIMP Ccssp::InterfaceSupportsErrorInfo(REFIID riid)
{
    static const IID* arr[] =
    {
        &IID_Icssp,
    };
    for (int i=0;i<sizeof(arr)/sizeof(arr[0]);i++)
    {
        if (InlineIsEqualGUID(*arr[i],riid))
            return S_OK;
    }
    return S_FALSE;
}
```

This method is invoked from the client to check if the component supports the IErrorInfo interface. This interface, in turn, supports passing error information from the component to the client. In the case of the Visual C++ component being invoked from within a VBScript block in an ASP page, the error information is accessed from the Err object. However, to create the error information, the ATL AtlReportError method is used.

The AtlReportError method basically adds information to the Error object using the methods exposed for the IErrorInfo interface. It is an overloaded function, which means that there are variations of the same function call, each accepting different sets of parameters. However, for creating an ASP object, the function prototype used most often is the following:

```
HRESULT WINAPI AtlReportError( const CLSID& clsid, LPCOLESTR lpszDesc,
const IID& iid = GUID_NULL, HRESULT hRes = 0 );
```

The parameters passed to the function are:

clsid

The component's class identifier, which can be found in the component's header file

lpszDesc

The description of the error

iid

The component's interface identifier, which can be found in the component's header file

hRes

The HRESULT for the error

The *clsid* and *iid* values can be pulled from the object's header file. For the example component created in this chapter, the values are CLSID_cssp and IID_ Icssp, respectively. The description is a string used to provide a meaningful error message to the ASP developer.

The HRESULT value is the result returned from the component. This is set to S_OK if no error occurs, and to a predefined error code for a specific error when an error occurs. The ASP application can access this value and provide different handling routines for different types of errors.

Example 11-7 shows a modified version of the MoveLeft method that adds AtlReportError and allows error handling in the ASP page that invokes the component and this method. First, rather than using standard HRESULT error codes, it uses error codes specific to Visual Basic. For instance, instead of using E_ OUTOFMEMORY, the constant CTL_E_OUTOFMEMORY, which is equivalent to VBScript error number 7, is used.

The MoveLeft method in Example 11-7 also contains an additional error check of the browser type. Instead of making the default browser Navigator (and generating DHTML source code for it by default), an error is generated if the browser type is neither IE 4.x nor Navigator 4.x.

Example 11-7. The ASP DHTML Component Method MoveLeft

```
STDMETHODIMP Ccssp::MoveLeft(BSTR bstrObject, int iBrowser, BSTR bstrValue, BSTR
*pbstrDHTML)
{

    HRESULT hr = S_OK;

    // to work with header
    CComBSTR bstrHeader("");
    if (!bstrHeader)
        return CTL_E_OUTOFMEMORY;

    // if browser type of 1 - IE
    if (iBrowser == 1) {
        bstrHeader=bstrObject;
        bstrHeader+=".style.top=";
        bstrHeader+=bstrValue;
    }
    else if (iBrowser == 2) { // Navigator
        bstrHeader = "document.";
```

Example 11-7. The ASP DHTML Component Method MoveLeft (continued)

```
            bstrHeader+=bstrObject;
            bstrHeader+=".top=";
            bstrHeader+=bstrValue;
        }
        else {
            hr = CTL_E_ILLEGALFUNCTIONCALL;
            LPCOLESTR lpError = L"An incorrect parameters was passed for browser";
            AtlReportError(CLSID_cssp,lpError,IID_Icssp,hr);
            return hr;
        }

        // assign to return variable, set CComBSTR m_str to null
        *pbstrDHTML = bstrHeader.Detach();

        return hr;
}
```

Notice that a variable of type **HRESULT** is created to hold the return value and is set to **S_OK** at the beginning of the method. The value of **CTL_E_OUTOFMEMORY** is still returned immediately if the **BSTR** can not be created to hold the generated results. Additionally, the type of browser is checked and an error of **CTL_E_ ILLEGALFUNCTIONCALL** is created if the browser number is not "1" or "2". An error message is passed with the **HRESULT** variable to the *AtlReportError* function. When this happens, the **HRESULT** value is returned, which triggers error handling within the ASP page. If no error occurs, the generated DHTML code is returned and the **HRESULT** variable is set to **S_OK** and returned.

Setting the **HRESULT** value returned by the MoveLeft method to something other than a success message raises an error within the ASP script. Consequently, the script must be modified to provide for error handling; otherwise, an unhandled exception error will occur. Example 11-8 shows the modified version of the ASP page that works with the component in Example 11-7.

Example 11-8. ASP Page to Traps Errors and Check the Err Object

```
<SCRIPT>
<!--

// function test moves paragraph object to
// the left and down
function test() {
<%
  ' find the browser using server variable
  On Error Resume Next
  Dim ua
  ua = ""
  Dim brwsr
  ua = Request.ServerVariables("HTTP_USER_AGENT")
  Dim ErrorCode
```

Example 11-8. ASP Page to Traps Errors and Check the Err Object (continued)

```
    ErrorCode = 0

    If Instr(1,ua, "MSIE",1) Then
        brwsr = 3
    Else
     brwsr = 2
    End If


     ' create the component instance
    Dim tmp
    Set tmp = Server.CreateObject("cssp.cssp")

     ' create the DHTML JavaScript string using a call to MoveLeft
     ' and MoveTop
     ' write out the strings
    Dim strng
    strng = tmp.MoveLeft("para1",brwsr,200)
    If Err.Number = 7 Then
        ErrorCode = Err.Number
        Response.Write("// Error description: " & Err.Description)
        Err.Clear
    ElseIf Err.Number = 5 Then
        ErrorCode = Err.Number
        Response.Write("// Error description: " & Err.Description & Chr(10))
        Response.Write("// parameter: " & Cstr(brwsr))
        Err.Clear
    Else
        Response.Write(strng & ";")
    End If
%>
//-->
}
</SCRIPT>
<BODY onload="test()">
<%
    If ErrorCode = 7 Then
        Response.Write("<H1>System Error, please contact WebMaster</H1>")
    ElseIf ErrorCode = 5 Then
        Response.Write("<p>DHTML is not supported for your browser")
    End If
%>
```

Notice the **On Error Resume Next** error-handling statement. This tells IIS to continue processing the first statement after the statement that generated the error. Notice also that when an out of memory error occurs (error number 7), an error message is actually written to the page so that the web page reader can view it. The invalid parameter error, on the other hand, prints out an error message as comments in the function as well as a message to the reader. To test the component, an invalid browser error can be deliberately generated.

Further Reading

For additional reading about the topics covered in this chapter, check out the following:

- An online Microsoft article about using ATL to build ASP pages is available at *http://www.microsoft.com/workshop/server/asp/comp.asp.*

- All the variations of AtlReportError can be seen at the Microsoft web site at *http://premium.microsoft.com/msdn/library/devprods/vs6/vc++/vcmfc/_atl_ atlreporterror.htm.*

- Don Box, the king of COM, wrote an especially helpful article on using ATL to create ASP pages at *http://premium.microsoft.com/msdn/library/periodic/ period97/f1/d4/s24618.htm.*

- Other useful articles can be read at Microsoft's web site by accessing the site search engine at *http://www.microsoft.com/search/* and using keywords such as "ATL" and "ASP."

12

The C++ ASP Built-in Interfaces

One of the advantages to writing ASP components in C++ is that you have such a fine level of control over how the component accesses, uses, and releases resources such as memory and threads. However, this depth of control does come with a cost. That cost is that several features of COM that are hidden when writing ASP components using a tool such as Visual Basic, or using a language such as Java, are exposed and must be managed explicitly within C++ code. For current Visual C++ users, this is not as much of a problem, since chances are you are pretty familiar with COM already. However, for C++ users unfamiliar with COM, a first exposure to COM can be intimidating, and the first exposure to COM when writing ASP components is likely to occur when accessing the ASP built-in objects.

Why access the built-in ASP objects? Mainly, you are likely to access these objects because they provide the paths of communication between the server application and the client. Without using the built-in ASP objects, communication is restricted primarily to the information passed as a parameter to or returned from a method.

The ASP objects consist of the Application, Session, Request, Response, and Server objects. The Application object is created when the ASP application is first loaded and maintains application-level information. The Session object is created for a specific web page reader session and maintains session-level information. The Server object is used for conversion and component instantiation. The Response object contains methods to communicate with the client, and the Request object contains information sent from the client to the server. The basic functionality of the ASP built-in objects are discussed in detail in Chapter 6, *Overview of the Intrinsic (Built-in) Objects*, which provides a built-in ASP object reference. This chapter concentrates on demonstrating how the built-in objects are accessed from within a Visual C++ ASP component written using the Active Template Library (ATL).

There are two techniques that can be used to access the built-in objects. The first technique was created for use with IIS 3.0 and is still supported for backward compatibility and for components that are not registered as part of the Microsoft Transaction Server (MTS). This technique accesses the built-in objects from a server component called the ScriptingContext object, using this object's interface, `IScriptingContext`. This technique is covered in this chapter primarily to assist those ASP component developers who might have to convert IIS 3.0 components to IIS 4.0. For IIS 4.0, the recommended approach to accessing the built-in objects is through an MTS object, ObjectContext. This object has two associated interfaces: `IObjectContext` and `IGetContextProperties`. Most of this chapter is devoted to accessing the objects using the MTS ObjectContext technique.

Chapter 6 provides an overview of the functionality of the ASP built-in objects, and Chapter 11, *Creating a Simple C++ ASP Component*, covers creating an ASP component using ATL and Visual C++. If you are unfamiliar with either of these topics, you might want to read these two chapters before reading this one.

Accessing Built-In Objects in IIS 3.0

The `IScriptingContext` interface can only be accessed as a parameter from the OnStartPage event handler when the ASP page is loaded. The code to access this interface can be handled automatically when a new ActiveX Server Component object is inserted into a project using the ATL Object Wizard. Selecting this type of ATL object opens a dialog with three tabs used to collect information pertinent to the new component. The first two tabs were covered in detail in Chapter 11. It is the last dialog page that is of interest in this section.

This last tab, ASP, has one checkbox, OnStartPage/OnEndPage, to include the optional OnStartPage and OnEndPage methods. Checking it enables the Request, Response, Session, Application, and Server options in the right side of the page. Checking any of these options includes support for that built-in object within the component. Checking all of the options includes support for all of the built-in objects.

When the OK button is clicked, the component class and interface are added to the existing Visual C++ project. Included with the interface are IDL entries for the two methods, OnStartPage and OnEndPage. Each of these interfaces has a matching C++ method. The prototypes for the event-handler methods are added to the component's header (*.h*) file, as shown in the following code.

```
public:
    //Active Server Pages Methods
    STDMETHOD(OnStartPage)(IUnknown* IUnk);
    STDMETHOD(OnEndPage)();
```

As stated earlier, the `IScriptingContext` interface can only be accessed from the OnStartPage event handler, which is invoked when the page accessing the ASP component is loaded by IIS. It has one argument, a pointer to `IUnknown`. To access the `IScriptingContext` interface, the COM function *QueryInterface* is used with the `IUnknown` pointer to query for an interface with an Interface ID (IID) of `IID_IScriptingContext`. A pointer to an interface pointer of the ScriptingContext object interface is passed as the second parameter to the function call, shown in the following generated code:

```
CComPtr<IScriptingContext> spContext;
HRESULT hr;

// Get the IScriptingContext Interface
hr = pUnk->QueryInterface(IID_IScriptingContext, (void **)&spContext);
if(FAILED(hr))
    return hr;
```

Once the pointer to the ScriptingContext interface has been returned, it can be used to access each of the five different ASP built-in objects. You can do this manually or have the code generated automatically by checking the box next to the object in the ATL Object Wizard's ASP tab. If the built-in object references are added automatically, Visual C++ defines a property for each object in the component's header file, and places the code to assign the object to the property in the component's C++ file. For example, checking the Request object generates the following in the component header file:

```
CComPtr<IRequest> m_piRequest;       //Request Object
```

This code uses the `CComPtr` smart pointer with `IRequest` to create a COM-wrapped pointer to a Request object interface. The `CComPtr` template is used, since it automatically handles reference counting through the AddRef and Release methods.

 As discussed in Chapter 3, *ASP Components and COM*, each new reference to an object must increment a reference counter, and every release of a reference to an object must decrement this same counter. When all references to an interface are released, the interface can be marked for unloading.

Visual C++ also includes *asptlb.h*, the Active Server Page type library header file.

Checking all five built-in objects in the ATL Object Wizard's ASP tab generates the following C++ code:

```
private:
    CComPtr<IRequest> m_piRequest;                //Request Object
    CComPtr<IResponse> m_piResponse;              //Response Object
    CComPtr<ISessionObject> m_piSession;          //Session Object
    CComPtr<IServer> m_piServer;                  //Server Object
    CComPtr<IApplicationObject> m_piApplication;  //Application Object
```

Each of the built-in objects is defined as a private property, accessible only by component member functions and from friend classes.

Within the component's C++ file created by Visual C++ and the ATL Object Wizard, code is also generated to get the interface for the built-in objects using specialized methods of the ScriptingContext object. As the following code fragment demonstrates, each object has its own associated method with a name of get_ *objecttype* that accepts as an argument the property created in the header file:

```
// Get Request Object Pointer
    hr = spContext->get_Request(&m_piRequest);
    if(FAILED(hr))
    {
        spContext.Release();
        return hr;
    }
```

If the reference to the object cannot be accessed, a failure result is returned and the **ScriptingContext** interface pointer is released.

Though the **ScriptingContext** interface must be accessed from within the OnStartPage event handler and the built-in objects must be instantiated within this same method, the object interfaces can be used *with caution* by other event handlers and methods. For instance, Example 12-1 shows a component that implements the OnStartPage and OnEndPage handlers and instantiates the **IResponse** object. This interface is then used to write out a value to the web page being returned to the client, in this case a value contained within an HTML tag.

Example 12-1. Accessing ASP Built-In Objects Using ScriptingContext

```
// first.cpp : Implementation of Cfirst
#include "stdafx.h"
#include "Two.h"
#include "first.h"

/////////////////////////////////////////////////////////////////////////////
// Cfirst

STDMETHODIMP Cfirst::OnStartPage (IUnknown* pUnk)
{
    if(!pUnk)
        return E_POINTER;
```

Example 12-1. Accessing ASP Built-In Objects Using ScriptingContext (continued)

```
    CComPtr<IScriptingContext> spContext;
    HRESULT hr;

    // Get the IScriptingContext Interface
    hr = pUnk->QueryInterface(IID_IScriptingContext, (void **)&spContext);
    if(FAILED(hr))
        return hr;

    // Get Response Object Pointer
    hr = spContext->get_Response(&m_piResponse);
    if(FAILED(hr))
    {
        return hr;
    }

    m_bOnStartPageCalled = TRUE;
    return S_OK;
}

STDMETHODIMP Cfirst::OnEndPage ()
{
    m_bOnStartPageCalled = FALSE;
    // Release all interfaces
    m_piResponse.Release();

    return S_OK;
}

STDMETHODIMP Cfirst::objWriteHeader()
{
    // create header and output
    CComVariant vtHeader(OLESTR("<H1>This is a test</H1>"));

    m_piResponse->Write(vtHeader);

    return S_OK;
}
```

Once this component is compiled and registered, it can be created within an ASP page like the one shown in Example 12-2. Loading the component using the CreateObject server method triggers the start page event. The OnStartPage event handler is invoked and the **Response** interface is created. Later in the ASP page, the *objWriteHeader* function is called, as shown in Example 12-2, and an <H1> tag is printed out to the web page returned from the server.

Example 12-2. Creating C++ Component and Invoking Method

```
<HTML>
<HEAD>
<TITLE>Response Test</TITLE>
```

Example 12-2. Creating C++ Component and Invoking Method (continued)

```
<BODY>
<%
  Dim myObject
  set myObject = Server.CreateObject("First.one")
%>
<H1>Test of Response Object</H1>
<%

  myObject.objWriteHeader()
%>

</BODY>
</HTML>
```

Because a reference to the Response object interface is maintained as a property of the ASP component, Response object methods are available for use until the ASP page is unloaded. When this occurs, the end page event is triggered, which invokes the OnEndPage event handler. This, in turn, calls the **CComPtr** Release method to decrement the **IResponse** reference count.

Using the combination of event handler methods and the **IScriptingContext** interface is a simple technique to access the built-in objects, but it is not a technique to be used with exposed method calls rather than event handlers. Nor is it a technique that is optimal for use with MTS.

MTS provides transaction management between components, for IIS, for other server components, and even for database transactions if the database supports Microsoft-based transaction management. In order to take advantage of MTS, and for ASP components created specifically for IIS 4.0 or later, you should consider using the MTS ObjectContext object, which is discussed in the next section.

IIS 4.0, MTS, and ObjectContext

With IIS 4.0 and MTS 2.0, Microsoft started providing support for transaction processing with ASP components by providing support for the built-in objects from the MTS ObjectContext object. The individual built-in object interfaces are accessed as properties of ObjectContext through an object interface, **IGetContextProperties**.

Accessing the built-in objects using **IGetContextProperties** is not as simple as having the ATL Object Wizard generate the code for you, but, once coded, the objects are available from any component method. To demonstrate the differences between the two approaches to accessing the built-in objects, let's use ObjectContext to recreate the component created in Example 12-1.

The first step to create the new ASP component is to use the ATL Object Wizard to generate the files supporting the component. Instead of creating the component as an ActiveX Server Component, create it as an MS Transaction Server Component. The dialog that opens is similar to that discussed in the previous section, except it has only two tabs: Names and MTS. The Names section is where the names of the C++ component class and its associated COM object are created, from which in turn the names of the C++ and header files, as well as the Prog ID and interface, are derived. This is no different than the Names tab used with the component in Example 12-1.

The MTS tab is where support for `IObjectControl` (which is discussed later) is added and where a dual or custom interface is selected. For the current example, the default of a dual interface is selected, but support for `IObjectControl` is not added. Figure 12-1 shows the tab page at this point.

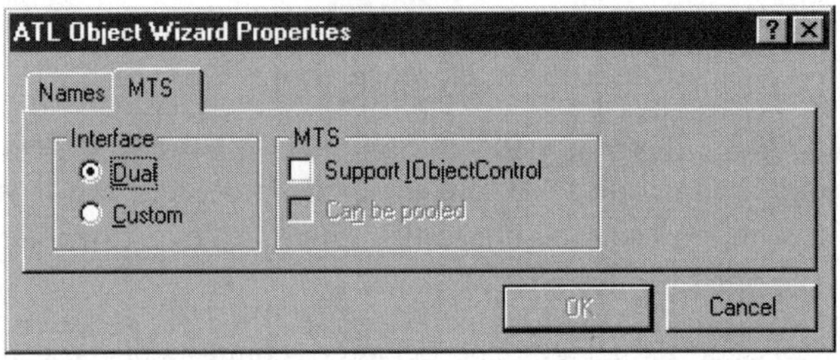

Figure 12-1. ATL Object Wizard Properties dialog for an MTS object

Clicking on the OK button creates the new component and adds the include statement for the MTS header file, *mtx.h*, to the component header file. You then add support for the ASP built-in objects to the component by manually including the *asptlb.h* header file, as shown in the following code:

```
#include <mtx.h>      // MTS Definitions
#include <asptlb.h>   // ASP Definitions
```

Once the component files are created, the next step in building the MTS/ASP component is to add a new method containing the code to write out the `<H1>` tag. The same method name is used for this component as it was for the component in the previous section, objWriteHeader. Add the method by right-clicking on the newly-generated interface in the Class View window and selecting the Add Method option. This adds both the interface code to the IDL file and the C++ skeleton code to support the method.

Once this code is generated, the next step is to add the code to retrieve a reference to the Response object and write out the header. Example 12-3 contains the complete code for the objWriteHeader method. First, `CComPtr` is used to create pointers to the `IResponse`, `IObjectContext`, and `IGetContextProperties` interfaces. Next, the built-in MTS GetObjectContext method is used to retrieve the pointer to the ObjectContext interface. If this method call succeeds, the COM QueryInterface method is used to query for the interface with the IID of `IID_IGetContextProperties`, and the processing to access the built-in Response object occurs.

Example 12-3. The objWriteHeader Method

```
STDMETHODIMP Cfirst::objWriteHeader()
{
    CComPtr<IResponse> piResponse;              //Request Object
    CComPtr<IGetContextProperties> pProps;      //Context Properties
    CComPtr<IObjectContext> pObjContext;        //Context object
    CComBSTR bstrObj;
    CComVariant vt;
    IDispatch* piDispatch = NULL;

    HRESULT hr = S_OK;

    // get ObjectContext
    hr = ::GetObjectContext( &pObjContext );
    if ( FAILED( hr ))
        return hr;


    // get Context Properties
    hr = pObjContext->QueryInterface( IID_IGetContextProperties,
               (void**)&pProps );
    if (FAILED(hr))
        return hr;

// get Response property
    bstrObj = "Response";
    hr = pProps->GetProperty( bstrObj, &vt ) ;

    if (FAILED(hr))
        return hr;

    piDispatch = vt.pdispVal;
    hr = piDispatch->QueryInterface( IID_IResponse,
                  (void**)&piResponse );

    if (!(FAILED( hr))) {
        // write out header
        CComVariant vtHeader(OLESTR("<H1>This is a test</H1>"));
        piResponse->Write(vtHeader);
        }

    return hr;
}
```

To access the `IResponse` interface, the `GetProperty` method of the `IGetContextProperties` interface is called, passing it the name of the object and a `CComVariant` pointer named *vt*. This pointer is then cast as an `IDispatch` interface. The `IDispatch` QueryInterface method is invoked, passing it the `IResponse` interface ID and a pointer to the pointer to `IResponse`. Once the `IResponse` interface pointer is successfully created, the Response object's Write method is used to write out an HTML header.

Using the Microsoft-Supplied CContext C++ Wrapper Class

Included with the IIS samples is one for a C++ ASP component that uses a C++ wrapper class to access built-in server objects. This class is located in the intermediate example section of the C++ components examples. The wrapper class is named `CContext` and is found in the *context.cpp* and *context.h* files.

Using the class is simple: add the *context.h* header file to your component's C++ file, following all other header references. Then obtain the built-in object reference using code similar to the following:

```
CContext cxt;
if ( FAILED( cxt.Init( CContext::get_Response ) ) )
{
    return E_FAIL;
}
```

Once the object reference is obtained, it can be used for all ASP built-in object reference, as the following demonstrates:

```
// write out header
CComVariant vtHeader(OLESTR("<H1>This is a test</H1>"));
hr = cxt.Response()->Write(vtHeader);
```

At first glance, it would seem that accessing the built-in objects using the MTS ObjectContext object and the associated GetContextProperties object is much more cumbersome than accessing the objects using the ScriptingContext object. To simplify the process, access to built-in objects can be wrapped in a C++ class or performed in an initialization method as a property of the component. This latter approach is discussed next.

Accessing a Built-In Object as a Property of a Component

An advantage to retrieving a reference to a pointer to a built-in object interface as a property of the component is that the code to access the interface can be created once and released once, but used many times. If the ASP component has several methods that require a pointer to the **IResponse** interface, for example, each method would use the same pointer rather than having to implement the code to access the object again and again.

To demonstrate, we'll create a new ASP component that has four methods and one property. The property is of type **IResponse**, is named m_piResponse, and is added as a private member to the component's header file, similar in manner to that shown in the following code:

```
private:
CComPtr<IResponse> m_piResponse;           //Response Object
```

The first method for the component is named Init, and it is used to retrieve the **IResponse** pointer and assign it to the component's m_piResponse property. The code for Init is shown in Example 12-4. Notice how it is identical to that shown in Example 12-3, but the method ends once m_piResponse is obtained.

Example 12-4. Storing a Pointer to IResponse in a Component Property

```
STDMETHODIMP Cprp::init()
{
    // define variables
    CComPtr<IGetContextProperties> pProps; //Context Properties
    CComPtr<IObjectContext> pObjContext;    //Context object
    CComBSTR bstrObj;
    CComVariant vt;
    IDispatch* piDispatch = NULL;

    HRESULT hr = S_OK;

    // get ObjectContext
    hr = ::GetObjectContext( &pObjContext );
    if ( FAILED( hr ))
        return hr;

    // get Context Properties
    hr = pObjContext->QueryInterface( IID_IGetContextProperties,
                (void**)&pProps );
    if (FAILED(hr))
        return hr;

    // get Response property
    bstrObj = "Response";
    hr = pProps->GetProperty( bstrObj, &vt ) ;

    if (FAILED(hr))
        return hr;

    piDispatch = vt. pdispVal;
    hr = piDispatch->QueryInterface( IID_IResponse,
                    (void**)&m_piResponse );
```

Example 12-4. Storing a Pointer to IResponse in a Component Property (continued)

```
    return hr;
}
```

Once the Init method is coded, and the pointer to the IResponse interface is stored as a component property, you can add the second method to the ASP component. This method is named releaseProps and is used to release m_piResponse when the component no longer needs the pointer reference. Since this pointer's scope now transcends a specific method, it is important to include property cleanup as well as property instantiation. The releaseProps method is shown in Example 12-5.

Example 12-5. The releaseProps Method

```
STDMETHODIMP Cprp::releaseProps()
{
    m_piResponse.Release();
    return S_OK;
}
```

The next method is an exact reproduction of the *objWriteHeader* function implemented earlier in this chapter, except now using the new m_piResponse property; it is shown in Example 12-6. As you can see, removing the code to implement the IResponse pointer has greatly simplified the process, as well as clarified the intent of the specific method.

Example 12-6. The objWriteHeader Method Using the m_piResponse Property

```
STDMETHODIMP Cprp::objWriteHeader()
{
    // write out header
    CComVariant vtHeader(OLESTR("<H1>This is a test</H1>"));
    m_piResponse->Write(vtHeader);

    return S_OK;
}
```

The final method for the component is a variation of *objWriteHeader*. This method writes out any content passed as a BSTR value to the method. This could be a header, a paragraph, anything. This method again makes use of m_piResponse, and is shown in Example 12-7.

Example 12-7. IResponse Interface Pointer Stored as a Component Property

```
STDMETHODIMP Cprp::objWriteSpecHeader(BSTR bstrHeader)
{

    CComVariant vtHeader(bstrHeader);
```

Example 12-7. IResponse Interface Pointer Stored as a Component Property (continued)

```
m_piResponse->Write(vtHeader);

return S_OK;
}
```

Example 12-7 really demonstrates the benefits of creating the pointers to the built-in object interfaces as properties of the component: the same pointer reference can be used with both methods. When this new component is instantiated in an ASP page, as Example 12-8 illustrates, the first method called for the component is the Init method to create the **IResponse** interface pointer. Then, either of the two methods to output content can be called. Last, the releaseProps method is called to release the pointer reference.

Example 12-8. Accessing the Component That Treats ASP Built-in Objects as Its Properties

```
<HTML>
<HEAD>
<TITLE>Component Property Test</TITLE>
<BODY>
<%
  Dim myObject
  set myObject = Server.CreateObject("FirstBltIn.one")
  myObject.init
%>
<H1>Test of Objects as Component Properties</H1>
<%
  Dim strng
  strng = "This Is a Test Header!"
  myObject.objWriteHeader()
  myObject.objWriteSpecHeader(strng)
  myObject.releaseProps()
%>

</BODY>
</HTML>
```

Forcing your ASP component clients to call methods to initialize and release component resources is time-consuming for the client, and dangerous for your component. You have to trust that the ASP developer remembers to call both methods. A better technique would be to have the component handle its own initiation and finalization by trapping component events and coding event handlers, or coding initialization and destruction tasks within the class constructor and destructor. Another approach is to incorporate the use of the **IObjectControl** interface provided with MTS, which is discussed in the next section.

Adding Support for IObjectControl and Pooling

Earlier in the chapter, I covered the ATL Object Wizard's MTS properties page, shown when creating an MTS component. At that time, the IObjectControl option was not selected for the component. In this section, the use of IObjectControl and the impact on the component when IObjectControl and the "Can be Pooled" options are selected are discussed.

The whole purpose for the IObjectControl interface is to add support for "just-in-time" activation to the component. What just-in-time activation means is that the component is not activated until a reference to one of its methods is invoked: when the component is created it is created as a deactivated object. It is only when one of the component's methods is directly accessed that the component is activated. When the component's transaction is completed, usually because of a SetComplete or SetAbort call or because the transaction the component is contained within finishes, the component is deactivated.

Creating an ASP component using the MTS ATL option and selecting the IObjectControl option does two things. First, m_spObjectContext, an Object-Context interface pointer, is created as a public property of the component. Second, two event handlers are added: Activate and Deactivate.

> To support just-in-time activation, the Activate method is called when the component is activated, and any component initialization occurs within this method. The Deactivate method is called when the component is deactivated, and component cleanup occurs within *this* method.

The ATL Object Wizard generates the Activate and Deactivate methods and includes instantiation of the IObjectContext pointer property. These two methods are ideal for instantiation and cleanup of ASP built-in objects. To demonstrate, Example 12-9 shows the Activate method for a component that includes code to create a pointer for each type of built-in ASP object.

Example 12-9. Component Activate Method

```
HRESULT Cmytest::Activate()
{
    HRESULT hr = S_OK;
    CComBSTR bstrObj;
    CComVariant vt;
    CComPtr<IGetContextProperties> pProps; //Context Properties

    IDispatch* piDispatch = NULL;
```

Example 12-9. Component Activate Method (continued)

```
// generated code
hr = GetObjectContext(&m_spObjectContext);
if (FAILED(hr))
    return hr;

// add in code to get built-in objects

// get Context Properties
hr = m_spObjectContext->QueryInterface( IID_IGetContextProperties,
            (void**)&pProps );
if (FAILED(hr))
    return hr;

// get Response property
bstrObj = "Response";
hr = pProps->GetProperty( bstrObj, &vt ) ;

if (FAILED(hr))
    return hr;

piDispatch = vt. pdispVal;
hr = piDispatch->QueryInterface( IID_IResponse,
                (void**)&m_piResponse );

if (FAILED(hr))
    return hr;

// get Request property
bstrObj = "Request";
hr = pProps->GetProperty( bstrObj, &vt ) ;

if (FAILED(hr))
    return hr;

piDispatch = vt. pdispVal;
hr = piDispatch->QueryInterface( IID_IRequest,
                (void**)&m_piRequest );

if (FAILED(hr))
    return hr;

// get Application property
bstrObj = "Application";
hr = pProps->GetProperty( bstrObj, &vt ) ;

if (FAILED(hr))
    return hr;

piDispatch = vt. pdispVal;
hr = piDispatch->QueryInterface( IID_IApplicationObject,
                (void**)&m_piApplication );
```

Example 12-9. Component Activate Method (continued)

```
    if (FAILED(hr))
        return hr;

    // get Session property
    bstrObj = "Session";
    hr = pProps->GetProperty( bstrObj, &vt ) ;

    if (FAILED(hr))
        return hr;

    piDispatch = vt. pdispVal;
    hr = piDispatch->QueryInterface( IID_ISessionObject,
                        (void**)&m_piSession );

    if (FAILED(hr))
        return hr;

    // get Server property
    bstrObj = "Server";
    hr = pProps->GetProperty( bstrObj, &vt ) ;

    if (FAILED(hr))
        return hr;

    piDispatch = vt. pdispVal;
    hr = piDispatch->QueryInterface( IID_IServer,
                        (void**)&m_piServer );

    return hr;
}
```

The built-in ASP object references are then released in the Deactivate method, as shown in Example 12-10.

Example 12-10. Component Deactivate Method

```
void Cmytest::Deactivate()
{
    // release pointer refs to built-in ASP objects
    m_piResponse.Release();
    m_piRequest.Release();
    m_piApplication.Release();
    m_piSession.Release();
    m_piServer.Release();

    // release ObjectContext - generated code
    m_spObjectContext.Release();
}
```

As shown in the code, the ASP objects are created as class properties. The declaration of these properties is included within the component header file, as shown in the following code block:

```
    private:
        CComPtr<IResponse> m_piResponse;
        CComPtr<IRequest> m_piRequest;
        CComPtr<IApplicationObject> m_piApplication;
        CComPtr<IServer> m_piServer;
        CComPtr<ISessionObject> m_piSession;
```

In addition, the MTS and ATL libraries are also included in the header file:

```
    #include <mtx.h>
    #include <asptlb.h>
```

The entire header file, including generated code and the code that we need to add, is shown in Example 12-11.

Example 12-11. Header File for MTS Component

```
#ifndef __MYTEST_H_
#define __MYTEST_H_
#include "resource.h"        // main symbols
#include <mtx.h>
#include <asptlb.h>


/////////////////////////////////////////////////////////////////////////////
// Cmytest
class ATL_NO_VTABLE Cmytest :
    public CComObjectRootEx<CComSingleThreadModel>,
    public CComCoClass<Cmytest, &CLSID_mytest>,
    public IObjectControl,
    public IDispatchImpl<Imytest, &IID_Imytest, &LIBID_ATLASTLib>
{
public:
    Cmytest()
    {
    }


DECLARE_REGISTRY_RESOURCEID(IDR_MYTEST)

DECLARE_PROTECT_FINAL_CONSTRUCT()

DECLARE_NOT_AGGREGATABLE(Cmytest)

BEGIN_COM_MAP(Cmytest)
    COM_INTERFACE_ENTRY(Imytest)
    COM_INTERFACE_ENTRY(IObjectControl)
    COM_INTERFACE_ENTRY(IDispatch)
END_COM_MAP()

// IObjectControl
public:
    STDMETHOD(Activate)();
    STDMETHOD_(BOOL, CanBePooled)();
    STDMETHOD_(void, Deactivate)();

    CComPtr<IObjectContext> m_spObjectContext;
```

Example 12-11. Header File for MTS Component (continued)

```
// Imytest
public:
    STDMETHOD(testtwo)();
    STDMETHOD(thetest)();
private:
    CComPtr<IResponse> m_piResponse;
    CComPtr<IRequest> m_piRequest;
    CComPtr<IApplicationObject> m_piApplication;
    CComPtr<IServer> m_piServer;
    CComPtr<ISessionObject> m_piSession;
};

#endif //__MYTEST_H_
```

This header is for a component named *mytest* that contains two methods, testtwo and thetest—so what can I say? I'm not very original.

Using MTS just-in-time activation is a terrific approach to creating and releasing pointers to the built-in ASP objects. Another advantage is that this technique can be combined with component pooling.

Pooling is the process of returning an object reference to a pool rather than marking the component to be unloaded from memory when the component is no longer active, such as when the ASP page containing the component is unloaded. With pooling, the time to create the ASP component can be decreased by pooling the component rather than destroying it and then having to recreate the component when it is accessed again. This is especially attractive for an ASP component that can be accessed many times within a short time period. The disadvantage to pooling is that the component maintains any resources it creates outside of using the Active and Deactivate methods. In the example just shown, the resource use is minimal, since the pointers to the built-in objects are created and then freed within the context of the activation process.

Using pooling requires that the component be marked as free- or both-threaded, rather than as apartment-threaded. Apartment threading requires that the component be created on the thread of the client creating the component. Pooling requires that the component be created in such a way that it can run under different threads. Because of this, setting a component to be apartment-threaded negates setting the component to be pooled. When an ASP component is created with the "Can be Pooled" option checked, it is automatically set to be a free-threaded component, which should work with pooling.

An interesting result of using just-in-time activation occurs when any activity using the built-in object properties occurs *after* a transaction is completed or aborted.

This is demonstrated in the next section, which also discusses some of the other methods available with the `IObjectContext` interface.

Adding Transaction Support with IObjectContext

 When coding a new ASP component that is also an MTS component, you need to do one of two things each time you change the component and recompile the DLL: reregister the component with MTS by running the utility *mtxrereg.exe* directly or by including this utility as a part of a custom build option in Visual C++. Visual C++ takes care of this for you when you add an MTS component to the DLL you are creating. You can also refresh the component directly in the MTS Console. If you do not reregister the component after a build, accessing the component locks up the ASP application.

The `IObjectContext` object provides several transaction support methods in addition to being able to return, indirectly, pointers to the ASP built-in objects. In fact, support for the built-in objects is actually a secondary feature of `IObjectContext`. Its primary purpose is for transaction support.

The primary methods `IObjectContext` exposes are SetAbort and SetComplete, used to mark a transaction as unsuccessfully or successfully finished, respectively. The DisableCommit method keeps a transaction from being committed, and EnableCommit turns transaction commitment capability back on. These latter two methods are useful for keeping a transaction from completing until certain operations have finished or certain conditions are met. The IsInTransaction method can return information about whether the component is within a transaction, the IsSecurityEnabled method returns a Boolean indicating if security is enabled for the component, and IsCallerInRole sets a Boolean to indicate whether the process calling the component is within a specific role. Finally, the CreateInstance method instantiates a COM object in the same transaction as the existing object.

Example 12-12 contains a new component that uses some of the `IObjectContext` methods. Specifically, the component uses the IsCallerInRole, IsSecurityEnabled, IsInTransaction, SetAbort, and SetComplete methods. In addition, once the component is created, it is installed as an MTS component, and the transaction property is set to Requires a Transaction, as discussed in Chapter 5, *Components, Transactions, and the Microsoft Transaction Server.*

Example 12-12. Using the IObjectContext Security and Transaction Support Methods

```
STDMETHODIMP Cobjcontextmethods::objTestMTS(BSTR bstrHeader)
{
    HRESULT hr = S_OK;
```

Example 12-12. Using the IObjectContext Security and Transaction Support Methods

```
BOOL bResult;
CComVariant vtResults;

// check security
bResult = m_spObjectContext->IsSecurityEnabled();
if (bResult)
    vtResults ="<p>Security is enabled";
else
    vtResults ="<p>Security is not enabled";
m_piResponse->Write(vtResults);

// check if in transaction
bResult = m_spObjectContext->IsInTransaction();
if (bResult)
    vtResults ="<p>Component is in transaction";
else
    vtResults ="<p>Component is not in transaction";
m_piResponse->Write(vtResults);

// check if in role
CComBSTR bstrRole("developer");

// check for role membership
hr = m_spObjectContext->IsCallerInRole(bstrRole,&bResult);
if (SUCCEEDED(hr) && (bResult))
    vtResults ="<p>Client is in role 'developer'<p>";
else
    vtResults ="<p>Component is not in role 'developer'<p>";
hr = m_piResponse->Write(vtResults);

// mark component for deactivating, and set success or failure
if (SUCCEEDED(hr))
    hr = m_spObjectContext->SetComplete();
else
    hr = m_spObjectContext->SetAbort();

// final write call, after set functions
vtResults = bstrHeader;
hr = m_piResponse->Write(vtResults);

return hr;
}
```

The example, as with all of the examples in this chapter, declares the ASP objects within the component headers, instantiates them in the Activate method, and destroys them in the Deactivate method, as discussed in Example 12-11 in the last section.

The component is created with support for IObjectControl and makes use of the Activate and Deactivate methods to assign pointers to the IObjectContext and IResponse interfaces. The method IsSecurityEnabled is called to see if security is enabled, and the result is displayed. Under MTS for Windows NT, this value is always True, because security is always enabled for any component that is not running directly within a client process. Under MTS for Windows 95/98, on the other hand, it is always False, since the underlying operating system does not support security. The next method checks to see if the component is within a transaction, and again, this returns True. The reason for this value is that when the component was registered with MTS, it was registered as requiring a transaction, which forces the component to run as part of a transaction.

The third method call, IsCallerInRole, checks to see if the client process calling the component was run within a certain role, in this case the "developer" role. This returns False, as the client process was not running within this role under MTS for WinNT. Since MTS for Win9x does not support roles, the method always returns True.

At the end, if the IsCallerInRole method had returned a failure code, the transaction would have been aborted with the use of SetAbort. Otherwise the transaction is marked as completed with SetComplete. Using the SetAbort method informs MTS that this component is finished processing, and that its processing has failed. Using the SetComplete method informs MTS that this component has finished processing, and that its processing has completed successfully. The success or failure of this component will impact on whether the transaction is committed or rolled back for all components operating in the same transaction. Another Write method call is issued on the Response object just after the component is listed as ready for deactivation. The reason for this is shown next.

One other piece of code is added to this component, an HTML <H1> tag that is written out when the Deactivate method is invoked, as shown in the code in Example 12-13.

Example 12-13. The Cobjcontextmethod Object's Deactivate Method

```
void Cobjcontextmethods::Deactivate()
{
    CComVariant vtHeader("<H1>Unloading Response Object</H1>");
    m_piResponse->Write(vtHeader);

    m_piResponse.Release();

    m_spObjectContext.Release();
}
```

Running the component results in output similar to that shown in the following block:

```
Unloading Response Object
Security is enabled
Component is in transaction
Component is not in role 'developer'
Unloading Response Object
```

This demonstrates that the Deactivate method is called once when the component is first created, and once after the transaction is completed. Notice, though, that the Deactivate method is queued, and the existing component method is allowed to finish before the method is called. This is shown by the "Unloading Response Object" message that appears after the final **IResponse** write method. If the Deactivate method had not been queued, the **IResponse** pointer would have been released, and attempting to use the pointer property would have resulted in an error.

One other capability the ObjectContext object provides is the ability to create an instance of a COM automation object and have the instance automatically share the transaction of the existing COM object if compatible transaction handling exists. To be compatible, both the new server component instance and the existing object must use transactions, and the new instance must be registered to support transactions. If the newly-created instance is defined to have its own transaction, it is created within its own transaction and not within the parent component's transaction.

To create a new instance of a COM object, use the ObjectContext method CreateInstance. This method takes the object's class and interface ID and a pointer to a reference of the same object type, as the following code demonstrates:

```
IObjectContext* pObjectContext = NULL;

Iem* psc = NULL;
// Get the object's ObjectContext.

hr = GetObjectContext(&pObjectContext);
// Use it to instantiate another object.

hr = pObjectContext->CreateInstance(CLSID_em, IID_Iem,
    (void **)&psc);

hr = psc->test();
```

In this example, a new pointer to an ObjectContext interface is created, and then used to create a pointer to an interface for an "em" object. Once the new instance is created, the object's functions can be accessed.

To include a COM object within your ASP or MTS/ASP component, use the #import directive, such as #import <embed.tlb>. This converts the contents of the type library into C++ classes for incorporation into your component. There are several different attributes that can be specified with the directive, such as the named_guids attribute, which directs the compiler to use old-style GUID variables.

After this overview of using the IObjectContext, IGetContextProperties, and IObjectControl interfaces, the next several sections will use these concepts to demonstrate how to work with each of the built-in ASP objects. Note that each of the following examples assumes that the component is created with support for IObjectControl, and that references to the built-in objects are retrieved in the Activate method and released in the Deactivate method.

The Application Object Interface

The Application object interface, IApplicationObject, can be used to store and retrieve information shared across all sessions. The information stored can be a single value or a reference to an object. The values are stored either in the Application object's Contents collection, which includes all values added dynamically to the Application object, or in the Application's StaticObjects collection, which includes all items added using the <OBJECT> tag in the *global.asa* file.

Microsoft has exposed the get_Contents and get_StaticObjects methods to access these two collections from the IApplicationObject interface. These collections are also available from ISessionObject, discussed in the next section. In addition to using these collections to access and set application-level information, you can also access values from either collection directly from IApplicationObject. The methods to directly access values are get_value and put_value, to get and set an application-level variable, respectively. Other application object methods are the Lock method to lock the application object against changes; the Unlock method to free the locked object; and the putref_Value method, which stores an automation object, a COM object, in the application object.

To demonstrate getting and setting a value using the Contents collection, as well as using the IApplicationObject's direct value-setting methods, we'll create a new example component whose primary method locks the Application object, gets a value directly from this object, uses the Response object to display it, resets the value, and then unlocks the Application object. In addition, the object also gets and sets an application-level object indirectly using the Contents collection. To accomplish this, the component also makes use of the `IVariantDictionary` interface.

To create the component, use the ATL COM AppWizard to generate a new COM project, name it what you would like, and accept the Wizard's defaults. Then create a new ATL Component using the MTS ATL Object Wizard type, and name this object Cmytest. Make sure you check the Support IObjectControl option from the MTS tab of the Object Wizard properties dialog.

Once the component is generated, copy the code from Example 12-9 to the Activate method in your new component, and the code from Example 12-10 to the Deactivate method. Also add in the *mts.h* and *asptlb.h* header files and ASP object properties, as demonstrated in Example 12-11. After creating this component framework, add a new method to the component, name it thetest, and add the code shown in Example 12-14 to use the `IApplicationObject` methods described two paragraphs ago.

Example 12-14. Using the IApplicationObject Interface

```
STDMETHODIMP Cmytest::thetest()
{
    HRESULT hr = S_OK;
    CComBSTR bstrValue("testers");
    CComVariant vtOut;
    CComVariant vtPara = "<P>"

    // get the application object value directly
    hr = m_piApplication->Lock();
    hr = m_piApplication->get_Value(bstrValue, &vtOut);

    // if failure, return
    if (FAILED(hr))
       return hr;

    // write out current value
    m_piResponse->Write(vtOut);
    m_piResponse->Write(vtPara);

        // add new value to application object
    vtOut = OLESTR("secondvalue");
    hr = m_piApplication->put_Value(bstrValue, vtOut);

    // unlock
    hr = m_piApplication->UnLock();

    // Get the Contents Collection
    CComPtr<IVariantDictionary> piVariantVariables;
    hr = m_piApplication->get_Contents(&piVariantVariables);

    // if failure, return
    if (FAILED(hr))
```

Example 12-14. Using the IApplicationObject Interface (continued)

```
    return hr;

  CComVariant vtIn(OLESTR("MyInfo"));

  // Get the item from the Contents collection
  hr = piVariantVariables->get_Item(vtIn, &vtOut);

  // again, check for failure
  if (FAILED(hr))
    return hr;

  // write value out
  m_piResponse->Write(vtOut);
  m_piResponse->Write(vtPara);

  // change value
  vtOut = OLESTR("newvalue");
  hr = piVariantVariables->put_Item(vtIn, vtOut);


    return S_OK;
}
```

Going through the code from the top, the Application object is locked by calling the Lock method. Then, the **IApplicationObject** interface get_value method is called, passing to it a **BSTR** object set to the name, or the *key* (which in this case is *testers*), of the value, and a **CComVariant** object. The latter object will receive the value of the data stored by the key name in the Application object. The retrieved variant is displayed using the Response object's Write method. No conversion is necessary on this value, since the Write method takes a value of type **VARIANT**. However, if conversion were necessary, the VariantChangeType method could be used to change the return value into the appropriate data type, such as **BSTR**. If the same **CComVariant** variable is used as both the source and the destination of the conversion, the variant is changed *in place*, as shown in the following code:

```
  hr = VariantChangeType(&vtOut, &vtOut, 0, VT_BSTR);
```

Once the current value of this application-level variable is displayed, the put_value method changes the variable's value to **secondvalue**.

The same sequence of method calls is used with the Contents collection, except that **IVariantDictionary** is used to access the collection, and its get_item and put_item methods are used to get and replace the value of the application-level variable *MyInfo*. The main difference between the two sets of get and put methods is that the **IApplicationObject**'s methods take a **BSTR** as the first parameter and a **VARIANT** as the second. The **IVariantDictionary** takes parameters of type **VARIANT** for both.

Storing information at the level of the application object is especially helpful for such things as maintaining counts of items in stock for an online catalog system, or perhaps maintaining a count of the number of people currently logged into the system. For information specific to the session, which is defined by the time a specific person logs into the application until they log out, the Session object must be accessed through the ISessionObject interface, discussed next.

The ISessionObject Interface

In C++, the Session object information and methods are accessed using the ISessionObject interface. The Session object is similar to the Application object in that variables and other objects can be stored within the object's Contents and StaticObjects collections, and accessed or altered as long as the Session object is in scope. The primary difference between Application and Session is that the Session object lasts from the time a person accesses the first web page of an ASP application until the person's session times out or he or she logs out of the application.

The Session object stores information, as the Application object does, but it also has information about the context of the session. This information includes what code page is used to display characters, accessed and altered using the ISessionObject get_CodePage and put_CodePage methods, and what locale is in use, modified and accessed with the get_LCID and put_LCID methods. The last two methods are especially important if your component must support a more international clientele.

The timeout of the session can be changed or read using the get_Timeout and set_Timeout methods. You can also access the specific session id with get_SessionID, but this should not be used directly by ASP developers. Session identifiers may not be unique across application runs.

The session can be abandoned using the Abandon method, which releases all resources currently held by the Session object. Finally, the component can access values directly from the Session object using get_Value and put_Value, and indirectly using the collections with the get_StaticObjects and get_Contents methods. Using the direct method means you can access a value in the same manner, regardless of how the value is instantiated—using the *global.asa* file or being set directly in code. However, the direct method does not support enumeration as the collections accessed using get_StaticObjects and get_Contents do.

Before demonstrating using the ISessionObject methods, we need to create a simple component to use with the demonstration. To do this, use the ATL COM AppWizard to generate a Component DLL as you did with other examples in this chapter, and then insert a new ATL object, again using the MTS component type. Name the project embed and the new ATL component *em*. You'll want to have the

Activate and Deactivate methods, so set the Support IObjectControl option when creating the new ATL object. This component uses the ASP Response object, which is instantiated in the Activate method and released in the component's Deactivate method, as shown in Example 12-15, which contains the entire C++ source code for the component.

Example 12-15. Creating a Reference and Writing a Message

```cpp
// em.cpp : Implementation of Cem
#include "stdafx.h"
#include "Embed.h"
#include "em.h"

/////////////////////////////////////////////////////////////////////////////
// Cem

HRESULT Cem::Activate()
{
    CComBSTR bstrObj;
    CComVariant vt;

    // generated code
    HRESULT hr = GetObjectContext(&m_spObjectContext);
    if (SUCCEEDED(hr)) {

        // add in code to get built-in objects
        CComPtr<IGetContextProperties> pProps; //Context Properties
        hr = m_spObjectContext->QueryInterface( IID_IGetContextProperties,
                (void**)&pProps );

        if (!FAILED(hr))
        {

            // get Response property
            bstrObj = "Response";
            pProps->GetProperty( bstrObj, &vt ) ;

            // cast to Response interface object
            if ((!FAILED(hr)) && ( V_VT(&vt) == VT_DISPATCH ))
            {
                IDispatch* pDispatch = V_DISPATCH(&vt);
                if ( pDispatch )
                {
                    hr = pDispatch->QueryInterface( IID_IResponse,
                            (void**)&m_piResponse );
                    if (FAILED(hr)) return hr;

                }
            }
        }
    }
    return hr;
}
```

Example 12-15. Creating a Reference and Writing a Message (continued)

```
BOOL Cem::CanBePooled()
{
   return FALSE;
}

void Cem::Deactivate()
{
   m_spObjectContext.Release();
}


STDMETHODIMP Cem::test()
{
   // TODO: Add your implementation code here

   CComVariant vtHeader("<H1>Hello from Embed</H1>");

   m_piResponse->Write(vtHeader);
   return S_OK;
}
```

Don't forget to add the ASP library to the component's header file, and to add the m_piResponse property. Once the component is compiled and registered, you can proceed to the next example, which uses the **ISessionObject** methods.

Example 12-16 contains a different version of the thetest method previously demonstrated in Example 12-14. To test it, keep the component you created for Example 12-14 the same, but replace the contents of the thetest method. In this version of the component method, **ISessionObject** interface methods are used. Specifically, the value of the Session timeout is accessed, displayed to a web page, and then changed to a value of 40 minutes, and an object is accessed from the StaticObjects collection. The code in Example 12-14 showed how to access a value from the Contents collection for **IApplicationObject**.

Example 12-16. Changing Session Timeout and Obtaining Access to COM Object

```
STDMETHODIMP Cmytest::thetest()
{
   HRESULT hr = S_OK;

   CComVariant vtOut;
   long lTimeout;

   // get timeout, print, and modify
   m_piSession->get_Timeout(&lTimeout);

   CComVariant vtTimeout(lTimeout);
   m_piResponse->Write(vtTimeout);

   lTimeout = 40;
```

Example 12-16. Changing Session Timeout and Obtaining Access to COM Object (continued)

```
    m_piSession->put_Timeout(lTimeout);

    // access object from global.asa
    Iem* pEm = NULL;

    // Get the Contents Collection
    CComPtr<IVariantDictionary> piVariantVariables;
    hr = m_piSession->get_StaticObjects(&piVariantVariables);

    // if failure, return
    if (FAILED(hr))
      return hr;

    CComVariant vtIn(OLESTR("MyInfo"));

    // Get the item from the Contents collection
    hr = piVariantVariables->get_Item(vtIn, &vtOut);

    VariantChangeType(&vtOut, &vtOut, 0, VT_DISPATCH);

    // cast to em interface object
    if (!FAILED(hr))
      {
      IDispatch* pDispatch = V_DISPATCH(&vtOut);
        if ( pDispatch )
        {
        hr = pDispatch->QueryInterface( IID_Iem,
                  (void**)&pEm );
        if (FAILED(hr)) return hr;
        }
    }

    hr = pEm->test();

    return hr;
}
```

 You can access the StaticObjects and Contents collections from either the **IApplicationObject** or the **ISessionObject** interface using the same technique.

Accessing and setting the timeout value is fairly straightforward. The code to access the StaticObjects collection object is not quite as simple. First, the server component being accessed from the StaticObjects collection is created using the following line in the *global.asa* file:

```
<OBJECT RUNAT=Server SCOPE=Session ID=MyInfo PROGID="embed.em">
</OBJECT>
```

To access the object, a reference to it is accessed as a pointer of type CComVariant, which is changed to a variant of type VT_DISPATCH. This is then used with *QueryInterface* to return a pointer to the object's interface, Iem. Once this interface pointer is obtained, it can be used to access the methods of the interface object.

The example accesses the component created in Example 12-15. When the component was compiled, a COM type library for the component was generated in addition to the component DLL. To complete the example shown in Example 12-16, the #import directive is used to pull in the interface's type library, and the object's header file is included with the component:

```
#import "embed.tlb" named_guids    // use old naming convention
#include "embed.h"
```

Without including the type library reference, the component cannot be successfully compiled and run.

Though the Session and Application objects are important, they are probably not accessed as much within ASP components as the next two built-in objects, the Request and Response objects. These objects are critical for communicating directly with the web page reader, and are covered in the next two sections.

The IRequestObject Interface

The Request object, and its associated C++ interface, IRequest, contain information about the client, such as what browser is being used; about client certification if used; the protocol; the server port; and so on. However, its primary importance is that it is used by the component to access information attached to the end of the URL of the page containing the component, and any information posted from an HTML form. It is the main object used to access information from the actual web page reader.

Most of the IRequest information is stored in collections, accessible by using the IRequestDictionary helper interface. For instance, one main reason to use the IRequest interface is to access values submitted from an HTML form. The particular collection for this information is the Form collection, and it can be accessed using the IRequest get_Form method, which returns a pointer to an IRequestDictionary object. The individual form elements are accessed using the IRequestDictionary get_Item method to access the form field value, or the get_key method to access the form field name. The form field names and values can also be accessed by using get_NewEnum to return an IEnumUnknown enumerator object. Enumerator objects have built-in methods to handle iteration through a fixed collection.

Example 12-17 demonstrates using an enumerator to access all the fields of a form and display both the field name as well as the field value. The **IRequest** get_ Form method returns a pointer to the **IRequestDictionary** object. This interface's get_NewEnum method is then used to create a pointer to an **IEnumUnknown** interface. The **IEnumUnknown** interface provides methods to enumerate through a collection of unknown object types. In the example, the enumerator interface's Next method is used to get each form field, one at a time, display the form field name, and then use the form field with the **IRequestDictionary** interface to get the field value.

Example 12-17. Enumerating the IRequest Interface ServerVariables Collection

```
STDMETHODIMP Cmytest::thetest()
{
    HRESULT hr = S_OK;
    CComVariant vt;
    IUnknown* pUnknown = NULL;
    IEnumVARIANT* pEnum = NULL;
    ULONG lValue;

    CComPtr<IRequestDictionary> piRequestVariables;
    hr = m_piRequest->get_Form(&piRequestVariables);

    // if failure, return
    if (FAILED(hr))
      return hr;

    // get enumerator object
    hr = piRequestVariables->get__NewEnum(&pUnknown);

    if (!FAILED(hr))
      {
      hr = pUnknown->QueryInterface( IID_IEnumVARIANT,
                  (void**)&pEnum );
        if (FAILED(hr)) return hr;
    }

    // return the server variable and associated value
    // until the return value from Next is not S_OK
    while(S_OK == (pEnum->Next(1,&vt,&lValue))) {
        CComVariant vtValue;

        // write out the field name and an equal sign
        m_piResponse->Write(vt);
        vtValue = "=";
        m_piResponse->Write(vtValue);

        // get the field value and write out, followed by a paragraph
        piRequestVariables->get_Item(vt, &vtValue);
        m_piResponse->Write(vtValue);
        vt = "<p>";
        m_piResponse->Write(vt);
```

Example 12-17. Enumerating the IRequest Interface ServerVariables Collection (continued)

```
  }

  return hr;
}
```

This type of code can be used to obtain the values for all of the collections associated with the `IRequest` object.

Another `IRequest` object collection is the ServerVariables collection, which has several server environment variables. A useful component for an ASP developer is one that will return all of the server environment variable names and associated values, if any. With this, you can check out the communication between client and server, how data is returned when accessed from `IRequestDictionary`, and what the identifying string for a specific browser looks like, for example.

I use an ASP test page with a component that contains code similar to that shown in Example 12-15 as a technique to determine what I can expect when accessing a specific environment variable. The only difference between the code for the component that prints out the form values and the one printing out the server variables is the following line:

```
  hr = m_piRequest->get_ServerVariables(&piRequestVariables);
```

which replaces the tenth line of code in Example 12-15. That's it to get the server variables instead of the form values. The same type of technique can be used to access values from the QueryString collection, which contains name-value pairs attached to the URL of the ASP page containing the component. In this case the `IRequest` get_QueryString method is used.

An example of an "entry" within the QueryString collection is something similar to the following:

```
  <a href="test.asp?test=one&test2=two&test3=three">Test</a>
```

Using the enumerator code shown, but with get_QueryString, would produce a result similar to that in the following block:

```
  test=one
  test2=two
  test3=three
```

However, if all three name-value pairs had the same name, as with:

```
  <a href="test.asp?test=one&test2=two&test3=three">Test</a>
```

The result would be:

```
  test=1,2,3
```

Assigning different values to the same name for any of the collection types results in a list of values being assigned to the same name.

If your site supports digital certificates for security and you need to access information about the client certificate, you can use the get_ClientCertificate method and access the certificate fields directly or again use enumeration, as shown in the previous examples.

Another use of IRequest collections is to access the Cookies collection using the get_Cookies method. In this case, you might actually want to access each cookie individually. The following code demonstrates how simple it can be to access one specific cookie:

```
CComVariant vt(OLESTR("cookie_name")), vtValue;
CComPtr<IRequestDictionary> piRequestVariables;
hr = m_piRequest->get_Cookies(&piRequestVariables);

// if failure, return
if (!FAILED(hr))

    piRequestVariables->get_Item(vt, &vtValue);
```

Once you have accessed an element from a collection, it's simple to use the same technique to access elements from all the collections. However, you can also access an item in any of the collections directly, without the use of IRequestDictionary, by using the IRequest get_Item method. This method takes a BSTR value that has the name of the value being accessed as its first parameter and returns a pointer to an IDispatch interface pointer.

If the value is contained within the ServerVariables, QueryString, or Form collections, the individual values can be accessed using the IStringList interface. As an example, assume that you want to retrieve the values of the item named test from Request Object. This item happens to be contained within the QueryString collection and contains an array of three values: 1, 2, and 3. The code to access these values using enumeration is contained in Example 12-18. Notice how similar this code is to that in Example 12-17, except that the value obtained with enumeration is the actual value, not the name.

Example 12-18. Listing the Array of Values Associated with a Specific QueryString Name

```
IDispatch* pDispatch;
IStringList* pList;
CComVariant vt;
IUnknown* pUnknown = NULL;
IEnumVARIANT* pEnum = NULL;
ULONG lValue;

    m_piRequest->get_Item(bstrName, &pDispatch);
```

Example 12-18. Listing the Array of Values Associated with a Specific QueryString Name

```
hr = pDispatch->QueryInterface( IID_IStringList,
                (void**)&pList );

// Get the item from the Contents collection
hr = pList->get__NewEnum(&pUnknown);

// cast to em interface object
if (!FAILED(hr))
  {
  hr = pUnknown->QueryInterface( IID_IEnumVARIANT,
              (void**)&pEnum );
    if (FAILED(hr)) return hr;
}

// return the server variable and associated value
while(S_OK == (pEnum->Next(1,&vt,&lValue))) {
   CComVariant vtValue;
   m_piResponse->Write(vt);
}
```

The `IStringList` interface also has a get_Item method to access a specific item by name. As with all enumerator type interfaces, it also has the get_Count method to return the count of items within the collection.

Just as the `IRequest` get_Item method is used to obtain a reference to a value contained in the Cookies collection, the `IReadCookies` interface provides similar access to the values associated with the specific name. For the ClientCertificate collection, the `IRequestDictionary` is used to obtain the values.

If the `IRequest` object processes information coming from the client to the server, the `IResponse` interface provides information back to the client, and is discussed next.

The IResponse Interface

The `IResponse` interface does not have as many collections as `IRequest`, but it does have the most methods of any of the built-in ASP objects. One of these methods, Write, has already been used extensively throughout this chapter to provide output from the server to the client.

In addition to creating output, the Response object and its associated C++ interface can control how and when the output is returned. This control occurs through the Buffer property. Setting this property to a Boolean value of **TRUE** turns page buffering on, which means that no content is returned to the page until all of the ASP scripts have finished. The default value is **FALSE**, meaning that content is returned to the page as it is processed. The Buffer property can be set using the put_Buffer method and retrieved using get_Buffer. Note, though, that the property must be set in the first line of the web page; otherwise, is it ignored. Because of this, the Buffer property is usually set directly within the ASP page using a line similar to the following:

```
<% Response.Buffer = true %>
```

Other methods that can determine when content is returned to the page are the Clear, End, and Flush methods. The Clear method is used to clear out the buffer contents in case of an error. This is helpful if a problem has occurred and you don't want any content returned to the web page reader:

```
CComVariant vtOut;
vtOut = "some contents";
m_piResponse->Write(vtOut);

// other activity occurs, and an error results
// clear buffer
m_piResponse->Clear();
```

The End method stops page buffering and returns the page contents directly at that point, while the Flush method returns output but does not turn buffering off. All three of these methods will return an error if buffering is not enabled.

The **IResponse** interface can also control caching. For instance, using the put_ Expires or put_ExpiresAbsolute methods controls when the page expires from the cache. The former method takes a long value representing the number of minutes before the page expires, and the latter takes an actual date. Example 12-19 shows one technique to set the absolute expiration of the page using the **SYSTEMTIME** data type.

Example 12-19. Setting the Expiration from Cache for the ASP Page

```
HRESULT hr = S_OK;
SYSTEMTIME stObject;
double dtTime;

// set day
stObject.wYear = 1998;
stObject.wMonth = 6;
stObject.wDay = 13;

// set time
stObject.wHour = 13;
stObject.wSecond = 13;
stObject.wMilliseconds = 13;

SystemTimeToVariantTime(&stObject, &dtTime);
hr = m_piResponse->put_ExpiresAbsolute(dtTime);

return hr;
```

SYSTEMTIME is a structure with members for each time field, including year, day, month, and seconds. The SystemTimeToVariantTime method is used to convert the SYSTEMTIME structure into a double, which is then passed to the put_ExpiresAbsolute method. To complement the "put_" methods, the IResponse interface also exposes the get_Expires and get_ExpiresAbsolute methods to obtain the current expiration times.

Other methods to control caching include two to get and set the CacheControl property. This property is used to control whether proxy servers can cache the ASP page contents. Passing in a BSTR value equal to "Public" to the put_Cache-Control method enables proxy caching.

The page return status code can be accessed and controlled using the put_Status and get_Status methods. For instance, the following results in a dialog requesting a username and password when the page is accessed:

```
CComBSTR bstrObj("401 Unauthorized");

m_piResponse->put_Status(bstrObj);
```

Entering a valid network username and password will allow entry to the page.

The IResponse interface's only collection is the write-only Cookies collection. Accessing this collection uses the IRequestDictionary interface, discussed in the last section. The same techniques to access and set cookies with the IRequest interface can be used with the IResponse interface. The main difference between the collections is that the IResponse cookies will actually set the cookie value in the client if not previously set, and they are write-only, while the IRequest interface returns cookies previously set, and are read-only.

Example 12-20 shows how to create and populate a cookie dictionary. Notice from the code that IRequestDictionary is used to pull in the write-only response object cookies collection, and a specific cookie dictionary is then accessed from the collection. For the write-only cookie collection, this returns an item that resolves to an IWriteCookie interface.

Example 12-20. Creating and Populating a Cookie Dictionary

```
HRESULT hr = S_OK;
    CComPtr<IRequestDictionary> piRequestVariables;
    IUnknown* pUnknown = NULL;
    IWriteCookie* piCookie = NULL;
    IDispatch *piDispatch = NULL;

    DATE    dtObject=36500.0;

    CComVariant vtOut, vtResponse;

    hr = m_piResponse->get_Cookies(&piRequestVariables);
```

Example 12-20. Creating and Populating a Cookie Dictionary (continued)

```
    // if failure, return
    if (FAILED(hr))
      return hr;

    // Get the item from the Contents collection
    CComVariant vtIn(_T("currentval"));
    hr = piRequestVariables->get_Item(vtIn, &vtOut);

  // if failure, return
   if (FAILED(hr)) {
     vtResponse = "Could not get item";
     m_piResponse->Write(vtResponse);
     return hr;
   }

    // get interface to write-only cookie
    piCookie = (IWriteCookie *)V_DISPATCH(&vtOut);

    // if failure, return
    if (FAILED(hr)) {
      vtResponse = "Could not get item";
      m_piResponse->Write(vtResponse);
      return hr;
    }

    // put cookie key-value pair
    CComVariant vtKey(OLESTR("first"));
    CComBSTR bstrValue("23.00");

    hr = piCookie->put_Item(vtKey, bstrValue);

    // put second cookie key-value pair
    vtKey = "second";
    bstrValue = "35.00";

    hr = piCookie->put_Item(vtKey, bstrValue);

    // set cookie props
    hr = piCookie->put_Expires(dtObject);

   return hr;
```

The `IWriteCookie` interface is derived from the variant returned from the `IRequestDictionary` get_Item method call. This is then defined as a variant of type `VT_DISPATCH`, and is cast to the `IWriteCookie` interface pointer. Once the `IWriteCookie` interface pointer is created, the first cookie key-value pair is added using the `IWriteDictionary`'s put_Item method. This is followed by the addition of a second key-value item, both to the same cookie dictionary, currentval. At the end, the expiration date of the cookie is set to a DATE value representing December 6, 1999.

Accessing this component within an ASP page using the Netscape Navigator browser when its cookies notification option is enabled results in a dialog similar to that shown in Figure 12-2. Notice that the cookie dictionary named currentval has two values, separated by an ampersand, URL-encoded, and set with the expiration date.

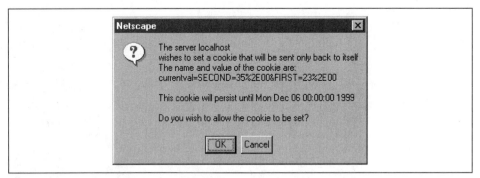

Figure 12-2. Cookie information from the component in Example 12-20

Another IResponse method, AppendToLog, appends to the IIS log file. This is a useful method to output information for debugging and tracking purposes. The response object's charset property can be set using the put_CharSet method. Writing to the web page without any Unicode-to-ANSI conversion is accomplished using the BinaryWrite method. Finally, to add a PICS label, discussed in more detail in Chapter 6, the PICS method is used.

The IServer Interface

The last ASP built-in object to be discussed is the Server object and its associated interface, IServer. This interface has few methods and no collections. It is mainly used to handle URL or HTML encoding, to create a new server object instance, or to set or get the script timeout value.

For encoding, the URLEncode and HTMLEncode methods take a string from the server and applies their own specific encoding, converting specific characters to special conversion values. As an example, URL encoding replaces spaces with the plus sign (+), and the percent sign with a hexadecimal value of "%25". HTML encoding replaces the left and right angle brackets with "&lt" and "&gt" respectively. Additional encoding methods exposed with the IServer interface are the URLPathEncode method, which applies URL encoding to all characters except those representing the path, such as the slash (/), and the MapPath method, which

on given a relative path and the current server loca-
icularly useful for accessing resources and opening

he encoding methods provided by `IServer`,
le for a component that outputs test strings, each of
of the encoding methods.

ferent IServer Interface Encoding Methods

```
a test</H1>"), bstrOut;
or("<p>");

, &bstrOut);


or);


++";
    &bstrOut);


m_piResponse->Write(vtSeparator);

// path encoding
bstrIn = "test/test2/this is a test";
m_piServer->URLPathEncode(bstrIn, &bstrOut);

vtOut = bstrOut;
m_piResponse->Write(vtOut);
m_piResponse->Write(vtSeparator);

// path mapping
bstrIn = "/test/test2/";
m_piServer->MapPath(bstrIn, &bstrOut);

vtOut = bstrOut;
m_piResponse->Write(vtOut);


return hr;
```

The actual Server object methods are pretty simple, with each taking an input
string as a BSTR data type, and each producing an output BSTR variable contain-

ing the encoded value. Error checking is not performed after each call of the
encoding method to keep the code lines down, but should be added for production components.

Accessing this component from within an ASP page generates results similar to the
following:

```
<H1>This is a test</H1>

%25+this+is+a+test+%25+%2B%2B

test/test2/this%20is%20a%20test

E:\Inetpub\wwwroot\New Folder\test2
```

Note that the first line, which contains the HTML encoded string, actually prints
out the <H1> HTML tags without producing HTML formatting.

The `IServer` object also can set the ASP script block timeout value. This controls
how long a specific scripting block can take for processing. The two methods to
access and set this value are get_ScriptTimeOut and put_ScriptTimeOut.

A final method the `IServer` interface exposes is CreateObject.

Earlier in this chapter, I demonstrated how to access a sever component from the
`ISessionObject`'s StaticObjects collection. This type of object is available from
any ASP page or component for the life of the session. However, accessing an ASP
component using the `IServer` object creates an instance that lasts only until the
page is processed and returned to the client. Example 12-22 demonstrates how to
create the object defined in Example 12-15 using the `IServer` interface.

Example 12-22. Accessing a Server Component Using CreateObject Within C++

```
HRESULT hr = S_OK;
    IDispatch* pDispatch = NULL;
    Iem* pEm = NULL;

    CComBSTR bstrProgID("Embed.em");

    hr = m_piServer->CreateObject(bstrProgID,&pDispatch);

        // cast to em interface object
    if (!FAILED(hr)) {
      hr = pDispatch->QueryInterface( IID_Iem,
                    (void**)&pEm );
      if (FAILED(hr)) return hr;
      }

    // invoke server component's method
    hr = pEm->test();

    return hr;
```

Instead of accessing identification information using the object's Interface ID (IID) and Class ID (CLSID), the same ProgID value used to access the object within scripting is used. This returns a pointer to an `IDispatch` interface pointer. The QueryInterface method is then used to retrieve a pointer to the server component's interface pointer. At that point, all of the server component's methods and public properties are available for access. The object does not have to be released, since its lifetime ends when the ASP script containing the enclosing component is finished.

Further Reading

For additional reading about the topics covered in this chapter, check out the following:

- Microsoft provides an online article discussing using ATL to build ASP pages at *http://www.microsoft.com/workshop/server/asp/comp.asp.*

- Microsoft has a reference page on ASP objects, located at *http://premium. microsoft.com/msdn/library/sdkdoc/iishelp/iis/htm/asp/introbj_1orp.htm.*

- See the article "Implementing with Visual C++," about implementing components using Visual C++, at *http://premium.microsoft.com/msdn/library/sdkdoc/ iisref/crtc4lgf.htm.*

- An excellent reference for the ASP C++ interfaces can be found at *http://premium.microsoft.com/msdn/library/sdkdoc/iishelp/iis/htm/sdk/crtcomp_ 1foz.htm.*

13

Integrating Data Access in C++ ASP Components with OLE DB

The ActiveX Data Objects (ADO) are actually a set of classes built on top of OLE DB. Microsoft created ADO primarily to simplify data access without having to use the more complex OLE DB. However, as you will find in this chapter, using OLE DB does not have to be a complicated process.

The ADO is also available for access from Visual C++. However, a more efficient approach to handling database access from C++ is to use the new OLE DB templates. These templates provide canned approaches to database access that don't require using the higher-level ADO objects and that can simplify the use of OLE DB.

This chapter covers using the new OLE DB templates from within ASP components. It begins by providing a general overview of OLE DB and continues by examining the OLE DB templates. These demonstrations and examples are all covered from a standpoint of usage within an ASP or any COM-based component.

OLE DB, ADO, and the OLE DB Templates

The principle behind OLE DB is the ability to use the same tools, API, and language to access an ISAM file, a relational database, or even a plain text document. OLE DB is based on Microsoft's concept of Universal Data Access (UDA). UDA is an initiative to define a set of tools and technologies that allow quick and efficient data access, regardless of where and how the data is stored. To achieve this, Microsoft based their approach on COM, thereby making use of an existing object-based implementation mechanism.

To support UDA, Microsoft created OLE DB. OLE DB is a COM implementation, and provides interfaces that can be used for all aspects of data access and management. To support existing data access methods, Microsoft also created OLE DB interfaces for existing sources by providing an OLE DB-to-ODBC bridge in addition to a direct OLE DB interface to SQL Server; these interfaces are termed OLE DB providers.

An *OLE DB Provider* is any implementation that contains and surrounds data. To access the data, an application developer creates or makes use of an *OLE DB Consumer*, which is an implementation that uses data. There is also an *OLE DB Service Component*, which acts as both a provider and a consumer. The latter type of component works by accessing data from another provider such as the OLE DB Provider for SQL Server, processes the data in some way, and then exposes the data for consumption by some consumer. It is this latter action that makes the service component a provider as well as a consumer.

OLE DB is an exciting prospect. Consider using the exact same technique to access data as a row from an object-oriented database, a relational database, an ISAM file, and a straight text file, and you can see the power of something such as this. However, the power does not come without a price: OLE DB is not an uncomplicated set of interfaces to use, and it requires a comfortable knowledge of COM. Because of this, Microsoft created ActiveX Data Objects (ADO), a set of classes implemented on top of OLE DB that hide most of the COM-specific aspects of OLE DB.

With ADO, instead of having to directly access an interface such as `IRowPosition` (discussed later), you can create an object of type Resultset and use this object to open a database connection, query for data, and process all the data returned. In particular, ADO simplifies OLE DB access in Visual Basic, as shown in Chapter 9, *Creating VB Data Access Components*, and in Java, as you will see in Chapter 17, *Integrating Java ASP Components with ADO and MTS*.

ADO can also be used with C++ components, but Microsoft also created simplified techniques to access OLE DB relatively directly through the use of the ActiveX Template Library (ATL). So, in addition to using ATL to create MTS and ASP components, you can also use it to create OLE DB provider and consumer components. The ATL Wizards generate the framework necessary to support each of these efforts. Not only do the OLE DB templates create a framework that allows us to develop more or less directly to the OLE DB, I have found that the OLE DB templates are actually easier to use in Visual C++ than using ADO. It is because of this that this chapter covers the templates rather than using ADO.

OLE DB Basics

 The OLE DB is included with Microsoft's Data Access SDK, version 2.0, at the time this was written. This can be accessed directly at *http://www.microsoft.com/data/*. In addition to the files supporting the technology, the SDK also includes complete and detailed documentation of the technologies, as well as a fairly comprehensive set of examples. The technologies, documentation, and examples are also included with Microsoft Visual C++ 6.0.

OLE DB actually has very few objects within its object model. Among them are the following:

Enumerator

An object that returns a set of data sources. For instance, an enumerator specific to SQL Server databases would return a listing of all databases that exist within the SQL Server implementation on the host machine where the enumerator resides. A data source in this instance is a SQL Server database. A special enumerator provided by Microsoft is the *root enumerator*, which traverses the registry for data sources and lists all of the sources regardless of the type of provider or data source.

Data Source Object

The data and the associated provider, which contains and manages the data. For instance, the Microsoft OLE DB Provider for SQL Server could act as a data provider for all SQL Server databases contained on the same machine as the provider. A data source would then be an element of one of these SQL Server databases.

Session

Used to control transactions, and can be used to create commands and rowsets. Following the conventions of COM, the Session object could be considered the *factory* for transactions, commands, and rowsets, in that it can be used to create objects of these types.

Transaction

Provides transaction management to an application.

Command

A text command such as a stored procedure call or an embedded SQL statement that may or may not result in a rowset. If a rowset is the result of a command, then the command is considered a factory of the rowset.

Rowset

> A rowset exposes data. One of the requirements for OLE DB is that all exposed data must be exposed in a tabular format, and a rowset exposes data in a tabular format.

Error

> All of the OLE DB objects can generate errors, and the Error object contains information about the error, similar to the errors that are trapped with exception handling within C++.

Each of these basic objects is implemented with one or more interfaces. For example, the data source is a specific object that must be created and, once created, exposes properties through an interface called **IDBProperties**. The rowset consists of four different interfaces, such as **IRowset**, which handles the row fetching, **IAccessor**, which handles the binding between column data and the application consuming the data, **IColumnsInfo**, containing information about the rowset columns, and **IRowsetInfo**, containing information specific to the rowset.

To detail how to create a simple OLE DB consumer, Microsoft provides an example application called SAMPCLNT that effectively demonstrates the interfaces used to create a simple OLE DB consumer. Creating OLE DB service components or providers goes beyond the scope of a book on writing ASP components. Please check the Microsoft documentation or books written specifically on creating OLE DB providers and service components. Additionally, there are several URLs at the end of this chapter that provide more detailed information on OLE DB. Additionally, most OLE DB consumers will most likely be written using the templates that Microsoft has provided to make the task simpler, which are discussed and demonstrated next.

Using the ATL OLE DB Templates

To simplify OLE DB access within a Visual C++ environment, Microsoft has provided a set of OLE DB templates that can be used within the context of ATL. To create an OLE DB component is as easy as creating a new project using the ATL AppWizard and then inserting a new ATL component. In addition to being able to create components that are MTS and/or ASP components, you can also create a data access component and implement it as either an OLE DB provider or an OLE DB consumer.

Rather than having to code to OLE DB directly, the templates provide a set of wizards that allow you to create either an OLE DB provider or consumer just by inserting a new ATL object and selecting whether to create a provider or consumer from the list of ATL data access object types. As stated in the previous section, the OLE DB provider is the component that allows access to an actual data source, and is usually provided by the data source (such as a database engine like SQL Server). As such, we are exploring its use with ASP component development. The OLE DB Consumer ATL templates, on the other hand, are useful, and this section contains a demonstration of creating such a consumer.

Though there are several ATL templates for use with OLE DB, those in the following list are the ones used in this chapter.

CDataSource
> Connection to a data source through a provider

CSession
> Database connection

CAccessor
> Binds data from columns to data in the application

CRowset
> The actual data manipulation tool, handling data in tabular form

CCommand
> Data source command

CTable
> Used for simple query-only table accesses

CDBPropSet
> Sets provider properties ·

To demonstrate how simple it is to create an OLE DB consumer using the templates, in this section we'll walk through the steps necessary to create a consumer component that connects to a SQL server database, accesses a database table, and creates a rowset for the table.

First of all, use the ATL AppWizard to create a new COM object, adding in support for MTS to the project and creating it as a DLL. Next, insert a new object using the ATL Object Wizard. In the Category list box, select Data Access, then select Consumer as the object type.

Pushing the Next button opens a dialog that contains several text fields that are grayed out, a set of options for Consumer type (Table or Command), and a set of options for the type of support provided (data update, insertions, and deletions). Selecting none of these latter options creates an OLE DB consumer that is a query only. Finally, the dialog also features a Select Datasource button. Clicking on it opens the Provider tab of the Data Link Properties dialog shown in Figure 13-1, which contains an enumeration of OLE DB providers registered on the machine.

Our example will access *pubs*, a SQL Server database, which means that the Microsoft OLE DB Provider for SQL Server should be chosen from the displayed

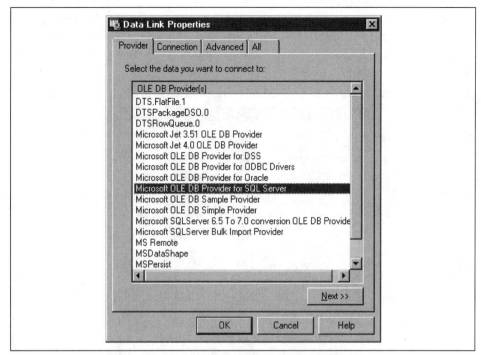

Figure 13-1. OLE DB providers available on the local machine

list. After selecting "Microsoft OLE DB Provider for SQL Server", click the Next button. This opens the Connection tab of the Data Link Properties dialog, where you can specify connection information for the provider, including server, database name, and userid and password. Figure 13-2 shows this dialog after all of the connection information for the example has been specified. For this example, the database used is the *pubs* sample database that comes with SQL Server, and the userid is the standard user sa.

After you finish with this page, another dialog opens that allows you to select a table, query, or stored procedure from the database. Select the authors table for the example. The ATL Object Wizard then uses the information from the selection to name the C++ class, objects, and files. Table 13-1 contains the names the Object Wizard derived.

Table 13-1. ATL Object Wizard Derived Names for OLE DB Consumer Example

Label	Value
C++ Short Name	Dboauthors
Class	Cdboauthors
Accessor	CdboauthorsAccessor
.H File	*dboauthors.H*

Don't select the options for Insert, Delete, or Change support, since we will create a query-only component. In addition, select the Table option in the Type group box to create the consumer as a Table query. Using a table-based query is equivalent to the standard `select * from table` type of query, and does not have the overhead of a command.

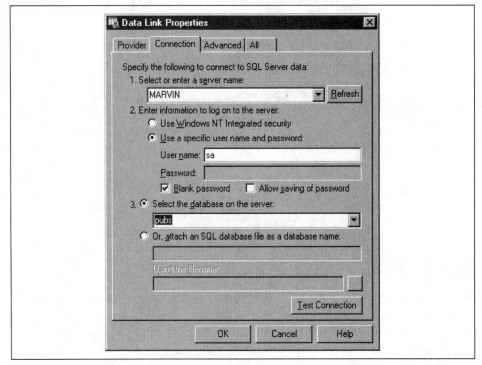

Figure 13-2. Dialog to specify connection information for the OLE DB data source

When you click OK, the ATL Object Wizard creates two new classes, one (the `Cdboauthors` class) for the rowset for the query, and the other (the `CdboauthorsAccessor` class) to perform the data binding. The class definition for the `CdboauthorsAccessor` object is discussed in the next section. The wizard places the definitions and initial methods into a header file. There is no associated C++ file; by creating the OLE DB consumer, the wizard has created the resource, and it is up to the developer to create the usage.

Looking at the Class view of the new objects, the `Cdboauthors` class has three new methods and a data member. The first method is Open, and all this does is call both of the other two methods. The first of these other methods is OpenDataSource, which sets the database properties and opens the session on the data source. Example 13-1 shows the code generated for this method in the *dboauthors.h* header file.

Example 13-1. Generated Code to Provide for an OLE DB Session on a Data Source

```
HRESULT OpenDataSource()
    {
        HRESULT      hr;
        CDataSource db;
        CDBPropSet   dbinit(DBPROPSET_DBINIT);

        dbinit.AddProperty(DBPROP_AUTH_PASSWORD, OLESTR(""));
        dbinit.AddProperty(DBPROP_AUTH_PERSIST_SENSITIVE_AUTHINFO, false);
        dbinit.AddProperty(DBPROP_AUTH_USERID, OLESTR("sa"));
        dbinit.AddProperty(DBPROP_INIT_CATALOG, OLESTR("pubs"));
        dbinit.AddProperty(DBPROP_INIT_DATASOURCE, OLESTR("MARVIN"));
        dbinit.AddProperty(DBPROP_INIT_LCID, (long)1033);
        dbinit.AddProperty(DBPROP_INIT_PROMPT, (short)4);
        hr = db.Open(_T("SQLOLEDB.1"), &dbinit);
        if (FAILED(hr))
            return hr;

        return m_session.Open(db);
    }
```

The second method is OpenRowset, which uses template syntax to create a new rowset using the **CAccessor** object created for the table. This rowset is then returned, as the code in Example 13-2 shows.

Example 13-2. Code to Provide for an OLE DB Rowset

```
HRESULT OpenRowset()
    {
        return CTable<CAccessor<CdboauthorsAccessor> >::
            Open(m_session, _T("dbo.authors"));
    }
```

By issuing the Open method on the **Cdboauthors** class, the application has effectively initialized a connection to the data source, created a session on the data source, opened a rowset, and created an accessor object to use to bind data from the data source to the application.

Though it's an interesting exercise to see how simple it is to create an OLE DB Consumer, the real proof of the template's value is to actually use it within an ASP application. Using the OLE DB consumer from an ASP/MTS component is detailed next.

Integrating OLE DB and ASP with MTS

So far, we've developed an OLE DB consumer component that creates an open rowset from the SQL Server authors table. To actually use this open rowset, we could do one of two things. We could extend the framework generated by the ATL Object Wizard and add new methods to access the rowset data, or even to make updates. Or we could create other components within the same or a different DLL that access the opened rowset. This section demonstrates the use of both techniques.

As stated, you don't have to use the ATL Object Wizard to create a separate component in order to use OLE DB within an ASP component. You can actually create the code directly within your existing COM components. To demonstrate, the following example uses a pre-existing MTS component with ASP support, such as those created in the examples in Chapter 12, *The C++ ASP Built-In Interfaces*.

To add OLE DB consumer support to an existing MTS/ASP component, first add the OLE DB header file to the *StdAfx.h* file for the project:

```
#include <atldbcli.h>
```

In addition, add the following header file to the *StdAfx.cpp* file:

```
#include <atlimpl.cpp>
```

Adding both of these files adds support for the OLE DB ATL Templates.

Once you've added the headers, the next step is to create a separate class file for the **Accessor** class. As discussed in the last section, the **Accessor** class is used to bind data query fields to actual component programming variables. The code shown in Example 13-3 uses the **CAccessor** class generated earlier when using the ATL Object Wizard to create an OLE DB consumer. The code is just copied to the header file for the MTS component, a technique you might want to keep in mind when adding OLE DB support to your existing MTS/ASP components.

Example 13-3. Code Copied from ATL Object Wizard OLE DB Code

```
class CAuthorsAccessor
{
public:
    TCHAR m_auid[12];
    TCHAR m_aulname[41];
    TCHAR m_aufname[21];
    TCHAR m_phone[13];
    TCHAR m_address[41];
    TCHAR m_city[21];
    TCHAR m_state[3];
    TCHAR m_zip[6];
    VARIANT_BOOL m_contract;
```

Example 13-3. Code Copied from ATL Object Wizard OLE DB Code (continued)

```
BEGIN_COLUMN_MAP(CAuthorsAccessor)
    COLUMN_ENTRY(1, m_auid)
    COLUMN_ENTRY(2, m_aulname)
    COLUMN_ENTRY(3, m_aufname)
    COLUMN_ENTRY(4, m_phone)
    COLUMN_ENTRY(5, m_address)
    COLUMN_ENTRY(6, m_city)
    COLUMN_ENTRY(7, m_state)
    COLUMN_ENTRY(8, m_zip)
    COLUMN_ENTRY_TYPE(9, DBTYPE_BOOL, m_contract)
END_COLUMN_MAP()
};
```

The **CAccessor** object is responsible for handling the binding between the rowset columns and the application variables. As you can see from the code, macros are used to define the column map. The **BEGIN_COLUMN_MAP** macro begins the column mapping, and includes a reference to the **CAccessor** object used in the application. Each of the columns is defined using the **COLUMN_ENTRY** macro, which specifies an ordinal number representing the location of the column in the retrieval, and the associated application variable. By default, the fields are defined as character data. The **COLUMN_ENTRY_TYPE** is an extension of **COLUMN_ENTRY** that allows a different data type definition as well as the data mapping.

Next, support is again added to the ASP/MTS component for the Response object as described in the previous section, and a new method is added to the MTS component called *Test* (I know, not very original). However, unlike the example in the previous section, you, not the ATL Object Wizard, have to add in all the code to create the rowset that is used to display the data.

To open the rowset, the component first has to initialize a connection to the database. The OLE DB template class for this is **CDataSource**. Additionally, certain properties have to be set or passed to **CDataSource** for initialization, and the **CDBPropSet** template class is used for this. **CDBPropSet** is a class wrapping the DBPROP structure to handle the data source properties. The class method AddProperty is used to add each property.

Once the data source is initialized, it is used to create a session using the template derived class **CSession**. Finally, the **CRowset** is created using the template class **CTable**, and this is opened with the session, as shown in Example 13-4.

Example 13-4. Accessing a SQL Server Data Source

```
STDMETHODIMP CobjFive::test()
{
    // variables
    CDataSource connection;
    CSession session;
```

Example 13-4. Accessing a SQL Server Data Source (continued)

```
CTable<CAccessor<CAuthorsAccessor> > authors;

_variant_t vbreak;
 vbreak = "<p>";


 // Define the DB Property Set
CDBPropSet   dbinit(DBPROPSET_DBINIT);

 // Set the connection properties
dbinit.AddProperty(DBPROP_AUTH_PERSIST_SENSITIVE_AUTHINFO, false);
dbinit.AddProperty(DBPROP_AUTH_USERID, OLESTR("sa"));
dbinit.AddProperty(DBPROP_INIT_CATALOG, OLESTR("pubs"));
dbinit.AddProperty(DBPROP_INIT_DATASOURCE, OLESTR("MARVIN"));
dbinit.AddProperty(DBPROP_INIT_LCID, (long)1033);
dbinit.AddProperty(DBPROP_INIT_PROMPT, (short)4);

 // initialize the database connection
connection.Open(_T("SQLOLEDB.1"), &dbinit);

 // open the session
 session.Open(connection);

 // open the rowset
authors.Open(session, "dbo.authors");

 // move through the records and output last name
authors.MoveFirst();

while (authors.MoveNext() == S_OK) {
    CComVariant vt(authors.m_aulname);
    m_piResponse->Write(vt);
    m_piResponse->Write(vbreak);
}


    return S_OK;
}
```

If you were expecting complicated code, I hope you are pleasantly surprised. What takes several hundred lines of code using OLE DB directly takes only about 20 lines of code with the OLE DB templates.

Of course, this example is relatively simple: creating a query and outputting one of the returned fields. However, even more complex data queries or stored procedure calls, including those with parameters, are still fairly simple with OLE DB templates, as shown in the next section.

I mentioned in the beginning of this section that the OLE DB consumer component and an ASP/MTS component can reside as separate components within the same DLL, rather than extending an existing MTS/ASP component directly. This technique has appeal, since the App Wizard can be used to generate both components, and the components can be tied together via the OLE DB component's header file. This section then extends the OLE DB Consumer component DLL created in the last section by adding in a new ATL object with support for both ASP and MTS.

Again, we use the ATL Object Wizard, except this time we are creating an MTS component and naming it *objThree*. To replicate this example, you should also add support for the ObjectControl object and object pooling, available from the MTS tab in the Object Wizard.

When you click OK, the Object Wizard generates the framework to support the MTS component. When ATL generates the component's files, include the ASP header file in the newly-created object header file by adding the following line to *objThree.h*:

```
#include <asptlb.h>
```

Adding this line adds in support for the ASP objects. In addition, add a new data member to the object by adding the following code to the header file and the class definition, following the public methods defined for the object:

```
private:
    CComPtr<IResponse> m_piResponse;
```

This gives the component access to the ASP Response object in order to output information to the ASP web page. The m_piResponse object is initialized in the MTS component's Activate method and released in the Deactivate method, as discussed previously in Chapter 12; the source code for the two events is shown in Example 13-5.

Example 13-5. Adding Initialization and Cleanup of Component Data Member

```
HRESULT CobjThree::Activate()
{
    HRESULT hr = S_OK;
    CComBSTR bstrObj;
    CComVariant vt;
    CComPtr<IGetContextProperties> pProps; //Context Properties

    IDispatch* piDispatch = NULL;

    // generated code
    hr = GetObjectContext(&m_spObjectContext);
    if (FAILED(hr))
        return hr;

    // add in code to get built-in objects
    // get Context Properties
    hr = m_spObjectContext->QueryInterface( IID_IGetContextProperties,
                (void**)&pProps );
```

Example 13-5. Adding Initialization and Cleanup of Component Data Member (continued)

```
    if (FAILED(hr))
        return hr;

    // get Response property
    bstrObj = "Response";
    hr = pProps->GetProperty( bstrObj, &vt ) ;

    if (FAILED(hr))
        return hr;

    piDispatch = vt.pdispVal;
    hr = piDispatch->QueryInterface( IID_IResponse,
                    (void**)&m_piResponse );
    return hr;
}

void CobjThree::Deactivate()
{
    // release pointer refs to built-in ASP objects
    m_piResponse.Release();

    // release ObjectContext - generated code
    m_spObjectContext.Release();
}
```

At this point, we have a new component that uses MTS object pooling, has access to the ASP built-in objects, and has a data member pointing to the ASP Response object that is created when the component is activated and released when the component is released.

Once the new component is created, it's a simple matter to integrate it with the OLE DB component. First of all, add the OLE DB header file to the MTS component's header file, *objThree.h*:

```
    #include "dboauthors.h"
```

This makes the class definition for the OLE DB consumer object available from within the new MTS component.

 It might seem a little odd to add a header file from one component to another component when both components reside in the same DLL. However, just because both components reside in the same DLL does not make them aware of each other.

Next, add a test method that takes no parameters to the MTS component; its source code is shown in Example 13-6. Within this method, the code accesses the author's last name from each row in the authors table rowset, wraps it with a CComVariant, and writes the value to the returned web page.

Example 13-6. Accessing Author Last Name from an OLE DB Consumer Rowset

```
STDMETHODIMP CobjThree::test()
{

    _variant_t vbreak;
    vbreak = "<p>";

    Cdboauthors author;
    author.Open();

    author.MoveFirst();

    while (author.MoveNext() == S_OK) {
        CComVariant vt(author.m_aulname);
        m_piResponse->Write(vt);
        m_piResponse->Write(vbreak);
    }

    return S_OK;
}
```

The result of invoking this component method is a display of all the authors' last names from the authors table in the *pubs* database.

Creating a Parameterized Stored Procedure Call

The OLE DB templates can be used for more complex data actions, such as parameterized queries or stored procedure calls. As shown in the last section, you can add the OLE DB template functionality manually or you can use the ATL Object Wizard to add most of the functionality for you. This was demonstrated in the last section for a fairly simple data source query. This section creates a parameterized query using ATL templates.

First, create a new DLL using the ATL AppWizard and add support for both MTS and MFC. Once the DLL support files are generated, use the ATL Object Wizard to add a new MTS component, including support for IObjectControl, object pooling, and a Dual interface. Call this object authorTitle.

Once you create the new MTS component, add ASP support to it by adding in the ASP header file and by adding a data member called m_piResponse, as detailed earlier in this chapter. This provides the ability to write the data returned by an operation to the web page returned to the client.

Finally, add a new method to the component called GetAuthorTitle with a single input parameter of type **BSTR**. Remember that this must be added to the interface derived for the new component in order to be accessible as a COM interface.

Next, this example uses the SQL Server *pubs* database and a new stored procedure called *sp_getauthortitle*. The stored procedure creates a query that returns a title and an author's last and first name, given an author's last name. You'll need to create the stored procedure; its code is as follows:

```
CREATE      PROCEDURE [sp_getauthortitle]
    (@author_name  VARCHAR(40) )

AS
BEGIN
SELECT title, au_lname, au_fname
FROM titles, authors, titleauthor
WHERE titleauthor.au_id = authors.au_id and titles.title_id =
    titleauthor.title_id and
    au_lname = @author_name
END
```

The next action is to use the ATL Object Wizard to create an OLE DB Consumer object. As with earlier examples, the provider will be "Microsoft OLE DB Provider for SQL Server" and the data source will be the *pubs* sample database, with a user-id of "sa" and no password. Clicking on the Select Datasource button opens a list of tables and stored procedures that are available from the data source. Select the stored procedure you just created. Once the data source is defined, the Object Wizard automatically fills in the names for the C++ classes and files. Set the OLE DB Consumer Type of the data source to Command rather than Table for this example. No updates to the data are being supported, so leave all the Support options unchecked.

 If you don't have SQL Server, you can still create this example by creating a stored procedure or canned query that takes a parameter and returns query results. The actual data source being used isn't important. The use of parameters is.

After the ATL Object Wizard generates the OLE DB consumer support code, you can see that the generated header file, *dbospgetauthortitle.h*, contains the class definition for the **CAccessor** class, as shown in Example 13-7.

Example 13-7. CAccessor Class for the OLE DB Consumer

```
class Cdbospgetauthortitle1Accessor
{
public:
```

Example 13-7. CAccessor Class for the OLE DB Consumer (continued)

```
    LONG m_RETURNVALUE;
    TCHAR m_authorname[41];
    TCHAR m_coltitle[81];
    TCHAR m_colaulname[41];
    TCHAR m_colaufname[21];

BEGIN_PARAM_MAP(Cdbospgetauthortitle1Accessor)
    SET_PARAM_TYPE(DBPARAMIO_OUTPUT)
    COLUMN_ENTRY(1, m_RETURNVALUE)
    SET_PARAM_TYPE(DBPARAMIO_INPUT)
    COLUMN_ENTRY(2, m_authorname)
END_PARAM_MAP()

BEGIN_COLUMN_MAP(Cdbospgetauthortitle1Accessor)
    COLUMN_ENTRY(1, m_coltitle)
    COLUMN_ENTRY(2, m_colaulname)
    COLUMN_ENTRY(3, m_colaufname)
END_COLUMN_MAP()

DEFINE_COMMAND(Cdbospgetauthortitle1Accessor,
              _T("{ ? = CALL dbo.sp_getauthortitle;1 (?) }"))

// You may wish to call this function if you are inserting a record and wish to
// initialize all the fields, if you are not going to explicitly set all of them.
    void ClearRecord()
    {
        memset(this, 0, sizeof(*this));
    }
};
```

Notice from the generated code that three sets of macros are used. The first defines the parameter map, with an input item of the author last name and with one output parameter, which is a stored procedure result return value. The second macro defines a column mapping between the fields returned by the stored procedure query and the component properties used to access these field values. The third macro defines the command itself. A ClearRecord method is also defined for the **CAccessor** object, which can be used to initialize a record for inserting a new row.

 Note that the parameter output value is required for an OLE DB stored procedure call, and removing it from the generated code, or not providing it with manually created code, will result in an error.

In addition to the CAccessor code, there is also code generated for database initialization, session opening, and creating the rowset, as shown in Example 13-8.

Example 13-8. Code to Handle Obtaining the Rowset for the OLE DB Consumer

```
class Cdbospgetauthortitle1 : public
    CCommand<CAccessor<Cdbospgetauthortitle1Accessor> >
{
public:
    HRESULT Open()
    {
        HRESULT        hr;

        hr = OpenDataSource();
        if (FAILED(hr))
            return hr;

        return OpenRowset();
    }
    HRESULT OpenDataSource()
    {
        HRESULT        hr;
        CDataSource db;
        CDBPropSet   dbinit(DBPROPSET_DBINIT);

        dbinit.AddProperty(DBPROP_AUTH_PERSIST_SENSITIVE_AUTHINFO, false);
        dbinit.AddProperty(DBPROP_AUTH_USERID, OLESTR("sa"));
        dbinit.AddProperty(DBPROP_INIT_CATALOG, OLESTR("pubs"));
        dbinit.AddProperty(DBPROP_INIT_DATASOURCE, OLESTR("MARVIN"));
        dbinit.AddProperty(DBPROP_INIT_LCID, (long)1033);
        dbinit.AddProperty(DBPROP_INIT_PROMPT, (short)4);
        hr = db.Open(_T("SQLOLEDB.1"), &dbinit);
        if (FAILED(hr))
            return hr;

        return m_session.Open(db);
    }
    HRESULT OpenRowset()
    {
        return CCommand<CAccessor<Cdbospgetauthortitle1Accessor> >
            ::Open(m_session);
    }
    CSession    m_session;
};
```

To use the generated code from within the MTS component, include the header file in the MTS component header file:

```
#include "dbospgetauthortitle1.h"
```

All that's left is to add the code to the MTS component's GetAuthorTitle method, which accesses the OLE DB rowset, passes in a name, which is passed to the method, and processes the returned data fields. Example 13-9 contains this code.

Example 13-9. Calling a Stored Procedure

```
STDMETHODIMP CobjSix::GetAuthorTitle(BSTR bstrName)
{
    AFX_MANAGE_STATE(AfxGetStaticModuleState())

    // created consumer object
    Cdbospgetauthortitle1 titleauthor;

    // copy string to buffer
    CString ctmp;
    ctmp = bstrName;
    strcpy(titleauthor.m_authorname, ctmp);

    // open rowset
    titleauthor.Open();

    m_piResponse->Write(_variant_t("<table>"));
    while (titleauthor.MoveNext() == S_OK)
    {
        m_piResponse->Write(_variant_t("<tr><td>"));
        m_piResponse->Write(_variant_t(titleauthor.m_coltitle));
        m_piResponse->Write(_variant_t("</td><td>"));
        m_piResponse->Write(_variant_t(titleauthor.m_colaulname));
        m_piResponse->Write(_variant_t("</td><td>"));
        m_piResponse->Write(_variant_t(titleauthor.m_colaufname));
        m_piResponse->Write(_variant_t("</tr></td>"));

    }
    m_piResponse->Write(_variant_t("</table>"));

    return S_OK;
}
```

The result of calling this method within an ASP page is a table containing the title, author last name, and author first name matching any authors with the last name passed to the query.

Instead of using generated code, the example could be built with manually entered code. The **CAccessor** class needs to be defined in a manner nearly identical to that shown in Example 13-7. The biggest difference is that the data source initialization, session creation, and rowset operations could be contained directly within the method.

In addition, the string for the command can be changed. For example, you can change the command string to use an embedded SQL statement that basically duplicates the stored procedure that was used. The new command string within the `DEFINE_COMMAND` macro then becomes:

```
DEFINE_COMMAND(Cdbospgetauthortitle1Accessor,
              _T("select title, au_lname, au_fname \
              from titles, authors, titleauthor where \
              titles.title_id = titleauthor.title_id and\
              titleauthor.au_id = authors.au_id and \
              authors.au_lname = '?'"))
```

Since a stored procedure is no longer being used, the return value parameter within the `PARAM_MAP` macros, and its defining type macro, can be removed. When this change is made and the component is accessed again, the results are exactly the same.

Queries aren't the only use for OLE DB templates. They can also be used to update data, demonstrated in the next section.

Updating Data

Creating OLE DB Consumers for data updating requires a change when using the ATL Object Wizard. As shown in Figure 13-3, you must check the option boxes in the main dialog page for the Wizard that specify whether the consumer provides support for Change, Insert, and/or Delete to provide for data update support. One, two, or all three of the options can be selected.

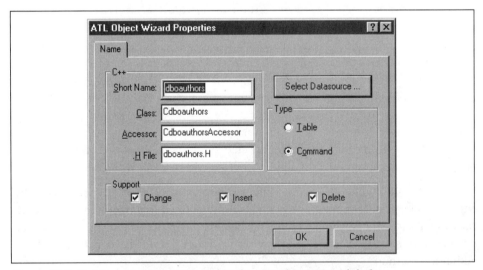

Figure 13-3. Checking update options within the ATL Object Wizard dialog

By adding in support for updates, there are changes made to the generated code as would be expected, though the changes are fairly small. Example 13-10 contains the code generated for the OpenRowset method used to open and return a rowset.

Example 13-10. Adding Update Capability for the OLE DB Consumer

```
HRESULT OpenRowset()
    {
        // Set properties for open
        CDBPropSet   propset(DBPROPSET_ROWSET);
        propset.AddProperty(DBPROP_IRowsetChange, true);
        propset.AddProperty(DBPROP_UPDATABILITY, DBPROPVAL_UP_CHANGE |
                            DBPROPVAL_UP_INSERT | DBPROPVAL_UP_DELETE);

        return CCommand<CAccessor<CdboauthorsAccessor> >
            ::Open(m_session, NULL, &propset);
    }
```

Comparing this code with that in Example 13-8, you can see that some properties are set to be used within the **CCommand** Open method that defines update capabilities on the **CRowset** object being returned, and that aren't used with a query.

Using the generated code to update data is no different from using the generated code to query the data. First, the header file containing the generated classes is added to the header file of the ASP/MTS component. After that, a variable of the same type of class created to return the rowset is instantiated. For example, the code in Example 13-11 contains a second method generated on the test MTS/ASP component that adds a new row to the authors table.

Example 13-11. Method to Insert Row into OLE DB Consumer Rowset

```
STDMETHODIMP CobjSix::InsertRow()
{
    AFX_MANAGE_STATE(AfxGetStaticModuleState())

    Cdboauthors author;

    try {

        // open CRowset and clear record
        // instantiating values
        author.Open();
        author.ClearRecord();

        // add in new values
        strcpy(author.m_auid, "999-99-9599");
        strcpy(author.m_aulname,"Testing");
        strcpy(author.m_aufname,"Iam");
        strcpy(author.m_phone,"617 555-1212");
        strcpy(author.m_address, "none");
        strcpy(author.m_city, "Brighton");
        strcpy(author.m_state, "MA");
        strcpy(author.m_zip, "02135");
```

Example 13-11. Method to Insert Row into OLE DB Consumer Rowset (continued)

```
        author.m_contract = false;

        // insert row
        hr = author.Insert();

    }
    catch (CException *e) {

      // write out error to returned Web page
      TCHAR   szError[255];
      e->GetErrorMessage(szError, 255);
      m_piResponse->Write(_variant_t(szError));
      }

    return S_OK;
}
```

The rowset is opened and the **CAccessor** ClearRecord method is called to instantiate all data values to a default empty value. These will act as placeholders in case not all of the fields are supplied with the insertion. Next, values are copied to the **CAccessor** data members that comprise the row being inserted. While these values are hardcoded, for your applications you would probably pass the values as parameters to the method. Following the data updates, the **CRowset** object's Insert method is called, which creates and inserts a new row with the **CAccessor** values into the database.

Deletes are just as easy. Instead of using the Insert method, move the rowset to the row you want to delete and call the Delete method.

Updates can be made by altering the **CAccessor** data members of a fetched row and then issuing the Update method call.

Instead of a **CCommand**, a **CTable** object can be used, which could improve the performance of the updates. **CTables** don't require some of the support that a **CComand** does. To use a **CTable**, just click the Table type when creating the new consumer object.

Additionally, as was demonstrated earlier in the query sections, the OLE DB templates can be used manually to update data as well as query it. It's important to remember the CDBPropSet object and to add the update properties when opening the rowset object.

Transaction management can also be handled within the component by accessing the **CSession** object's StartTransaction and Commit or Abort methods. A **CSession** object is created automatically as a data member of the same class that generates the rowset.

Further Reading

For additional reading about the topics covered in this chapter, check out the following:

- See the online article "Using Visual C++ OLE DB Provider Templates," at *http:/ /msdn.microsoft.com/developer/news/feature/vcjune98/vc6oledbprov.htm*.

- Microsoft's main data web site is located at *http://www.microsoft.com/data/*.

- More general information about OLE DB can be found at *http://www. microsoft.com/data/oledb/*.

- The SAMPCLNT OLE DB Sample consumer mentioned earlier in the chapter can be downloaded from *http://premium.microsoft.com/msdn/library/devprods/ vs6/vc++/vcsample/vcsmpsampclnt.htm*.

14

Persistence with ASP Components Using ATL and MFC

In Chapter 11, *Creating a Simple C++ ASP Component*, I mentioned that using the ActiveX Template Library (ATL) does not preclude using the Microsoft Foundation Classes (MFC). In fact, for the examples created in this chapter, we'll see that the two technologies blend to create some simple but powerful ASP components.

Also in earlier chapters, you had a chance to store information into the ASP Session or Application objects, persisting this information for the session or until the ASP application was shut down. What happens, though, when you need information that lasts beyond the application?

This chapter discusses two approaches for maintaining information. The first is to write and read the information from a file; the examples use the MFC `CFile` class for this. The second is to persist an entire object—its structure as well as its data—to a file. This technique uses the MFC `CFile`, `CArchive`, and `CObject` classes to first create a serializable class, and then to archive and reretrieve this object from a file.

Most ASP components are created on the client thread, in this case a thread created by IIS, and most ASP components perform their work within this thread. There may be times, though, when you are performing a time-consuming operation and you don't want to wait for the operation to finish before returning feedback to the web page. This chapter provides a demonstration of creating a separate thread for managing the serialization of our object, discussed earlier.

By the end of the chapter, you should come away with the realization that file-based I/O, object serialization, and threads are not as complicated as you might have originally thought—with a little help from ATL and MFC, of course.

Combining MFC and ATL

Usually you won't want to include a large framework such as MFC when creating small, lightweight controls, but there are advantages to using MFC. One such advantage is the built-in class support for objects such as `CString` and `CStdioFile`. Another advantage is the built-in macros that do things such as simplify thread creation. Plus, when creating server-side components, the size of the component is not as much of an issue as with components embedded into client-side applications, and ASP components are definitely server components. This section demonstrates adding MFC support for an ATL component by creating a component that's used in the rest of the examples in this chapter.

First of all, create a component named *Ctest2APP* using the ATL COM AppWizard and selecting the options to add support for MFC and MTS. The result of adding MFC support to the ASP component is the addition of two header files to include the MFC core and automation functionality, *afxwin.h* and *afxdisp.h*. Also, the wizard automatically alters the DLL support code to include `CWinApp` as part of the application, as shown in Example 14-1.

Example 14-1. Code to Provide Support for the MFC Class CWinApp

```
class CTest2App : public CWinApp
{
public:

// Overrides
    // ClassWizard generated virtual function overrides
    //{{AFX_VIRTUAL(CTest2App)
    public:
     virtual BOOL InitInstance();
     virtual int ExitInstance();
    //}}AFX_VIRTUAL

    //{{AFX_MSG(CTest2App)
       // NOTE - the ClassWizard will add and remove member functions here.
       //    DO NOT EDIT what you see in these blocks of generated code !
    //}}AFX_MSG
    DECLARE_MESSAGE_MAP()
};
```

In addition, the wizard implements two methods, InitInstance and ExitInstance, within the project's main C++ file. When creating a component that incorporates MFC, the initialization and termination functionality is really invoked within the context of the Microsoft Foundation Framework, meaning that initialization code is included within the `CWinApp` InitInstance method, and termination code is included within the **CWinApp** ExitInstance method. The code the wizard generates to handle this is very similar to that shown in the Example 14-2.

Example 14-2. Code to Add MFC Instance Management

```
CTest2App theApp;

BOOL CTest2App::InitInstance()
{
    _Module.Init(ObjectMap, m_hInstance, &LIBID_TEST2Lib);
    return CWinApp::InitInstance();
}

int CTest2App::ExitInstance()
{
    _Module.Term();
    return CWinApp::ExitInstance();
}
```

The ATL COM AppWizard also generates the following line of code for every COM method when MFC is incorporated into the project:

```
AFX_MANAGE_STATE(AfxGetStaticModuleState());
```

The **AFX_MANAGE_STATE** macro protects exported methods and is used by MFC when managing the state of data. This is mainly used with DLLs that might do such things as open a dialog window and that have to manage window resources. Since you don't use windows with an ASP component, it can be removed, or you can leave it in—there's no harm to its inclusion.

Adding MFC to the DLL does not affect how ATL components are added to the DLL. For the example created for this chapter, add a new component by using the ATL Object Wizard and then selecting the MS Transaction Server Component object. Name the component *Advanced*, select the options for Dual Interface, support of **IObjectControl**, and object pooling from the MTS tab, and generate the component. To add support for ASP, include the following in the header file for the component, following the line that includes the MTX header file:

```
#include <asptlb.h>
```

This adds support for the built-in ASP objects.

Once the MTS/ASP component is created, add a new private data member, m_piResponse, to the class header file to support the ASP Response object:

```
CComPtr<IResponse> m_piResponse;
```

The data member is set in the component's Activate method and released in the component's Deactivate method, as discussed in Chapter 12, *The C++ ASP Built-In Interfaces*. To repeat the code here, the member is set in the Activate event handler method:

```
HRESULT Cmytest::Activate()
{
    HRESULT hr = S_OK;
    CComBSTR bstrObj;
    CComVariant vt;
    CComPtr<IGetContextProperties> pProps; //Context Properties

    IDispatch* piDispatch = NULL;

    // generated code
    hr = GetObjectContext(&m_spObjectContext);
    if (FAILED(hr))
        return hr;

    // add in code to get built-in objects

    // get Context Properties
    hr = m_spObjectContext->QueryInterface( IID_IGetContextProperties,
                (void**)&pProps );
    if (FAILED(hr))
        return hr;

    // get Response property
    bstrObj = "Response";
    hr = pProps->GetProperty( bstrObj, &vt ) ;

    if (FAILED(hr))
        return hr;

    piDispatch = vt. pdispVal;
    hr = piDispatch->QueryInterface( IID_IResponse,
                    (void**)&m_piResponse );

    return hr;
}
```

The member is released in the component's Deactivate event handler method, as repeated from Chapter 12 in the following code block:

```
void Cmytest::Deactivate()
{
    // release pointer refs to built-in ASP objects
    m_piResponse.Release();
}
```

The next section discusses file I/O from an ASP component.

File Access from ASP Components

By adding support for MFC, you also add support for MFC classes such as `CFile` and the classes derived from `CFile`, such as `CMemFile`, `CSocketFile`, and

CStdioFile. These classes provide techniques to control I/O such as reading and writing to a file, standard input and output, memory, or even operations across a network.

Some forms of I/O don't make much sense from an ASP component. As an example, writing to standard input and output such as an NT console is not very meaningful for a component that does not have access to the console, or when the communication to the standard input is not monitored. However, file-based I/O not only makes sense, but, along with database access, it is probably the most common technique for storing information outside of an IIS application.

There is more than one approach to file-based I/O. Using CFile directly provides for reading and writing of unbuffered binary data, whether to memory or to disk. CStdioFile, a class derived from CFile, is used mainly for text input and output. For writing simple text to a file, either of these classes can be used, with the main difference between them being that CStdioFile does not support some of the locking methods implemented in CFile.

To demonstrate file I/O using CStdioFile, add two methods to the CAdvanced component. The first method is called set_info and contains one input parameter of type BSTR; the method in its entirety can be seen in Example 14-3. The method instantiates a new object of type CStdioFile, which by default opens the file as well as creating the object. The CStdioFile class is then used to write out the parameter string value to the file. Standard C++ exception handling is used to catch and process any exceptions that might result from this activity.

Example 14-3. The set_info Method

```
// write out parameter to disk file
STDMETHODIMP CAdvanced::set_info(BSTR name)
{
    AFX_MANAGE_STATE(AfxGetStaticModuleState())

    // write object to file
    try {

        // file name
        char* pFileName = "e:\\test1.dat";

        // open file using text type, create, write modes, and exclusive share
        CStdioFile stdFile( pFileName, CFile::modeCreate | CFile::modeWrite |
            CFile::shareExclusive | CFile::typeText);

        // if successful on opening file, write out parameter
        CString bstrName = name;
        stdFile.WriteString(bstrName);
        stdFile.Close();
    }
```

Example 14-3. The set_info Method (continued)

```
// error handling
catch (CFileException *e) {

    // write out error to returned Web page
        TCHAR    szError[255];
     e->GetErrorMessage(szError, 255);
    CComVariant vt = CComVariant(szError);
    m_piResponse->Write(vt);
    }
return S_OK;

}
```

The first parameter to the **CStdioFile** constructor is the location and name of the file being opened, in this case *e:\test1.dat*. The first backslash in the text tells the compiler that the second backslash should be read literally.

The second parameter to **CStdioFile** specifies the file-opening options. These options include **modeCreate**, which will create the file if it does not already exist, **modeWrite**, which opens the file for writing, **typeText**, which sets the output to text mode, and **shareExclusive**, which opens the file for exclusive access and denies other access, whether read or write. This latter prevents another web page access from opening the file until the contents are written out. Once the string is written out to the file, it is closed. This releases the exclusive lock on the file.

Using **CFile** directly also provides for file locking on a specific byte range through the LockRange and UnlockRange methods.

If a **CFileException** had occurred, the error message associated with the exception would have been printed to the returning web page. To catch all exceptions, I could have instead used **CException**, as will be demonstrated next.

To retrieve the string from the file, add another method, get_info, to the **CAdvanced** class. This method takes a **BSTR** as a return value. Example 14-4 contains the complete source code for this method.

Example 14-4. The get_info Method

```
// access string in file and return
STDMETHODIMP CAdvanced::get_info(BSTR *pbstrName)
{
    AFX_MANAGE_STATE(AfxGetStaticModuleState())

    // read object from file
    try {
```

Example 14-4. The get_info Method (continued)

```
        // file name
        char* pFileName = "e:\\test1.dat";
        CString strName;

        // create file object and open file for read
        CStdioFile stdFile( pFileName, CFile::modeRead | CFile::typeText);

        // read string, close file and return string
        stdFile.ReadString(strName);
        stdFile.Close();
        CComBSTR bstrName(strName);
        *pbstrName = bstrName.Detach();
    }

    // error handling
    catch (CException *e) {

        // write out error to returned Web age
        TCHAR   szError[255];
        e->GetErrorMessage(szError, 255);
        CComVariant vt = CComVariant(szError);
        m_piResponse->Write(vt);
    }
    return S_OK;

}
```

Like the set_info method, get_info creates a **CStdioFile** object and uses it to read the string from the file and return the string to the requesting web page. Also, as with set_info, the **CStdioFile** activity is contained within C++ exception handling, but this method uses the **CException** class rather than the derived **CFileException**. This will capture all of the exceptions that could occur with the method, not just those that are I/O-based.

The ASP page that contains the ASP component creates the component using the Server object's CreateObject method:

```
    Dim myobj
    Set myobj = Server.CreateObject("test2.Advanced")
```

The value to be stored persistently is set by calling the set_info method, passing in the string to be saved:

```
    Dim strng
    Strng = "Shelley Powers 12/12/98 1:5 100"
    myobj.set_info(strng)
```

Accessing the value uses the get_info method:

```
    Strng = myobj.get_info()
```

Accessing information from a file within an ASP component is relatively simple. What are some of the problems associated with file access from an ASP component? First and foremost is handling file access when several people may be requesting ASP pages that try to access the same file at the same time. Using share privileges and locks can prevent deadlock problems. Other problems can occur due to permissions for the file activity. If a write occurs to a subdirectory that is not opened for writing by the anonymous Internet user account (usually named `IUSR_COMPUTER`, where *COMPUTER* is the name of the computer), an error will occur. In addition, any activity that makes a change to the server opens the door to hackers, so security is a consideration when using file I/O.

Still, the `CStdioFile` class is useful for fairly standard text I/O, but other classes, or even `CFile` itself, are better suited to other tasks. One such task is to provide for object serialization, discussed next.

Creating a Serializable Class

Serialization is used to maintain object state. By this I mean that an object, including the object structure and current values, can be written out in some persistent form and recovered at a later time. The persistent form is usually a disk file, but it could also be a memory file for actions such as undoing a change.

To create a serializable object, you first need to create the class that can *be* serialized. Microsoft has actually provided five easy steps for creating a serializable object, steps which are demonstrated in this section.

The first requirement for creating a serialized object is to derive the class for it from the MFC `CObject` class or from an object that is itself derived from `CObject`. In the case of our example, the class we'll create is called `CGame`, and its purpose is to store information about an online game winner, perhaps to maintain a listing of high scores. Within an existing ATL project, the class can be added by selecting the Insert → New Class option, then selecting either MFC Class or Generic Class from the "Class type" drop-down list box. In the Derived From list box, enter `CObject` so the new generic class is derived from `CObject` as the base class.

CObject provides only a few methods. IsSerializable checks whether the object derived from `CObject` is serializable, and Serialize actually performs the serialization. IsKindOf allows runtime comparison between an instance of a class and the class type. GetRuntimeClass allows you to access a runtime structure describing the class. This structure contains information such as a string with the class name, a pointer to the object's constructor, and all other information necessary to support the serialization and instantiation of an object from serialized store.

Once **CGame** has been created, use the right mouse button from the Class View to
add the following four data members: m_date, m_score, m_gametime, and m_
name. All of the data members are public. (This would also be the time to add any
methods for the object, but in the interest of keeping the example simple, no
class-specific methods are created for the class.) The data types and the resulting
code generated by adding the elements are shown in the following code block,
copied from the game object's header file, *game.h*:

```
class CGame : public CObject
{
public:
    DECLARE_SERIAL( CGame )

    // Constructor
    CGame();

    // define members
    LONG m_gametime;
    WORD m_score;
    CTime m_date;
    CString m_name;

    // define methods
     void Serialize( CArchive& ar );
    virtual ~CGame();

// Implementation
protected:
};
```

The next step in creating the object is to override the Serialize method for the
CObject base class by right-clicking on the **CGame** class in Class View and selecting the Add Member Function from the context menu. Add the Serialize method,
which takes the address of a **Carchive** object as a parameter. (The **CArchive**
class is used to store complex objects in a persistent, binary form.) Once Visual
C++ has generated the header for the method in the C++ file, *game.cpp*, add in the
rest of the code, which is shown in Example 14-5.

Example 14-5. Overridden Serialize Method for New Class

```
void CGame::Serialize( CArchive& archive )
{
    // call base class function first
    // base class is CObject in this case
    CObject::Serialize( archive );

    // now do the stuff for our specific class
    if( archive.IsStoring() )
        archive << m_name << m_date << m_gametime << m_score;
```

Example 14-5. Overridden Serialize Method for New Class (continued)

```
    else
        archive >> m_name >> m_date >> m_gametime >> m_score;
}
```

The first part of the Serialize method is the call to the base object to perform its serialization process. The rest of the method passes data to the **CArchive** object, if the object is being stored, or accesses data from **CArchive**, if the object is being retrieved.

The **CArchive** IsStoring method returns 0 if the archive is in a load state; otherwise, it returns a non-zero value. The archive state is described a bit later. The double angle bracket operators (<< and >>) are used to store or retrieve the simple data types for the object.

The next step to provide for a serializable object is to use the DECLARE_SERIAL macro with the object:

```
    DECLARE_SERIAL( CGame )
```

This macro is called from within the public declaration section of the object and must be the first line of the class definition. The DECLARE_SERIAL macro generates the C++ header code to support serialization of the **CObject** type.

After creating a class derived from **CObject**, adding in the serializing data members, coding the Serialize method, and adding the DECLARE_SERIAL macro, the next requirement for creating a serializable object is to have a default constructor for the class that contains no arguments. This requirement is met for us automatically; when the class was created using Insert → New Class, it was automatically created with a default constructor and destructor, the constructor without parameters.

Another macro must also be used, and so the final step to creating a serializable object is to include in the C++ implementation file for the class a line similar to the following:

```
    IMPLEMENT_SERIAL( CGame, CObject, 1 )
```

This generates the C++ code in the implementation file for a dynamic **CObject**-derived class at runtime. This code should be included just before the methods for the default constructor and destructor, as shown in the following code block:

```
    IMPLEMENT_SERIAL( CGame, CObject, 1 )


    CGame::CGame()
    {

    }
```

```
CGame::~CGame()
{

}
```

Once all of the serialization requirements have been met, any object instantiated from the class can be serialized, as demonstrated next. Just to summarize, the requirements for serializing the object are:

1. Create a new object by inheriting from `CObject`.

2. Add the object's data members.

3. Override the `CObject`'s Serialize method in the new object, and provide serialization specific to the object's data members.

4. Include the `DECLARE_SERIAL` macro in the new object's header file.

5. Define a constructor with no parameters.

6. Add the `IMPLEMENT_SERIAL` macro to the C++ file after the header file section and before the object's methods.

Persistence Through Object Serialization

The key to serialization is the `CArchive` class passed to the Serialize method of the object class. `CArchive` has a constructor that takes a pointer to a file for the first parameter, a flag that sets the load or store state as the second parameter, and an optional buffer size and buffer. The latter two parameters are to contain the internal buffer used by the archive object. Usually the buffer that `CArchive` creates by default is sufficient, and these two parameters are not used. The file pointer actually references an open file, which is then used for the I/O-specific parts of the serialization process.

To perform the serialization, the serializable class was included within the component created earlier in the chapter, `CAdvanced`. For this example, the `CGame` object is going to be compiled into the application rather than created at runtime, so the header file for the new class is all that is required in the `CAdvanced` C++ implementation file:

```
#include "Game.h"
```

To support serialization using the `CGame` object, you must add two new methods to the `CAdvanced` class. One, set_score, is used to create a `CGame` object and archive it to disk; Example 14-6 shows the complete code for the set_score method. The `CFile` class is used for the serialization instead of one of the derived file types. The Open method for `CFile` does not require exception handling, since the `CFileException` exception is actually returned as one of the parameters in the Open method. Error checking occurs by testing the returned value of the Open method, with a **False** return being a failed open condition and a **True** value representing a successful condition.

 Why does the Open method for **CFile** not throw exceptions? Because failed attempts to open a file are expected failures rather than unexpected failures. Processing is actually meant to continue from the point where the method is called, regardless of the return value.

Example 14-6. The set_score Method

```
// serialize the CGame object to disk
STDMETHODIMP Cagain::set_score(BSTR name, int score, int time)
{
    AFX_MANAGE_STATE(AfxGetStaticModuleState())

    // create new version of Game class
    CGame *m_game = new CGame();

    // set information
    m_game->m_date = CTime::GetCurrentTime();
    m_game->m_gametime = time;
    m_game->m_name = name;
    m_game->m_score = score;

    // serialize object to file
    CFile f;
    CFileException e;
    char* pFileName = "e:\\test.dat";

    // open file, check for error
    if( !f.Open( pFileName, CFile::modeCreate | CFile::modeWrite |
        CFile::shareExclusive, &e ) )
    {
        CComVariant vt(OLESTR("Could not Store Game Results"));
        m_piResponse->Write(vt);
    }
    else {

        // serialize the object
        CArchive archive(&f, CArchive::store);
        m_game->Serialize(archive);
        archive.Close();
        f.Close();
    }
    return S_OK;
}
```

The method has three parameters: a name, a score, and a game time. It creates a new instance of **CGame** and assigns the parameters to the appropriate class members. In addition, the time the object was created is also set using the CTime class method GetCurrentTime to get the current system time. After the object's data members are set, the CFile object is created and the disk file is opened. If the file is opened successfully, the CArchive object is created and serialization can start.

Notice from the code in Example 14-6 that the instance of the CArchive class is set to a "store state" when created. This will result in the CArchive IsStoring method call shown in Example 14-5 returning a True value. When this happens, the object is serialized to the file. After the object is serialized, first the archive object and then the file are closed.

Another method, called get_score, is necessary to retrieve the data; its complete source code is shown in Example 14-7. This method has three parameters, two of type VARIANT and one of type pointer to BSTR. The VARIANT data types are necessary to return values by reference to VBScript in the ASP page that references the method. The last parameter is returned as a return value from the function within the scripting page, and can be of any data type. In this case, the value being returned is a string, and the COM compatible BSTR value is used.

In Example 14-7, a new object of type CGame type is created, as well as new objects of CFile and CArchive. Instead of using CArchive to write to the disk file, the file is now opened for read access, and CArchive is set to a load state. When the Serialize object is called for CGame, the data members for the game object are set to the previously saved values.

Example 14-7. The get_score Method

```
// retrieve the CGame object from disk
STDMETHODIMP Cagain::get_score(VARIANT* score, VARIANT* time, BSTR *pbstrName)
{

    AFX_MANAGE_STATE(AfxGetStaticModuleState())

    // create new version of CGame class
    CGame *m_game = new CGame();

    CFile f;
    CFileException e;
    char* pFileName = "e:\\test.dat";

    // open file and check for error
    if( !f.Open( pFileName, CFile::modeRead, &e ) )
    {

        CComVariant vt(OLESTR("Could not access Game Results"));
        m_piResponse->Write(vt);
    }
    else {
```

Example 14-7. The get_score Method (continued)

```
        // restore object state
        CArchive archive(&f, CArchive::load);
        m_game->Serialize(archive);

        // return values as Variants
        CComVariant *vtScore = new CComVariant(m_game->m_score);
        vtScore->Detach(score);
        CComVariant *vtGametime = new CComVariant(m_game->m_gametime);
        vtGametime->Detach(time);
        m_game->m_name.AllocSysString();

        // return name as BSTR
        *pbstrName = m_game->m_name.SetSysString(pbstrName);
    }
    return S_OK;
}
```

Once the data members of the **CGame** object have been set, the appropriate data member values are assigned to the appropriate parameters for return to the calling ASP program. Example 14-8 contains the complete ASP page to run this component's methods.

Example 14-8. ASP Page to Retrieve Game Scores

```
<HTML>
<HEAD>
<BODY>
<H1>test</H1>
<%
  Dim authorsObject

  Set authorsObject = Server.CreateObject("Test2.again.1")

  Dim str
  str = "Shelley"
  authorsObject.set_score str, 555, 6666

  Dim int1, int2
  Dim str2
  str2 = authorsObject.get_score(int1, int2)

  Response.Write("<H3>" & str2 & " is the winner with a score of " &
             CStr(int1) & " and a time of " & _
             Cstr(int2) & "</H3>")
%>
</BODY>
</HTML>
```

Many times, object serialization is used to maintain object state in a distributed environment. As an example, an object may be serialized before being passed as a parameter in a method from one component on one machine to another component on another machine. Then, the object is serialized again and the persisted object on the originating machine is destroyed. Using this approach, if a transaction fails at any point in the application, recovery can begin at the point of failure rather than at the beginning of the process.

However, there's no reason that object serialization can't be used to maintain persistence for a complex object within an Internet application, as the game example has demonstrated in a simplified manner. It doesn't replace a database for more extensive transactions, but it can be an effective approach for isolated information.

So far, this chapter has demonstrated two different techniques of storing information to a disk file. One of the disadvantages to using file I/O in an Internet application is that the reply to the web page reader can be held up by the time required to make the file transaction. This leads us to the next and last section in this chapter, using threads to handle file I/O.

Using Threads for Background Processes

In a Windows environment such as Windows 9x or NT, when you print a document, the printing actually occurs in the background. You can continue doing other work and do not have to wait for the document to finish. This is an example of using a separate *worker* thread to perform a background process, such as printing the document, while the main thread of the application continues to process the user's interactive requests. This use of threads was discussed in Chapter 4, *ASP Components and Threads*.

With an ASP application, the use of threads becomes more a matter of returning a web page to a reader as soon as possible after the reader has initiated some action. The longer it takes to return a page to the reader, the greater the chance that the ASP page script will time out or the reader will lose patience and go on to other web pages.

Within an Intranet, using a separate thread to handle printing makes a whole lot of sense. A document could be requested from a web page and routed to a printer on the server. Additionally, as demonstrated earlier in this chapter, file access can also be processed on a separate worker thread, speeding up page returns to the user.

To assist in using threads, Microsoft has created an MFC function, *AfxBeginThread*, that performs a couple of tasks. First, it instantiates a new object using the `CWinThread` class. Next, it calls the `CWinThread` method CreateThread to start the thread. In addition, the function also provides checks that test for failures on the thread and provides for clean up of all objects if the thread process does fail.

There are two versions of *AfxBeginThread*, one to create a worker thread and one to create a user-interface thread. The thread created in this example for the ASP component is a worker thread, which runs without interaction from the user.

The *AfxBeginThread* function takes a function name as its first parameter, and a parameter to be passed to that function as the second parameter. Additional optional parameters are the thread priority, the stack size of the thread, whether the thread is created in a suspended state, and a pointer to a SECURITY_ ATTRIBUTES structure. The latter is used to provide a security descriptor for the object, and is a standard parameter for most functions that return handles to an object. The *AfxBeginThread* function returns a pointer to a CWinThread object. The two prototypes for *AfxBeginThread*, as they are defined in Microsoft documentation, are:

```
CWinThread* AfxBeginThread( AFX_THREADPROC pfnThreadProc,
LPVOID pParam, int nPriority = THREAD_PRIORITY_NORMAL, UINT nStackSize = 0,
DWORD dwCreateFlags = 0, LPSECURITY_ATTRIBUTES lpSecurityAttrs = NULL );

CWinThread* AfxBeginThread( CRuntimeClass* pThreadClass, int nPriority =
THREAD_PRIORITY_NORMAL, UINT nStackSize = 0, DWORD dwCreateFlags = 0,
LPSECURITY_ATTRIBUTES lpSecurityAttrs = NULL );
```

For the last example shown in this chapter, we'll create a new function to handle the object serialization using the techniques discussed earlier. However, instead of creating a method of the CAdvanced object, we'll create a function that must follow a specific function declaration. The declaration is:

```
UINT TheThreadedFunction( LPVOID pParam );
```

The return value for the function must be an unsigned integer, and its only parameter is a long pointer to a void (otherwise known as star (*) void).

As Example 14-9 shows, the first thing the function does is check to make sure that the object passed to the function is the correct type. If it is, the object is serialized. Otherwise a value of one (1) is returned. Once this test has been successfully passed, the by-now-familiar serialization can occur.

Example 14-9. Serialization of an Object on a Separate Worker Thread

```
// serialization process, run on separate worker thread
UINT MyThreadProc( LPVOID pParam ){

    CGame* pGame = (CGame*)pParam;

    // if pGame is not valid return with error condition
    if (pGame == NULL ||
        !pGame->IsKindOf(RUNTIME_CLASS(CGame)))
    return 1;

    // serialize object to file
```

Example 14-9. Serialization of an Object on a Separate Worker Thread (continued)

```
    CFile f;
    CFileException e;
    char* pFileName = "e:\\test.dat";

    // open file, check for errors
    if( !f.Open( pFileName, CFile::modeCreate | CFile::modeWrite
        | CFile::shareExclusive, &e ) )
    {
        return 1;
    }
    else {

        // serialize the object
        CArchive archive(&f, CArchive::store);
        pGame->Serialize(archive);
        archive.Close();
        f.Close();
    }
    return 0;    // thread completed successfully}
}
```

Notice that the main difference between the serialization code in this function and that shown in Example 14-6 is that this code does not access the **CAdvanced** object's *m_piResponse* member variable to write out an error message. All it does is return a value of 1 for an error.

Once the thread function has been created, all that's left is to write the **CAdvanced** method that creates the **CGame** object and begins the thread. Example 14-10 contains the code for this method.

Example 14-10. Method to Start a Worker Thread, Passing to It a Thread Process

```
// serializing the CGame object using a worker thread
STDMETHODIMP CAdvanced::set_extended_score(BSTR name, int score, int time)
{
    AFX_MANAGE_STATE(AfxGetStaticModuleState())

    // create new version of Game class
    CGame *m_game = new CGame();

    // set information
    m_game->m_date = CTime::GetCurrentTime();
    m_game->m_gametime = time;
    m_game->m_name = name;
    m_game->m_score = score;

    // begin thread and return
    AfxBeginThread(MyThreadProc, m_game);
    return S_OK;
}
```

When *AfxBeginThread* is called, the first parameter is the name of the function shown in Example 14-8, and the second parameter is the CGame object created within the method. None of the optional parameters are specified, which means each is set to its default value. The third parameter sets the priority, and defaults to THREAD_PRIORITY_NORMAL. The fourth parameter, the stack size, is set to a value of zero (0) by default. Doing this creates a stack size equal to that of the calling thread. The fifth parameter determines whether the thread is created in suspend mode or is begun as soon as the thread is created. By default, the thread is started as soon as it is created. The sixth and final parameter, which is not used in this example, is a pointer to a security attributes structure.

By using a worker thread to handle the file-based object serialization, the web page is returned as soon as *AfxBeginThread* is called, not when the object has actually been serialized. Calling the new component method that uses threads is no different than calling the methods that didn't use threads (demonstrated in Example 14-8), except that the page return should, hopefully, be a little faster, and the method name is changed:

```
authorsObject.set_extended_score str, 555, 6666
```

 As you can imagine, if you must return the results of an operation to the web page reader or provide some form of feedback, using threads is not as viable an option. Use the following scenario to determine whether to use threads: when you print a document, you aren't notified of a successful print, only an unsuccessful print. Would a similar process work if you weren't notified of either event? If so, use threads. If not, continue to use the serial processing.

Further Reading

For additional reading about the topics covered in this chapter, check out the following:

- To find out more about threads in general, I recommend the book *Advanced Windows*, authored by Jeffrey Richter and published by Microsoft Press.

- An example of using ATL in an MFC server, "MFCATL: Using ATL COM Objects in an MFC Server," is available at *http://premium.microsoft.com/msdn/ library/devprods/vs6/vc++/vcsample/_sample_atl_mfcatl.htm.*

- Another article discussing combining ATL and MFC is "Create an ATL Project that supports MFC," at *http://premium.microsoft.com/msdn/library/devprods/ vs6/vc++/vccore/vchowcreateatlprojectthatsupportsmfc.htm.*

- Read more about serialization in the article "Serialization: Making a Serializable Class," at *http://premium.microsoft.com/msdn/library/devprods/vs6/vc++/vccore/_core_serialization.3a_.making_a_serializable_class.htm.*

- An overview of COObject can be found at *http://premium.microsoft.com/msdn/library/devprods/vs6/vc++/vccore/_core_cobject_class.3a_.specifying_levels_of_functionality.htm.*

- Read more about creating worker threads in the article "Multithreading: Creating Worker Threads," at *http://premium.microsoft.com/msdn/library/devprods/vs6/vc++/vccore/_core_multithreading.3a_.creating_worker_threads.htm.*

IV

Developing ASP Components with Visual J++

15

Creating a Simple Java Component

ASP components are COM objects, but as long as a particular development environment supports COM, there is no limitation on which tool or programming language can be used to build the component. This includes Java and the Visual J++ programming tool, Microsoft's entry into the Java IDE market.

As a COM object, there are certain requirements the object must meet, such as exposing certain interfaces and requiring the use of pointers to these same interfaces. Java, however, does not support the concept of a pointer. The inference based on these two statements is that Java cannot be used to create ASP components. In this case, though, the logic fails. Java can be used to create ASP components. Not only that, but these same ASP components can also be used within Microsoft Transaction Server (MTS) as MTS-based ASP components.

Java-based ASP components are created as Java code classes or as non-visual *Java-Beans*. JavaBeans are separate components that can be incorporated into an application in much the same manner that ActiveX controls can be used within applications. A *Java code class* is no different than any other language's code class: it is included in an application and does not have a beginning "main" program. The primary purpose of a code class is to provide access to a basic set of functionality, such as the functionality included into an ASP component through the addition of the ASP object library.

This chapter provides an overview of the JavaBean concept and how it compares to and differs from ActiveX components. As JavaBeans are primarily visual, the chapter concentrates more on converting Java code classes into ASP components. However, the same techniques that can be used to convert nonvisual JavaBeans can be used to convert Java code classes. This chapter also discusses how to access components written in Visual Basic or C++ from within a Java component.

At the time this was written, several legal decisions were pending regarding Microsoft's Java VM and the use of directives, such as the COM directive mentioned later in this chapter. Microsoft may make changes to Visual J++ in order to comply with these court orders, and this may impact—hopefully slightly—how the Visual J++ tool works with COM objects. Please check the Microsoft Visual J++ web site, at the URL given at the end of the chapter, for detailed information relating to Visual J++ before proceeding to try the examples in this chapter.

What Are JavaBeans?

Sun created JavaBeans to encompass independent software components that could be accessed by a visual tool. They are very similar to ActiveX components, except that JavaBeans are platform-neutral, requiring the existence of a Java Virtual Machine, while ActiveX components are language-neutral, and must have support libraries in the environment in which they are used.

When a component is made available for access within a visual tool, this does not mean it has to provide a visual interface. This just means that the component can be added to an application at design time, and the component's properties, methods, and events are exposed for access within the application.

A characteristic of a JavaBean is that it must be persistent, and the bean's properties, methods, and events can be "found" with the process of *introspection*. Introspection is a mechanism that allows the application builder, or visual tool, to query the bean to see what methods it provides, and what properties and events it supports. It is very similar to **IUnknown**, discussed in Chapter 3, *ASP Components and COM*, which is used to query a component for interface support.

ActiveX components can be accessed from within beans, and beans can be accessed by ActiveX components, but only in an integrated environment supported by the Microsoft Virtual Machine (VM). Java is not compiled to a machine-dependent binary code as C++ is, but is instead compiled to *byte* code, which is then interpreted on virtual machines that are created for the platforms that support Java. Virtual machines have been created for most operating systems, but the Microsoft VM, however, is not cross-platform-compatible, and to take advantage of the ActiveX-Java integration, the Java component/application must have access to the Microsoft VM. This could be a problem with user interface components built for a variety of applications and on a variety of machines. However, this isn't a problem, for the most part, with ASP components. ASP components, and by this I mean components meant to be directly accessed from within an ASP page, run in environments supported by Microsoft's VM.

Actually, with the porting of DCOM to Unix and the support of ASP on other platforms and with other web servers, this is no longer necessarily true. Additionally, Sun has provided the JavaBeans Bridge for ActiveX and the JavaBeans Migration Assistant for ActiveX, which allow ActiveX/Bean communication without having to use Microsoft's VM. However, we can safely say that, *for the most part*, ASP components written in Java will be run within a Windows environment, using Microsoft's VM if ActiveX integration is supported.

Component Execution and Threads

Java has thread capability built directly into the language, and thread management is actually relatively simple. A class that can run on a separate thread is subclassed from the Java **Thread** class, and the run method is overridden to include the thread-specific code.

Creating threads within a Java ASP component is not as much of an issue as is creating thread-safe components. It is up to the component developer to ensure that the Java-based component is thread-safe. One way to ensure this is to protect the component's global data from inadvertent access, such as a both-threaded component accessing and changing global data while another both-threaded component is still processing a method and expecting the global data to retain its original value. This problem was demonstrated in Chapter 4, *ASP Components and Threads*.

Another way of ensuring that a method within a Java component is thread-safe is to use the "synchronized" method modifier, discussed in the next section, which serves to prevent a thread from entering a method currently accessed by another thread.

Access to a component may be marshaled or not, depending on the threading model used for the component and the one used with the client. How COM handles marshaling and Java component instantiation depends on the threading model used with the component. The Microsoft VM determines on which thread to create the component, and this determines if the calls to the component are marshaled.

If the component is designated as using the free- or both-threading model, the component is instantiated on the calling thread and all method calls are direct to the object. If the component is designated as single-threaded, the component is created on the application's main thread, and all calls to the component are marshaled if the calling thread is not the main thread. If the component is apartment-threaded, it is instantiated on the calling thread if this thread is capable of hosting an apartment-threaded component. Otherwise, the component, and all other apartment-threaded components, are instantiated on a special thread that the VM creates. All components must then share this one thread, and all component calls must be marshaled.

Unfortunately, cross-thread marshaling has about the same performance considerations as cross-process marshaling, since the method parameters must be pulled from the client's local stack, converted into a flat data stream, and then converted back in the component.

Creating the Java Class

The component that we'll create in this chapter is no different, behaviorally, than the ones created in Chapter 7, *Creating a Simple Visual Basic ASP Component*, and Chapter 11, *Creating a Simple C++ ASP Component*. In those chapters, a small ASP component that generates dynamic HTML (DHTML) was created. DHTML can be used to alter the appearance or position of HTML elements both before and after the page has been loaded. The purpose of the ASP component is to write out the browser-specific code to perform the DHTML action associated with each component method. The browsers supported by the component are Netscape Navigator 4.x and Internet Explorer 4.x. The type of browser is indicated as a parameter to the function. The DHTML will be applied to HTML elements, and the identifier for the element being manipulated with the DHTML is also passed in, as are any additional values necessary to perform the action.

The component has the following four methods:

MoveLeft
> Generates the browser-specific JavaScript to move a positioned and named HTML element to the left

MoveTop
> Generates the browser-specific JavaScript to move a positioned and named HTML element to the top

Hide
> Generates the browser-specific JavaScript to hide a positioned and named HTML element

Show
> Generates the browser-specific JavaScript to show a positioned and named HTML element

To create this example component in Visual J++, select the New Project option from the File menu. In the New File dialog, choose Components as the type of project, and select COM DLL as the component type. Provide a name for the project, in this case dhtml.

Creating the Class Definition

A default Java class is automatically created for the project, which includes a directive to register the class as a COM object. The class is created simply, with no inheritance implied, as shown in the following code block:

```
public class Class1
```

When developing a Java component, you will most likely change the name of the class and its associated file. In fact, if you rename the class, you *have to* rename the file or an error occurs. For the example, rename the Java class and file to **Positioning**.

You might also add annotation for the class. For example, the following shows a class that is renamed to **MyConcatenator** with the **final** modifier:

```
final class MyConcatenator
```

The **final** modifier applies to the class declaration and prevents the class from being overridden or subclassed. Another class modifier, **abstract**, is used with classes that contain abstract functions. An abstract function is one that does not have an implementation in the ancestor, but must have an implementation in a descendant or an error will result. By default, all classes are defined with the **public** modifier, which means the class is visible to applications that use the class.

Inheritance in Java is through the use of the **extends** clause, and if the class is an extension of an existing Java class, this information is added to the class declaration. When one class is an ancestor, or *superclass*, of another, it is listed in the **extends** clause of the descendent, or *subclass*, as shown here:

```
class MyInsertConcatenator extends MyConcatenator
```

Since the original class, **MyConcatenator**, was defined with the **final** modifier, inheriting from the class will result in an error. To inherit from **MyConcatenator**, its class declaration would need to be modified:

```
public class MyConcatenator
class MyInsertConcatenator extends MyConcatenator
```

The class for the example in this chapter is called **position**; it does not extend any other class, and the **public** modifier is explicitly stated. The declaration for this class is:

```
public class position
```

Adding Methods to the Class

All the generated Java file contains at this point is the empty class declaration. Methods for the class can be added directly to the class file. However, you can add methods in Visual J++ by using the Add Method dialog, which is accessible from the menu opened by right-clicking on the class in the Class Outline window.* Use the dialog to create the first method, MoveLeft, as shown in Figure 15-1. Note that the return type for the method is defined to be a `java.lang.String`, an option you can select from the Return Type drop-down combo box.

As Figure 15-1 shows, the Access type for the method is defined as `public`, meaning that the method is accessible from outside the class. A `private` method is available only within the class or any internal nested classes. A `protected` method is available within a class, the classes package, or within any classes derived from the class and the derived class package.

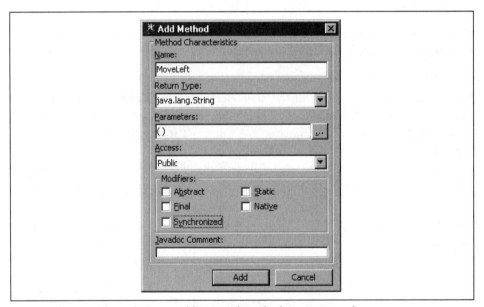

Figure 15-1. Visual J++ dialog to add MoveLeft method to new Java class

The method has three parameters. These are added by clicking the button with the ellipses (...) next to the Parameters field. In the Edit Parameter List dialog that opens, add the three parameters one at a time. The first parameter is defined as a `String` type and is called *strObject*. The last two are created with the `int` basic type and are called *intBrowser* and *intLeft*. Figure 15-2 shows the Edit Param-

---

* If the Class Outline window isn't visible, you can display it by selecting View → Other Windows → Document Outline.

eter List dialog that should appear before you click the OK button to confirm the parameters you've added.

Figure 15-2. Edit Parameter List dialog to add parameters to the newly-created method

The Add Method dialog lists the following method modifiers:

static
    Gives all instances of a class access to one, and only one, copy of the method or variable

final
    Indicates that a method or variable cannot be subclassed

synchronized
    Marks the method as thread-safe, meaning that only one thread has access to the method at any one time

native
    Used if a method is implemented in a native language such as C

None of the modifiers are checked for the new method.

Add the other three methods using the same technique. The second method is MoveTop, which returns a `String`, and has a `String` and two `int` parameters that are identical to MoveLeft. The third method is Hide, and it returns a `String` and contains two parameters, a `String` and an `int`. The fourth and final method is Show, and its declaration is identical to that for Hide.

After adding the method definitions, we'll need to add code for each method. The code for each of the methods checks for the browser type and uses browser-specific DHTML and the passed-in HTML element and parameters to create a string that performs the specified action, but which is geared specifically to the browser. This string is then returned to the client application.

When finished, the code for the new COM class object looks similar to that shown
in Example 15-1.

Example 15-1. Simple Java Component with One Class and One Method

```
/**
 * This class is designed to be packaged with a COM DLL output format.
 * The class has no standard entry points, other than the constructor.
 * Public methods will be exposed as methods on the default COM interface.
 * @com.register ( clsid=397D0C90-592C-11D2-8079-204C4F4F5020,
    typelib=397D0C91-592C-11D2-8079-204C4F4F5020 )
 */
//
// Positioning
//

public class position
{

    // create DHTML string to move object to left
    public String MoveLeft (String strObject, int intBrowser, int intLeft)
    {
        String strOutput;
        if (intBrowser == 1)
            strOutput = strObject + ".style.left=" + intLeft;
        else
            strOutput = "document." + strObject + ".left=" + intLeft;
        return (strOutput);
    }

    // create DHTML string to move object's top position
    String MoveTop (String strObject, int intBrowser, int intTop)
    {
        String strOutput;
        if (intBrowser == 1)
            strOutput = strObject + ".style.left=" + intTop;
        else
            strOutput = "document." + strObject + ".left=" + intTop;
        return (strOutput);
    }

    // create DHTML string to hide object
    String Hide (String strObject, int intBrowser)
    {
        String strOutput;
        if (intBrowser == 1)
            strOutput = strObject + ".style.visibility='hidden'";
        else
            strOutput = "document." + strObject + ".visibility='hidden'";
        return (strOutput);
    }

    // create DHTML string to show object
    String Show (String strObject, int intBrowser)
```

Example 15-1. Simple Java Component with One Class and One Method (continued)

```
    {
        String strOutput;
        if (intBrowser == 1)
            strOutput = strObject + ".style.visibility='inherit'";
        else
            strOutput = "document." + strObject + ".visibility='inherit'";
        return (strOutput);
    }
}
```

All four methods return a **String** object containing the DHTML used to perform the action associated with the method. All four methods also include the type of browser used to access the ASP page. A simpler approach would be to set a class variable or property when the component is first loaded. The variable or property would then be accessed by all the methods. Additionally, information about which browser accessed the page can be pulled in directly by the component. Accessing the built-in objects using a set of predefined Java interfaces is covered in detail in Chapter 16, *The Java Interfaces.*

Once the Java class has been created, it is compiled into a Java class file. The Java class is compiled, by default, into a both-threaded component. This threading model can be changed with the use of the OLE/COM Viewer, discussed in "Examining and Altering Component Properties with the OLE/COM Viewer" later in this chapter.

Registering and Installing a Java Component Using javareg

Earlier versions of Visual J++ required the use of a utility to register a COM object created using Java. Visual J++ 6.0 does not require a separate step for this—it compiles the Java class directly to a DLL, including an associated type library. The DLL can then be registered using *regsvr32* or installed using the Microsoft Transaction Server. However, for those people using an earlier version of Visual J++ or other Java tools, this section provides an overview of the Java registration utility, *javareg.exe.* This utility is a command-line tool that registers the Java class within the Registry, and which can also assign a progid to the class and generate a class identifier. The *javareg* switches are shown in Table 15-1.

Table 15-1. Switches for javareg.exe

Switch	Description
/?	Displays utility switches and usage
/register	Registers the Java class as an ActiveX component

Table 15-1. Switches for javareg.exe (continued)

Switch	Description
/unregister	Unregisters the Java class
/codebase	Used while registering a class to return base location of the component
/control	Used while registering a class to designate that the component is an ActiveX control
/typelib	Used while registering a class to generate type library for file
/q	Suppresses messages
/class	Java class being registered
/clsid	CLSID for class
/progid	COM program ID for class
/surrogate	Used when Java class is run as a DCOM server
/remote	For remote access, server where remote component is located

Not all of the switches listed are required. For example, if the **clsid** switch and a class ID are not given, the utility generates one for the class. Use the **clsid** switch only if the class ID was generated outside the utility and is used in registering the class. In addition, the **progid** switch is needed only if the class is being accessed by its progid value using the CreateObject method. The **remote** and **surrogate** switches are needed only if the class is accessed through DCOM.

To generate a class ID outside of the utility, you can use *guidgen. exe*. Both this and *javareg.exe* should be available for download at the Microsoft Java web site at *http://www.microsoft.com/java/*. Look for them to be a part of the Microsoft Java SDK. The *javareg.exe* utility is also installed as part of the IIS sample installation.

To use the *javareg* utility on **position**, the example class just created, run the following command from the NT console:

```
javareg /register /class:position /progid:Project1.position.1
```

Additionally, when using the *javareg* utility, the java class should be moved to a location on the Java **CLASSPATH**.

Unless a problem occurs, a message similar to that shown in Figure 15-3, which states that the Java class has been successfully registered and gives the class identifier used with the component, should pop up.

The component should then appear in the OLE/COM Object Viewer, a tool that is included with the Visual Studio 6.0 tools and with the Windows platform SDK.

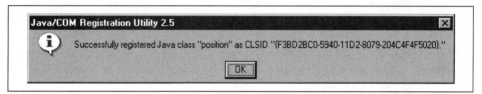

Figure 15-3. Success message after registering Java ASP component using javareg

This tool was discussed in Chapter 3, but the next section goes into detail about using it to alter the properties of the component.

Examining and Altering Component Properties with the OLE/COM Viewer

After the Java component is built and registered, you can view and modify the COM settings using the OLE/COM Viewer. When you open the Viewer, the component can be found under the main heading of "Object Classes," and then under the folder called "Java Classes." The component has the name "Java Class: position." Clicking on the component opens the OLE/COM Viewer in the right side, which contains several tab pages labeled Registry, Implementation, Activation, Launch Permissions, and Access Permissions, as shown in Figure 15-4.

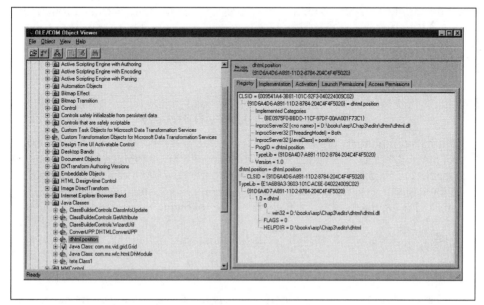

Figure 15-4. View of Visual Basic component using OLE/COM Object Viewer utility

The tool opens with the Registry page as the first displayed. Examining the Registry information for the object shows that the in-process server is *msjava.dll*, which is the Microsoft Java VM. The component is also created with the threading model of both, which is the default threading model for a Java COM object. The progid, position, is the one specified when using the *javareg* utility, or when the component was registered directly using Visual J++ 6.0.

The component compiled directly into a COM DLL using Visual J++ 6.0 has a progid of Project1.position. Additionally, Visual J++ compiles the component with the both-threaded threading model.

The next tab opens the Implementation page. This page can be used for specifying implementations for a local server and an in-process handler. The page can also be used to specify the path for a custom surrogate for the component if remote invocation is used. The fields originally populated are the implementation path for the component, which is the Java class name, and the threading type.

The next page in the OLE/COM Viewer is the Activation page. This page can be used to change whether the Java component is launched as an interactive user, whether At Storage activation is supported, and to specify a remote machine name. The interactive user option is for interactive distributed applications and does not apply to ASP components, since ASP interaction occurs through the browser. The At Storage option controls whether, if an object is accessed using Monikers, it is instantiated in the same location where the persisted state of the object is stored.

Java Component Monikers

Java ASP components are usually accessed with the Server object's CreateObject method, but an alternative approach is to use a Java Moniker. Monikers are specified as class names. When encountered, the Java VM looks up the progid in the Registry to get the class identifier for the object. The object reference is returned using the GetObject method, as the following demonstrates:

```
Dim tmp
Set tmp = GetObject("java:ConvertJPP.position")
```

The fourth OLE/COM Viewer property page is the Launch Permissions page. This page can be used to change the default permissions for launching the component. Clicking on the page's Modify button opens another dialog listing the users and groups with launch privileges. Clicking on the Add button in this page opens yet another dialog to add other groups or users. Figure 15-5 shows the Launch Permissions window after a user, highlighted in the window, has been added.

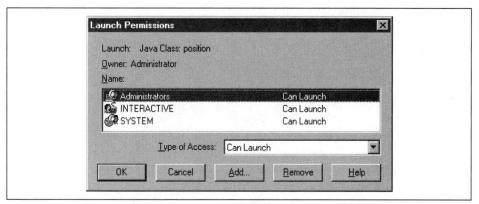

Figure 15-5. Adding a user to the Launch Permissions for the component

The last OLE/COM property page is the Access Permissions page, which can be used to modify the access permission for a component for users and/or groups in a manner similar to that used with the Launch Permissions page.

No changes are made to the simple component being created in this chapter, except for the addition of the user in the Launch Permissions page; the default values in the OLE/COM dialog pages are accepted as is.

Testing the Java Component

Once the Java component has been built and successfully registered using *javareg*, or has been successfully compiled into a COM DLL using Visual J++ 6.0 and up, it can be accessed as any other ASP or COM component is accessed. To demonstrate this, create the ASP page shown in Example 15-2, which contains two HTML DIV elements, each positioned using absolute positioning—positioned using CSS in such a way that they are exposed to scripting using DHTML. In an ASP scripting block, calls are made to all four of the methods to alter the web page returned to the reader. The progid used is `Project1.position`. The MoveLeft and MoveTop methods are called for one element, the DIV block containing the HTML paragraph. The DIV block containing the HTML header is hidden, and the one containing the paragraph is made visible.

In Example 15-2, note that the Request object's ServerVariables collection is accessed to determine the type of browser accessing the page.

Example 15-2. ASP Page to Test New Java ASP Component

```
<!DOCTYPE HTML PUBLIC "-//W3C//DTD HTML 4.0//EN">
<HTML>
<HEAD>
<TITLE>DHTML Positioning Object Test</TITLE>
<STYLE type="text/css">

BODY { margin: 0.5in }
</STYLE>
<SCRIPT>
<!--

// function test moves paragraph object to
// the left and down
function test() {
<%
  ' find the browser using server variable
  Dim ua
  ua = ""
  Dim brwsr
  ua = Request.ServerVariables("HTTP_USER_AGENT")
  If Instr(1,ua, "MSIE",1) Then
      brwsr = 1
  Else
      brwsr = 0
  End If

  ' create the component instance
  Dim tmp
  Set tmp = Server.CreateObject("dhtml.position")

  ' create the DHTML JavaScript string using a call to MoveLeft
  ' and MoveTop, Hide and Show
  ' write out the strings
  Dim strng
  strng = tmp.MoveLeft("para1",brwsr,200)
  Response.write(strng & ";")
  strng = tmp.MoveTop("para1", brwsr,200)
  Response.write(strng & ";")
  strng = tmp.Hide("h1", brwsr)
  Response.write(strng & ";")
  strng = tmp.Show("para1", brwsr)
  Response.write(strng & ";")
%>
//-->
}
</SCRIPT>
<BODY onload="test()">
<DIV id="h1" style="position:absolute; left: 10; top: 10">
<H1> Testing Positioning Component</H1>
</DIV>
<DIV id="para1" style="position:absolute; left: 10; top: 10; visibility:hidden">
<p style="font-family: Arial; color: red; font-style: italic">
```

Example 15-2. ASP Page to Test New Java ASP Component (continued)

```
This is the paragraph
</p>
</DIV>
</BODY>
</HTML>
```

The object is created with the Server object's CreateObject method, and then the four Java component methods are accessed in turn to create the client-side Java-Script function. The function will reposition the paragraph, display it, and hide the header, all using browser-specific code.

Invoking a COM Object in a Java Component

The Java component in Example 15-1 provides methods to be called from other COM components, but it does not call any COM methods itself. Invoking COM methods within a Java class could be complicated. However, again, Visual J++ has provided automated support to add the necessary Java wrappers to a COM object so the object can be invoked within a Java class. In addition, for older versions of Visual J++ and for Java development products other than Visual J++, Microsoft has provided another utility, *JActiveX*, to assist in creating a Java COM wrapper.

To demonstrate accessing a COM object in Java, create a new Visual Basic project and select ActiveX DLL as the project type. VB generates a project and a VB class. Rename the project to vbtest and the class to **test**. Add the function shown in Example 15-3 to the class. Note that the component takes one parameter of type Integer and returns a string. Compile the VB component as *vbTest.dll* and register it if necessary using *regsvr32*.

Example 15-3. The testObject Method of the vbtest.test Component

```
Public Function testObject(intValue As Integer) As String
    If intValue = 1 Then
        testObject = "Value is 1"
    ElseIf intValue = 2 Then
        testObject = "Value is 2"
    Else
        testObject = "Some other value"
    End If
End Function
```

The next two sections show how a COM wrapper can be added to a Java class using Visual J++ 6.0 and the utility *JActiveX*.

Adding a COM Wrapper Class to the Component Using Visual J++

To access this new VB COM component from within the existing DHTML Java class shown in Example 15-1, open this Java project again. Right-click on the `position` class and from the context menu select Add → Add COM Wrapper. A dialog will open listing the available COM objects registered on the machine. Find and check the *vbtest* component in the list.

Adding a COM wrapper to the project generates the Java code to wrap the VB component and attaches this code as a dependency to the project. You can actually view the Java code for the class and the associated interface code by selecting the classes from the Project view window. The code block contained in `test.java` is shown in Example 15-4.

Example 15-4. Adding a COM Wrapper for a VB COM Component

```
//
// Auto-generated using JActiveX.EXE 5.00.2748
//   ("E:\Microsoft Visual Studio\VJ98\jactivex.exe"  /w /xi /X:rkc /l "C:\TEMP\
jvc86D.tmp" /nologo /d "C:\WINNT\Profiles\Administrator\Personal\
    Visual Studio Projects\Project1" "D:\books\asp\chap15\vbtest.dll")
//
// WARNING: Do not remove the comments that include "@com" directives.
// This source file must be compiled by a @com-aware compiler.
// If you are using the Microsoft Visual J++ compiler, you must use
// version 1.02.3920 or later. Previous versions will not issue an error
// but will not generate COM-enabled class files.
//

package vbtest;

import com.ms.com.*;
import com.ms.com.IUnknown;
import com.ms.com.Variant;

/** @com.class(classid=D6D26D58-5946-11D2-8079-204C4F4F5020,DynamicCasts)
    @com.interface(iid=D6D26D5A-5946-11D2-8079-204C4F4F5020,
        thread=AUTO, type=DUAL)
*/
public class test implements IUnknown,com.ms.com.NoAutoScripting,vbtest._test
{
  /** @com.method(vtoffset=4, dispid=1610809344, type=METHOD, name="testObject",
addFlagsVtable=4)
      @com.parameters([in,out,size=1,elementType=I2,type=ARRAY] intValue,
                      [type=STRING] return) */
  public native String testObject(short[] intValue);


  public static final com.ms.com._Guid iid =
new com.ms.com._Guid((int)0xd6d26d5a, (short)0x5946,
```

Example 15-4. Adding a COM Wrapper for a VB COM Component (continued)

```
(short)0x11d2, (byte)0x80, (byte)0x79, (byte)0x20, (byte)0x4c, (byte)0x4f,
    (byte)0x4f, (byte)0x50, (byte)0x20);

  public static final com.ms.com._Guid clsid =
new com.ms.com._Guid((int)0xd6d26d58, (short)0x5946, (short)0x11d2,
(byte)0x80, (byte)0x79, (byte)0x20, (byte)0x4c, (byte)0x4f, (byte)0x4f,
(byte)0x50, (byte)0x20);
}
```

Notice how the generated class includes imports for the necessary COM interface, **IUnknown**. Additionally, the class also includes the Variant class, to handle most unknown or object parameter types. Code that looks very much like Interface Definition Language (IDL) is used to define both the VB component's method and the method parameters.

Once the COM wrapper is added to the class, compiling the class also compiles the COM wrapper for Java. The wrapped object is discussed in the section "Using the COM Wrapped Class."

Using JActiveX to Wrap a COM Object

For earlier versions of Visual J++, and for other Java development tools, there is another utility to make your development task a whole lot easier. However, there is a catch to this simplicity, as you will see later in the section.

In order to call a COM method in the past, the Java Type Library Wizard tool had to be run against whatever component contained the method or methods. This would generate a set of class libraries containing Java wrappers for the object. The Java Type Library Wizard tool is installed, in Visual J++ 1.1, in the Tools menu of Visual J++, and is relatively easy to work with. However, beginning with the Java SDK 2.01, a new tool was created, *Jactivex.exe*, a command-line tool that can be used to create *.java* (not class) files to wrap the COM interfaces, making them accessible from a Java component.

 The JActiveX tool also requires that the Java compiler recognize @COM directives in the Java files. The version for Visual J++ should be 1.02.3920 or higher. Additionally, the Java compiler that comes with the Microsoft Java SDK also recognizes the @COM directive.

The JActiveX tool creates a Java class for each COM object within a type library. A type library is any COM-based object with a *.tlb*, *.olb*, *.ocx*, *.dll*, or *.exe* extension.

The JActiveX tool switches that deal directly with the COM/Java transaction are shown in Table 15-2, while output switches of particular interest are shown in Table 15-3.

Table 15-2. JActiveX Translation-Specific Switches

Switch	Description
/javatlb	Specifies typelib translation
/r	Registers all type libraries
/w	Disables warnings
/wx	Treats warnings as errors
/x2	Maps VT_I2 and VT_UI2 (variant types) to char rather than short, which is the default mapping
/xc	Ignores all coclasses in the type libraries
/xd	Prevents creation of the default Java classes; two Java classes are created for each dispinterface, a default and one used when the interface is not the default for the coclass
/xi	Duplicates method and COM declarations to be duplicated in coclass file so that objects can be accessed without having to cast to an interface pointer
/x:m	Disables thread switching, implemented by default for non-thread safe components

Table 15-3. Output Switches for the JActiveX Tool

Switch	Description
/cj	Generates a template file for every coclass in the file with name *<coclass>*Impl.java; the templates can then be used to create the actual method implementations
/d	Places generated files in the specified subdirectory rather than the default subdirectory, which is the Java trusted library
/e	Generate files only for specified type libraries
/p	Specifies a package name used when generating the subdirectory to contain the Java files. By default, the name is the name of the type library

All of the switches can be seen just by running the following command:

```
jactivex /?
```

The test case for using this tool is started in the next section.

Running JActiveX Against the Visual Basic Component

Once the VB *vbtest* component (discussed earlier) is registered, the JActiveX tool can be used on it to create the Java-COM classes. The command line used with this component is:

```
jactivex /javatlb /xi vbtest.dll
```

This creates a subdirectory, *vbtest*, located in the Java trusted library. Contained in this subdirectory are three generated *.java* files, *_test.java*, *_testDefault.java*, and *test.java*, each with an associated compiled class file. The *test.java* file generated by JActiveX is shown in Example 15-5.

Example 15-5. COM Wrapper Class Code Generated by JActiveX

```
//
// Auto-generated using JActiveX.EXE 5.00.2924
//    (jactivex /javatlb /xi vbTest.dll)
//
// WARNING: Do not remove the comments that include "@com" directives.
// This source file must be compiled by a @com-aware compiler.
// If you are using the Microsoft Visual J++ compiler, you must use
// version 1.02.3920 or later. Previous versions will not issue an error
// but will not generate COM-enabled class files.
//package vbtest;

package vbtest;

import com.ms.com.*;
import com.ms.com.IUnknown;
import com.ms.com.Variant;

/** @com.class(classid=D6D26D58-5946-11D2-8079-204C4F4F5020,DynamicCasts)
    @com.interface(iid=D6D26D5A-5946-11D2-8079-204C4F4F5020,
    thread=AUTO, type=DUAL) */
public class test implements IUnknown,com.ms.com.NoAutoScripting,vbtest._test
{
  /** @com.method(vtoffset=4, dispid=1610809344, type=METHOD, name="testObject")
      @com.parameters([in,out,size=1,elementType=I2,type=ARRAY] intValue,
[type=STRING] return) */
  public native String testObject(short[] intValue);


  public static final com.ms.com._Guid iid =
  new com.ms.com._Guid((int)0xd6d26d5a,
(short)0x5946, (short)0x11d2, (byte)0x80, (byte)0x79, (byte)0x20, (byte)0x4c,
(byte)0x4f, (byte)0x4f, (byte)0x50, (byte)0x20);

  public static final com.ms.com._Guid clsid =
new com.ms.com._Guid((int)0xd6d26d58, (short)0x5946,
(short)0x11d2, (byte)0x80, (byte)0x79, (byte)0x20, (byte)0x4c, (byte)0x4f,
(byte)0x4f, (byte)0x50, (byte)0x20);
}
}
```

Comparing Example 15-4 and Example 15-5, you can see that the code is virtually identical. To use the JActiveX generated code, compile the classes using Visual J++ or the Java Compiler that comes with the Java SDK.

Once the COM Wrapper classes have been generated and compiled, either by using Visual J++ 6.0 directly or by using JActiveX, the wrapped class can be used within a Java component.

Using the COM Wrapped Class

After the COM wrapper classes have been generated and compiled, all it takes to access the component's methods within a Java component is to include an import statement for the file at the top of the Java class file, as follows:

```
import vbtest.*;
```

To see how the component's methods are accessed, let's create another method for the Java *position* component. The method, which is shown in Example 15-6, does nothing more than take a short value passed from the client, pass it to the VB method, and then return the string the VB method generates.

Example 15-6. Invoking a COM Method from Within a Java Component

```
// invoke COM method
public String ReturnValue (short shrtValue)
    {
    String strTest;
    short x[] = new short[1];
    x[0] = shrtValue;
    test objTest = new test();
    strTest = objTest.testObject(x);
    return (strTest);
    }
```

Note that the **Integer** type from Visual Basic has been mapped to a **short** type in Java, since VB's integer is only a 16-bit value and Java's **int** type is a 32-bit value. Also, notice that the method uses a one-element array to pass the value to the VB component. The reason for this is that in the original VB component, the parameter is passed by reference because **ByVal** is not explicitly specified with the parameter. Visual Basic passes parameters by reference by default. However, passing an element by reference involves pointers, something Java does not support, and this is where things get a bit more complicated.

Java cannot support pointers, but a way around this is to pass one-element arrays, since Java does pass arrays by reference. So for the Visual Basic example, an array of data type **short** is created with one element, which is then passed to the VB method, as shown in Example 15-6.

To avoid having to use arrays, the VB method can be changed and the **ByVal** modifier added to the parameter, as in the following declaration:

```
Public Function testObject(ByVal intValue As Integer) As String
```

The VB component must be recompiled, and either the JActiveX tool can be run on the resulting DLL file to update the generated files, or the component can be removed from Visual J++ and added back to pick up the modified method. Next, modify the Java class, accessing the component so that it uses a discrete short value, as the following code shows:

```
// invoke COM method
public String ReturnValue (short shrtValue)
{
String strTest;
test objTest = new test();
strTest = vbtest.testObject(shrtValue);
return (strTest);
}
```

More on data types and mappings between COM and Java is included in the next section. For now, the new Java method is called from within the test ASP file with the lines:

```
strng = tmp.ReturnValue(1)
Response.write("/* " & strng & "*/")
```

These two lines generate a comment in the web page being returned that looks similar to:

```
/* Value is 1*/
```

 If you are having a hard time recompiling either the VB component or the Java component for this test, unload the ASP application containing the ASP test page by opening the IIS Internet Service Manager, clicking on the ASP application, and choosing Unload from the properties dialog. In addition, if component changes are not showing up in the ASP application, again unload the application to refresh the component. More on this in Chapter 2, *Setting Up and Maintaining the ASP Development Environment.*

Java/COM Data Type Mappings

A rule to handle data type mappings for COM/Java development is to use ODL (Object Description Language) data types, which have a default mapping from COM to Java. Other data types, and more complex data types, can require custom marshaling. For the most part, the available data types should match most needs. The Java SDK, which can be downloaded from *http://www.microsoft.com/java/* and is available on CD if you have a membership in the Microsoft Developer Network, lists the data type mappings. The mappings work for Visual C++ and Visual

Basic components being used within Java components, but there are some differences.

For an integer value, as shown earlier, a VB integer is only a 16-bit value, but an int for C++ and Java is a 32-bit value. To map correctly to Visual Basic, the Java component will need to use a short value, which is 16-bit.

The Visual Basic Variant data type maps to a Java ODL VARIANT type, which maps in turn to a com.ms.com.Variant class. Microsoft documentation also states that any out parameters in Java should be in the Variant data type also.

The String data type maps straight through, though the String class is immutable in Java. An immutable class is one that is never versioned and never revised.

You have had a chance to see two different techniques to create a COM object out of a Java class, and two different techniques to access a COM object from within a Java class. This chapter will close with a discussion of error handling.

Adding Error Handling

If you have worked with Java before, the first thing you probably noticed about the Java component in this chapter is that the standard Java language try... catch error handling is not included within the component.

COM uses a return value of type HRESULT, which is a 32-bit error or success code. Microsoft has defined a Java wrapper class for this code, called ComException, with a full class path of com.ms.com.ComException. This class is used to process errors returned from COM to a Java component.

To see how to incorporate error handling into the Java component and use ComException, let's modify the ASP component created in this chapter one more time to add error handling to one of the methods. The newest method, Return-Value, which invokes another COM component, is a perfect candidate for error handling. Any component that invokes methods external to it and outside its control should include error handling for potential problems.

Modify the method to use ComException and to return an error message rather than the derived string if an error occurs. The modified ReturnValue method is shown in Example 15-7.

Example 15-7. The ReturnValue Method Modified to Support Error Handling

```
// invoke COM method
public String ReturnValue (short shrtValue)
{
    try {
        String strTest;
```

Example 15-7. The ReturnValue Method Modified to Support Error Handling (continued)

```
    test testObj = new test();
    strTest = testObj.testObject(shrtvalue);
    return (strTest);
    }
catch (com.ms.com.ComFailException e) {
    return (e.getMessage());
    }
}
```

Note that the Java class is fully specified, as the `com.ms.com` package is not imported into the class. The method used with the exception object, getMessage, can be used to access any error message, and the method getHResult returns the `HRESULT` value returned by the COM method.

Errors can also be written out directly from the Java component by accessing the ASP built-in objects. Chapter 16 provides details on using the built-in objects.

Unfortunately, there is no way to continue passing the exception to the ASP page itself. VBScript relies on error handling occurring through the use of the Err object, which is not supported in Java. In addition, throwing an error in Java does not trigger error handling within VBScript. Error handling between the component and the ASP page will have to rely on return values.

Further Reading

For additional reading about the topics covered in this chapter, check out the following:

- Read more about Visual J++ at Microsoft's Visual J++ web site at *http://msdn.microsoft.com/visualj/*.

- Read more about Microsoft's implementation of Java at *http://www.microsoft.com/java/*.

- You can access the Javasoft Java Developer Kit (JDK) at *http://www.javasoft.com/*.

- An excellent site at which to read more about Java is the online magazine JavaWorld, at *http://www.javaworld.com/*.

- Read a multiple-page article about COM and Java integration at *http://www.q-tek.com/scripting/JavaDocs/contents/sdk0211.htm*.

- For more on ActiveX and JavaBeans, see the document titled "Using Java-Beans with Microsoft ActiveX Components" at *http://java.sun.com/products/plugin/1.1.1/docs/script.html.*

- Chili!Soft has a COM-to-Java bridging tool called Chili!Beans. You can find out more about this at *http://www.chilisoft.com/CaspSamp/beansamp/default.asp.*

16

The Java Interfaces

Microsoft has provided several different built-in objects that provide information about the environment and allow for communication between the client and server. These objects, known as the ASP built-in objects, are the ObjectContext object, provided by the Microsoft Transaction Server (MTS), and the ASP Application, Session, Server, Request, and Response objects. The Application object can be used to store information available from throughout the ASP application that persists until the application is shut down. The Session object, though, is used to store session-level information only, with a session beginning when a person logs on and lasting until the same person logs off or is timed out, or the person's connection fails. Communication from the client to the server occurs through the Request object, and communication back to the client occurs through the Response object. Finally, the Server object is mainly used to create new instances of objects.

Prior to the release of IIS 4.0, all intrinsic objects were accessed via the Scripting-Context object, which, in turn, is passed as a parameter to the onStartPage event handler. This technique required only the presence of the ASP library. With IIS 4.0, the built-in objects can be accessed via the MTS `IGetContextProperties` interface from any event or method. In addition, the MTS `IObjectContext` interface adds transaction capability to the ASP component. Techniques using both Scripting-Context and `IGetContextProperties` are covered in this chapter.

ASP objects are COM-based, which means that Java wrappers must be provided in order for a Java component to access these objects. To facilitate the use of the ASP built-in objects from within a Java component, Microsoft has also provided a set of Java classes that can be imported into the component. The purpose of the Java classes is to provide a more Java-like interface to the ASP objects, including the use of more familiar Java data types. This is also demonstrated in the chapter.

Each of the built-in objects, their properties, and their methods are discussed in detail in Chapter 6, *Overview of the Intrinsic (Built-in) Objects*. The rest of this chapter demonstrates the Java interfaces for these objects, but assumes the reader has read Chapter 6 or has worked previously with these objects. Additionally, Chapter 15, *Creating a Simple Java Component*, covers the steps to take to compile and register a Java ASP component. If you have never created an ASP component using Java, you should read Chapter 15 before proceeding with this chapter. Finally, Chapter 8, *The Visual Basic Built-in Object Interfaces*, covers accessing the built-in objects using Visual Basic, and Chapter 12, *The C++ ASP Built-in Interfaces*, covers accessing the built-in objects using C++. It might be of interest to compare how the built-in objects are accessed using the different tools and languages.

IIS 3.0 and the IScriptingObject Interface

With IIS 3.0, Microsoft provided access to the built-in objects from an event handler via a special object, the ScriptingContext object. From Java, this object is accessed via its interface, **IScriptingObject**, as a parameter to the OnStartPage event handler.

Each of the built-in objects can be accessed from the **IScriptingContext** interface using the appropriate method:

getResponse
> Returns an interface to the Response object

getRequest
> Returns an interface to the Request object

getApplication
> Returns an interface to the Application object

getServer
> Returns an interface to the Server object

getSession
> Returns an interface to the Session object

In order to access **IScriptingContext**, the Java ASP classes must be added to the project. This is accomplished by importing the appropriate class, in this case the ASP classes, as shown in the following line of code:

```
import com.ms.asp.*;
```

Add **package** or **import** statements before the generated COM directive code, not between this code and the class declaration. To do otherwise will most likely generate an error when the component is built into a Java class. Additionally, if you copy these examples to test for yourself, remember not to copy the generated COM directive comment. This needs to be generated for your own copy of the COM object using either Visual J++ or the techniques discussed in Chapter 15.

In addition to importing the ASP classes, the Java ASP component will also need to have access to the Microsoft COM classes to provide access to Microsoft-only data types, such as **Variant**. These classes are incorporated into the component with the following line:

```
import com.ms.com.*;
```

To demonstrate how the **IScriptingContext** interface works, we'll create a small Java component whose **OnStartPage** event accesses the Response object and invokes its Redirect method. To do this, create a new project of type COM DLL, naming the project tstASP. After Visual J++ generates the class file, rename it to *aspTest.java* and change the class name to match by calling it **aspTest**. Next, add the **import** statements, making sure to add these *before* the comments generated to hold the COM directive.

Next, add the OnStartPage event handler function, including its **IScripting-Context** parameter. The event handler uses it to create a reference to the Response object by calling its getResponse method. The Response object reference is used to redirect the output by calling the Response object's Redirect method. The complete source code for the application is shown in Example 16-1.

Example 16-1. Accessing the Response Object Using the IScriptingContext Interface

```
import com.ms.com.*;
import com.ms.asp.*;

/**
 * This class is designed to be packaged with a COM DLL output format.
 * The class has no standard entry points, other than the constructor.
 * Public methods will be exposed as methods on the default COM interface.
 * @com.register ( clsid=CD8C7700-59F8-11D2-8079-204C4F4F5020,
 *                 typelib=CD8C7701-59F8-11D2-8079-204C4F4F5020 )
 */

public class aspTest
{
    // create object and redirect input
    public void OnStartPage(IScriptingContext objContext){
```

Example 16-1. Accessing the Response Object Using the IScriptingContext Interface (continued)

```
        IResponse iobjResponse = null;
        iobjResponse = objContext.getResponse();
        String s = new String("temp.htm");
        iobjResponse.Redirect(s);
    }
}
```

After the component is created and compiled into a DLL, it is automatically registered using Visual J++ 6.0, or it can then be registered using *regsvr32* or MTS if using an earlier version of Visual J++.

To test the component, create an ASP test page like the one shown in Example 16-2. This page creates an instance of the new Java component, and when the instance is created, the OnStartPage event handler method is invoked. (You might also want to create an HTML file named *temp.htm*, since this is the page to which the component redirects the browser.)

Example 16-2. aspTest.ASP, an ASP Test Page for the Java aspTest Component

```
<HTML>
<HEAD>
</HEAD>
<BODY>
<%
Dim tst
Set tst = Server.CreateObject("aspBigTest.aspTest")
%>
</BODY>
</HTML>
```

When the example is run, though, instead of the contents of *temp.htm* showing, an error message similar to the following appears:

```
The HTTP headers are already written to the client browser. Any HTTP
header modifications must be made before writing page content.
```

The reason for the error message is that HTTP requires that any redirect operation occur before any of the HTTP header is written. Since the server-side script is included within the body of the document in *aspTest.asp*, the HTTP header has already been written by the time the component method is invoked. Moving the ASP scripting block to the top of the page, before the beginning <HTML> tag, prevents this error from occurring.

Any of the built-in objects (Request, Response, Application, Session, Server) can be accessed from the ScriptingContext object via their associated interfaces, but the limitation to this approach is that the objects can only be referenced within the OnStartPage event handler. Accessing the ScriptingContext object outside of this event results in an error. Another limitation is that the ASP component itself can be created as a local object or as a session-level object, but not as an application-level object. The reason for this is that the `OnStartPage` event is not fired when the application starts, only when a page is accessed or the first page of a session is accessed. The section titled "Accessing the Built-In Objects in IIS 3.0" in Chapter 8 contains a demonstration of this using a VB component; the same principles apply to a component created using Java.

Microsoft supports `IScriptingContext` in IIS 4.0 primarily for backward compatibility. New components should use the MTS ObjectContext and GetContextProperties objects, discussed next.

IIS 4.0 and the IObjectContext and IGetContextProperties Interfaces

 The examples in the rest of this chapter exist within an IIS test environment as well as an MTS test environment. See Chapter 2, *Setting Up and Maintaining the ASP Development Environment*, for information on setting up the IIS test environment, and Chapter 5, *Components, Transactions, and the Microsoft Transaction Server*, for details on setting up an MTS test environment.

When Microsoft released IIS 4.0, the company also released version 2.0 of the Microsoft Transaction Server (MTS). MTS provides a mechanism to enhance the scalability of a distributed system by allowing the transaction server to control the creation and release of objects and other resources.

Another change that resulted from the integration of MTS with IIS is that ASP components can be created as MTS components, regardless of whether the component is registered with MTS, and regardless of whether the component uses the transaction support MTS provides. To access the built-in ASP objects, the MTS GetContextProperties object is used; the component does not need to be registered with MTS to use GetContextProperties. If the component is using transaction management, then it will also need access to ObjectContext, and will need to be registered with MTS.

The IGetContextProperties Interface

I'll discuss ObjectContext in a moment, but let's begin with GetContextProperties. This object and its associated interface, `IGetContextProperties`, are used to access the built-in objects. It is created by accessing the `Mtx` class, which is included within the MTS Java import file *com.ms.mtx*. The GetContextProperties object contains a method, GetObjectContext, used to return a reference to either `IGetContextProperties` or to `IObjectContext`, depending on whether the return value is cast to `IGetContextProperties` or not. `IGetContext-Properties` has the following three methods:

Count
> Returns a count of object context properties

EnumNames
> Returns the names of object context properties (Response, Request, Session, Server, Application)

GetProperty
> Returns a named property

The GetProperty method returns a `Variant` data type, which then needs to be cast to the appropriate built-in object type. To include the MTS objects in a project, the following import is added to the existing import statement to include the ASP objects:

```
import com.ms.mtx;
```

This includes Microsoft's prebuilt Java-wrapped references to the MTS interfaces.

To demonstrate adding in MTS capability, create a new Visual J++ COM/DLL project, naming this project tstjava. After the tool generates the class file, rename the file to *props.java* and the class itself to props. Add a method named objWrite-Header to the class; it takes a single `String` parameter named *s* and does not return a value. Then add the source code shown in Example 16-3 to your project. The objWriteHeader method uses `IGetContextProperties` to obtain a reference to a Variant object. The Variant object is used, in turn, to obtain a reference to the `IResponse` interface by using the Variant's getDispatch method. The `IResponse` interface reference is then used to write a header to the web page using the IResponse write method. Notice from this code that the Response object is accessed from the interface `IGetContextProperties`, rather than through `IScripting-Context`.

Example 16-3. Accessing IResponse Persistently

```
import com.ms.com.*;
import com.ms.mtx.*;
import com.ms.asp.*;

/**
 * This class is designed to be packaged with a COM DLL output format.
 * The class has no standard entry points, other than the constructor.
 * Public methods will be exposed as methods on the default COM interface.
 * @com.register ( clsid=44F22086-5A06-11D2-807A-204C4F4F5020,
 *                 typelib=44F22087-5A06-11D2-807A-204C4F4F5020 )
```

Example 16-3. Accessing IResponse Persistently (continued)

```
 */
public class props
{
    // write header using response object
    public void objWriteHeader(String s) {

        // get Context Object Props
        IGetContextProperties iObjProps = null;
        IResponse iObjResponse = null;
        Variant vResponse = new Variant();
        iObjProps = (IGetContextProperties)MTx.GetObjectContext();

        // get Response object
        vResponse = iObjProps.GetProperty("Response");
        iObjResponse = (IResponse)vResponse.getDispatch();

        // write out new header
        Variant v = new Variant("<H1>" + s + "</H1>");
        iObjResponse.Write(v);
    }
}
```

In Example 16-3, the `IGetObjectContext` object is instantiated with a call to GetObjectContext from the MTx object, defined within the **com.ms.mtx** package. The call is cast to the appropriate instance object type, in this case `IGetContextProperties`. This object is then used to create a Response object by using GetProperty to get the Response object returned as a **Variant** data type, and then using the **Variant** object's getDispatch method and casting the value returned to a reference to an `IResponse` interface object type. The Response object's methods can then be invoked. Example 16-4 contains the HTML and ASP script to access this Java component and its associated method.

Example 16-4. ASP Page and Script to Access ASP Component tstjava.props

```
<HTML>
<HEAD>
<BODY>
<%
  Dim authorsObject
  Set authorsObject = Server.CreateObject("tstjava.props")

  authorsObject.objWriteHeader "test"
%>

</BODY>
</HTML>
```

The `IGetContextProperties` interface is used to access the context object's properties as built-in objects, but transaction management is not incorporated into the component. To include transaction management, an instance of the IObject-Context object interface is used in the project. This is covered in the next section.

Using IObjectContext

The MTS `IObjectContext` object is used to instantiate instances of other objects within a transaction, to commit or roll back a transaction, or to check the state of the object. By "state of the object" I mean whether the object is participating in a transaction, which can be determined using the object's IsInTransaction method. The method returns `True` if the component is executing within a transaction. The DisableCommit and EnableCommit methods can be used to control whether a component is in a state that can be successfully committed or not. The IsCallerIn-Role method can be used to check what role a caller is participating in, and the IsSecurityEnabled method to determine whether security is enabled for the object. Security is enabled for a component by default unless it is running within the client's process. The CreateInstance method can be used to create an instance of an object that participates in the same transaction as the component creating the instance.

Including the `IObjectContext` interface as part of an ASP component and then installing that component into a transaction package provides hooks for MTS to actually catch all invocations of the component. The transaction server then handles all references to the component. By doing this, when a component marks that it has finished its processing by calling SetAbort or SetComplete from the `IObjectContext` interface, MTS marks the component for unloading even if the client still has a reference to it. This allows the system to unload the component and any resources it contains from memory. When the client calls one of the component's methods again, using the reference to the pointer the client *thinks* it has, MTS either creates and loads a new instance of the ASP component or pulls a reference from an available pool of the same component. This on-demand activation of an ASP component is referred to as *just-in-time activation.*

Recall from Chapter 5 that managing an ASP component from MTS allows for improved scalability of the object. For a web site that could have considerable activity, this could mean the difference between a user successfully accessing the application and one who receives the equivalent of a web "busy" signal.

To demonstrate some of the methods of the `IObjectContext` interface, we'll create another Java component that includes a reference to the component we created in Example 16-2; this will allow us to test the CreateInstance method, in particular. Start a new Visual J++ project named objcont, and again select COM DLL as the component type. Rename the Java class and its associated file to `ObjectContext`. Next, create a COM wrapper for the Java component in Example 16-2 by selecting the Add COM Wrapper option from the Project menu.

In the COM Wrappers dialog, either select the component created in Example 16-2 in the Installed COM Components list box, or click the Browse button to locate the DLL of the test component. Visual J++ then generates two Java source files within the Java project.

 Any COM component created in any language or within any tool can be used in this example, as long as the component has at least one method that can be called.

Next, to include the newly wrapped COM package along with MTS, ASP, and other COM functionality, add the following statements to the beginning of *ObjectContext.java*:

```
import com.ms.com.*;
import com.ms.mtx.*;
import com.ms.asp.*;
import tstjava.*;
```

The last imported Java class is the class for the COM object being used within this new example.

You'll create an instance of the COM wrapped object next. To do this, copy the code shown in Example 16-5 to your new Java class. As the code demonstrates, the wrapped COM object is used in the ObjectContext CreateInstance call, and has as parameters the CLSID property of the class and the IID property of the class interface. Both of these properties are accessible from the COM wrapper code generated by Visual J++ for the project. As the COM object is called props, the CLSID and IID are accessed directly from the props object. The component also determines whether security is enabled for the new component by calling the IsSecurityEnabled method. Security is always enabled by default for server components, so this method should return a **True** value. The call to IsInTransaction returns **True** if the component is in a transaction, **False** otherwise. This value can change based on the transaction settings used in the ASP page calling the component, or by changing the transaction settings within MTS for the component itself.

Example 16-5. Instantiating an Instance of an Existing COM Object

```
import com.ms.com.*;
import com.ms.mtx.*;
import com.ms.asp.*;
import tstjava.*;

/**
 * This class is designed to be packaged with a COM DLL output format.
 * The class has no standard entry points, other than the constructor.
 * Public methods will be exposed as methods on the default COM interface.
```

Example 16-5. Instantiating an Instance of an Existing COM Object (continued)

```
 * @com.register ( clsid=A67A8C30-5ACA-11D2-807C-204C4F4F5020,
                   typelib=A67A8C31-5ACA-11D2-807C-204C4F4F5020 )
 */
public class ObjectContext
{
 public void objTestMTS() {

    // new instances of MTS objects
    IObjectContext objContext = null;
    IGetContextProperties objProps = null;

    // Response object
    IResponse iObjResponse = null;

    // previously created props object
    props_Dispatch prpObject = null;

    // variant for using with Response
    Variant v = new Variant();

    // get ObjectContext, Context Properties
    objContext = (IObjectContext) MTx.GetObjectContext();
    objProps = (IGetContextProperties)MTx.GetObjectContext();

    // Get the Response object
    v = objProps.GetProperty("Response");
    iObjResponse = (IResponse)v.getDispatch();

    v.VariantClear();
    boolean bResult = false;

    try {
        // create instance of test component, call method
        prpObject = (props_Dispatch)objContext.CreateInstance(props.clsid,
                    props_Dispatch.iid);
        prpObject.objWriteHeader("From within Component");
        iObjResponse.Write(v);
        v.VariantClear();

        // test security
        if (objContext.IsSecurityEnabled()) {
            v.putString("Security is enabled <P>");
            iObjResponse.Write(v);
        }
        else {
            v.putString("Security is not enabled <P>");
            iObjResponse.Write(v);
        }
        v.VariantClear();

        // test transaction
        if (objContext.IsInTransaction()) {
```

Example 16-5. Instantiating an Instance of an Existing COM Object (continued)

```
            v.putString("Component is in transaction ");
            iObjResponse.Write(v);
      }
      else {
            v.putString("Component is not in transaction ");
            iObjResponse.Write(v);
      }

      // mark component finished,
      // successful
      objContext.SetComplete();
      }

      // exception handling - mark component finished
      catch(Exception e) {
         bResult = false;
         v.putString(e.getLocalizedMessage());
         iObjResponse.Write(v);
         objContext.SetAbort();
      }
   }
}
```

The functionality to create the instance of the COM object and to call the other ObjectContext methods is contained within a Java `try...catch` exception-handling block. If the component completes successfully, SetComplete is called. Otherwise, SetAbort is called from the exception-handling block.

Note, though, that using transaction management calls such as those shown in Example 16-5 requires that the component be registered with MTS. After the Java component is compiled, both it and the Java test component are added to the MTS test environment package, as outlined in Chapter 5. Each component's transaction property is checked to make sure it supports a transaction.

Finally, test the component. Example 16-6 shows an ASP test page that contains a script directive to require a transaction for the page, creates the Java component, and invokes the object's method.

Example 16-6. ASP Test Page for the MTS Java Component

```
<%@ TRANSACTION=Required %>
<HTML>
<HEAD>
</HEAD>
<BODY>
<%
  Dim MyObject
  Set MyObject = Server.CreateObject("objcont.ObjectContext")
  MyObject.objTestMTS()
%>
```

Example 16-6. ASP Test Page for the MTS Java Component (continued)

```
</BODY>
</HTML>
```

The result of calling objTestMTS is a header with the words "From within Component" followed by two lines of text, similar to the following:

```
Security is enabled
Component is in transaction
```

If an error had occurred, the error message would have been displayed from within the catch block.

Both `IObjectContext` and `IGetContextProperties` have been demonstrated in this section. The next section goes into detail about the built-in object interfaces and how they are used within Java components.

The ASP Built-In Object and Helper Interfaces

As we've seen, there are five built-in objects that can be used for communication between the client and server and the server component with the server environment. These are the Response, Request, Session, Application, and Server objects. Each of these objects are discussed and demonstrated in turn in the following sections.

In addition to the ASP built-in objects, the `com.ms.asp` package also has other interfaces to facilitate working with the collections returned from several methods. These interfaces are `IVariantDictionary`, `IReadCookie`, `IWriteCookie`, `IStringList`, and `IRequestDictionary`. The `IVariantDictionary` interface provides support for the `IApplicationObject` and `ISessionObject` interfaces; the `IRequestDictionary` interface provides support for the `IRequest` and `IResponse` interfaces; `IReadCookie` and `IWriteCookie` provide support for reading and writing to Netscape-style cookies.

The Application Object and Its Associated Interface, IApplicationObject

The Application object contains application-level information that persists for the life of the ASP application. A variable can be set to a beginning default value when the application starts, and the value and any changes to this value persist until the application is shut down. This makes application-level variables useful for storing values that must persist for the life of the application and must be accessible by all sessions within the application.

Application-level variables are defined either by setting values directly in the Application object, or by defining a static variable in the *global.asa* file for the application.

 The *global.asa* file is a single, static file located in the root directory of the IIS application. It contains references to application- and session-level variables, as well as some event handlers. This file is discussed in more detail in Chapter 6.

The Application object's functionality is accessible from Java components through the `IApplicationObject` interface, defined in `com.ms.asp`. This interface provides the following methods:

getContents
> Returns an `IVariantDictionary` interface pointer that points to the Contents collection. The Contents collection includes all of the objects created with CreateObject within the Application object.

getStaticObjects
> Returns an `IVariantDictionary` interface pointer that points to the StaticObjects collection. The StaticObjects collection includes all of the objects created with the `OBJECT` tag within the *globals.asa* file.

getValue
> Returns a value stored in the Application object.

putValue
> Sets a value in the Application object.

Lock
> Locks out access of the Application object variables.

UnLock
> Unlocks access of the Application object variables.

The `IVariantDictionary` interface is returned from calls to the getContents and getStaticObjects methods. This *helper* interface has the following methods that facilitate working with the Application object:

getCount
> Returns a count of the number of objects in either the StaticObjects collection or the Contents collection

getItem
> Returns a specific item from either the StaticObjects or Contents collection

getKey

Returns an identifier for an item in the StaticObjects or Contents collection

get_NewEnum

Returns a reference to an **IUnknown** interface pointer for the enumerator

putItem

Sets a specific item in either the StaticObjects or Contents collection

The **IVariantDictionary** interface is an *enumerator* interface, which means that it has methods to access a single object, or methods that can be used to iterate through the entire collection of objects managed by the enumerator.

 An example of using enumeration is provided in the section covering **IRequest**.

To try using **IVariantDictionary** to access a specific value, create the example shown in Example 16-7. The component does several things. First, it creates a reference to the **IGetContextProperties** interface, which it uses to create a reference to the **IApplicationObject** and **IResponse** interfaces. Following this, the **IApplicationObject** interface method getContents is called to return a reference to the **IVariantDictionary**, which in turn contains a reference to the Contents collection. To access a specific value in the Contents collection, two Variant objects are used, one for the Contents item key and one for the Contents item value. The key with a value of **tstVariable** is used to retrieve an item from the contents collection by using the **IVariantDictionary** method getItem. The new component then outputs the value using the Response object. At the end of the method, the component changes the value for the **tstVariable** Contents item by using the **IVariantDictionary** method putItem.

Example 16-7. The Combination of IApplicationObject and IVariantDictionary

```java
import com.ms.com.*;
import com.ms.mtx.*;
import com.ms.asp.*;

/**
 * This class is designed to be packaged with a COM DLL output format.
 * The class has no standard entry points, other than the constructor.
 * Public methods will be exposed as methods on the default COM interface.
 * @com.register ( clsid=C27308D5-5AD3-11D2-807D-204C4F4F5020,
                   typelib=C27308D6-5AD3-11D2-807D-204C4F4F5020 )
 */
public class application
{
```

Example 16-7. The Combination of IApplicationObject and IVariantDictionary (continued)

```
// test function
public void tstApplication() {

    // program variables
    IGetContextProperties objProps = null;
    IApplicationObject iObjApplication = null;
    IVariantDictionary iObjDictionary = null;
    IResponse iObjResponse = null;
    Variant v = new Variant();
    Variant v2 = new Variant();

    // get Context Properties
    objProps = (IGetContextProperties)MTx.GetObjectContext();

    // Get the Application object
    v = objProps.GetProperty("Application");
    iObjApplication = (IApplicationObject)v.getDispatch();

    // get response object to output info
    v.VariantClear();
    v = objProps.GetProperty("Response");
    iObjResponse = (IResponse)v.getDispatch();
    v.VariantClear();

    // access dictionary interface for Contents collection
    try {
        iObjDictionary = iObjApplication.getContents();
        v.VariantClear();

        // get contents item for key "tstVariable"
        v.putString("tstVariable");
        v2 = iObjDictionary.getItem(v);
        iObjResponse.Write(v2);

        // reset value
        v2.VariantClear();
        v2.putString("this is a new value");
        iObjDictionary.putItem(v, v2);
        }
    catch(Exception e) {
        v.putString(e.getLocalizedMessage());
        iObjResponse.Write(v);
    }
  }
}
```

Accessing this component from within the ASP page shown in Example 16-8 results in a page that has one line that reads "this is a test." followed by another line that reads "this is a new value."

Example 16-8. ASP Page to Test the Java Application Class

```
<HTML>
<HEAD>
</HEAD>
<BODY>
<%
  Application("tstVariable") = "this is a test"
  Dim MyObject
  Set MyObject = Server.CreateObject("javaObjs.application")
  MyObject.tstApplication()
  Dim theValue
  theValue = Application("tstVariable")
  Response.Write("<p>" + theValue)
%>
</BODY>
</HTML>
```

If the item being accessed had been created within the *global.asa* file, using syntax such as the following:

```
<OBJECT RUNAT=Server SCOPE=Application ID=MyInfo
        PROGID="tstComponent.somecomponent">
</OBJECT>
```

referencing the StaticObjects collection item with the getStaticObjects method, then accessing this collection using getItem with a key of **MyInfo**, would return a reference to this item.

Two other **IApplicationObject** methods are getValue and putValue. These can be used to access variables that are assigned directly to the Application object. For example, the following code block would get the string value for an Application-level variable named *tstString*, display its value using the **IResponse** interface, and then change it:

```
try {

    // get application value
    v = iObjApplication.getValue("tstString");
    iObjResponse.Write(v);
    v.putString("new value");
    iObjApplication.putValue("tstString",v);
    }
catch(ClassCastException e) {
    v.VariantClear();
    v.putString(e.toString());
    iObjResponse.Write(v);
    }
```

The final two methods for the **IApplicationInterface** interface are Lock and UnLock. These methods can be handy to lock access to the application-level variables while a transaction is in process or while the values of application-level variables are being modified, and then to unlock the Application object when the transaction is finished. However, their use should be limited, and the lock should be released as soon as possible, since no other changes to the Application object can be made while it is locked.

The Session object is similar to the Application object and is discussed in the next section.

The Session Object and Its Associated Interface, ISessionObject

Like the Application object, the Session object persists beyond a specific web page. Unlike the Application object, the Session object persists for the length of time that one person (as a session) is connected to the ASP application.

Session-level variables can be created by direct assignment to the Session object, or by declaration in the *global.asa* file. The variables are initialized when a specific user accesses the first page for the ASP application, and persist until the user's session times out or the user logs out.

The Session object is accessible from within Java components through the `ISessionObject` interface. This interface supports the following methods:

Abandon
> Destroys all variables associated with the session and releases any associated resources

getCodePage
> Returns an integer representing the CodePage property, which determines how characters are displayed

getContents
> Returns an `IVariantDictionary` reference pointing to the Contents collection

getLCID
> The locale identifier

getSessionID
> The unique identifier for the session

getStaticObjects
> Returns an `IVariantDictionary` reference pointing to the StaticObjects collection

getTimeout
> Returns the timeout period for the session, in minutes

getValue
> Returns a specific session variable value

putCodePage

> Sets the CodePage property

putLCID

> Sets the locale identifier

putTimeout

> Sets a new time out value

putValue

> Sets the value for a specific session variable

The getContents, getStaticObjects, getValue, and putValue methods operate the same with the **ISessionObject** interface as they did with **IApplicationObject**. The main difference is, of course, that the values impacted by these methods persist only through the session of the person currently logged into the application. Session-level variables might be used, for example, to maintain a running total for a catalog system, or to provide a user identifier for database entries.

The getCodePage and getLocale methods are unique to the Session object, and are of interest if you are working with international web page applications. For example, the CodePage value defines the keyboard mapping for a system, allowing for specialized characters based on a country, or language, character set. The Locale is used to determine regional character settings, such as the use of metrics for numbers, or which characters are used with currency. In the United States, currency uses the dollar sign ($), but the United Kingdom uses the pound sign, which I really can't show because I am using a system based on the United States locale. The following code fragment displays the CodePage and Locale currently in use on a system:

```
try {
    // session object
    v = objProps.GetProperty("Session");
    iObjSession = (ISessionObject)v.getDispatch();

    // get application value
    int i;
    i = iObjSession.getCodePage();

    v.putInt(i);

    // response object defined earlier
    iObjResponse.Write(v);
    iObjResponse.Write("<P>")
    i = iObjSession.getLCID();
    v.putInt(i);
    iObjResponse.Write(v);
    }
```

```
catch(Exception e) {
   v.putString(e.getLocalizedMessage());
   iObjResponse.Write(v);
   }
```

The CodePage and Locale can be changed using the associated putCodePage and putLCID methods. Both the CodePage and Locale can be used to return content based on the settings for the browser accessing the ASP page.

Two other methods that are useful with the Session object are the Abandon and putTimeout methods. The Abandon method can be used to destroy the Session object and free any resources currently in use by the session. The method shown in Example 16-9 can do whatever processing is necessary when a person logs out of a session, including destroying the Session object itself.

Example 16-9. Releasing Resources When User Logs Out

```
public class session
{
   // test function
   public void sesnLogout() {
      IGetContextProperties objProps = null;
      ISessionObject iObjSession = null;
      IResponse iObjResponse = null;
      Variant v = null;

      // get Context Properties
      objProps = (IGetContextProperties)MTx.GetObjectContext();

      v = objProps.GetProperty("Response");
      iObjResponse = (IResponse)v.getDispatch();

      try {
         // session object
         v = objProps.GetProperty("Session");
         iObjSession = (ISessionObject)v.getDispatch();

         // ...other processing

         v.putString("Thanks for stopping by!");
         iObjResponse.Write(v);

         // free Session
         iObjSession.Abandon();
         }
      catch(Exception e) {
         v.putString(e.getLocalizedMessage());
         iObjResponse.Write(v);
         }
      }
}
```

Other information specific to the server can be accessed or changed using the ISERVER object, discussed next.

The Server Object and Its Associated Interface, IServer

The Server object can be used to create new instances of other COM classes, including MTS classes. In addition, it can also be used to derive encoded strings, using either HTML encoding or URL encoding, or to map a relative location to a physical location.

The Java interface for the Server object is IServer, and its methods are:

CreateObject
> Creates an instance of a COM object

getScriptTimeout
> The script timeout value set for the server

HTMLEncode
> Converts HTML special characters into equivalent values that can display as characters within a web page

URLEncode
> Converts URL special characters into equivalent values that can be passed as-is within a URL

URLPathEncode
> Converts all URL special characters except those specific to URL paths into equivalent values that can be passed as-is within a URL

MapPath
> Maps a relative path to a physical path

putScriptTimeout
> Sets the script timeout value for the server

The CreateObject method is useful to create another instance of an object, one that exists for the life of the page and is destroyed when the page display is finished. Remember that a Java component requires a Java wrapper to access the COM object from within the component. Once the wrapper class is created, it is imported into the component and the object can then be created, as shown in the following code fragment:

```
import tstjava.*;

//...other code
IGetContextProperties objProps;
IServer iServer;
```

```
IinstanceCk tst;

// get Context Properties
objProps = (IGetContextProperties)MTx.GetObjectContext();

try {
    // session object
    v = objProps.GetProperty("Server");
    iServer = (IServer)v.getDispatch();

    // ...create object and invoke one of its methods
    tst = (props_Dispatch) iServer.CreateObject("tstjava.props");
    tst.objWriteHeader("test");
    }
```

Unlike using the CreateInstance method of **IObjectContext**, the progid for the COM object is used with the Server object's CreateObject method.

The **IServer** interface can also be used to encode strings. For example, the angle brackets (<, >) are used to delimit HTML tags, such as <p> for a paragraph or <H1></H1> to define a header. To actually output the angle brackets as is, without triggering formatting, special encoding characters are used. The left angle bracket is encoded using the sequence "<", and the right angle bracket is ">". The **IServer** method HTMLEncoding encodes all HTML-specific characters into their associated encoded values. So, the following code:

```
str = iServer.HTMLEncode("<H1>test</H1>");
v.putString(str + "<p>");
iObjResponse.Write(v);
```

would output the following string:

```
&lt;h1&gt;test&lt;/h1&gt;
```

which would output the following to the web page that is viewed:

```
<H1>test</H1>
```

rather than creating the header.

The URLEncode method maps the URL special characters into their associated encoded character sequences. The following code:

```
str = iServer.URLEncode("% this/is a test % +");
v.putString(str + "<p>");
iObjResponse.Write(v);
```

would result in the following string:

```
%25+this%2Fis+a+test+%25+%2B
```

with the percent sign, space, slash, and plus sign encoded. This is similar to how the URLPathEncode method works, except that it does not try to include the slashes. The MapPath method doesn't encode any characters, but instead prepends whatever string is passed to the method with the actual physical location where the ASP application is running. This is especially helpful when performing any access that depends on a physical location. The following code:

```
str = iServer.MapPath("/test/test2");
v.putString(str);
iObjResponse.Write(v);
```

results in the following string, based on the physical directory location where my ASP component testing occurs:

```
E:\Inetpub\wwwroot\New Folder\test2
```

In addition to methods to create COM instances and encode strings, the getScriptTimeout and putScriptTimeout methods can be used to check the current script run times and to increase the value for components that may take time, such as those that access a database or do some other time-consuming operation. The getScriptTimeout returns an integer, and the putScriptTimeout takes an integer, both representing the number of minutes for the timeout.

The Request Object and Its Associated Interface, IRequest

The Request object contains information that the web page reader is sending to the ASP application. Any time a form is submitted, information is appended to the end of a URL, or a Netscape-style cookie is set, an item is added to one of the Request object's collections. Among the collections that can be accessed through the Request object are:

cookies
> Small, persistent bits of information that can be stored on the client and accessed from the ASP application via an HTTP request

Server variables
> A list of environment variables

form
> The name/value pairs submitted from an HTML form

query string
> The name/value pairs appended to the URL of the ASP page

client certificate
> Client certification fields for certification requests

Cookies originated with Netscape and are bits of information stored on the client side and indexed by the URL of the page that set the cookies. They allow an application to maintain information between the client and the application that persists beyond a specific web page. The cookies collection contains the Netscape-style cookies for the page. The Server variables collection contains information about the client, client certification object, HTTP request, browser, and other information pertaining to the client, server, and the communication between the two. The query string and form collections both contain name/value pairs, with the name forming the key that's used to access its associated value. Lastly, the client certificate collection contains the fields of the client certificate issued with the request, in support of the SSL3.0/PCT1.0 security protocol.

The Request object is accessed with the `IRequest` interface in Java. The methods of this interface are:

BinaryRead
> Returns raw, unformatted data from a POST request; the data is returned in a *safe array*—an array that also includes information about its dimensions and bounds

getBody
> Returns the message body when working with the Microsoft Message Queue Server

getClientCertificate
> Returns information about the client certificate

getCookies
> Returns the cookie collection of the client

getForm
> Returns a collection containing a form's field/value pairs

getItem
> Looks for a value matching a key name within all the collections of the Request object

getQueryString
> Returns an item from the query string collection

getServerVariables
> Returns a value for a specified environmental variable

getTotalBytes
> Indicates the size of the raw, unformatted data from a POST request

Most of these methods are used to access collection information. In order to access specific values, the `IRequestDictionary` interface is used.

One use of the `IRequest` and `IRequestDictionary` interfaces is to access the information resulting from user interaction with a page. As an example, if an ASP page has a form whose results are submitted using the POST method, the form's field/value pairs can be accessed within an ASP component using the `IRequest` getForm method and the `IRequestDictionary` getItem method, as shown in Example 16-10.

Example 16-10. Access Item from Forms Collection and Store in Session Variable

```
try {
    // get session object
    v = objProps.GetProperty("Session");
    isesnObject = (ISessionObject)v.getDispatch();

    // get Request object and form collection
    v = objProps.GetProperty("Request");
    iRequest = (IRequest)v.getDispatch();
    iRqstDict = iRequest.getForm();

    // get reader's last name
    v.putString("lastname");
    v = iRqstDict.getItem(v);

    // store in Session object
    isesnObject.putValue("name",v);
    }
catch(Exception e) {
    v.putString(e.toString());
    iObjResponse.Write(v);
}
```

In this component, the web page reader's last name is accessed from the submitted form and stored as an item in the Session object. This makes the last name available to all session-level ASP pages. The getForm method returns a reference to an `IRequestDictionary` interface, which is used to access the form collection. The form's lastname field is assigned to a **Variant** object passed to getItem. This method, in turn, returns the value associated with the lastname field. The value is stored persistently for the session by using the `ISessionObject` object's putValue method. If the form had been submitted using a GET rather than a POST request, the query string collection would have been populated instead of the forms collection. However, the same approach would work with both collections.

Another use of the `IRequest` and `IRequestDictionary` combination is to access the sever variables collection, which contains environment information about the browser, the server, and the connection between the two. This collection can be accessed using the getServerVariables method. The server variables collection contains information such as the URL of the requesting page, the request method (GET or POST), the IP address of the requestor, the protocol used, even the NT user account the reader is logged in as. The information can be accessed discretely by using the getItem method, or the get_NewEnum method can be used to access the Java enumerator interface, `IEnumVariant`.

One handy use of the `IEnumVariant` enumerator and the server variables collection is to print out all of the variables and their associated values. This allows the developer to have a better idea of what variables are available, the format the values take, and how changes in the environment can impact the variables. Example 16-11 shows the complete Java code for a component that can be used to list all of the environment variables and their associated values. In the example, once the `IRequest` interface is accessed, the getServerVariables method is called to return the `IRequestDictionary` interface. The get_NewEnum method is then used to return an `IEnumVariant`. To enumerate through the items in the collection, a count is obtained of the number of items in the collection and the Next method is called. This method takes three parameters: an integer that indicates the number of items to return, an open-ended Variant array to hold the items, and an integer array to indicate the number of items returned.

Example 16-11. Outputting All the Environment Variables from the Request

```java
import com.ms.com.*;
import com.ms.mtx.*;
import com.ms.asp.*;

/**
 * @com.register ( clsid=B5B569B2-DC65-11D1-AB93-204C4F4F5020,
 * typelib=7DA12223-D865-11D1-AB86-204C4F4F5020 )
 */
public class request
{
    // test function
    public void tstRequest() {
        IGetContextProperties objProps;
        IRequest iRequest;
        IRequestDictionary iRqstDict;
        IResponse iObjResponse;
        Variant v = null;

        // get Context Properties
        objProps = (IGetContextProperties)MTx.GetObjectContext();

        v = objProps.GetProperty("Response");
        iObjResponse = (IResponse)v.getDispatch();

        try {

            // get Request object and environment variables collection
            v = objProps.GetProperty("Request");
            iRequest = (IRequest)v.getDispatch();
            iRqstDict = iRequest.getServerVariables();

            // get enumerator
            IEnumVariant ienum;
            ienum = (IEnumVariant) iRqstDict.get_NewEnum();
```

Example 16-11. Outputting All the Environment Variables from the Request (continued)

```
                // set up enumeration
                int[] iItems = new int[1];
                iItems[0] = 0;

                int iCount = iRqstDict.getCount();
                Variant[] vt = new Variant[iCount];
                ienum.Next(iCount,vt,iItems);

                // print out environment variables
                v.putString("<table>");
                iObjResponse.Write(v);
                for (int i = 0; i < iCount; i++) {
                    v.putString("<TR><TD>");
                    iObjResponse.Write(v);
                    iObjResponse.Write(vt[i]);
                    v.putString("</TD><TD>");
                    iObjResponse.Write(v);
                    iObjResponse.Write(iRqstDict.getItem(vt[i]));
                    v.putString("</TD></TR>");
                    iObjResponse.Write(v);
                    }
                v.putString("</table>");
                iObjResponse.Write(v);
                }
            catch(Exception e) {
                v.putString(e.toString());
                iObjResponse.Write(v);
                }
        }
    }
}
```

Once the **Variant** array is populated, a **for** loop is used to display the environment variable names and their associated values using HTML table cell and row elements, with each label and its associated value output in a separate table row.

To test the component, use the ASP file shown in Example 16-12.

Example 16-12. ASP Page to Test the Component in Example 16-11

```
<HTML>
<HEAD>
</HEAD>
<BODY>
<%
Dim MyObj
Set MyObj = Server.CreateObject("javaObjs.request")
MyObj.tstRequest()
%>
</BODY>
</HTML>
```

The same techniques to individually access a collection item or to enumerate through a collection can be used with all of the collections obtained using IRequestDictionary.

The Request object has information about a request being submitted to the server. The Response object, on the other hand, contains information to be returned to client and is discussed next.

The Response Object and Its Associated Interface, IResponse

The Response object and the Java IResponse interface have been used throughout this chapter to write information to a web page returned to the client browser. However, the write method is not the IResponse interface's only useful function. The Response object can also control how content is buffered before being sent to the browser and whether ASP pages are cached. The object can also determine if the client is still connected, control what status to return to the client, and define what type of content is being returned. This is in addition to directing the browser to another location, altering the header for the HTML output, and appending information to the IIS log file.

The IResponse interface actually has the most methods of any of the built-in objects, as shown in the following list:

Add
    Appends a string to an existing HTTP response header

AddHeader
    Adds an HTTP header to the response

AppendToLog
    Adds a string to the IIS log file

BinaryWrite
    Writes data to the client without conversion

Clear
    Erases buffered HTML output

End
    Ends script processing and returns any output

Flush
    Returns any buffered output immediately

getBuffer
    Gets the current buffer setting (True or False)

getCacheControl

Gets the current cache control setting

getCharSet

Gets the current character set value

getContentType

Gets the current content type setting

getCookies

Returns an `IRequestDictionary` collection of write-only cookies

getExpires

Retrieves the expiration time of the cached page in minutes

getExpiresAbsolute

Retrieves the absolute expiration time

getStatus

Retrieves the HTTP status

isClientConnected

Determines whether the client is still connected

PICS

Adds a value to the PICS field of the header

putBuffer

Sets the buffer on or off

putCacheControl

Sets caching on or off

putCharSet

Sets the current character set

putContentType

Sets the current content type

putExpires

Sets cache expiration time, in minutes

putsExpiresAbsolute

Sets an absolute expiration time for the cache

putStatus

Sets the HTTP status

Redirect

Directs the browser to connect to different URL

Write

Outputs HTML content

The Response object's control of output can be manipulated by several of the **IResponse** methods, such as Clear, End, and Flush. Using these methods in conjunction with transaction management can be particularly effective. Consider the scenario of an ASP application consisting of several different actions, all performed within one transaction. If any one of the actions fails and the transaction is rolled back, much of the output that is already generated can be controlled with Response buffering. For example, the following code turns buffering on:

```
iObjResponse.putBuffer(true);
```

Since the putBuffer method controls how output is returned to the client, any component calling this method must be instantiated in the ASP page and must call the method before any other output is returned to the client, or an error will result.

With buffering enabled, output can be returned or not, based on the success or failure of any one of the component actions, as the following code demonstrates:

```
try {

    //...other code
    iObjResponse.Flush();
    objContext.SetComplete();
    }
catch(Exception e) {

    // clear existing output
    iObjResponse.Clear();

    v.putString(e.getLocalizedMessage());
    iObjResponse.Write(v);
    objContext.SetAbort();
    }
```

In earlier chapters I pose the question whether buffering should be controlled from a component. The main reason why this would be of concern is that changing buffering from within a component overrides any other behavior that the developer specifies within an ASP script, and this can have unexpected results. So, as a matter of form, control buffering from within a component sparingly, and document the effects.

The **IResponse** object can also be used to set whether an ASP page is cached or not. If content is unlikely to change within the same ASP application session, the caching expiration time should be set to a high value, using code such as the following, so that the page is pulled from the client cache rather than the server:

```
iObjResponse.putExpires(300);
```

In addition to controlling caching and buffering, the **IResponse** interface can also be used to change the status of the HTTP response, such as setting the status or redirecting the output, as the following code demonstrates:

```
iObjResponse.Redirect("http://www.somewhere.com/someother.htm")
```

The advantage of using redirection is that the component can query for information, such as browser type and version, and then direct the client to a set of pages created specifically for the browser/version.

Another method of the **IResponse** interface that can be particularly handy is put-ContentType. One example of its use is for web pages that provide buttons for people to see the actual HTML source. When a user chooses this option, the page is returned as **text/plain** rather than **text/HTML**, as the following demonstrates:

```
if (type == 0) {
    v.putString("HTML");
    iObjResponse.Write(v);
    iObjResponse.putContentType("text/HTML");
    }
else    {
    v.putString("plain");
    iObjResponse.putContentType("text/plain");
    iObjResponse.Write(v);
    }
```

To display the page as HTML, a value of zero (0) is sent with the component method call. Otherwise, a value other than zero is sent with the method, and the HTML is returned as plain text without any processing of the HTML tags.

As handy as it is to access the built-in objects from within a Java component, the process can be a bit cumbersome at times. Consider that to obtain a reference to one of the objects, such as the **IRequest** object, an interface to the **IGetContextProperties** as well as the **IRequest** object must be obtained, and a Variant must be used to access the **IRequest** object. In addition, Variants have to be used elsewhere to handle any Java-to-COM data type communication mapping. To circumvent this, Microsoft created a set of Java classes that provide a more "Java-like" interface to the built-in objects; this framework is discussed next.

The Java Component Framework

To make things a bit easier, Microsoft has created a framework that encapsulates much of the ASP Java built-in component class functionality. The framework, called the Java Component Framework (JCF), is installed with other IIS samples when IIS 4.0 is installed. To use the framework, the JCF classes must be moved to a subdirectory named *aspcomp* directly off of the *java\TrustLib* directory. Installation instructions and additional documentation are included with the classes.

JCF provides Java wrappers that hide most of the Microsoft COM-specific functionality, making access of the built-in objects more Java-like and less COM-like. To demonstrate, the following code uses the `com.ms.asp` classes directly to write a string to the client:

```
import com.ms.com.*;
import com.ms.mtx.*;
import com.ms.asp.*;
...
IGetContextProperties objProps;
IResponse iObjResponse;
Variant v = null;

// get Context Properties
objProps = (IGetContextProperties)MTx.GetObjectContext();

// get Response, write output
v = objProps.GetProperty("Response");
iObjResponse = (IResponse)v.getDispatch();
v.putString("test");
iObjResponse.Write(v);
```

However, with the JCF framework, the following three lines of code generate the same result:

```
import aspcomp.*;
...
Response response = AspContext.getResponse();
response.write("test");
```

In addition, the JCF also hides the COM-specific data types, wrapping them within Java data types, again making the COM classes easier to use for traditional Java programmers. For example, a Java programmer will be comfortable working with **Strings**, and not as comfortable having to use the **Variant** object to handle Java-to-COM communication.

In this chapter, I'll demonstrate how the JCF classes can be used and highlight the key differences between using the framework and directly accessing `com.ms.asp` components.

First, each of the five built-in objects has been implemented within the JCF, in addition to a reference to the **IObjectContext** interface. The previous code fragment shows how to implement a Response object, and the others are equally easily implemented using the appropriate AspContext method call:

```
Request rqstObject  = AspContext.getRequest();
Server srvrObject = AspContext.getServer();
```

```
Application appObject = AspContext.getApplication();
Session sesnObject = AspContext.getSession();
```

The only Java class library that needs to be included to work with the framework is **aspcomp**, but in order to access the **IObjectContext** interface, the **com.ms. mtx** class library should also be included, as demonstrated in the following code:

```
import aspcomp.*;
import com.ms.mtx.*;
iObjectContext iobjContext = AspContext.getObjectContext();
```

Without including the **com.ms.mtx** class library, an error occurs when trying to compile the Java component.

Once the objects are accessed, their object methods can be invoked. With Visual J++ 6.0, the syntax for each method is displayed while typing out the method calls. Note that primarily due to using traditional Java data types instead of using the Variant, the method calls are different between the framework and the lower-level ASP methods. To demonstrate this, the following code provides the same functionality as that shown in Example 16-10, except that the former uses the WFC:

```
Response response = AspContext.getResponse();
try
    {
    Session sesnObject = AspContext.getSession();

    Request rqstObject = AspContext.getRequest();
    RequestDictionary rqstDictObj = rqstObject.getForm();

    // access and set name
    String str;
    str = rqstDictObj.getString("lastname");
    sesnObject.setString("name",str);
    }
catch (Exception e)
    {
    response.write(e.toString());
    }
}
```

Note that instead of using a **Variant** to create the argument for the Write method, a string is passed directly to the method.

As can also be seen in the example, not only are the built-in objects implemented in the JCF, their helper interfaces are too. In the code, a RequestDictionary object is returned when the form collection is accessed on the Request object, and is then used to pull out the web page reader's last name. This is added as a session-level variable.

One other difference between accessing the **com.ms.asp** and **com.ms.mtx** classes directly and using the JCF is important to note. In order to implement a more traditional Java-like interface, the JCF objects also require that exception handling be implemented for some of the object methods. In the earlier examples in the chapter using the direct COM classes, any exception handling was more a matter of form than a requirement. However, with some of the JCF methods, exception handling is a requirement, and you will get a compile-time error if the method is not invoked within a `try` block.

As stated earlier, Microsoft has provided documentation on using the JCF, and you should review this before using the classes.

Further Reading

For additional reading about the topics covered in this chapter, check out the following:

- "Writing Microsoft Transaction Server Components in Java," at *http://premium. microsoft.com/msdn/library/bkgrnd/html/msdn_mtsjava.htm.*

- "Developing MTS Components with Java," at *http://premium.microsoft.com/ msdn/library/sdkdoc/mts20sp1/building_965d.htm.*

- "Java Class and Interface Definitions," at *http://premium.microsoft.com/msdn/ library/sdkdoc/iishelp/iis/htm/sdk/crtcomp_39f7.htm.*

- "Java Classes," at *http://premium.microsoft.com/msdn/library/sdkdoc/iisref/ buil3foz.htm.*

- "Writing Microsoft Transaction Server Components in Java with Visual J++ 6.0," at *http://premium.microsoft.com/msdn/library/techart/msdn_mtsjava.htm.*

17

Integrating Java ASP Components with ADO and MTS

Data access from a Java component has existed since Sun released the Java Database Connectivity API preceding the release of the Java Developer's Kit version 1.1. The JDBC provided techniques to connect to, query, and update data for a specified data source. These activities could be accomplished by using ODBC and the JDBC-ODBC Bridge or by using a variety of drivers provided by independent toolmakers or the database vendors themselves.

Microsoft supported, and still supports, JDBC access within Visual J++. Additionally, Microsoft provides alternative methods of database access, including Remote Data Objects (RDO) and Data Access Objects (DAO). In addition, support for Microsoft's new Universal Data Access technology, called ActiveX Data Objects (ADO), has also been provided. This chapter briefly discusses the differences between these approaches when used with Java, but concentrates on ADO.

The use of ADO within Visual J++ has been facilitated by a set of new classes included within the Windows Framework Classes (WFC). This chapter demonstrates how to use WFC to connect to a data source and create several types of result sets using different types of queries.

The chapter ends with demonstrations of using WFC to update data and to support transaction control, both as an aspect of ADO and as a Microsoft Transaction Server (MTS) technology.

 Though this chapter can serve as a good overview of the ADO techniques as implemented within the WFC, the demonstrations are all provided within the context of ASP/MTS components, and focus specifically on server-side components. This chapter does not provide an in-depth coverage of ADO or WFC, which are beyond the scope of this book. In addition, the chapter also uses the *pubs* database that comes with Microsoft SQL Server for the database examples.

DAO, RDO, OLE DB, and ADO

If you have programmed with Visual Basic, chances are you have used DAO, which is still the most commonly used data access technique for VB. DAO is supported in 16-bit as well as 32-bit environments, accesses data using the Microsoft Jet Engine, ODBC, or both, and can be used to access ISAM databases such as those supported by dBase or Btrieve. The disadvantages to DAO are that it does not scale well, consumes more resources than other data access techniques, and offers inferior performance when compared to other methods such as RDO.

A new version of DAO, ODBCDirect, does provide ODBC access for DAO with improved performance. However, Microsoft has stated that DAO should be confined to small, standalone systems, and ADO is recommended for larger, distributed systems.

RDO, on the other hand, is more efficient, can be used with distributed systems, and provides more controlled access to data. The main disadvantage to using RDO is that ISAM access is actually much more complicated than accessing a database such as Oracle or Microsoft's SQL Server, both relational database systems.

While RDO is an effective approach, another disadvantage to this technique is the hierarchical approach to accessing data. For instance, you must open a database connection, then create a record set, then retrieve the record set, and then close the record set, and so on, each operation requiring an instance of a specific type of object to perform the action. With ADO, you can actually open a database connection, create a record set, and retrieve the set with one command and one object, rather than with several commands and objects. Or you can continue using the multi-command object approach—whichever works best.

As an example of how different this flattened approach can be, the following code fragment shows the Java ADO commands that create a separate database connection, a data source command, and a recordset to hold and work with the results of the command:

```
Connection conn = new Connection();
Command cmd = new Command();
Recordset rs = new Recordset();
String strvalue;

// open connections
conn.setConnectionString("Provider=SQLOLEDB;driver={SQLServer};
    server=MARVIN;uid=sa;pwd=;database=pubs");
conn.open();

// create command
```

```
cmd.setCommandText("select * from authors");
cmd.setActiveConnection(conn);

// create record set
rs.setCommand(cmd);
rs.open();
```

With RDO, you would need to create an rdoEnvironment object to manage the connection transactions, then use this to create an rdoConnection object for the actual connection. This in turn would be used to create an rdoResultset, and so on.

There can be advantages to creating objects of each type, such as a Connection, Command, or Recordset object. The advantage is primarily that other commands can use the same connection, other recordsets can use the same command, and so on. However, if the purpose of the component is to access and display one or more fields from a specific recordset, the component could be rewritten as follows to create only a Recordset object and to use its methods to set both the data source and the connection:

```
// create and open record set
Recordset rs = new Recordset();

rs.setActiveConnection("Provider=SQLOLEDB;driver={SQLServer};
   server=MARVIN;uid=sa;pwd=;database=pubs");

rs.setSource("select * from authors");
rs.open();
```

In addition to allowing component instantiation outside of the object hierarchy, ADO has also decreased the number of objects within its data access model. There are 7 ADO objects, compared to 14 for RDO, but for each of the ADO components there are more properties and methods. This model simplification does not necessarily result in a loss of services or performance. The primary area left out of ADO is the support for Data Definition Language (DDL) and the ability to create ODBC data sources. Considering the focus of ADO, which is simplified, fast access and update capability within a distributed application, the absence of data object creation capability is not a serious functional loss.

Aside from simplifying coding, ADO can support access to ISAM data sources as easily as relational databases. Based on what Microsoft describes as Universal Data Access, a set of interfaces called the OLE DB interfaces provide data manipulation support for all types of data sources. The problem with using OLE DB directly, though, is that it is implemented as C++, and is not necessarily easy to work with. ADO provides simple-to-use wrapper classes of the lower-level OLE DB interfaces. Because of this, ADO provides access to OLE DB's performance and flexibility without forcing the developer to deal with the complex interfaces that make up OLE DB.

The combination of a flattened data object model on an underlying low-level support infrastructure means that a component, such as an ASP component, can access only those objects it needs, keeping the component small, without having to access the data through too many layers, which then keeps the component fast.

 Another advantage to ADO? Microsoft has provided a set of built-in objects to access ADO from Java.

As stated, ADO was created mainly for use within Internet and Intranet applications and other distributed types of applications. To support this, ADO provides batch caching of data changes and support for submitting them to a server at one time. Additionally, ADO objects are created as free-threaded objects, meaning that accessing any of the objects will not force serialization of the ASP component incorporating ADO. Different cursor types are also supported, as are stored procedures and multiple recordsets. The OLE DB provider associated with the ODBC driver used defines the limit on what an ASP component can do with ADO. Setting the ADO provider is discussed in the next section on establishing an ADO connection.

Connecting to a Data Source with ADO

To add support for ADO to a Java component, an import statement is added to the component, which pulls in the WFC classes for ADO:

```
import com.ms.wfc.data.*;
```

This adds support for the Java-wrapped ADO classes supported through the WFC.

An ADO connection is a specific database session. Within an ASP application, the connection can be either a direct database connection or a network connection if the data source is remote to the ASP component. The ADO connection may or may not be represented by a specific instantiation of a Connection object. As shown in the previous code fragment, a connection to the database can be created without having to specifically create a Connection object. However, if the connection is used for more than one record set, it is more efficient to create a separate Connection object that is usable for all queries and database commands.

A Connection object has several methods and properties. For instance, the Open method is used to create the database connection and can optionally take a connection string, a userid, a password, and an open option, as shown in the following prototypes, taken from the Microsoft Connection class documentation.

```
public void open()
public void open(String connectionString)
public void open(String connectionString, String userID)
public void open(String connectionString, String userID, String password)
public void open(String connectionString, String userID, String password,
                 int options)
```

The connection string itself consists of a set of key=value pairs, each separated by a semicolon (;). All connection strings, regardless of the OLE DB provider, require that certain information, such as the server and the database, or the DSN for the data source, the userid and the password, be included in the connection string. An example of a connection string is the following:

```
Provider=SQLOLEDB;DSN=pubs;uid=sa;pwd=;database=pubs;
pwd=somepassword;Driver={SQL Server}
```

The first keyword shown in the string defines the OLE DB provider for the database. The provider listed in the example is for the Microsoft SQL Server database. If no provider is given, the default is a generic OLE DB for ODBC provider, **MSDASQL**. The following connection string uses this default provider to connect to an Access database:

```
DSN=books;uid=sa;Driver={Microsoft Access Driver(*.mdb)}
```

Check the documentation for your database to see if an OLE DB provider is given. If none is provided, you can still use the generic OLE DB for ODBC provider if the database provides an ODBC 3.0 or above driver.

In addition to the provider, the connection string can also contain a driver name, which is a reference to the database server, such as {SQL Server} for Microsoft SQL Server, and {Microsoft Access Driver (*.mdb)} for Access. You can take this information from the ODBC Data Source Administrator. Instead of, or in addition to, the server, you can also specify a Data Source Name (DSN) or a File Data Source Name (FileDSN). The DSN references data sources installed on the computer, and the FileDSN represents data sources installed and configured in such a way to be accessible by all users that have access to the installed driver. For ASP components, the data source can be configured using either the DSN or FileDSN. If the DSN is provided in the connection string, the database source does not need to be provided, though this is a good technique to ensure you can connect to the correct database.

The user identifier and password can be specified separately within the connection string as optional Open method parameters. In addition, other keyword/value pairs may be required for each OLE DB provider; if so, they should be documented with the provider.

In addition to the connection string and the user identifier and password, the Connection object's Open method can establish an asynchronous database connection by specifying an optional parameter of type **AdoEnums.ConnectOption** and a value of **ASYNCCONNECT**. The value used with the parameter is accessible by adding the import statement for the WFC ADO classes, accessing the AdoEnums package, and then accessing the specific parameter. Visual J++'s autofill capability will provide a listing of enumerated objects. By setting the connection to be asynchronous, processing can continue while the connection is being made. However, there must be a means by which the component is informed when a connection is made and when the connection itself can be used. This occurs through ADO event trapping and using the ADO event-handler functions.

An event is fired when the Connection object establishes a connection. The event has an associated event handler and can be trapped through the use of the connection complete event handler, onConnectComplete. Example 17-1 shows a component that adds an onConnectComplete event-handler function, invokes the Connection object's Open method synchronously, and processes a record set within the event handler. A message is displayed just before the connection is established and just after the connection event handler function has finished.

Example 17-1. Using Delegation and an Event Handler

```
import com.ms.com.*;
import com.ms.wfc.data.*;
import com.ms.mtx.*;
import com.ms.asp.*;

/**
 * This class is designed to be packaged with a COM DLL output format.
 * The class has no standard entry points, other than the constructor.
 * Public methods will be exposed as methods on the default COM interface.
 * @com.register ( clsid=C27308E9-5AD3-11D2-807D-204C4F4F5020,
                   typelib=C27308EA-5AD3-11D2-807D-204C4F4F5020 )
 */
public class tstado
{
    // data members
    // response object
    IResponse iObjResponse = null;

    // connection object
    Connection conn = new Connection();

    // define connection event handler
    ConnectionEventHandler ceHandler =
        new ConnectionEventHandler(this, "onConnectComplete");
```

Example 17-1. Using Delegation and an Event Handler (continued)

```java
// connection event handler
public void onConnectComplete(Object sender,ConnectionEvent e)
   {
   Variant vtConnection = new Variant();

   // check status
   if (e.adStatus == AdoEnums.EventStatus.ERRORSOCCURRED) {
      vtConnection.putString("Connection failed");
      iObjResponse.Write(vtConnection);
      return;
      }

   // some other work
   Recordset rs = new Recordset();
   rs = conn.execute("select * from authors");

   String str;
   Variant vtOutput = new Variant();
   Field fld;
   rs.moveFirst();
   while (!rs.getEOF()) {
      str = rs.getFields().getItem("au_lname").getValue().toString();
      vtOutput.putString(str + "<br>");
      iObjResponse.Write(vtOutput);
      rs.moveNext();
      }
   return;
}


// create connection, response object
public void test() {

   // access Response object
   IGetContextProperties iObjProps;
   iObjProps = (IGetContextProperties)MTx.GetObjectContext();
   Variant vResponse = new Variant();

   // Get the Response object
   vResponse = iObjProps.GetProperty("Response");
   iObjResponse = (IResponse) vResponse.getDispatch();

try
{
   // add handler
   conn.addOnConnectComplete(ceHandler);

   // waiting...
   Variant vtMessage = new Variant("Waiting for connection...<p>");
   iObjResponse.Write(vtMessage);
```

Example 17-1. Using Delegation and an Event Handler (continued)

```
    // open connection
    String str = "Provider=SQLOLEDB;database=pubs;Driver={SQL Server}";
    conn.open(str,"sa","");

    vtMessage.putString("Finished with connection...");
    iObjResponse.Write(vtMessage);

    // other work ...

    conn.close();

    // remove event handler
    conn.removeOnConnectComplete(ceHandler);
    }
  catch( Exception e )
    {
    Variant vtError = new Variant(e.getLocalizedMessage());
    iObjResponse.Write(vtError);
    }
  }
}
```

This component has several public data members, including ones for the Response object, the Connection object, and one of type ConnectionEventHandler for the event handler. The latter object is passed the object that receives the event, which happens to be the current object, denoted by the use of the class pronoun **this**. In addition, the ConnectionEventHandler constructor also receives the name of the event handler function, in this case *onConnectionComplete.*

Following the declaration of the class members, the onConnectionComplete event handler is created. This method first checks to see if the connection opened without an error. If an error occurs, a message is output and the event handler is exited. If the connection is successful, a Recordset object is derived as a result of running a query directly from the Connection object, and the value of a field is pulled from all the record set's rows.

The code for the event-handler method is followed by the code for test, the method that is invoked from an ASP page. This method creates the Response object data member and writes out a message about opening the Connection. The ConnectionEventHandler is added to the Connection object using the addOnConnectionComplete method. This is then followed by the call to the Connection object's Open method. After the post-connection processing, a last message that the connection to the database is being closed is output to the web page.

The result of running this component within an ASP page is a page with a message about connecting to the database, a list of author last names from the *pubs* demo database for SQL Server, and a message at the end of the list about the connection being closed. Since the connection is not opened asynchronously, the last message is not displayed until the connection event handler has returned.

In addition to the ConnectionOpen event handler, other events that can be trapped for the Connection object are those for transaction management, discussed later in the chapter, and an event handler for trapping the connection disconnect. This is in addition to event handlers for events that fire when the execution method is finished and that occur just before a connection is made or an execution statement is run. However, for incorporating into ASP components, the most useful, trappable events are the **OpenConnection** event and the following events:

Disconnect
> The event handler for this event is addOnDisconnect, which is invoked when the connection is disconnected. This event can be used to perform post-connection cleanup, or to reopen the connection if it has terminated.

ExecuteComplete
> The event handler for this event is addOnExecuteComplete, which is invoked when the Execute method call (which executes a query, a SQL statement, a stored procedure, or some provider–specific command) is complete. Again, if the ASP component is operating asynchronously, this event handler can be used to provide any post-execution processing.

Some event handlers, such as addOnWillExecute, are more useful in front-end components, since they enable the user to examine or modify the pending statement before it is invoked. Another use of the pre-event handlers is to cancel a pending action—such as a specific query or an update—just by setting a status variable, one of the parameters passed to the event handler.

 Microsoft uses *delegation* event handling for the ADO event handlers. This is a different technique than that supported for Java-Beans, and you must not use the two different techniques at the same time within the same component.

Other Connection object methods are used specifically to control database access and transaction management, two issues critical for a multi-user system such as an Internet or Intranet application. Database access can be controlled by using the setMode method to control whether the access is read/write or read- or write-only, and if the database is opened in such a way as to deny other connections. The following code prevents others from opening a connection to the database while the existing connection is active (open):

```
conn.setMode(AdoEnums.ConnectMode.SHAREEXCLUSIVE);
conn.open(str,"sa","");
```

Another property of the Connection that can impact on database access is the isolation level. Database transactions supported by ADO default to a type of `AdoEnums.IsolationLevel.CHAOS` and `AdoEnums.Isolationlevel.CURSORSTABILITY`. The `CHAOS` isolation level means that pending changes from isolated transactions cannot be overwritten by actions of the component. The `CURSORSTABILITY` Isolationlevel setting means that other ADO transactions operating on the same server-side database can only view changes in this specific transaction after these changes have been committed. The ADO provider determines the types of isolation level supported, and trying to use unsupported types can result in a different level of isolation being set or in an error.

Transactions can be controlled directly for a connection with the use of the Connection object's beginTrans, commitTrans, and rollbackTrans methods. This is an effective approach to take to fine-tune transaction control for a specific set of database activities, rather than controlling the transaction for several components using MTS transaction control. Using beginTrans creates a new transaction on the Connection, and using commitTrans or rollbackTrans impacts on the activity for the specific connection only.

To begin a new transaction, use the following code:

```
conn.beginTrans();
```

After creating changes on the database, the transaction can be committed using the following command:

```
conn.commitTrans();
```

The transaction can be rolled back by using the following:

```
conn.rollbackTrans();
```

The rollbackTrans method ends the transaction without committing any pending changes to the database for the specific database connection. Each of the transaction methods also has associated event handlers: onBeginTransComplete, onCommitTransComplete, and onRollbackTransComplete. These event handlers can be used to return a message with the transaction status to the ASP application user. Adding transaction handling to the Connection object is demonstrated in more detail later in this chapter in the section "Updating the Data."

One last method that I did not mention was the Connection Close method. You will want to close every connection as soon as possible, since there are a finite number of database connections possible. Creating a connection and then not closing it locks out other users when they access the application and the application attempts to create a new connection.

Querying the Data

As demonstrated in "Connecting to a Data Source with ADO," database retrievals can be executed using the Connection object, with a Recordset object returned as a result. In addition to the retrieval being managed by the Connection object, a database can be read directly from a Recordset object or by using a Command object. For the latter, parameters can be passed with the query.

Database queries can fall into several categories:

- Simple one-table queries, such as "select au_lname from authors"

- More complex multiple-table join queries, such as "select authors.au_lname, titles.title from authors, titles, titleauthor where titles.title_id = titleauthor.title_id and authors.au_id = titleauthor.au_id"

- Simple or complex queries using parameters

- Retrieving data for updates

- Calling stored procedures

These types of queries are covered in the next several sections. In addition, the impact of each type of query on other possible data transactions is explored.

Simple Data Queries

You might think that a simple, one-table query to return and output information to an ASP page would have no real effect on any other transaction activity. However, any data action impacts all other actions, even one as simple as the following:

```
Recordset rs = new Recordset();
Variant vtSource = new Variant("select * from authors");
rs.open(vtSource, (Connection)conn, AdoEnums.CursorType.FORWARDONLY,
        AdoEnums.LockType.READONLY, AdoEnums.CommandType.TEXT);
```

This query selects all the fields from the AUTHORS table using an existing Connection object and a forward-only cursor—meaning that the cursor is read from the first record to the last. In addition, a read-only lock is applied with the query, which prevents any modifications to the retrieved information. This is probably the simplest type of query to make: no joined tables or stored procedure calls, no passed parameters, and no updates on the returned data. What possible impact can something like this have on any other transactions?

One possible impact is the use of resources to fulfill the command. There is only so much CPU and memory to handle all database transactions, and this small one does take its own piece. It also impacts the network traffic to support the query. This query returns a small number of rows, but querying a table with a thousand, or even a million, rows without any form of selection criteria can require all system processes as well as much of the available server bandwidth to return the query. This is in addition to a possible timeout of the existing ASP request, as well as a very slow response time for the web page reader.

To control the number of rows returned, criteria are usually applied to database retrieval. In addition, the Recordset object's setMaxRecords method controls the number of records that are returned for a particular result set, regardless of any other criteria.

Adding Selection Criteria

The next simplest data query adds selection criteria, otherwise known as adding a WHERE clause to the SQL SELECT statement. Again, this can be used with a single table query, or with a more complex multi-table join. As an example of the latter type of query, the following code fragment contains a query with a three-table join in which one specific column is accessed from the Recordset result set and output to the returning web page:

```
// create recordset and select
Recordset rs = new Recordset();
str = "select * from titles, titleauthor, authors where ";
str+= "au_lname = 'Ringer' and titleauthor.au_id = authors.au_id ";
str+= "and titles.title_id = titleauthor.title_id";

Variant vtSource = new Variant(str);
rs.open(vtSource, (Connection)conn, AdoEnums.CursorType.FORWARDONLY,
        AdoEnums.LockType.READONLY, AdoEnums.CommandType.TEXT);

// print out title
Variant vtOutput = new Variant();
rs.moveFirst();
while (!rs.getEOF()) {
    str = rs.getFields().getItem("title").getValue().toString();
    vtOutput.putString(str + "<br>");
    iObjResponse.Write(vtOutput);
    rs.moveNext();
    }
rs.close();
```

Though more complex than a single-table query with no selection criteria, the impact on the ASP application is the same for this type of query. The number of rows being returned is not likely to be large unless the selection criteria are not very restrictive, but another problem can occur with a multiple-table join. A valid but not well-thought-out query can actually force the database engine to do full table scans of all tables involved with the query. If the tables are large, this activity can take a considerable amount of time. The amount of time to process the query can cause a timeout on the Connection object, the transaction containing the connection, or the ASP page containing the component.

The best approach to take in building queries with multiple table joins is to test the selection out using a SQL tool such as I-SQL, and to use optimization on the database, such as indexes on the tables. The optimization tools provided with most database systems perform analysis on queries and can help define a more efficient query just by rearranging the WHERE clause, making use of indexes, or controlling other factors.

Using a query such as the one demonstrated in the previous code fragment, where the query string itself is built using hardcoded parameter values, is not that likely in a "real world" database application. What is more likely is the use of user-specified parameters, discussed in the next section.

Using the Command Object and Parameters

For most ASP components, database queries will be based on selection criteria that are all or in part provided by the web page reader's interaction with the ASP application. The criteria can be accessed using the built-in ASP Request object. The criteria are then retrieved from the form or query string collection, depending on the method of submitting the form or whether the values are submitted using a query string. The values can be concatenated—added—to the query string used with the Recordset. Example 17-2 shows such a component that accesses books by an author's last name.

Example 17-2. Query Using Value Passed to Component with Query Request

```
String str;
Variant vtMessage = new Variant();
Variant vtRequest = new Variant();
IRequest iObjRequest = null;
IRequestDictionary iObjReqDictionary = null;
IGetContextProperties iObjProps;
iObjProps = (IGetContextProperties)MTx.GetObjectContext();

try
    {
    // get Request object and form collection

    vtRequest = iObjProps.GetProperty("Request");
    iObjRequest = (IRequest)vtRequest.getDispatch();
    iObjReqDictionary = iObjRequest.getForm();

    // get author's last name
    vtRequest.putString("lastname");
    vtRequest = iObjReqDictionary.getItem(vtRequest);

    // create recordset and select
```

Example 17-2. Query Using Value Passed to Component with Query Request (continued)

```
    Recordset rs = new Recordset();
    str = "select * from titles, titleauthor, authors where ";
    str+= "authors.au_lname = '" + vtRequest.toString();
    str+= "' and titleauthor.au_id = authors.au_id ";
    str+= "and titles.title_id = titleauthor.title_id";

    vtMessage.putString(str + "<p>");
    iObjResponse.Write(vtMessage);
    Variant vtSource = new Variant(str);
    rs.open(vtSource, (Connection)conn, AdoEnums.CursorType.FORWARDONLY,
            AdoEnums.LockType.READONLY, AdoEnums.CommandType.TEXT);

    // print out title
    Variant vtOutput = new Variant();
    rs.moveFirst();
    while (!rs.getEOF()) {
            str = rs.getFields().getItem("title").getValue().toString();
            vtOutput.putString(str + "<br>");
            iObjResponse.Write(vtOutput);
            rs.moveNext();
            }
    rs.close();

    }
catch( Exception e )
    {
    Variant vtError = new Variant(e.getLocalizedMessage());
    iObjResponse.Write(vtError);
    }
}
```

In addition to listing book titles, Example 17-2 also displays the query string, a good technique to use while developing components that access a database. Then you'll be able to see at a glance what the query string is in case problems occur. Just remember to remove the relevant call to the Write method before publishing the component.

This approach is very effective, since the web page reader has a chance to determine what data is returned, leading to more efficient uses of database and other resources.

If more than one parameter is provided, or if the recordset retrieval procedure is run multiple times with different names each time, using parameters with a Command object would probably be a better approach than using a Recordset object. Using a command caches the query for reuse, allowing you to change the parameter value rather than having to reissue the query directly. When using a Command object instead of concatenating the query values into the query string, you can create parameters for the command and use the search values to set these parameters. Example 17-3 uses the Command object, the Command object's Parameters collection, and the Parameter object to create the same query as shown in Example 17-2.

Example 17-3. Query Using a Parameter Object to Pass the Query Criteria

```
vtRequest = iObjProps.GetProperty("Request");
iObjRequest = (IRequest)vtRequest.getDispatch();
iObjReqDictionary = iObjRequest.getForm();

// get author's last name
vtRequest.putString("lastname");
vtRequest = iObjReqDictionary.getItem(vtRequest);

Command cmd = new Command();
cmd.setActiveConnection(conn);

// query string
str = "select * from authors, titles, titleauthor where ";
str+= "titleauthor.au_id = authors.au_id and ";
str+= "titles.title_id = titleauthor.title_id and ";
str+= "au_lname = ?";

// set command prperties
cmd.setCommandText(str);
cmd.setPrepared(true);
cmd.setCommandType(AdoEnums.CommandType.TEXT);

// parameter
Parameters parms = cmd.getParameters();
Parameter parm = new Parameter();
parm.setType(AdoEnums.DataType.VARCHAR);
parm.setSize(40);
parm.setString(vtRequest.toString());
parms.append(parm);

Recordset rs = cmd.execute();

// print out title
Variant vtOutput = new Variant();
rs.moveFirst();
while (!rs.getEOF()) {
    str = rs.getFields().getItem("title").getValue().toString();
    vtOutput.putString(str + "<br>");
    iObjResponse.Write(vtOutput);
    rs.moveNext();
    }
rs.close();
```

In this example, the Command object's properties are set first, the query by using the setCommandText method to assign the SQL **SELECT** statement to the Command object's CommandText property, and the command type specifier by using the setCommandType method. To add the parameter for the query, the Parameters collection is accessed from the Command object. Next, a new Parameter object is created, and its data type, size, and value are set using the setType, setSize, and setString methods, respectively. The new parameter is then appended to the Parameters collection. (For more than one query criteria, more than one parameter can be created and appended to the Parameters collection.) Finally, the query is run by calling the Command object's execute method. The result of the operation returns a Recordset object, which is then used to process the returned records in a manner similar to that shown in Example 17-2.

Queries are not the only operation performed with ASP components. Components can update data as well as query it; updating data using ADO is covered in the next section.

Updating the Data

ASP components using ADO can delete records, insert new records, or modify existing data. Each of these operations can be performed directly on the database, or can be performed on a recordset, with updates committed to the database. As an example, we'll create a component that deletes all entries from the AUTHORS table where the last name of the author is Ringer. The example uses the delete database command and the executeUpdate method for the Command object.

Create a Visual J++ component and name the project adoupdate. Once the ASP component class is generated, rename the class and its associated file to updateasp. Add the following line to import the WFC classes:

```
import com.ms.wfc.data.*;
```

Then add a method for the component named DeleteAuthor.

To the new ASP component, add the Connection object and set its properties to allow both reads and writes to the database:

```
Connection conn = new Connection();
conn.setMode(AdoEnums.ConnectMode.READWRITE);
conn.setCursorLocation(AdoEnums.CursorLocation.CLIENT);
conn.open("Provider=SQLOLEDB;database=pubs;Driver={SQL Server}","sa","");
```

Next, create a Command object and set its type to be text, since you will be passing an embedded SQL delete command:

```
// create command
Command cmd = new Command();
cmd.setActiveConnection(conn);
cmd.setCommandType(AdoEnums.CommandType.TEXT);
```

Once the Command object is created, add the command string, which deletes all records from the authors table for an author with a last name of Ringer:

```
// set command
str = "delete from authors where au_lname = 'Ringer'";
cmd.setCommandText(str);
```

Finally, issue the command, enclosing it within a transaction in order to roll back the changes (you don't want to make permanent modifications to your test database at this time):

```
// make transaction
conn.beginTrans();
cmd.executeUpdate();
conn.rollbackTrans();
```

If you build this ASP component and access its method from an ASP page, you'll most likely get an "com.ms.wfc.data.AdoException" error similar to the following:

```
com.ms.wfc.data.AdoException: DELETE statement conflicted with COLUMN
REFERENCE constraint 'FK__titleauth__au_id__1312E04B'. The conflict
occurred in database 'pubs', table 'titleauthor', column 'au_id'
error '800a0cae'
```

What's happened is that you have run up against the first line of defense of transaction management, which is the referential integrity of the database, in this case enforced through the use of foreign key constraints. In other words, you can't delete rows from a parent table when there is an associated row in a dependent or child table, such as the associated TITLEAUTHOR table for AUTHORS. To delete the records within the AUTHORS table, all matching rows within the TITLE-AUTHOR table must be deleted first. Only then can the application proceed with the deletion from the parent table.

To modify the deletion operation to handle the integrity constraint, create a new recordset containing all of the author IDs for the specified author name as shown in the following block of code:

```
// create command
Command cmd = new Command();
cmd.setActiveConnection(conn);
cmd.setCommandType(AdoEnums.CommandType.TEXT);

// set command
str = "select au_id from authors where au_lname = 'Ringer'";
cmd.setCommandText(str);

// make transaction
conn.beginTrans();
Recordset rs = cmd.execute();
```

Next, a second Command object is created to be used for deleting rows from AUTHOR:

```
// make second command
Command cmdupdate = new Command();
cmdupdate.setActiveConnection(conn);
cmdupdate.setCommandType(AdoEnums.CommandType.TEXT);
```

Each row is accessed from the Recordset returned with the first Command object. The au_id field from each row is accessed and is used to create a delete statement for the second, updateable command:

```
// get each author id
rs.moveFirst();
while (!rs.getEOF()) {
    String auid = rs.getField("au_id").getValue().toString();
    String strupdate = "delete from titleauthor where au_id = '";
    strupdate = strupdate + auid + "'";
    cmdupdate.setCommandText(strupdate);
    int iResult = cmdupdate.executeUpdate();
    rs.moveNext();
    }
```

Finally, the command to delete the rows from the AUTHORS table is executed:

```
str = "delete from authors where authors.au_lname='Ringer'";
cmdupdate.setCommandText(str);
int iResult = cmdupdate.executeUpdate();
```

All of the deletions are contained within a transaction, which is started with the Connection object's beginTrans method and can be rolled back using rollback-Trans.

Though this technique is workable, it's not very efficient. If the database being accessed is located on a remote machine, the record set retrieval as well as each deletion must occur over a network. A better approach would be to "package" the deletions of both the TITLEAUTHOR and AUTHORS table into one stored procedure call and invoke it instead. Next, we'll discuss using a stored procedure from within an ASP component.

Multiple SQL Statements and Batch Updates

If any operation is going to be costly in terms of performance, it is one that includes actions that occur over a network, whether internally over a LAN or externally via the Internet. By their very nature, ASP applications are based, at least in part, on being at the other end of some connection. In addition, ASP applications that access data frequently access databases that are themselves on separate machines, usually with some form of firewall surrounding the database to keep the data secure. Considering all of this, when creating a data access layer using ASP components, keep in mind that your component should make the most of infrequent database calls.

The previous section demonstrated an ASP component that deleted all references to an author in the *pubs* SQL Server example database. In order to maintain the foreign key integrity defined for the database, the component had to first delete all references to the author from the associated table, TITLEAUTHOR. The previous example did this by creating a query for the author identifier of the author being deleted, then deleting all entries for that author from the associated table. Only then did the component delete the author from the AUTHORS table. Though a workable approach, this technique results in three separate SQL statements to the database.

Instead of embedding SQL statements directly into the ASP component, a better approach is to create a stored procedure for the statements and then invoke this stored procedure directly.

Using stored procedures has a couple of advantages. First, the stored procedure is stored in the database as compiled code, and performance can be improved by not having the SQL pass through a SQL engine for processing. Another advantage is that optimization can be performed on the stored procedure to ensure its quick execution. A third advantage is that the stored procedure can include several different SQL statements, thereby decreasing the number of references to the database and the number of traversals across the network. There is a fourth advantage, but this is discussed in the sidebar titled "Another Advantage to Using a Stored Procedure."

Though techniques differ from database to database, a stored procedure will, for the most part, appear similar to the one shown in Example 17-4, which is created for use with Microsoft's SQL Server.

Example 17-4. Stored Procedure for ASP Component Examples

```
if exists (select * from sysobjects where id = object_id('dbo.remauthor')
          and sysstat & 0xf = 4)
   drop procedure dbo.remauthor
GO

CREATE PROCEDURE remauthor @lastname varchar(20)
AS
BEGIN
delete from titleauthor where au_id in
(select au_id from authors where au_lname = @lastname)
delete from authors where au_lname = @lastname
END
GO

GRANT  EXECUTE  ON dbo.remauthor  TO public
```

Example 17-4. Stored Procedure for ASP Component Examples (continued)

```
GO

GRANT  EXECUTE  ON dbo.remauthor  TO guest
GO
```

This stored procedure includes code to drop the stored procedure first if it has already been created, and then includes the syntax to create the actual stored procedure. The stored procedure itself is named remauthor and takes one parameter, the author's last name, defined as a **VARCHAR** value. The procedure contains two SQL statements, grouped as a block using **BEGIN** and **END** statements. The first statement deletes all rows from TITLELAUTHOR where the au_id field is found in the selection set returned from a nested query. This nested query pulls back all author identifiers that belong to any author with the last name passed to the stored procedure. Following this statement, a second statement completes the operation by deleting the entries from the AUTHORS table. At the end of the script are commands to grant permissions to execute the stored procedure to those users belonging to the public or guest groups.

The Visual J++ ASP component that calls the stored procedure can be seen in Example 17-5. This code is not the complete component—it includes only those portions having to do with getting the author's last name, creating the ADO Command object to execute the stored procedure, and performing error handling.

Example 17-5. ASP Component to Call a Stored Procedure, with Error Handling

```
try
{
    // get Request object and form collection
    vtRequest = iObjProps.GetProperty("Request");
    iObjRequest = (IRequest)vtRequest.getDispatch();
    iObjReqDictionary = iObjRequest.getForm();

    // get author's last name
    vtRequest.putString("lastname");
    vtRequest = iObjReqDictionary.getItem(vtRequest);

    // create command
    Command cmd = new Command();
    cmd.setActiveConnection(conn);
    cmd.setCommandType(AdoEnums.CommandType.STOREDPROC);
    cmd.setCommandText("remauthor");

    // create parameter
    Parameters parms = cmd.getParameters();
    Parameter parm = cmd.createParameter("lastname",
        AdoEnums.DataType.VARCHAR, AdoEnums.ParameterDirection.INPUT,
        20, vtRequest.toString());
```

Example 17-5. ASP Component to Call a Stored Procedure, with Error Handling (continued)

```
    // append to command parameters
    parms.append(parm);

    // execute
    conn.beginTrans();
    cmd.execute();
    conn.rollbackTrans();

    //end message
    Variant vtMessage = new Variant("Transaction Successful");
        iObjResponse.Write(vtMessage);
    }
    catch(com.ms.wfc.data.AdoException e) {
        Variant vtError = new Variant (e.getLocalizedMessage());
    iObjResponse.Write(vtError);
    }
}
```

After the ASP IRequest object is used to access the last name sent from an HTML form, a new Command object is created and defined to be a stored procedure command object by setting the command type property to AdoEnums.CommandType.STOREDPROC. It is connected to the database using an existing Connection object, and is passed the name of the stored procedure, remauthor.

Next, the Command object's Parameters collection is accessed and a new Parameter is created. This holds the value of the author's last name. Notice that when it is created, the parameter is defined to be an input parameter of type VARCHAR with a size of 20 characters. After the parameter is defined, the stored procedure is executed using the Command object's execute method. As the stored procedure does not return a result set, no Recordset object is assigned as a result of the execute statement.

To trap and process any errors, the AdoException object is used within a catch statement, and any error message is displayed on the returned page. If no error occurs, the message "Transaction Successful" is displayed on the returned web page.

In addition to handling updates, stored procedures can return multiple result sets, and can return database state information as well as make updates. It is important to understand how to handle these conditions within the ASP component.

First, handling multiple result sets is actually fairly simple. As an example, the following code block shows a stored procedure that queries the authors table to get author information, and then queries the titles table to get the author's titles and year-to-date sales:

```
CREATE PROCEDURE getauthor @lastname varchar(20)
AS
```

Another Advantage to Using a Stored Procedure

Earlier I mentioned that there is another advantage to using stored procedures from within ASP components. Notice from the code shown in Example 17-5 that we can delete an author without necessarily knowing that there is a foreign key reference defined for the authors table, or even without knowing that there is an authors table. This is, to me, a real advantage to using stored procedures: data abstraction, or hiding the data details from the process implementation.

Consider the scenario where the database schema changes, and the result is that the author ID is now defined as two fields, not one—an author classification identifier and the author's own specific subclassification number. If the ASP components accessing the database accessed the tables directly using SQL, each of these components would need to be modified to handle the changes. This becomes an expensive operation. Add to this the fact that some implementations of the application may be using an older database, one that does not have the split author ID, and you have a version as well as implementation problem.

Now, if the data access layer were itself implemented as stored procedures, the ASP component would access the same stored procedure name, remauthor, and pass in the same parameter, the author last name. The database stored procedure would handle the actual processing, and would work with a one-field author ID in an older database, and a two-part author ID in newer databases. The processing components would require no changes at all.

```
BEGIN
select * from authors where au_lname = @lastname
select title, ytd_sales from titles where title_id in
(select title_id from titleauthor where
    au_id in (select au_id from authors where au_lname = @lastname))
END
```

Next, Example 17-6 shows some of the code from an ASP component that calls the new stored procedure, this time assigning the results to a Recordset object. Note that again, a parameter is retrieved from a form to pass to the parameterized stored procedure call.

Example 17-6. Processing Multiple Result Sets from One Stored Procedure Call

```
try
    {
    // get Request object and form collection

    vtRequest = iObjProps.GetProperty("Request");
    iObjRequest = (IRequest)vtRequest.getDispatch();
    iObjReqDictionary = iObjRequest.getForm();
```

Example 17-6. Processing Multiple Result Sets from One Stored Procedure Call (continued)

```java
    // get author's last name
    vtRequest.putString("lastname");
    vtRequest = iObjReqDictionary.getItem(vtRequest);

    // create command
    Command cmd = new Command();
    cmd.setActiveConnection(conn);
    cmd.setCommandType(AdoEnums.CommandType.STOREDPROC);
    cmd.setCommandText("getauthor");

    // create parameter
    Parameters parms = cmd.getParameters();
    Parameter parm = cmd.createParameter("lastname",
                     AdoEnums.DataType.VARCHAR,
                     AdoEnums.ParameterDirection.INPUT,
                     20, vtRequest.toString());

    // append to command parameters
    parms.append(parm);

    // execute
    Recordset rs = cmd.execute();
    Variant vtOutput = new Variant();
    rs.moveFirst();
    while (!rs.getEOF()) {
        str = rs.getFields().getItem("au_fname").getValue().toString();
        vtOutput.putString(str + "<br>");
        iObjResponse.Write(vtOutput);
        rs.moveNext();
        }
    vtOutput.putString("<p>");
    rs = rs.nextRecordset();
    rs.moveFirst();
    while (!rs.getEOF()) {
        str = rs.getFields().getItem("title").getValue().toString();
        vtOutput.putString(str + "<br>");
        iObjResponse.Write(vtOutput);
        rs.moveNext();
        }
    rs.close();

    //end message
    Variant vtMessage = new Variant("Transaction Successful");
    iObjResponse.Write(vtMessage);
    }
catch(com.ms.wfc.data.AdoException e) {
    Variant vtError = new Variant (e.getLocalizedMessage());
    iObjResponse.Write(vtError);
    }
```

The call to the Command object's execute method returns a Recordset object, which we have seen in earlier examples. The code loops through the result set until the end is reached, and the author's first name is displayed with each loop. Unlike previous examples, though, instead of closing the Recordset object at the end of the loop, a call to the nextRecordset method is made, which gets the next recordset returned from the stored procedure call. This is reset to the same Recordset object, and looped through in turn to get the titles associated with the author, though if more than one author is associated with the name, there is nothing in this code to keep the authors and titles synchronized.

Handling a result set from an update is also fairly simple. Assign the value returned by the stored procedure to a Recordset object, and access the Recordset object as you would a query-based result set. This approach can be used to do such things as show a before-and-after result to a database change, or process a user-defined message.

As an example of a compound statement stored procedure, the following code shows a stored procedure named giveraise that executes a query, updates one of the data fields from the query, and then performs the same query. This results in three result sets, of which the first and third contain data:

```
CREATE PROCEDURE giveraise @percentage VARCHAR(4)
AS
BEGIN
select au_lname, au_fname, title, royaltyper from authors,
    titleauthor, titles where titleauthor.au_id = authors.au_id
    and titles.title_id = titleauthor.title_id
update titleauthor set royaltyper = royaltyper +
    Convert (int, @percentage)
select au_lname, au_fname, title, royaltyper from authors,
    titleauthor, titles where titleauthor.au_id = authors.au_id
    and titles.title_id = titleauthor.title_id
END
GO
```

Portions of the code for the ASP component that processes the first and third result sets and outputs the results into two HTML tables are shown in Example 17-7. The routine first assigns the value returned by the Command object's execute method to a Recordset object. It then processes the first result set, uses the nextRecordset method to access and discard the next result set generated by the update, and then uses the nextRecordset method to get the final result set, which contains the "after" query.

Example 17-7. ASP Component That Processes Three Result Sets

```
try
{
    // get Request object and form collection
```

Example 17-7. ASP Component That Processes Three Result Sets (continued)

```
vtRequest = iObjProps.GetProperty("Request");
iObjRequest = (IRequest)vtRequest.getDispatch();
iObjReqDictionary = iObjRequest.getForm();

// get author's last name
vtRequest.putString("lastname");
vtRequest = iObjReqDictionary.getItem(vtRequest);

// create command
Command cmd = new Command();
cmd.setActiveConnection(conn);
cmd.setCommandType(AdoEnums.CommandType.STOREDPROC);
cmd.setCommandText("giveraise");

// create parameter
Parameters parms = cmd.getParameters();
Parameter parm = cmd.createParameter("percentage",
    AdoEnums.DataType.VARCHAR, AdoEnums.ParameterDirection.INPUT,
    4, vtRequest.toString());

// append to command parameters
parms.append(parm);

// execute
conn.beginTrans();
Recordset rs = cmd.execute();
conn.rollbackTrans();

Variant vtOutput = new Variant();
vtOutput.putString("<H3>Before</H3><table cols=3>");
iObjResponse.Write(vtOutput);

// process 'before' query
rs.moveFirst();
while (!rs.getEOF()) {
    str = rs.getFields().getItem("au_lname").getValue().toString();
    vtOutput.putString("<tr><td>" + str + "</td>");
    iObjResponse.Write(vtOutput);
    str = rs.getFields().getItem("title").getValue().toString();
    vtOutput.putString("<td>" + str + "</td>");
    iObjResponse.Write(vtOutput);
    str = rs.getFields().getItem("royaltyper").getValue().toString();
    vtOutput.putString("<td>" + str + "</td></tr>");
    iObjResponse.Write(vtOutput);
    rs.moveNext();
    }

vtOutput.putString("</table>");
iObjResponse.Write(vtOutput);

// discard next value, result of update
rs = rs.nextRecordset();
```

Example 17-7. ASP Component That Processes Three Result Sets (continued)

```
        vtOutput.putString("<H3>After</H3><table cols=3>");
        iObjResponse.Write(vtOutput);

        // get 'after' results
        rs = rs.nextRecordset();
        rs.moveFirst();
        vtOutput.putString("test");
        iObjResponse.Write(vtOutput);
        while (!rs.getEOF()) {
            str = rs.getFields().getItem("au_lname").getValue().toString();
            vtOutput.putString("<tr><td>" + str + "</td>");
            iObjResponse.Write(vtOutput);
            str = rs.getFields().getItem("title").getValue().toString();
            vtOutput.putString("<td>" + str + "</td>");
            iObjResponse.Write(vtOutput);
            str = rs.getFields().getItem("royaltyper").getValue().toString();
            vtOutput.putString("<td>" + str + "</td></tr>");
            iObjResponse.Write(vtOutput);
            rs.moveNext();
            }
        vtOutput.putString("</table>");
        iObjResponse.Write(vtOutput);
        rs.close();

        //end message
        Variant vtMessage = new Variant("Transaction Successful");
        iObjResponse.Write(vtMessage);
        }
    catch(com.ms.wfc.data.AdoException e) {
        Variant vtError = new Variant (e.getLocalizedMessage());
        iObjResponse.Write(vtError);
        }
```

The result of accessing this component is two HTML tables, one containing the records and the "before update" royalty percentage, the second containing the "post update" royalty percentage, as shown in Figure 17-1.

Multiple result sets can also be returned just by creating a compound statement directly in the Command or Resultset object, as shown in this SQL statement:

```
select * from titles; select * from authors;
```

Example 17-7 used transaction processing to prevent the actual update from occurring to the data—we are trying to preserve the test database data as much as possible for future development efforts. Using transactions is discussed in the next, and final, section of this chapter.

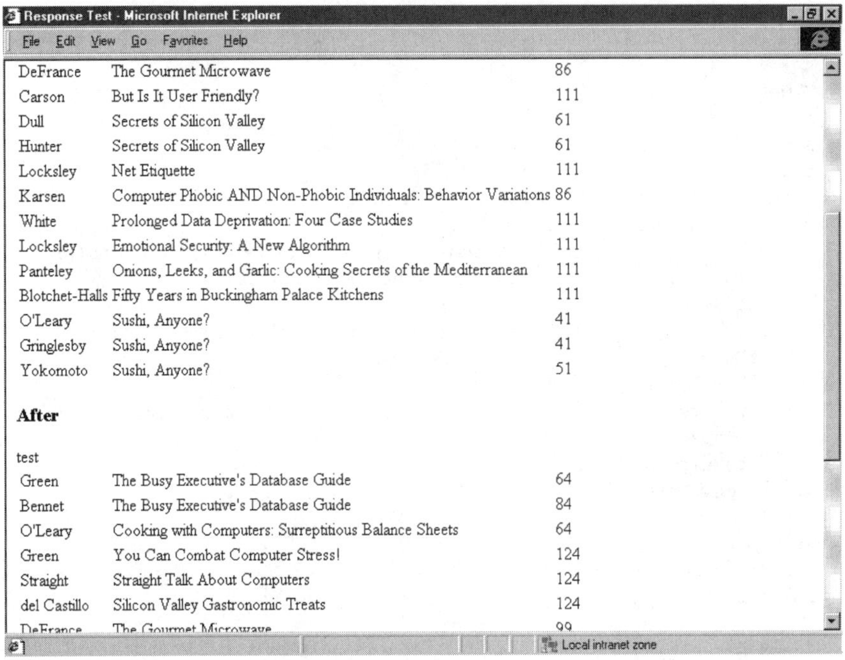

Figure 17-1. Web page containing "before" and "after" update query results

Transaction Management Across Multiple ASP Components

ASP components that query a database don't have to exist as part of a transaction, though they can. ASP components that perform some form of update should be enclosed within a transaction in order to ensure consistent data updates. For some components, all aspects of their transactions are contained completely within the component, and the ADO database transaction methods beginTrans, commitTrans, and rollbackTrans can be used. Other times, though, several components are used to create a business transaction, and the updates that each performs must be committed or rolled back consistently across all components. In these cases, it is essential to use MTS and the associated Distributed Transaction Controller or DTC. This section discusses the use of MTS, and its impact on Java ASP components accessing data through ADO.

To support MTS-based transactions, the component must be registered with MTS, and transaction support must be enabled for the object. Transaction support is added by changing the transaction property for the component once the component is added to MTS. By default the component is added without support for transactions.

 Using MTS and the DTC, and adding a component to MTS, is discussed in Chapter 5, *Components, Transactions, and the Microsoft Transaction Server.*

To incorporate transaction processing into an ASP component, created using Visual J++ or otherwise, you use the ObjectContext object that is created concurrently for every COM component registered with MTS. ObjectContext can be accessed directly within the Java ASP component using the built-in MTX object and the GetObjectContext method used earlier in the chapter to get the object context properties. However, instead of casting the method return to `IGetContextProperties`, it is cast to `IObjectContext`, as shown in the following block of code:

```
IObjectContext iObjContext;

// get instance of ObjectContext associated with ASP component
iObjContext = (IObjectContext)MTx.GetObjectContext();
```

Once the component's associated ObjectContext object is accessed, it can be used to control the component's transaction by using the SetComplete and SetAbort methods.

Within the component, the use of SetComplete does not necessarily commit the update. Instead, it indicates that the component is finished processing and that any updates it has made can be committed. Each component should use SetComplete any time a successful update to the data has occurred. If the component is only one of many participating within a transaction, the updates contained within all the components are only committed when all of the components have issued the SetComplete method call, or at least have not issued the SetAbort method call. One call to SetAbort aborts the entire transaction.

How the component's transaction property is set determines within which transaction the component exists, if any. If the component is registered with a transaction property of "Requires a Transaction" or "Supports Transactions," the component is created within the calling object's (the *client's*) transaction. If the client does not have a transaction, a new one is created for the component if a transaction is required, but one is not created for the component if transaction management is supported but not required. If the component is registered with MTS with a transaction property of "Requires a new transaction," a new transaction is created for the component regardless of whether the client itself has a transaction.

Nested transactions are processed in a recursive fashion. If the component does not support transactions, and the transaction property is set to "Does not support transactions," use of the setComplete or setAbort method is ignored. However, if the client that calls the component invokes SetAbort and the client requires a transaction, any pending database changes for the component are not committed.

If a component is accessed from an ASP page that has started a transaction and tries to start another transaction using the Connection's object's beginTrans method, an error similar to the following results:

```
Only one transaction can be active on this session.
```

Based on this, if the component tries to perform transaction management using just the Connection object's transaction methods, and the component is called from a client that requires transaction processing, the component will never be able to bypass the client's transaction management, preventing possibly inconsistent or unexpected results.

ASP component transactions can be included as part of the client transaction by creating the component within another component's transaction using CreateInstance, or by accessing the component within an ASP page that begins with the @TRANSACTION directive, as the following code fragment shows:

```
<%@ Transaction = Required %>
<HTML>
<HEAD>
</HEAD>
<BODY>
<H1>test</H1>
<%
  Dim myObject

  Set myObject = Server.CreateObject("adomts.adomts")

  myObject.make_connection

  myObject.test

  myObject.cleanup

  // ... some code

  ObjectContext.SetAbort
%>
</BODY>
</HTML>
```

This example demonstrates how the code within the ASP page actually controls the transaction management for the component. Regardless of what the component does, any changes it makes are rolled back by invoking the SetAbort method.

If the component created in the listing in Example 17-7 but minus the transaction management from the Connection object is run from an ASP page, such as that shown in the previous code fragment, no changes would be committed to the database. However, if the SetComplete method were called in the ASP page instead of the SetAbort method, the database changes would be saved.

Transactions that access a database engine that supports MTS, such as Microsoft's own SQL Server, must have the Distributed Transaction Coordinator (DTC) started within the database engine. Otherwise an error similar to the following occurs:

```
MSDTC Service not running
```

```
/test/testr.asp
```

```
Transactional web pages cannot be run if the MSDTC service is not running.
```

If multiple components are created as part of a single transaction, either by using the @TRANSACTION directive or by creating the components from another component's ObjectContext using the CreateInstance method, issuing the SetComplete method call commits all pending changes for all components. MTS does this using a two-phase commit approach, with the first pass or phase used to ask each component if it is ready to be committed. If all components answer in the affirmative, the second pass then commits each component. Using a two-phase approach prevents incomplete updates, with one component committed successfully while another fails.

The component indicates that it is ready to be committed invoking the SetComplete method call, or by not invoking the SetAbort method call and having the component successfully finish processing without any error. The code to call the SetComplete method call within a Java component is:

```
iObjContext.SetComplete();
```

This uses the instance of the ObjectContext object accessed using the code shown earlier in this section. By issuing the SetComplete method call, two private properties are set within the ObjectContext object. The first property is Consistent, which is set to **True** when the component is ready to have its changes committed. The second is Done, which is set to **True** to indicate that the component has finished all of its processing. To abort the transaction, the following is used:

```
iObjContext.SetAbort();
```

This sets the Consistent property to **False**, which means that the transaction should not be committed to prevent inconsistent updates. The Done property is still set to **True**, though, since the transaction is finished. To prevent a transaction from being committed before the transaction is finished, the ObjectContext object's DisableCommit method can be called to prevent commits from occurring until an associated EnableCommit method call is made, as illustrated in the following code fragment:

```
iObjContext.DisableCommit();
...some processing
iObjContext.EnableCommit();
iObjContext.SetComplete();
```

Further Reading

For additional reading about the topics covered in this chapter, check out the following:

- "Introduction to the WFC Application Model" at *http://premium.microsoft.com/ msdn/library/devprods/vs6/vj/vjconintroductiontowfcapplicationmodel.htm.*

- The Microsoft ADO web page is accessible at *http://www.microsoft.com/data/ ado/default.htm.*

- Read a comparison of JDBC and ADO/WFC at *http://www.microsoft.com/data/ ado/adotechinfo/adovsjdbc.htm.*

- Read the article "ADO Events in ADO/WFC" at *http://www.microsoft.com/data/ reference/ado2/mdevents_7cof.htm.*

- Explore the WFC package at *http://premium.microsoft.com/msdn/library/ devprods/vs6/vj/package-com.ms.wfc.data.html.*

- For a description of the PUBS database tables, see *http://premium.microsoft. com/msdn/library/sdkdoc/sql/tsqlref/src/append_b_8885.htm.*

18

Java ASP Components and J/Direct, Native Code, and Marshaling

Anything not written in Java—and usually something written in C/C++—is referred to as *native code* primarily because Windows itself and the API to access Windows services, known as the Windows SDK, are written in C. Based on this, any code written in C is usually considered to be faster executing and more efficient than code written in some other language—particularly when that language happens to be Java.

Java can be less efficient than C because a compiled Java class is byte code capable of running only within a Virtual Machine (VM). There are techniques, though, that enable a Java-based ASP component to access functionality written in C. These techniques do have a cost, in that the Java component must run on specific Java VMs, such as the Microsoft VM, and the component may not be port-able to other environments. However, for server-based components such as ASP, that usually only run within a Windows environment, this cost may be negligible.

One of the first native code access techniques has already been demonstrated, particularly in Chapter 16, *The Java Interfaces*. This technique depends on COM integration and the use of Java wrappers around COM components. Another approach is to use the Raw Native Interface, which is a technique to create C components that are accessible by Java; this is particularly valuable when performance is a critical factor. A limitation with this approach is that the C component must be created specifically for access by JNI, which can limit the usefulness of this technique.

A third approach that does not require a COM wrapper and also does not require modification of the C functionality is J/Direct. J/Direct is a technique to access the Windows SDK directly from Java, without having to provide any supporting C or

C++ code. The first section of this chapter discusses each of these approaches, when to use which, and the advantages and disadvantages of each.

Regardless of what method is used to call native methods, consideration must be given to marshaling the data types between Java and the C or C++ functions. For instance, Java does not have pointers, which are prevalent in C/C++. Additionally, C/C++ structures are created to fill a contiguous block of non-movable memory, while Java classes, the equivalent of a structure, are created in whatever blocks of memory are free, and may be moved as a result of garbage collection.

Once marshaling is understood, any Win32 API can be called using J/Direct; this chapter demonstrates this, using Java directives and the new Win32 Java classes.

Sun and Microsoft are currently in the courts over Microsoft's additions to the Java language, and this includes the addition of *directives*. This chapter and J/Direct are totally dependent on the use of directives. Before reading through this chapter, you should check out the Microsoft Java and Visual J++ sites—their URLs are available in the "Further Reading" section at the end of this chapter—to see what impact the court rulings have on J/Direct.

The Different Native Code Approaches

You access native code from Java when you access the built-in ASP components. This access is facilitated through the use of COM and the use of Java wrappers. Prior to Visual J++ 6.0, you would have to use a tool, JAVATLB, to create the wrapper. However, with Visual J++ 6.0, all you have to do is choose the "Add COM Wrapper..." option from the Project menu, and then check the registered COM object to create the wrapper. The tool automatically adds in Java wrappers for the COM object. When the component is compiled, the COM wrappers get compiled. Simple!

However, as simple as it is to access a wrapped COM object, one of the downsides to this approach is that performance takes a hit. The reason for this is that the methods are invoked through a Java-native language layer, rather than invoking the native language method directly. If performance is a real issue, you might want to access the native language directly using the Raw Native Interface (RNI).

RNI is not for the faint of heart, and should only be considered when performance is very critical for the application. RNI is a way of invoking native code that is specifically written to be accessed by a Java component. Right away, this eliminates any of the Windows API or most third-party Dynamic Link Libraries (DLLs).

If you do use RNI to access native code DLLs, be aware of the fact that Java's built-in garbage collection can be a problem. DLLs tend to expect to find certain structures in specific locations in memory—structures that the garbage collection may remove. Speaking of garbage collection, this must be managed within the Java component, and you won't be able to rely on that nice built-in garbage collection facility that was probably one of the reasons you selected Java in the first place.

I won't go into detail on using RNI, since this approach is geared more towards Java applications rather than Java ASP components, and may not be easily compatible with ASP component technology. However, if you want more information on RNI, you can access the Microsoft Java web site, listed in the "Further Reading" section at the end of this chapter.

Another approach to accessing native services is the Java Native Interface, or JNI, proposed by Sun. JNI is in some ways similar to a blend of the COM method and RNI, in that Java wrappers access a native code interface, which is in turn written specifically to be accessed by Java.

There is another approach that is fairly simple to use, which allows you to access the Win32 API functions. This approach is J/Direct, covered in the next section.

An Overview of J/Direct

Luckily for us, Microsoft has provided fairly easy access to the Win32 API with a set of Java classes called the J/Direct classes. These classes provide access to all of the Window's functions, including those from the following critical Window's dynamic link libraries:

user32.dll
> Contains user-based methods, such as MessageBox, that are not of much interest for an ASP component developer

kernel32.dll
> Provides basic Windows methods and services

gdi32.dll
> The graphics library, again not especially useful for an ASP developer

advapi32.dll
> "Advanced" library providing crypto, event logging, and registry access

shell32.dll
> Interface to the Windows shell

winmm.dll
> Library of multimedia routines not likely to be used for ASP development

spoolss.dll

Supports spooling

Although most of the methods exposed in the Win32 API aren't of much interest to the ASP component developer (because they cover front-end presentation), some of the libraries and their associated methods are useful. For instance, the kernel32 methods allow you to open, copy, and move files, as well as manipulate directories—operations that can be very handy for ASP component development. The *spoolss.dll* methods are handy for adding and monitoring equipment, such as printers, or adding jobs to printers—again something that might be managed from a backend application.

 Just because you can, doesn't mean you want to. Many of the techniques discussed in this chapter should be used with caution, since they open a doorway into your system. Unless protective safeguards are in place, you won't want to allow Internet access to ASP components that may do things such as remove a printer or add a subdirectory. However, these same functions could be very helpful in an Intranet environment.

J/Direct works by embedding a compiler directive into the Java code just in front of the prototype for the external Win32 method. This directive then keys the Java compiler into embedding the reference to the method as *byte* code directly in the Java class. This allows the call to the method to be invoked directly rather than through any form of interface. Additionally, the method call itself is the standard C-based Win32 method and does not require that the dynamic link library be modified, which is necessary for RNI, or that the function call be wrapped, as JNI requires.

To see J/Direct in action, we'll use Java to create a simple ASP component that invokes the kernel32 CreateDirectory method to create a subdirectory named *thetest* directly off the root of the C drive. The prototype for this method is:

```
BOOL CreateDirectory(LPCTSTR lpPathname,
    LPSECURITY_ATTRIBUTES lpSecurityAttributes)
```

As parameters, the method takes a pointer to a null-terminated string and a pointer to a **SECURITY_ATTRIBUTES** structure.

The following sections detail the steps necessary to invoke this Win32 kernel API from Java using J/Direct.

Marshaling Scalar Types

To define the prototype for the CreateDirectory method, it's necessary to marshal each C data type to an equivalent Java type. This is actually simple for the first parameter, since the Java String type will work for the LPCSTR data type. Java strings can be used for any form of output parameter. In fact, most scalar data types have a fairly simple conversion type, as can be seen in Table 18-1, adapted from a table presented by Dr. GUI in his series of online articles on J/Direct.

Table 18-1. Scalar C to Java Type Conversions

C or C++ Type	Java Equivalent Type
BYTE or CHAR	Byte
SHORT or WORD	Short
INT, UINT, LONG, ULONG, DWORD	Int
TCHAR	Char
_int64	Long
Float	Float
Double	Double
BOOL	Boolean
LPCTCSR	String
LPTSTR	StringBuffer
BYTE* or CHAR*	Byte[]
SHORT* or WORD*	Short[]
TCHAR*	Char[]
INT*, UINT*, ULONG*, DWORD*	Int[]
float*	Float[]
double*	Double[]
_int64*	Long[]

Some of these scalar conversions deserve further explanation. For example, a Java long value is a 64-bit value, not a 32-bit value as it is in C/C++. Second, Java does not support pointers, but it does pass a reference to an array. In order to emulate a C/C++ pointer in Java, a one-element array is used for the value, so that it is equivalent to a pointer to a scalar value in C/C++. A final note is that the LPCTSTR and LPTSTR types cannot be used for return values, except for the LPCTSTR value in OLE mode, to be discussed in a later section.

For many methods, these simple scalar types are all that is necessary. However, the CreateDirectory method has a pointer to a structure as its second parameter. Working with C structures and other more complex parameters is discussed in the next section.

Handling Complex Data Types

If every Win32 API method took simple scalar data types, our job would basically be over. However, most methods have parameters with more complex data types, such as pointers to structures. Fortunately, J/Direct provides a fairly simple way of handling these data types.

If you are thinking, as I did when I first started working with J/Direct, just to use a class in place of a structure, consider one major difference between a Java class and a C structure. A C structure, unlike a Java class, is guaranteed to occupy a contiguous block of memory. Java, with its built-in garbage collection, may use noncontiguous memory, and may even move an element within memory. However, the C/C++ Win32 DLLs expect that the structure will occupy a fixed block of memory.

To accommodate the differences between Java and C, J/Direct provides a directive, `@dll.struct`, which informs the Java Virtual Machine (VM) that it should create a contiguous block of fixed memory for the class/structure.

As an example, the `SECURITY_ATTRIBUTES` structure, passed as the second parameter to CreateDirectory, is defined as follows:

```
typedef struct _SECURITY_ATTRIBUTES {
DWORD nLength;
LPVOID lpSecurityDescriptor;
BOOL bInheritHandle;
} SECURITY_ATTRIBUTES;
```

To convert the C/C++ data structure to a Java class, you should replace the references to `DWORD` and `BOOL` with their equivalent Java types: `int` and `boolean`. However, the `lpSecurityDescriptor` data type is really a pointer to a `void` type, something Java just does not support. Instead, you can use an integer in place of this pointer to a structure, since pointers really are integer values. The converted structure is:

```
/** @dll.struct() */
class SECURITY_ATTRIBUTES {
    int nLength = DllLib.sizeOf(this);
    int lpSecurityDescriptor;
    boolean bInheritHandle;
}
```

There is no loss in functionality by using an integer in the place of a pointer to a `void` type, because if the `lpSecurityDescriptor` value is not specified, the security descriptor of the calling process (in this case, the parent process of the component) is used as the default one. Additionally, this member of the structure is ignored in Windows 95 and 98. Since for the purposes of our example, we have no interest in any finer control over the CreateDirectory method, an actual pointer to a security descriptor is not necessary.

The value for *nLength* isn't required except for compatibility in an NT environment, and should be set to the size of the SECURITY_ATTRIBUTES structure. Since the size must be specified in a manner meaningful to the C DLL, we need access to a method that "translates" between the two languages. This method can be found in the DllLib class of the Java support package, com.ms.dll. The DllLib class has a sizeOf method, which does exactly what we need: returns the size of the structure in bytes.

 When working with J/Direct, you should become familiar with the Java DllLib support class in the com.ms.dll package. As you can see in this chapter, you won't get far calling native code methods without it.

Finally, the last element of the structure, *bInheritHandle*, controls whether any handle created by the process call that contains the SECURITY_ATTRIBUTES structure is returned to the calling process. As the CreateDirectory method does not return a handle, this value can be set to **False** without impairing its functionality.

If a pointer to a structure is returned from a function call, a class can be defined for the returned structure, and this class can then be used to *cast* the pointer using the DllLib.ptrToStruct method:

```
POLY poly = (poly)DllLib.ptrToStruct(POLY.class, rawptr);
```

In this example, the DllLib.prtToStruct method protects the pointer from standard garbage collection.

In the prototype for the CreateDirectory method, an instance of the newly created SECURITY_ATTRIBUTES class is passed as the second parameter, as shown in the following code:

```
/** @dll.import("KERNEL32") */
static native boolean CreateDirectory(String str, SECURITY_ATTRIBUTES
security);
```

Note that the prototype is preceded by the @dll.import directive that includes a reference to the dynamic link library containing the method. This is the directive that instructs the VM to return the byte code for the actual DLL method call.

As this example demonstrates, processing a C structure within a Java call does not have to be difficult with J/Direct to simplify the process. Other complex data type mappings supported by J/Direct are given in Table 18-2. The asterisks (*) denote pointers in C or C++.

Table 18-2. Complex C to Java Data Type Conversions

C or C++ Data Type	Java Equivalent Data Type
pointer to structure	object
COM Interface	Interface
SAFEARRAY*	com.ms.com.SafeArray
GUID, IID, CLSID	com.ms.com._Guid
VARIANT*	com.ms.com.Variant
pointer to struct	@dll.struct class
pointer to struct	@com.struct class
VOID	void

As with the scalar types, there are some restrictions with the complex data types. The void data type can be used for a return value only, but the SafeArray data type *cannot* be used as a return type. In OLE mode, discussed later, the object reference is an **IUnknown*** instead. Note that the equivalent of the pointer to struct used in the preceding example is the **@dll.struct** directive, as shown in Table 18-2.

An additional constraint on complex objects has to do with complex objects being nested within other complex objects. In this case, the embedded structure is created first, with its own **@dll.struct** directive. Then the class is referenced directly within the structure class definition that contains the embedded structure.

Additionally if a structure contains a fixed-length string or an array of some form, another directive, **@dll.structmap**, is used to specify the size of the array. For example:

```
CHAR c[4]
```

maps to:

```
/** @dll.structmap([type=FIXEDARRAY, size=4]) */ char c[];
```

in the structure class definition.

For parameters that are *polymorphic*, which can change based on the context of the function call, the **Object** data type can be used to define an indeterminate data type, and J/Direct determines what the reference is at run time.

A final note on values returned as strings: the String data type is read-only. In order to receive strings, the calling function must create a pre-buffered **StringBuffer** data type, sized to fit the return value. This is then freed in the calling Java component. In addition, any String reference is mapped to an ANSI value rather than a UNICODE value, unless the **unicode** modifier is used within the **@dll.import** directive, as follows:

```
/** @dll.import("KERNEL32", unicode) */
```

All strings are treated as UNICODE in OLE Mode.

Once the data conversion issue is resolved, it's time to create the ASP component.

Invoking the Win32 API function

Once a prototype for the Win32 API function is created, the method can be invoked from Java code just as any other method is invoked. Example 18-1 contains the complete code for the ASP component that creates a prototype for the Win32 *CreateDirectory* function and uses the J/Direct directives.

Example 18-1. Calling Kernel32 API Method CreateDirectory

```
import com.ms.com.*;
import com.ms.dll.*;
import com.ms.mtx.*;
import com.ms.asp.*;

/** @dll.struct() */
class SECURITY_ATTRIBUTES {
   int nLength = DllLib.sizeOf(this);
   int lpSecurityDescriptor;
   boolean bInheritHandle;
}


/**
 * This class is designed to be packaged with a COM DLL output format.
 * The class has no standard entry points, other than the constructor.
 * Public methods will be exposed as methods on the default COM interface.
 * @com.register ( clsid=C27308EE-5AD3-11D2-807D-204C4F4F5020,
                   typelib=C27308EF-5AD3-11D2-807D-204C4F4F5020 )
 */
public class kernal
{
   // add prototype call here
   /** @dll.import("KERNEL32") */
   static native boolean CreateDirectory(String str,
                                       SECURITY_ATTRIBUTES security);

   public void test() {
      IGetContextProperties objProps;
      IObjectContext objContext;
      IResponse iObjResponse;
      Variant v = null;
      boolean bResult;

      // get Context Properties
      objProps = (IGetContextProperties)MTx.GetObjectContext();
```

Example 18-1. Calling Kernel32 API Method CreateDirectory (continued)

```
    // get response object for outputs
    v = objProps.GetProperty("Response");
    iObjResponse = (IResponse)v.getDispatch();

    // enclose Win32 API calls within try...catch blocks
    try {
        SECURITY_ATTRIBUTES sec = new SECURITY_ATTRIBUTES();
        sec.bInheritHandle = false;

        // create directory
        bResult = CreateDirectory("c:\\thetest",sec);

        // print out results
        if (bResult)
            v.putString("Directory created");
        else
            v.putString("Directory could not be created");
        iObjResponse.Write(v);
    }
    catch (Exception e) {
        v.putString(e.getLocalizedMessage());
        iObjResponse.Write(v);
    }
  }
}
```

Notice from the code that the **SECURITY_ATTRIBUTES** class with its **@dll.struct** directive is created first, and then the prototype is given. The **@dll.import** directive will include the Java byte code to handle pulling in the method. From then on the Java is pretty basic.

A Response object is created to display the result of creating the subdirectory, and a new **SECURITY_ATTRIBUTES** class is created. The native code CreateDirectory method is called with a string containing a subdirectory name and the **SECURITY_ ATTRIBUTES** class/structure. The subdirectory string is *escaped*, meaning that the "\" escape character is placed in front of the directory slash character (\) to instruct the application to pass the character through as-is.

A Boolean value is used to capture the return code for the Win32 CreateDirectory call. If the call is successful and the subdirectory is created, a value of **True** is returned and a message is output about the success of the operation. If the call is not successful but no error occurs, a value of **False** is returned, and a message is output accordingly. The operation may not be successful if the process invoking the component does not have directory create permission, or if the directory has already been created.

Accessing an ASP page that contains the new Java ASP component results in the creation of a new subdirectory named *thetest* in the C drive. Running the same page again results in CreateDirectory failing, since a subdirectory of that name has already been created.

If the process of having to create a class for the SECURITY_ATTRIBUTES structure and using the directives seems cumbersome, there is a shortcut you can use. The Win32 API functions have been created as classes that can be included within Java components. These classes are discussed in the next section.

Using the com.ms.win32 Classes

Instead of using the Win32 J/Direct directives, you could also include the Win32 classes, which contain the conversion information. The Win32 classes are in the Win32 package, and there is one class for each Win32 library, as shown in the following list:

- Kernel32.class for the *kernel32.dll*
- Gdi32.class for the *gdi32.dll*
- User32.class for the *user32.dll*
- Advapi32.class for the *advapi32.dll*
- Shell32.class for the *shell32.dll*
- Winmm.class for the *winmm.dll*
- Spoolss.class for the *spoolss.dll*

In addition to the classes above, the com.ms.win32 package also includes predefined constants matching the associated C/C++ SDK constants. They can be accessed from the win class, com.ms.win32.win.

Example 18-2 is the same as Example 18-1, except that it uses the built-in Win32 classes. Notice how, instead of having to create the SECURITY_ATTRIBUTES class, it is already created for us. Best of all, it actually matches our own implementation of SECURITY_ATTRIBUTES.

Example 18-2. Using Kernel32 Function CreateDirectory

```
import com.ms.com.*;
import com.ms.mtx.*;
import com.ms.asp.*;
import com.ms.win32.*;
/**
 * This class is designed to be packaged with a COM DLL output format.
 * The class has no standard entry points, other than the constructor.
 * Public methods will be exposed as methods on the default COM interface.
 * @com.register ( clsid=C27308F2-5AD3-11D2-807D-204C4F4F5020,
```

Example 18-2. Using Kernel32 Function CreateDirectory (continued)

```
                        typelib=C27308F3-5AD3-11D2-807D-204C4F4F5020 )
'*/
public class jdirect

{
   // test
   public void test() {
      IResponse iObjResponse;
      IGetContextProperties objProps;
      boolean b;
      Variant v = new Variant();

      // get response object
      objProps = (IGetContextProperties)MTx.GetObjectContext();
      v = objProps.GetProperty("Response");
      iObjResponse = (IResponse)v.getDispatch();

      // create directory using classes
      try {
         SECURITY_ATTRIBUTES sec = new SECURITY_ATTRIBUTES();
         sec.nLength = com.ms.dll.DllLib.sizeOf(sec);
         sec.bInheritHandle = false;
         b = Kernel32.CreateDirectory("C:\\test2",sec);

         // write out response
         if (b)
            v.putString("Directory Created");
         else
            v.putString("Directory not Created");
         iObjResponse.Write(v);
      }
      catch( Exception e) {
         v.putString(e.getLocalizedMessage());
         iObjResponse.Write(v);
      }
   }
}
```

To better understand how to convert data types between C/C++ and Java, create a class for one of the Win32 structures and check against the equivalent structure declared in com.ms.win32. If the two match, chances are you have a pretty good handle on the Java/C/C++ data conversion.

As you can see from Example 18-2, there is much less code involved with using the imported classes. In addition, the cumbersome **@directives** do not have to be used.

Running the code from this second example results in a subdirectory called *mytest* being created the first time the ASP page containing the Java component is invoked. Running the page again results in a message about the directory not being created, because it already exists.

Using J/Direct in OLE Mode

A final note on J/Direct concerns using the OLE mode modifier to invoke OLE functions. The modifier is added as a parameter to the @dll.import directive, as demonstrated in the following line:

```
/** @dll.import("OLE32", ole) */
```

The use of OLE mode results in different behaviors for the invoked functions. First, most OLE functions return a 32-bit status, HRESULT. In addition, OLE functions are Unicode, while Win32 functions can be ANSI, unless the Unicode modifier is used. Another difference is that prebuffering works with strings returned by a Win32 function call. With an OLE function call, the String data type can be used as a return value.

To pass GUIDS, IIDs, and CLSIDs in OLE mode, the com.ms.com._GUID class provides the necessary data types.

To work with COM interface pointers, you must use the Java/COM interface generation techniques discussed in Chapter 3, *ASP Components and COM*, and in Chapter 16.

Further Reading

For additional reading about the topics covered in this chapter, check out the following:

- Microsoft has a site on Java, located at *http://www.microsoft.com/java/*.

- You can see more about J/Direct at the J/Direct resource page at *http://www.microsoft.com/java/resource/jdirect.htm*.

- Read more about accessing Win32 SDK functions and Java-to-C data mappings in the article "Using J/Direct to Call the Win32 SDK API from Java" at *http://premium.microsoft.com/msdn/library/periodic/period98/html/jdirect.htm*.

- The Microsoft Visual J++ web site is at *http://msdn.microsoft.com/visualj/*.

Index

A

Abandon method, 128, 193, 195, 419
abstract base class, 58
Activate method, 107, 306
activation
    component, 119
    MTS, 112
ActiveX DLL, 152
    generation, registration, installation and
        testing, 162–166
    instancing, 154
    JavaBeans vs., 378
    testing, 169
ActiveX exe, 156
Add, 155, 383
AddHeader, 205
AddHeader method, 142
adLockPessimistic value, 253
ADO (ActiveX Data Objects), 21, 211,
    334–335
    interactive query, 225–230
    Java, 434–437
    libraries, 221
    RDS and, 221
    use of, 212–220
    Visual Basic, 220, 222–225
ADO connection, 224
    Java, 437–443
    queries, 444–449
    updates, 449–451
ADODB (ActiveX Data Objects 2.0
    Library), 213, 221

ADOM (ActiveX Data Objects
    (Multidimensional)), 221
adOpenKeyset value, 253
ADOR (ActiveX Data Objects Recordset 2.0
    Library), 213, 221
adPessimisticLock value, 260
ADSI (Active Directory Service
    Interface), 25
    Container Object properties and
        methods, 45–46
    properties, 34–36
ADsPath, 31, 35–36
AfxBeginThread, 370–373
aggregation, 62, 79, 81, 96–99, 277
ALL_HTTP - HTTP environment
    variable, 140
ALL_RAW environment variable, 140
Apache web server, 5
apartment-threading model, 68, 80, 85–90
    ADO, 224
    C++, 276
    Visual Basic, 156–158, 180
AppendToLog method, 142, 205
application component, 123
Application object, 90, 122–127
    C++, 315–318
    Java, 412–417
    Visual Basic, 178–179, 181, 190–193
APPL_MD_PATH environment
    variable, 140
APPL_PHYSICAL_PATH environment
    variable, 140

AppServer object, 106, 109
argument method, 161
ASP (Active Server Pages)
    Application object, 90
    built-in objects, 121
    description of, 8–10
    history, 7
    scripting syntax, 122
ASP component
    ADO
        interactive query, 225–230
        objects, 220–225
    C++, 267–292
    data access, 231–234
    description and use of, 11–13
    functionality, 3
    interaction of, xiii
    Java, 377–399
    MTS
        component, 105–111
        environment, 113–117
    multiple transaction
        management, 460–464
    thread-safe, 11
    Visual Basic, 151–171
        methods, 159–162
        n-tier, 238–263
AspAllowOutOfProcComponents
        property, 38
AspAllowSessionState property, 40
AspBufferingOn property, 40
AspCodepage property, 40
AspEnableParentPaths property, 41
AspExceptionCatchEnable property, 41
AspLogErrorRequests property, 42
AspMemFreeFactor property, 42
AspQueueTimeout property, 42
AspScriptEngineCacheMax property, 43
AspScriptErrorMessage property, 43
AspScriptErrorSentToBrowser property, 43
AspScriptFileCacheSize property, 43
AspScriptLanguage property, 44
AspScriptTimeout property, 44, 133
AspSessionTimeout property, 45
asynchronous method calls, 94
ATL (ActiveX Template Library), 14, 267,
        335
    method interface data types, 280
    MFC, 268, 356–359

ATL AppWizard, 268
    ATL object, 274
    C++, 338
    DLL, EXE, server option, 270
    generated files, 272
    Project Files, 269
    Project Options, 271
ATL COM AppWizard, 63, 91
    MFC, 357–359
ATL Object Wizard, 64, 91, 268
    ASP page, 278
    C++, 300, 339–341
        MTS, 345
    code changes for object addition, 278
    OLE DB Consumer object, 348–352
    properties, 96
    Properties Attributes, 275–278
AtlReportError, 289
audit trail, 258
authentication, 205
AUTH_PASSWORD environment
        variable, 140
AUTH_TYPE environment variable, 140
AUTH_USER environment variable, 140
Auto List Member, 180
automation server, 48, 70

B

background processes, threads
        for, 370–373
batch updates, 263, 451–459
BeginTrans method, 250
binary communication, COM, 49
binary reusability, 52
BinaryRead method, 133, 199
BinaryWrite method, 143, 202
BLOBs (binary large objects), 219
Books application, 238–242
    ASP data access component, 252–254
    business rule, 247–251, 255
    presentation in ASP
        component, 242–246
Boolean data type, 280
Borland, 13
both-threaded model, 80, 96–99
    ADO, 224
    C++, 277
    Visual Basic, 181

bottleneck, 82, 86
Brockschmidt, Kraig, 75
BSTR data type, 281
Buffer property, 142–143, 145, 202
built-in objects, 3, 121
    C++, 294–333
    Java, 401–433
    JCF, 431
    ObjectContext access, 182
    Visual Basic, 173–209
business processing layer, 235–236
byVal, byRef modifiers, 161

C

CAccessor object, 338, 342, 348, 354
CacheControl property, 142
caching, 203, 327
CanBePooled method, 107–108
C++Builder, 13
CComBSTR class, 66, 288
CCommand object, 338, 354
CComPtr class, 296, 300
CContext class, 302
CDataSource object, 338, 343
CDBPropSet object, 338, 343, 354
CERT_COOKIE environment variable, 140
CERT_FLAGS environment variable, 140
CERT_ISSUER environment variable, 140
CERT_KEYSIZE environment variable, 140
CERT_SECRETKEYSIZE environment
        variable, 140
CERT_SERIALNUMBER environment
        variable, 140
CERT_SERVER_ISSUER environment
        variable, 140
CERT_SERVER_SUBJECT environment
        variable, 140
CERT_SUBJECT environment variable, 140
Certificate property, 137
certificates, 137
    (see also ClientCertificate collection)
CGI (Common Gateway Interface), 5
Char data type, 280
Charset property, 142
Chili!ASP, 15
Chili!Soft, 15, 50
class name, 36
Clear method, 143–144, 202
client proxy, 79, 81

ClientCertificate collection, 134, 137, 200,
        326
client-server system, 102
client-side scripting, 138, 227
CLSID (class identifier), 51, 60
CoCreateFreeThreadedMarshaler
        function, 81, 96
CoCreateInstance function, 60
CoCreateInstanceEx function, 60
CodePage property, 128, 193, 418
CoInitalizeEx function, 60
CoInitialize function, 60
COM (Component Object Model), 48
    implementation, 55–62
    initialization methods, 80
    overview, 49–55
    web site, 76
    wrapped object, 409–411, 466
COM component
    C++, 63–67, 268, 285, 314
    functionality, 3
    Java, 70–74, 377
        wrappers, 73, 391–398
    Visual Basic, 68–70
@COM directives, 71, 393
COM-CORBA Bridge, 4, 15
COM/DCOM (Component Object
        Model/Distributed Component
        Object Model), 50, 101
Command object, 21, 214, 219, 336, 448
Commit method, 250
com.ms.asp classes, 412–413, 431, 439
com.ms.com classes, 403, 439
com.ms.dll package, 471
com.ms.mtx classes, 405, 432, 439
com.ms.wfc.data classes, 437, 439
com.ms.win32 classes, 475–477
com.ms.win32.win classes, 475
component
    activation, 119
    built-in object as property of, 302–305
    COM, 48, 53
    data access, 252–254
        library, 231–234
    in-process, 50, 80–81
        out-of-process vs., 152
    instancing, 153
    Java execution, 379
    MTS, 114, 117–120

component (*continued*)
  name, 165
  out-of-process, 80–81
  owner name, 165
  pooling, 306–311
  reusability, 62
  single-threaded vs. multithreaded, 82–85
  thread-safe, 11, 68, 180, 379
Component Object Model Specification, 51
component-based system, 102
compute-bound thread, 77
Connection object, 21, 214, 216, 437–443
connection point, 61, 69, 276
containment/delegation, 62
CONTENT_LENGTH variable, 140
CONTENT_TYPE variable, 140
Contents collection, 125, 129, 191, 194–195,
  259, 317, 320
ContentType property, 142, 144, 203
cookies, 128, 134, 194
  collection, 137, 146, 200, 204, 325, 328
CORBA-based components, 4, 15
Count method, 181
Counters ASP component, 124
court rulings, J/Direct, 466
CreateDirectory, Java, 468–477
CreateInstance method, 60, 106, 110, 181
CreateObject method, 130, 163, 175, 183,
  207, 332
cross-process marshaling, 79
cross-thread marshaling, 79, 156, 158, 161
CRowset object, 338, 343, 354
CRUD (Create, Read, Update, and
  Delete), 258
CSession object, 338, 343, 354
CTable object, 338, 343, 354
Currency data type, 281
CursorType property, 253

D

DAO (Data Access Objects), 19, 21, 211
  Java, 435–437
data
  abstraction, 455
  connections, 18
  consumer, 20
  display component, 245
  layer, 235–236
  output, 243–246
  provider, 20

queries
  C++, 347–352
  Java, 444–449
  Visual Basic, 225–230
types
  COM/Java mappings, 397
  complex, 470–473
updates, 16
  Java, 449–451
  OLE DB, 352–354
  Visual Basic, 258–263
data access, 19–22
  C++ with OLE DB, 334–354
  component library, 231–234
  Java, 434–464
  separate layer, 252–254
  Visual Basic, 211–234
  n-tier, 235–263
Data Source object, 336
DB-Library, 19
DCE (Distributed Computing
  Environment), 51, 56
DCOM runtime, 79
DDL (Data Definition Language), 436
Deactivate method, 107–108, 308
deadlock, 78
debugging, 24, 41
  Visual Basic, 169–171
delegation event handling, 442
Delphi, 13
dependent object, 155, 157
  Private instancing type, 159
design-time vtable binding, 276
DHTML (Dynamic HTML), 13, 153, 380
directive, 128
  @COM, 393
  @dll.import, 471, 474, 477
  @dll.struct, 470, 474
  @dll.structmap, 472
  Java, 403
  J/Direct, 466
  JScript, 213
  @TRANSACTION, 462
  VBScript, 213
DisableCommit method, 106, 181
Disconnect method, 442
DISPID, 58
DISPPARAMS, 59
distributed application, 16

distributed system, 102
(see also MTS)
DLL (Dynamic Link Library), 38, 50, 80, 152
C++, 269
loading/unloading, 272
native code, 466
proxy/stub code, 271
Windows, 467
@dll.import directive, 471, 474, 477
@dll.struct directive, 470, 474
@dll.structmap directive, 472
documentation, 33
DoEvent method, 158
Domain property, 147
double data type, 280
DTC (Distributed Transaction Controller), 12, 16, 463
dual interface, 59

E

early binding, 59, 175, 180
embedded SQL, 252, 351, 452
EnableCommit method, 106, 181
encoding
server, 207
URL and HTML, 131
End method, 143–144, 202
enumerator, 45, 414, 424
Enumerator object, 336
error handling, 108, 110
C++, 288–292
Java, 398
MTS, 116
Visual Basic, 166–169, 185, 189, 205, 240, 250
error number, 167
Error object, 22, 214, 219, 337
event handling, delegation, 442
exception handling, 166, 288, 433
Execute method, 216
ExecuteComplete method, 442
Expires property, 142, 203
ExpiresAbsolute property, 142, 203
export, MTS server package, 118

F

Field object, 21, 214, 219
Fields collection, 252

file-based IO, 356, 359–363
FileDSN (File Data Source Name), 438
final modifier, 383
fixed thread pool, 157
Flags property, 137
Float data type, 280
Flush method, 143–144, 202
foreign key constraint, 257, 450
Form collection, 133, 136, 197, 325
free-threaded
component, 277
marshaler, 79, 277
model, 80, 90–95
functionality, 3, 12
COM, 49, 54

G

garbage collection, 466–467, 470
GATEWAY_INTERFACE environment variable, 140
Get method, 37
GetDirectCallerName method, 107
GetDirectCreatorName method, 107
GetEx method, 37
GetObjectContext method, 106, 109, 181–182
GetOriginalCallerName method, 107
GetOriginalCreatorName method, 107
global
access, 155
data protection, 86–89
free-threaded component data, 90–95
setting, 41
variable
memory leak, 159
Request object, 183
global.asa, 123, 129–130, 190–192, 194, 413, 416
GlobalMultiUse instancing type, 154
GlobalSingleUse instancing type, 154
GUID (Globally Unique Identifier), 36, 51
guidgen.exe, 386

H

hidden field, 251
Hide method, 160, 280
history, 5–8
HRESULT data type, 281

HTMLEncode method, 131, 208, 330, 421
HTTPS environment variable, 140
HTTPS_KEYSIZE environment variable, 140
HTTPS_SECRETKEYSIZE variable, 140
HTTPS_SERVER_ISSUER variable, 140
HTTPS_SERVER_SUBJECT variable, 140

I

IADSContainer interface, 45
IApplicationObject interface, 315–318,
         412–417
IClassFactory interface, 59
IConnectionPoint interface, 69
IConnectionPointContainer interface, 69
IConnectionPointer interface, 61
IConnectionPointerContainer interface, 61
identifier, 51
IDHTMLConvertCPP interface, 66
IDispatch data type, 282
IDispatch interface, 58, 66, 268, 279
IDispatchEx interface, 73
IDL (Interface Definition Language), 56,
         268, 273, 278
    data types, 281
IEnumVariant interface, 424
IErrorInfo interface, 289
IExternalConnection interface, 61, 69
IGetContextProperties interface, 295, 299,
         405–408
IIS Admin Object, 25
    methods, 36
    properties, 38–45
IIS Admin objects, 32
IIS Base Admin Object, 46
IIS (Internet Information Server)
    C++, 278
    documentation, 33
    test environment, 25–31
    version 3.0
        C++, 295–299
        Java, 402–405
        out-of-process component, 152
        Visual Basic, 174–179
    version 4.0, 24, 179
        C++, 299–315
        Java, 405–412
        Visual Basic, 180–190
IIS Metabase, 24, 31
    values, 133

IIsComputer object, 32
IIsWebDirectory object, 32
IIsWebServer object, 32
IIsWebService object, 32
IIsWebVirtualDir object, 32
IMarshal interface, 61
implicit search, 199
IMSAdminBase interface, 46
Inprise, 13
in-process component, 80–81, 270
    ActiveX DLL, 152
    argument method, 161
    instancing, 154
InProcServer32 registry key, 80
input parameters, C++, 282
installation, MTS server package, 118
INSTANCE_ID environment variable, 140
INSTANCE_META_PATH environment
         variable, 140
instancing, 153
Int data type, 281
int64 data type, 281
interface
    as semantic contract, 49
    C++ data types, 280
    COM, 52, 61
    com.ms.asp, 412
    pointer, 53–54, 60, 70, 81
    referencing, 53
    virtual function table, 55
    Visual Basic, 69
internationalization, 129, 194, 196, 418
interoperability, 14
introspection, 378
invoke method, 58
IObjectContext interface, 295, 311–315,
         408–412
IObjectControl interface, 306–311, 313
Iona's COM-CORBA Bridge, 4
IP address 127.0.0.1, 10, 29
IProvideClassInfo interface, 61, 69
IProvideClassInfo2 interface, 73
IRequest interface, 422–427
IRequestDictionary interface, 423
IRequestObject interface, 322–326
IResponse interface, 302–305, 326–330,
         427–430
ISAM database, 19, 211
ISAPI (Internet Server Applications
         Programming Interface), 7

IsCallerInRole property, 106, 181, 188
IsClientConnected property, 142, 146, 205
IScripting interface, 402–405
IScriptingContext interface, 295–299
IServer interface, 330–333, 420–422
ISessionObject interface, 318–322, 417–420
IsInTransaction property, 106, 181, 187
IsSecurityEnabled property, 106, 181
Issuer property, 137
ISupportErrorInfo interface, 61, 69, 276, 289
Item property, 181
IUnknown data type, 282
IUnknown interface, 57, 66, 268, 278
IVariantDictionary interface, 413–415

J

JActiveX, 391, 393–396
Java, 13
    (see Visual J++)
    ADO
        connection, 437–443
        MTS transaction
            management, 460–464
        queries, 444–449
        updates, 449–451
    Application object, 412–417
    built-in objects, 401
    C++ type conversions, 469
    class
        creation, 380
        definition, 381
        methods, 382–385
    code class, 377
    COM
        object wrappers, 391–393
        settings, 387
        wrapped class, 396
    com.ms.win32 classes, 475–477
    component execution and threads, 379
    DAO, RDO, OLE DB, and
        ADO, 435–437
    error handling, 398
    IIS
        3.0 built-in objects, 402–405
        4.0 IObject Context and
            IGetContextProperties, 405–412
    JActiveX, 393–396
    Moniker, 388
    registration and installation, 385

Request object, 422–427
Response object, 427–430
SDK, 393, 397
Server object, 420–422
Session object, 417–420
SQL statements and batch
        updates, 451–459
testing, 389
VM (Virtual Machine), 13, 267, 378, 465, 470
Win32 API function, 473–475
JavaBeans, 70, 377–379
    Bridge for ActiveX, 379
    Migration Assistant for ActiveX, 379
javareg.exe, 385
JavaScript code block, 165
JAVATLB, 466
JCF (Java Component
        Framework), 430–433
JDBC (Java Database Connectivity), 434
J/Direct, 465
    complex data types, 470–473
    marshalling scalar types, 469
    OLE mode, 477
    overview, 467
    Win32 API function, 473–475
Jet database, 19
JNI (Java Native Interface), 465, 467
JScript, 213
just-in-time activation, 18, 119, 306, 310

L

language
    choice of, 13
    default, 44
late binding, 59, 175, 192, 276
LCID property, 129, 194
libraries
    ADO, 221
    ATL, 267, 335
    data access components, 231–234
    Windows DLLs, 467
library activation, 112
load balancing, 157
local setting, 41
LOCAL_ADDR environment variable, 140
Locale property, 418
LocalHost address, 10, 29, 31, 35
Lock method, 126
LockType property, 253, 260

LOGON_USER environment variable, 140
Long data type, 281
loopback address, 10, 29

M

main subroutine, 161
Make Project, 162
MapPath method, 131, 208
marshaling, 79, 85, 152, 156, 158, 161
    C++, 270–271
memory
    contiguous vs. non-contiguous, 470
    leak, 159
methods
    C++, 279–288
    Java, 427
MFC (Microsoft Foundation Classes), 268
    ATL, 356–359
Microsoft
    Active Server Pages Object Library, 106,
        175
    ActiveX Data Objects 2.0 Library
        (ADODB), 213, 221
    ActiveX Data Objects (Multidimensional)
        (ADOM), 221
    ActiveX Data Objects Recordset 2.0
        Library (ADOR), 213, 221
    Developer Network web site, 137
    Internet Explorer, 222
    Java and, 14
    J/Direct, 466
    Script Debugger, 24, 41
    Transaction Server Type Library, 106,
        180
    web server extension, 7
modular code, 12
Moniker, 54, 388
MoveLeft method, 160, 279, 284, 290
MoveTop method, 160, 280
MTA (Multiple Threaded Apartment), 85
MTS (Microsoft Transaction Server), 7, 101,
    103
    ASP components, 15–19, 105–111
    ASP integration, 113–117
    C++, 272, 299–315
    component criteria, 105
    component management, 117–120
    Java, 405–412, 434
        transaction management, 460–464

ObjectContext, 180–190
OLE DB in C++, 342–347
    package, 111, 118, 185
    test environment, 111–113
    Transaction Statistics, 116
MTSTransactionMode, 107, 155
multiple
    CPU system, 75, 77, 84, 157
    interface, 52
    threads, 77
multithreaded
    component, 82–85
    model, 11
multi-tier application model, 235
MultiUse instancing type, 154

N

n-tier application, 102, 222, 235–242
    data access layer, 252–254
    database updates, 258–263
    multiple tables, 246–251
    presentation layer "helper", 242–246
    row deletion and foreign key
        constraints, 254–258
Name property, 34
native code, 465–466
native modifier, 383
Netscape, 15, 50
    cookies, 204, 330, 422
    RDS and, 222
    website, 201
NT Option Pack documentation, 33
NT service, 271

O

O'Reilly website, xvi
object
    application-wide access, 125
    serialization, 356, 363–366
        persistence through, 366–370
OBJECT tag, 130, 190, 194
ObjectContext object, 15, 17, 95, 102, 106,
    108
    C++, 295, 299–315
    MTS component access, 184–189
    transaction control, 189
    Visual Basic, 173, 180–184, 250, 256
ObjectControl method, 18, 107–108, 119

objRequest, 199
objResponseMethod, 183
objWriteHeader, 177–179, 183, 195, 300
   m_piResponse, 304
ODBC, 213
   driver, 19, 211–212
ODBCDirect, 19
ODL (Object Definition Language), 56, 397
OLE automation server, 48
OLE DB, 7, 211
   C++
      data update, 352–354
      with MTS, 342–347
   consumer, 335, 342
   introduction to, 334–337
   Java, 435–437
   J/Direct, 477
   parameterized stored procedure
      call, 347–352
   provider, 212, 335, 438
   service component, 335
   templates, 20, 337–341
OLE/COM viewer, 63, 69, 73, 387
On Error Resume Next, 292
OnEndPage event, 174, 295
OnStartPage event, 174, 178–179, 183, 191,
      194, 295
OpenSchema method, 216
Oracle, 213
orphaned row, 254
OSF (Open Software Foundation), 51, 56
out-of-process component, 80–81, 152,
      156, 270
   argument method, 161
output, altering, 144

P

PageCounter component, 130
Parameter object, 22, 214, 219
parent-child relationship, 36
Parent property, 36
PATH_INFO environment variable, 140
PATH_TRANSLATED environment
      variable, 140
performance
   ADO in ASP components, 224
   C++ threading, 277
   object method, 161
   OBJECT tags, 130

RNI, 466
server, 102
server-side applications, 6
stored procedures, 452
system, 77
threading, 156, 158
Perl script, 5
persistence, using ATL and MFC, 356–373
persistent storage, 54
Petzold, Charles, 75
PICS, 142, 202
pointer, 52–55, 60–61, 70, 79, 81
   Java, 470
Pointer data type, 281
polymorphic parameters, 472
pooling, 310
Positioning object, 153, 163
PowerBuilder, 13
presentation layer, 235–236
   ASP "helper", 242–246
Private instancing type, 154
ProgID (programmatic identifier), 165
project defaults, 63
Property object, 22, 214
proxy/stub code, 271
PublicNotCreatable instancing type, 154,
      157, 159
pubs database, 213, 225, 255, 338
   properties, 215
   URL, 237
Put method, 37
putBuffer method, 429
PutEx method, 38
PWS (Personal Web Server), 4
   ASP changes, 10
   independent applications, 26
   testing, 169
   use of, 80

Q

QUERY_STRING environment variable, 140
QueryInterface function, 53
QueryString collection, 133–136, 197, 324

R

RDO (Remote Data Object), 19, 21,
      435–437
RDS (Remote Data Service), 211, 221, 263

Recordset object, 21, 214, 216–219, 240, 243, 252, 259, 446
Redirect method, 143, 175, 205
reference counter, 296
referential integrity rules, 246–251
registration, 185
  C++, 279, 311
    COM, 285
  Java, 385, 404
  MTS, 105, 111, 114, 405, 460
  Visual Basic, 162
registry file, 50
  ADO, 224
RegSvr32 application, 50, 162
  Java, 385, 404
relational data, 19, 211
remote access, 152, 271
REMOTE_ADDR environment variable, 140
REMOTE_USER environment variable, 140
REQUEST_METHOD environment variable, 141
Request object, 8, 122, 133–141
  C++, 322–326
  global variable, 183
  Java, 422–427
  Visual Basic, 196–201
reregistration, C++, 311
resource management, 18, 119
Response object, 8, 122, 141–147, 179
  C++, 326–330
  Java, 427–430
  Visual Basic, 175–176, 178, 192, 201–206
result sets, multiple, 454
Resultset passing, 238–242
reusable code, 4, 12, 52, 62
Richter, Jeffrey, 75
RNI (Raw Native Interface), 465–466
Rollback method, 250
rolled back changes, 16
'round robin' approach, 77, 157
row deletion, 254–258
Rowset object, 337
RPC (Remote Procedure Call) IDL, 56
runtime binding, 192

S

SafeArray array, 133, 199, 281
SafeRef method, 106
sample programs, xvi

scalar conversions, 469
schema class, 36
SCM (Service Control Manager), 79
SCODE data type, 281
SCRIPT_NAME environment variable, 141
scripting, 4, 8
  default language, 44
  untested component, 166
ScriptingContext, 107, 174–179
ScriptingContext object, 173, 183, 295
ScriptTimeout, 133, 209
search, implicit, 199
Secure property, 147
security issues, CGI, 6
Security method, 181
SecurityProperty method, 107
selection criteria, 445
serialized method calls, 95, 156, 276
SerialNumber property, 137
server
  activation, 112
  directory, 162
SERVER_NAME environment variable, 141
Server object, 122, 130–133
  C++, 330–333
  Java, 420–422
  Visual Basic, 206–209
SERVER_PORT variable, 141
SERVER_PORT_SECURE variable, 141
SERVER_PROTOCOL variable, 141
SERVER_SOFTWARE variable, 141
server-side
  applications history, 5–8
  caching, disadvantages of, 228
  scripting, 3
ServerVariable collection, 134, 138–141, 324
service component, 271
Session object, 122, 127–130
  C++, 318–322, 336
  Java, 417–420
  Visual Basic, 193–196, 259–263
SessionID property, 194, 196
SetAbort method, 17, 106, 109, 119, 181, 189, 250, 253, 311
SetComplete method, 106, 109, 119, 181, 189, 250, 253, 256, 311
SetInfo method, 38
Short data type, 281
Show method, 160, 280

single-threaded
    component, 82–85
    model, 11, 80, 276
SingleUse instancing type, 154
Software AG, 15, 50
SQL Server, 16, 19–20, 104, 213, 225, 237
    DTC, 463
    version 7.0, 215
SQL statements, Java, 451–459
STA (Single Threaded Apartment), 85
static modifier, 383
StaticObjects collection, 125, 191, 194, 318, 320
Status property, 142, 145
stored procedure, 250
    Java, 452–461
    OLE DB, 349
    row deletion, 254–258
stub function, 79, 271
subclass, 381
Subject property, 137
superclass, 381
surrogate application, 153
Sybase, 13
symbols, xvi
synchronization, thread, 78
synchronized modifier, 383
SYSTEM account, 85, 90, 95, 99
system, component-based, 102

T

tables, multiple, 246–251
testing
    application, 25–31
    C++, 285
    Java, 389
    MTS environment, 111–113
    Visual Basic component, 163–166, 169–171
threading
    C++, 276
    models, 80
threads
    background processes in C++, 370–373
    classification, 85
    definition of, 75–81
    Java, 379
    synchronization, 78
thread-safe component, 11, 68, 180, 379
three-tier application, 236

TimeOut property, 129, 194, 196
TotalBytes method, 133, 199
@TRANSACTION directive, 462
transaction, 104
    C++ support, 311–315
    control with ObjectContext, 189
    management, 7, 12, 15–17
    MTS requirements, 115
    multiple components, 460–464
    ObjectContext, 184–189
    ObjectContext object, 184–189
Transaction object, 336
Transaction Server Explorer, 111, 185
type library, 58, 155
typographic conventions, xv

U

UDA (Universal Data Access), 20–22, 334
UDT (Uniform Data Transfer), 54
Unattended Execution, 156
Unix, COM components, 15
Unlock method, 126
URL environment variable, 141
URLEncode method, 131, 208, 330, 421
user security account, 99
UUID (Universally Unique Identifier), 51

V

validation, data entry, 253
ValidFrom property, 137
ValidUntil property, 137
Values, accessing, 141
variable
    application, 125
    environment, 138, 424
    global, 183
    Session, 129
Variant data type, 281
vbObjectError constant, 167
VBScript, 44, 213
    block, 8
Virtual Directory, 25–31
virtual function table, 55
Visual Basic, 13, 32
    ADO, 213, 220–225
        interactive query, 225–230
    Application object, 190–193
    ASP component, 29, 151
    built-in objects, 173

Visual Basic (*continued*)
    COM component, 63, 68–70
    component
        execution and threads, 156–159
        generation, registration, installation
            and testing, 162–166
        in-process vs. out-of-process, 152
        methods, 159–162
    CStr function, 261
    IIS
        3.0 built-in objects, 174–179
        4.0, 180–190
    Java, 394–398
    MTS-aware ASP component, 105
    multiple threading model, 85
    n-tier ASP application, 238–263
    Request object, 196–201
    Response object, 201–206
    Server object, 206–209
    Session object, 193–196
    testing and debugging, 169–171
    version 5.0, 153, 155–156
        debugging, 171
    version 6.0, 151
Visual C++, 13
    adding methods, 279–288
    ADO support, 213
    Application object, 315–318
    ASP component, 267
    ATL
        AppWizard, 269–274
        object, 274–279
    built-in objects, 294
    COM component, 63–67
    error handling, 288–292
    file-based IO, 359–363
    IIS
        3.0 built-in objects, 295–299
        4.0 ObjectContext, 299–315
    Java type conversions, 469
    object serialization, 363–366
    OLE DB, 334
        data update, 352–354
        parameterized stored procedure
            call, 347–352
        templates, 20, 337–341
        with MTS, 342–347

persistence
    ATL and MFC, 356–359
    object serialization, 366–370
Request object, 322–326
Response object, 326–330
Server object, 330–333
Session object, 318–322
threading, 276
    background processes, 370–373
Visual J++, 13
    (see Java)
    ADO support, 213
    COM
        component, 63, 70–74
        object wrappers, 391–398
    Java COM object registration, 385
VM (Virtual Machine), 70, 378
Void data type, 281
vtable interface, C++, 276, 279
vtbl, 55
    binding, 59

W

web server
    development history, 5–8
    global and local settings, 41
    test environment, 25
WFC (Windows Framework Classes), 432,
        434
    ADO connection, 437–443
Win32
    API function, 467, 473–475
    classes, 475
    environment, 50
Windows
    NT, 157
    Registry, 31
    SDK, 465
wrappers, 14, 19, 66, 73
    C++, 267–268, 296, 302, 343
    Java, 391–398, 401, 406, 409, 437,
        465–466
    JCF, 431
    Visual Basic, 231–234
Write method, 143, 145, 202

About the Author

Shelley Powers is a consultant/author with her own company, YASD, currently located in Boston, Massachusetts. In the last several years, she has worked with a variety of distributed and/or web development applications, with a variety of tools and on a variety of platforms. In addition, Shelley has also authored or coauthored books on Dynamic HTML, JavaScript, Java, CGI, Perl, general web technologies, and more. She can be reached at *shelleyp@yasd.com*.

Colophon

Our look is the result of reader comments, our own experimentation, and feedback from distribution channels. Distinctive covers complement our distinctive approach to technical topics, breathing personality and life into potentially dry subjects.

The animal on the cover of *Developing ASP Components* is an asp, which is a term applied to various venomous snakes, including the depicted asp viper (*Vipera aspis*) of Europe as well as the Egyptian cobra (*Naja haje*), thought to have been the means of Cleopatra's suicide.

Needing to eat at least 5–6% of their body weight in food per week, European asp vipers hunt by lying in wait for approaching prey. After grabbing and biting a small rodent or other prey, they release it and wait several minutes for it to stop moving; the generally sluggish viper rarely chases prey. Vipers know their home territory very well, which allows quick escape from their asp-kicking natural enemies, serpent eagles and hedgehogs. This trick hasn't helped them escape from their greatest threat, the expansion of human civilization, which frequently wipes out large sections of their territory.

The chemical composition of asp viper venom can vary from one population to the next, hampering initial antivenin development until 1896, but few viper bite fatalities occur in Europe today.

Ellie Fountain Maden was the production editor and copyeditor for *Developing ASP Components*; Sheryl Avruch was the production manager; Mary Anne Weeks Mayo, Maureen Dempsey, and Jeffrey Liggett provided quality control. Abby Myers and Sarah Jane Shangraw proofread the book. Robert Romano created the illustrations using Adobe Photoshop 4 and Macromedia FreeHand 7. Mike Sierra provided FrameMaker technical support. Lynn Hutchinski wrote the index.

Hanna Dyer designed the cover of this book, based on a series design by Edie Freedman. The image is a 19th-century engraving from the Dover Pictorial Archive. The cover layout was produced by Kathleen Wilson using QuarkXPress 3.3 and the ITC Garamond font. Whenever possible, our books use RepKover™, a durable and flexible lay-flat binding. If the page count exceeds RepKover's limit, perfect binding is used.

The inside layout was designed by Nancy Priest and implemented in FrameMaker 5.5 by Mike Sierra. The text and heading fonts are ITC Garamond Light and Garamond Book. This colophon was written by Nancy Kotary.

How to stay in touch with O'Reilly

1. Visit Our Award-Winning Web Site

http://www.oreilly.com/

★ "Top 100 Sites on the Web" —*PC Magazine*
★ "Top 5% Web sites" —*Point Communications*
★ "3-Star site" —*The McKinley Group*

Our web site contains a library of comprehensive product information (including book excerpts and tables of contents), downloadable software, background articles, interviews with technology leaders, links to relevant sites, book cover art, and more. File us in your Bookmarks or Hotlist!

2. Join Our Email Mailing Lists

New Product Releases

To receive automatic email with brief descriptions of all new O'Reilly products as they are released, send email to:
listproc@online.oreilly.com
Put the following information in the first line of your message (*not* in the Subject field):
subscribe oreilly-news

O'Reilly Events

If you'd also like us to send information about trade show events, special promotions, and other O'Reilly events, send email to:
listproc@online.oreilly.com
Put the following information in the first line of your message (*not* in the Subject field):
subscribe oreilly-events

3. Get Examples from Our Books via FTP

There are two ways to access an archive of example files from our books:

Regular FTP

- ftp to:
  ftp.oreilly.com
  (login: anonymous
  password: your email address)
- Point your web browser to:
  ftp://ftp.oreilly.com/

FTPMAIL

- Send an email message to:
  ftpmail@online.oreilly.com
  (Write "help" in the message body)

4. Contact Us via Email

order@oreilly.com
To place a book or software order online. Good for North American and international customers.

subscriptions@oreilly.com
To place an order for any of our newsletters or periodicals.

books@oreilly.com
General questions about any of our books.

software@oreilly.com
For general questions and product information about our software. Check out O'Reilly Software Online at **http://software.oreilly.com/** for software and technical support information. Registered O'Reilly software users send your questions to: **website-support@oreilly.com**

cs@oreilly.com
For answers to problems regarding your order or our products.

booktech@oreilly.com
For book content technical questions or corrections.

proposals@oreilly.com
To submit new book or software proposals to our editors and product managers.

international@oreilly.com
For information about our international distributors or translation queries. For a list of our distributors outside of North America check out:
http://www.oreilly.com/www/order/country.html

O'Reilly & Associates, Inc.
101 Morris Street, Sebastopol, CA 95472 USA
TEL   707-829-0515 or 800-998-9938
          (6am to 5pm PST)
FAX   707-829-0104

O'REILLY®

International Distributors

UK, EUROPE, MIDDLE EAST AND AFRICA (EXCEPT FRANCE, GERMANY, AUSTRIA, SWITZERLAND, LUXEMBOURG, LIECHTENSTEIN, AND EASTERN EUROPE)

INQUIRIES
O'Reilly UK Limited
4 Castle Street
Farnham
Surrey, GU9 7HS
United Kingdom
Telephone: 44-1252-711776
Fax: 44-1252-734211
Email: josette@oreilly.com

ORDERS
Wiley Distribution Services Ltd.
1 Oldlands Way
Bognor Regis
West Sussex PO22 9SA
United Kingdom
Telephone: 44-1243-779777
Fax: 44-1243-820250
Email: cs-books@wiley.co.uk

FRANCE

ORDERS
GEODIF
61, Bd Saint-Germain
75240 Paris Cedex 05, France
Tel: 33-1-44-41-46-16 (French books)
Tel: 33-1-44-41-11-87 (English books)
Fax: 33-1-44-41-11-44
Email: distribution@eyrolles.com

INQUIRIES
Éditions O'Reilly
18 rue Séguier
75006 Paris, France
Tel: 33-1-40-51-52-30
Fax: 33-1-40-51-52-31
Email: france@editions-oreilly.fr

GERMANY, SWITZERLAND, AUSTRIA, EASTERN EUROPE, LUXEMBOURG, AND LIECHTENSTEIN

INQUIRIES & ORDERS
O'Reilly Verlag
Balthasarstr. 81
D-50670 Köln
Germany
Telephone: 49-221-973160-91
Fax: 49-221-973160-8
Email: anfragen@oreilly.de (inquiries)
Email: order@oreilly.de (orders)

CANADA (FRENCH LANGUAGE BOOKS)

Les Éditions Flammarion ltée
375, Avenue Laurier Ouest
Montréal (Québec) H2V 2K3
Tel: 00-1-514-277-8807
Fax: 00-1-514-278-2085
Email: info@flammarion.qc.ca

HONG KONG

City Discount Subscription Service, Ltd.
Unit D, 3rd Floor, Yan's Tower
27 Wong Chuk Hang Road
Aberdeen, Hong Kong
Tel: 852-2580-3539
Fax: 852-2580-6463
Email: citydis@ppn.com.hk

KOREA

Hanbit Media, Inc.
Sonyoung Bldg. 202
Yeksam-dong 736-36
Kangnam-ku
Seoul, Korea
Tel: 822-554-9610
Fax: 822-556-0363
Email: hant93@chollian.dacom.co.kr

PHILIPPINES

Mutual Books, Inc.
429-D Shaw Boulevard
Mandaluyong City, Metro
Manila, Philippines
Tel: 632-725-7538
Fax: 632-721-3056
Email: mbikikog@mnl.sequel.net

TAIWAN

O'Reilly Taiwan
No. 3, Lane 131
Hang-Chow South Road
Section 1, Taipei, Taiwan
Tel: 886-2-23968990
Fax: 886-2-23968916
Email: benh@oreilly.com

CHINA

O'Reilly Beijing
Room 2410
160, FuXingMenNeiDaJie
XiCheng District
Beijing, China PR 100031
Tel: 86-10-86631006
Fax: 86-10-86631007
Email: frederic@oreilly.com

INDIA

Computer Bookshop (India) Pvt. Ltd.
190 Dr. D.N. Road, Fort
Bombay 400 001 India
Tel: 91-22-207-0989
Fax: 91-22-262-3551
Email: cbsbom@giasbm01.vsnl.net.in

JAPAN

O'Reilly Japan, Inc.
Kiyoshige Building 2F
12-Bancho, Sanei-cho
Shinjuku-ku
Tokyo 160-0008 Japan
Tel: 81-3-3356-5227
Fax: 81-3-3356-5261
Email: japan@oreilly.com

ALL OTHER ASIAN COUNTRIES

O'Reilly & Associates, Inc.
101 Morris Street
Sebastopol, CA 95472 USA
Tel: 707-829-0515
Fax: 707-829-0104
Email: order@oreilly.com

AUSTRALIA

WoodsLane Pty., Ltd.
7/5 Vuko Place
Warriewood NSW 2102
Australia
Tel: 61-2-9970-5111
Fax: 61-2-9970-5002
Email: info@woodslane.com.au

NEW ZEALAND

Woodslane New Zealand, Ltd.
21 Cooks Street (P.O. Box 575)
Waganui, New Zealand
Tel: 64-6-347-6543
Fax: 64-6-345-4840
Email: info@woodslane.com.au

LATIN AMERICA

McGraw-Hill Interamericana
Editores, S.A. de C.V.
Cedro No. 512
Col. Atlampa
06450, Mexico, D.F.
Tel: 52-5-547-6777
Fax: 52-5-547-3336
Email: mcgraw-hill@infosel.net.mx

O'REILLY®

TO ORDER: **800-998-9938** • *order@oreilly.com* • *http://www.oreilly.com/*
OUR PRODUCTS ARE AVAILABLE AT A BOOKSTORE OR SOFTWARE STORE NEAR YOU.
FOR INFORMATION: **800-998-9938** • **707-829-0515** • *info@oreilly.com*